MW00654025

Affordable Housing in New York

Affordable Housing in New York

The People, Places, and Policies That Transformed a City

Edited by Nicholas Dagen Bloom
and Matthew Gordon Lasner

With photographs by David Schalliol

PRINCETON UNIVERSITY PRESS
Princeton and Oxford

Published by Princeton University Press, 41 William Street, Princeton, New Jersey 08540
In the United Kingdom: Princeton University Press, 6 Oxford Street, Woodstock, Oxfordshire OX20 1TW
press.princeton.edu

Cover illustrations: (*front*) NYCHA playground (unidentified), Bronx. Courtesy of The New York City Housing Authority Photograph Collection, La Guardia and Wagner Archives, La Guardia Community College/The City University of New York. (*back*) Via Verde, 2014. Photo by David Schalliol.
Library of Congress Cataloging-in-Publication Data
Affordable housing in New York : the people, places, and policies that transformed a city / edited by Nicholas Dagen Bloom and Matthew Gordon Lasner.
pages cm
Includes bibliographical references and index.
ISBN 978–0-691–16781–7 (hardcover : alk. paper) 1. Public housing—New York (State)—New York—History—20th century. 2. Low-income housing—New York (State)—New York—History—20th century. 3. Housing policy—New York (State)—New York—History—20th century. I. Bloom, Nicholas Dagen, 1969– II. Lasner, Matthew Gordon.
HD7288.78.U52N7185 2016
363.5'8097471—dc23
2015003568
British Library Cataloging-in-Publication Data is available
Publication of this book has been aided by the New York State Council on the Arts with the support of Governor Andrew Cuomo and the New York State Legislature.
The editors express appreciation to the Schoff Fund at the University Seminars at Columbia University for their help in publication. Material in this work was presented to the University Seminar: The City.
Cover and interior design by Jason Alejandro
This book has been composed in Palatino and ITC Avant Garde Gothic
Printed on acid-free paper. ∞
Printed in China
10 9 8 7 6 5 4 3 2 1

Government credit at low interest and amortization rates should be made available for public housing wherever it is most needed, not only now in the emergency, but as a permanent public policy.

—Mary Simkhovitch, "Housing as a Permanent Municipal Service," Radio Address, WEAF, February 19, 1934

Contents

Acknowledgments

The combined effort of many talented individuals, across numerous fields, defines *Affordable Housing in New York: The People, Places, and Policies That Transformed a City*. A project that would have consumed many years as a solitary undertaking was finished in just three as a result of this collaboration. This process nicely parallels the cooperative spirit that defined so much of the housing discussed. As with real housing cooperatives, then, this book belongs to the many "co-owners" who built and sustained it, especially our authors: Matthias Altwicker, Hilary Ballon, Lizabeth Cohen, Andrew S. Dolkart, Peter Eisenstadt, Yonah Freemark, Brian Goldstein, Richard Greenwald, Jennifer Hock, Benjamin Holtzman, Christopher Klemek, Lilian Knorr, Jeffrey A. Kroessler, Karen Kubey, Nancy H. Kwak, the late Steven Levine, Nadia A. Mian, Karina Milchman, Mariana Mogilevich, Stephen Petrus, Annemarie Sammartino, Susanne Schindler, David Smiley, Jonathan Soffer, Fritz Umbach, Nader Vossoughian, and Samuel Zipp.

The keen eye and determination of photographer and sociologist David Schalliol generated many of the breathtaking images in this book. Chair of the New York Institute of Technology (NYIT) School of Architecture Matthias Altwicker and advanced architecture students Alexander MacVicar, Christopher Alvarez, and Kevin Kawiecki constructed models and floor plans that illustrate the changing standards in affordable housing design. Noted photographer Eduard Hueber of Archphoto captured the models for the comparative galleries following chapters 2 and 4 and the conclusion. Cartographer Minna Ninova created the original map found in the book's introduction (fig. 0.4) that provides a sense of scale to the city's housing efforts. Mark Willis and Sean Capperis of the Furman Center for Real Estate and Urban

Policy at New York University provided most of the map's data. The superior organizational skill of research assistant Oksana Miranova ensured that the collection was completed on time.

Many direct participants in the production and maintenance of affordable housing in New York provided feedback and assistance as the book developed. Thanks first to the residents, managers, and staff of housing developments across the city who graciously hosted the researchers. We hope that the results confirm their faith in our open-mindedness. Architects Fernando Villa and Petr Stand of Magnusson Architecture and Planning arranged for multiple visits to the Melrose district that deepened the coverage of this neighborhood. Lisa Diaz, the former federal liaison and senior policy advisor to the chairman at the New York City Housing Authority (NYCHA) was a hidden treasure in the vast bureaucracy that is New York City government. She generously set up interviews and tours of developments because she believes deeply in the value of public housing. Architect Mary Rusz of NYCHA's capital division provided floor plans and other details. Millie Molina arranged for permission to use many of the agency's vast collection of images, past and present.

For access to and much assistance with images we thank Douglas Di Carlo at the LaGuardia and Wagner Archives at LaGuardia Community College, who efficiently organized the retrieval and scanning of many, including those of the NYCHA collection. The *New York Times*, especially Phyllis Collazo, provided access to their unrivaled collection of photographs documenting the urban crisis and more recent renaissance. For help with these extraordinary pictures, many taken by some of the *Times*'s most esteemed photographers, we also thank Rosemary Morrow and Jack Rosenthal. Lo-Yi Chan, Dan Wakin, Marc Miller of Co-op City, Don Shulman of Bell Park Gardens, Michele Hiltzik Beckerman at the Rockefeller Archive Center, Devon Meave Nevola at Columbia University, and Katherine Reagan at Cornell University all helped secure other archival images. Photographers Joe Conzo, Norman McGrath, Stephen Nessen, Grace Madden, Michael Moran, Alan Zale, Mel Rosenthal, Nancy Siesel, and Nancy Kaye generously shared their own.

Michelle Komie, executive editor of art and architecture at Princeton University Press, has been a long-time supporter of the project and we are honored that she took on the challenge of such a complicated manuscript. We thank the anonymous peer reviewers for their suggestions, many of which we adopted, as well as the strong vote of confidence by the Princeton University Press editorial board. Detailed feedback on earlier versions of the text by Alex Schwartz of the Milano graduate program at the New School proved timely and useful. Additional comments by Carol Lamberg, who hosted a tour of Settlement House developments in the Bronx, were also helpful in shaping the narrative.

The strong support of George McCarthy, former director of the Ford Foundation's Metropolitan Opportunity division and now president of the Lincoln Institute of Land Policy, enabled the book's timely completion. We are also grateful to Jerry Maldonado and Rowena Nixon of the Ford Foundation, and Candice Homan of the Institute of International Education, Inc., for the grant that funded research assistance and index preparation. We hope that the final product matches, and perhaps even exceeds, the initial proposal. Similarly we are grateful for support for research, production, and photography from the Individual Projects program of the New York State Council on the Arts, overseen by the Van Alen Institute.

Nicholas Bloom thanks the administration of the New York Institute of Technology including NYIT president Edward Guiliano, provost Rahmat Shoureshi, College of Arts and Sciences dean Roger Yu, NYIT counsel Catherine Flickinger, and social science chair Ellen Katz. Matt Altwicker and I also benefited from NYIT's generous Institutional Support for Research and Creativity (ISRC) grant program. I also received timely feedback from many people including Lawrence Vale, Lizabeth Cohen, Theodore Liebman, and Alexander Garvin. The project benefited from comments made during a presentation of the research at the Columbia University Seminar on the City. The LaGuardia and Wagner Archives—including director Richard K. Lieberman, the late education director Steven Levine (who also contributed to this volume), and educational associate Tara Jean Hickman—is a vital institution that is always a pleasure to visit. My students, many of whom grew up in below-market housing communities, have provided additional depth and insight in various classes over the years. My family was a strong supporter of the book, and I owe them a debt of gratitude, including my daughter, Roxie Bloom, and wife, Leanne Bloom, who had to tolerate a very busy father/husband over the past few years. My parents, Naomi Dagen Bloom and Ronald L. Bloom, while living far away, are still conversant in all matters of New York housing and remain good sounding boards for new ideas.

Matthew Gordon Lasner thanks David Schalliol for agreeing to come to New York for several weeks to take photographs and for his ongoing enthusiasm for the project as a whole. Oksana Mironova provided hugely important assistance conducting research as well crucial logistical support preparing the manuscript. My students at Hunter College, especially Allison Blanchette, Michael Fivis, and Jennifer Yip in the spring of 2013, did a superior job conducting fieldwork. I also thank Vernon Cooper at Co-op City and Jose Taveras for helping to facilitate efforts there; Naomi Goldstein, Mario Mazzoni, Walter Mankoff, and Karen Smith at Penn South; Paul Stein at Bell Park Gardens; and Frank Marcovitz and Theresa Markevich at Queensview. For financial assistance I thank Hunter College's president Jennifer Raab and dean of the School of Arts and Sciences, Andrew Polsky. I am especially grateful to my husband, Dan Goldstein, and son, Amos, for accommodating the many long hours I needed to take on this project, and to my parents, Richard and Edith Lasner, and parents-in-law, Sandra and Ronald Goldstein, for all their support.

Many administrators, managers, tenants, and homeowners helped David Schalliol produce his photographs. They include Joe Boiko, Mitch Berkowitz, and the Department of Public Safety at Co-op City; Barbara Nienaltowski and Tracy Winston at the Dunbar Apartments; Matt Altwicker, Marcia Cole, and Dleanna Hoosain at Roosevelt Landings (Eastwood); Kathie Shoulders and Wallace Duprey at the Harlem River Houses; Anthony Winn and Ana Melendez at Melrose Common and Nos Quedamos; Carmelia Goffe, Erica Townsend, and Katie Gilbert at Nehemiah Houses; Lisa Diaz, Millie Molina, Leroy Williams at NYCHA; Karen Smith and Mario Mazzoni at Penn South; Tabia Heywot and Kenneth Simpson at Polo Grounds Houses; Dorothy and Milton Wilner, John Marsh, and Frank Marcovitz and the entire staff at Queensview; Norm Sherman at Queensview North; Yvette Caban and Pedro Carrion at Rangel Houses; Carol Wilkins at Ravenswood; Eric Allen and Penny Wisneski at Reliant Realty Services, Inc. (Twin Parks); Alex Freedman and Jeffrey Hicks at Rochdale Village; and the numerous other residents and staff who helped introduce David to their neighborhoods.

Affordable Housing in New York

Introduction

In 1957, future Supreme Court Justice Sonia Sotomayor's family moved from an old walk-up tenement to a "pristine" apartment in the Bronxdale Houses (1955), a brand-new public housing complex. When the family's finances improved a decade later, they moved again, buying an apartment in Co-op City (1968–73), another new complex in Bronx, whose more than fifteen thousand units were being developed by labor unions with financial assistance from New York State (see fig. 0.10). The future Supreme Court justice soon left for college at Princeton University, but her family remained in their new home for decades.[1]

Justice Sotomayor's career may be exceptional, but the investment made by government in housing her family was typical of postwar New York City, when hundreds of thousands came to live in bright, clean apartments constructed or financed through a wide range of government programs. In 2015, 8 percent of the city's rental apartments (178,000 units) were still in government-owned and -operated public housing developments. Some individual public housing complexes, such as Queensbridge Houses (1940), with 3,149 apartments, were larger than the entire public housing stock of many U.S. cities. Hundreds of thousands more New Yorkers lived in privately owned below-market buildings, both rental and owner-occupied, developed with government aid and very often still subsidized by it, like Co-op City. The large scale and rich history of New York's subsidized housing developments have no parallel in the United States.

New York, America's most densely developed and politically progressive city, has an exceptional history both in terms of substandard housing conditions and the heroic attempts to overcome them. To those residing far from the city, all this effort has often seemed perplexing. Most Americans have long lived well and continue to do so

0.1: Cold-water apartment, 124 Moore St., Brooklyn, 1955

today: better than anywhere else, in any period, of human history. For the most part this high standard of living has been accomplished privately, in new houses and apartments for middle- and upper-income groups, and filtered (secondhand) or manufactured housing (trailers) for the poor. What makes these high standards possible is the powerful combination of lightly regulated, abundant land with indirect government subsidies including federal highway construction, tax breaks for many homeowners, and the mortgage insurance programs of the Federal Housing Administration.[2]

In New York City conditions are quite different—and they have been for at least two centuries. Massive, centralized, and expensive, America's biggest metropolis condenses and magnifies social inequality. Its poor historically lived in the worst tenements anywhere this side of Dickens's London, while sky-high prices meant nearly everyone, in every era, has endured deficiencies and inconveniences unimaginable elsewhere in the United States (fig. 0.1). Twentieth-century road-building and tax-deduction programs encouraged decentralization and urban disinvestment, but these initiatives did not change New York's fundamental nature: the city remained crowded, ill-housed, and costly. But just as its privations were unmatched, so too were the aggressive responses by reformers in working to ameliorate poor conditions, marshaling untold billions of dollars in city, state, federal, and private philanthropic aid to the cause.[3]

At the turn of the twentieth century, city leaders had yet to articulate the need for subsidized housing. With the exception of a few thousand families in low-cost projects developed by philanthropists, New Yorkers lived at the mercy of the market. Conditions were abysmal despite decades of tenement reform. No government offered tax abatements, let alone cash grants, for low-rent housing. No court this side of the Atlantic supported taking of private property for this purpose. Rent control was unthinkable. No trade union built cooperatives. Even with a burgeoning tenants' movement, laissez-faire ideology dominated, and most leaders believed the housing question would be solved privately, through the process of decentralization that was already gradually unfolding, or in model tenements built by philanthropists.[4]

As early as the 1910s, however, New York housing reformers began to comprehend that only government subsidies could make the kinds of dramatic changes they believed were necessary. Under the influence of these "housers," and after much debate, in 1926 Governor Alfred E. Smith (1919–20; 1923–28) passed the nation's first program of financial support for below-market urban housing. So began a rich tradition in New York that continues today. In the 1930s and 1940s New York's progressive U.S. senator Robert F. Wagner (1927–49) led the national fight for federal aid for public housing; in the 1950s and 1960s New York labor leader Abraham Kazan lobbied for support for low-cost cooperatives, such as Co-op City; in the 1970s and 1980s New York planners and neighborhood activists pioneered new forms of public-private partnerships, resulting in such innovative projects as Charlotte Gardens (1983–87) and Nehemiah Houses (1983–present) (fig. 0.2). Over time subsidies included cash grants for construction and maintenance; favorable construction and mortgage loans, often at below-market interest rates and for unusually long terms; and discounts on

0.2: Rev. Bertram G. Bennett, Jr., left, and Tony Aguilar with model of Nehemiah Houses, Bronx, by Edward Keating, 1991

0.3: "Today—Yesterday," NYCHA exhibit, 1948

property taxes. The housers invested the subsidies they fought for not only in construction and maintenance but also in innovative organizations to achieve their goals, such as the New York City Housing Authority (NYCHA) for public housing created in 1934, the United Housing Foundation for union-financed nonprofit, or limited-equity, cooperatives in 1949, and the city's Department of Housing Preservation and Development in 1977, which has managed a growing number of new low- and middle-income programs since the 1980s.

The New York approach has been remarkable not just for getting things done and for its creativity, but also for its flexibility in response to changing social, economic, and political circumstances. Initial efforts in the era of congestion and overcrowding before the Great Depression targeted poor foreign immigrants living in East Side slums. Many lived in squalid conditions that were at odds with American norms. Reformers based in settlement houses—college graduates, American-born, and middle class—worked to make life in the "foreign wards" more salubrious by fighting for better housing and sanitation standards. These efforts, including betterment of housing, were intended to offer humanitarian relief, but also to teach tenement dwellers to become more "American" before setting off for what housers hoped were better-quality neighborhoods, mostly in the boroughs or beyond.

As immigration waned and suburbanization threatened to undermine the viability of the city as a whole, housing leaders reimagined their role. From the 1930s to the 1960s they sought state and federal subsidies, and pioneered municipal housing programs, not just to help families with very low incomes, particularly African Americans and Puerto Ricans, but to help remake New York in a more up-to-date, middle-class image (fig. 0.3). Housers used these robust subsidies to develop no-frills low-income public complexes like Jacob Riis Houses (1949) as well as higher-quality middle-income projects like Queensview (1950) that were conceived to appeal to the types of second-generation families increasingly choosing to leave the city. By the 1970s amid the deepening urban crisis, housing activists were using subsidies as a form of triage to stabilize neighborhoods.

Since the 1980s a new generation of housers has employed subsidies to yet different ends: to prevent displacement by gentrification amid a rising real estate tide in a second Gilded Age. Meanwhile, as foreign immigration resumed, nonprofit developers such as Asian Americans for Equality once again began using subsidized housing as a bridge for those just beginning their American journeys.

As a result of these ever-changing efforts, New York City today boasts a remarkable range of below-market subsidized housing (fig. 0.4). Approximately half a million New Yorkers live in government-owned and -operated low-income public housing. Perhaps a million more live in privately developed below-market apartments made affordable through federal, state, and local subsidies. These include an estimated 225,000 individuals in complexes financed with the help of the Federal Housing Administration's nonprofit multifamily programs after World War II, such as Bell Park Gardens (1950) in Bayside, Queens; 350,000 in other federally aided low-income developments; 200,000 in middle-income projects built with New York City and State funds under the Mitchell-Lama program, including those developed by the New York State Urban Development Corporation, such as Eastwood (1976) on Roosevelt Island; and more than 210,000 in housing built with the help of federal Low-income Housing Tax Credits, such as the much celebrated Via Verde (2012) in the Bronx. And these figures say nothing of the more than 120,000 households receiving federal rent vouchers, or the astonishing half of all renters who live in rent-stabilized or -controlled apartments. Millions of city residents, both yesterday and today, have thus benefited from below-market rents made possible by the diversity and scale of New York's housing programs.[5]

The enduring belief among New York City leaders and voters that high-quality housing is a right of urban citizenship regardless of income has sustained the city's housing program through many twists and turns. As with all reform movements, the path to implementation has rarely been smooth. Between the 1930s and the 1960s "slum clearance" scattered hundreds of thousands of families, along with many small businesses, with minimal relocation assistance. In their haste to see old housing replaced with new, important questions about the value of material betterment were ignored. As terrible as conditions could be, tenement interiors were often as spotless as courtyards were filthy. Lax rules meant tenants could take in boarders or extra family as necessary. "Underconsumption" of housing as some described it also allowed families to save to build social capital, through things like a college education that encouraged upward mobility. Rock-bottom rents, especially in rooming houses, flophouses, and single-room occupancy hotels (SROs), also allowed huge numbers of the very poor to afford accommodation without subsidy. By contrast, new developments, including public housing, engaged in careful tenant screening, resulting in what historian Lawrence Vale has called "purging the poorest."[6]

The social price of slum clearance might matter less today if the utopian environments promised by housers had been realized fully. Life in new developments, however, has invariably been more complex than envisioned by policymakers and designers. Financial calculations made in one decade often fell short in the next.

COLOR KEY

- NYCHA public housing
- Mitchell-Lama
- FHA limited-dividend/-equity
- other subsidized 1926-1973
- subsidized 1974-2011
- rent control or stabilized

ICON KEY

CHAPTER 1 *(~1926-1933)*
early subsidized housing
philanthropic, 1926 housing law, federal limited-dividend (pre-FHA), private limited-equity

CHAPTER 2 *(~1934-1941)*
public housing pre-WWII
PWA NYCHA, 1937 housing act NYCHA

CHAPTER 3 *(~1948-1973)*
public housing post-WWII
1949 housing act NYCHA, state- and city-financed NYCHA

CHAPTER 4 *(~1938-1973)*
middle-income housing
FHA limited-dividend/-equity, UHF, 1942 redevelopment companies, Title I, NYS Division of Housing, Mitchell-Lama

CHAPTER 5 *(~1960-1975)*
experimental housing
community-led redevelopment, Title I, UDC, Mitchell-Lama, private limited-equity

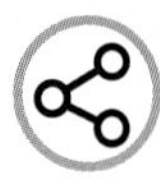

CHAPTER 6 *(~1969-2014)*
decentralized housing network
community development corporations, homesteading, HPD, federal tax credits, supportive housing

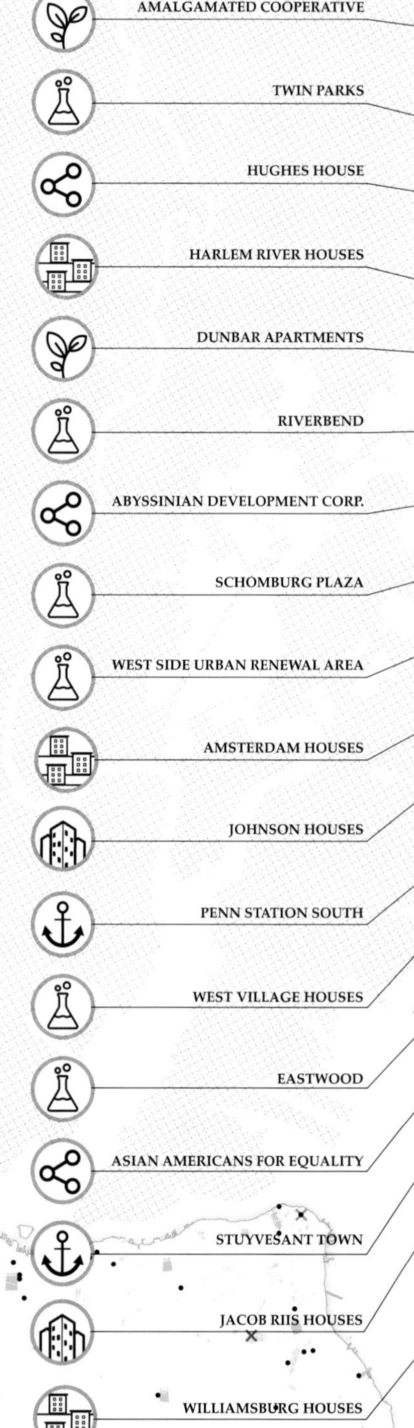

Data sources: *Public housing courtesy of NYCHA, 2011; Mitchell-Lama and subsidized 1926-2011 courtesy of Furman Center for Real Estate and Urban Policy, New York University, 2011; FHA Sec. 207, 608, 213 chiefly from Citizen's Housing and Planning Council of New York,* Directory of Large-scale Rental and Cooperative Housing, *1957; rent control or stabilized represents all 4+ unit buildings built before 1971 courtesy of New York City Department of Planning PLUTO data, 2014; base data courtesy of ESRI*

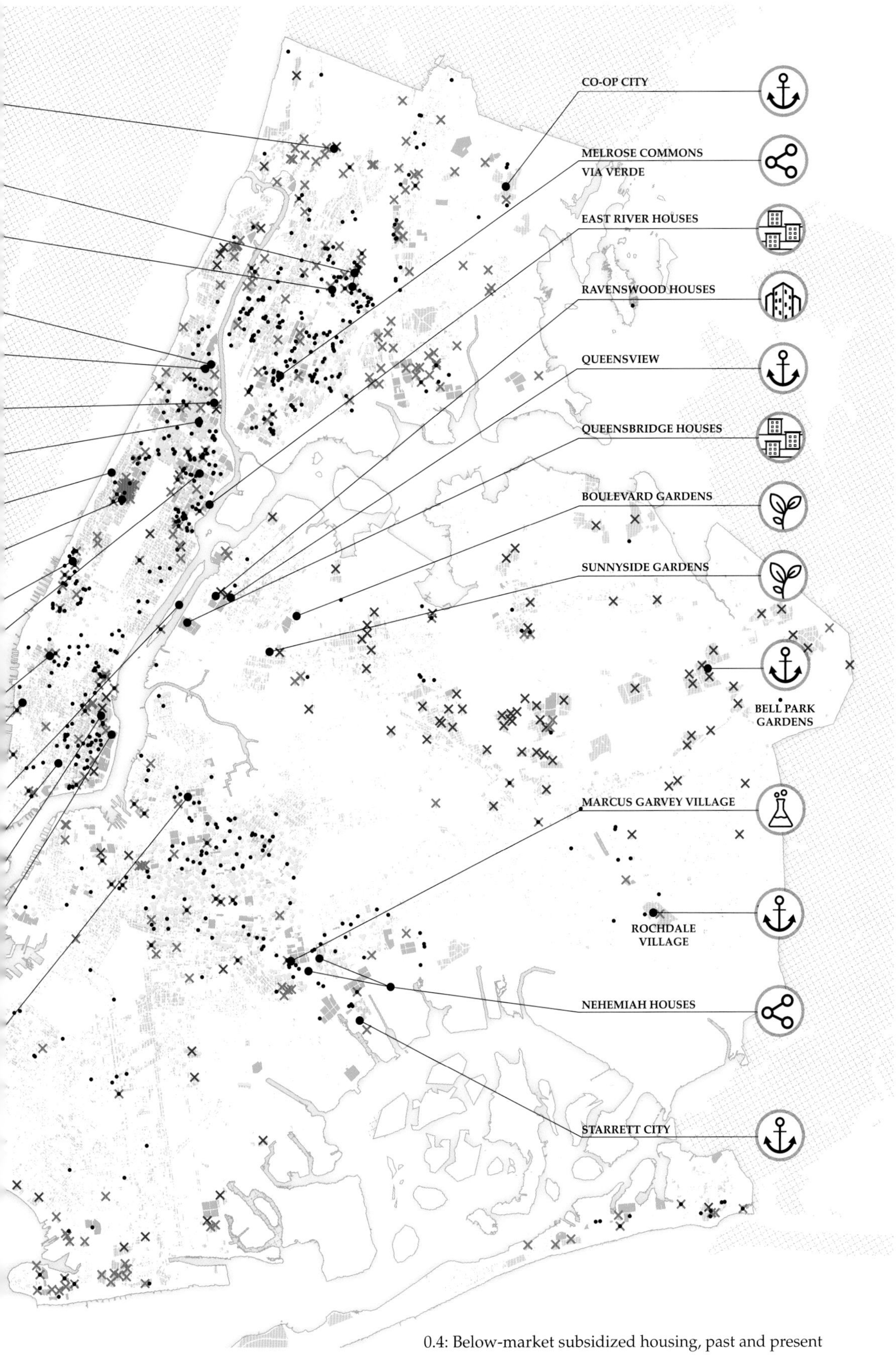

CO-OP CITY

MELROSE COMMONS

VIA VERDE

EAST RIVER HOUSES

RAVENSWOOD HOUSES

QUEENSVIEW

QUEENSBRIDGE HOUSES

BOULEVARD GARDENS

SUNNYSIDE GARDENS

BELL PARK GARDENS

MARCUS GARVEY VILLAGE

ROCHDALE VILLAGE

NEHEMIAH HOUSES

STARRETT CITY

0.4: Below-market subsidized housing, past and present

Architects and administrators too often dismissed neighborhood context, traditions, and family needs in community design. Subsidy programs often failed to maintain below-market rents or quality housing in the long term. Social problems frequently persisted.

Despite the distance between idea and building, we believe New York City's efforts constitute a success. We also believe it to be a singular one, not least because unlike in most other American cities, New York housers remained committed to the complexes they built and worked creatively, against many odds, to maintain them, physically and socially. *Affordable Housing in New York* thus calls into question stubborn American beliefs, drawn mainly from the experience of other cities, about the essential nature of big-city, below-market subsidized housing.

Chief among these is the idea that this housing is unsustainable. Outside New York, where the market has adequately housed all but the very poor and, as a consequence, public support for below-market housing has been weak except when deployed as a strategy of racial containment, subsidized projects were grievously neglected. From St. Louis's Pruitt-Igoe (1956) to Chicago's Robert Taylor Homes (1962) to San Francisco's Sunnydale (1940), political considerations led leaders to starve projects of essential resources, allowing them to become places of last resort for families living on public assistance. Meanwhile, there emerged a mismatch between the very low incomes of residents and the available subsidies, especially for maintenance, leading to rapid decay. Things fell apart so quickly and deeply that by the 1980s and 1990s the most expedient management strategy—and one embraced by leaders in most big cities—became to give up entirely: to raze everything except seniors-only projects and scatter tenants by providing them with "Housing Choice" (Section 8) vouchers (fig. 0.5).[7] In New York City, by contrast, where below-market subsidized housing has always been in great demand and enjoyed substantial political support, the housing authority, private owners, and tenant-owners (in the case of cooperatives), have proven the system not only workable but essential to the city's well-being. The greater range of income groups served even in low-cost public housing has also allowed for more sustainable financial models. This commitment is evident in low rates of turnover and long waiting lists, as well as in many of the spirited efforts to defend complexes against privatization.

0.5: Demolition of Chicago Housing Authority's Stateway Gardens (1958), 2007

It is not hard to imagine why residents of new, privately managed, below-market apartments in Manhattan find great satisfaction in their homes. But even most residents of low-income public housing—70 percent according to a 2010 survey—rate their apartments positively, despite specific complaints about issues such as crime and maintenance.[8] For low—often very low—rents, they get spacious, well-equipped units, many

0.6: View from apartment in NYCHA's Polo Grounds Towers (1968), Manhattan, 2014

with spectacular views, and well-tended lawns (fig. 0.6). In NYCHA developments and many of the larger cooperatives like Penn Station South (1962) they also might enjoy on-site social services and other community resources (fig. 0.7). Most tenants recognize how fortunate they are. For the poor, the alternatives might be homelessness, doubling up, or one of the city's illegal and unsafe subdivided or basement apartments. For middle- and moderate-income families it might be a less-favored neighborhood, a much smaller space, or leaving for the suburbs. At a time when a third of New York City households spend more than half their income on housing, below-market subsidized tenancies allow those fortunate enough to secure one not only a humane environment, but also protection from the vicissitudes of the market and money for other life essentials.[9]

The experience of below-market subsidized housing in New York City also raises questions about the widespread belief, again based chiefly on the experience of other U.S. cities, that subsidized housing is a waste of public resources. The majority of writing on affordable housing in the United States, even in New York City, frames government-aided projects as a failed experiment. Whole genres of scholarship, film, and art examine subsidized housing, especially public housing in big cities like Chicago, Baltimore, and St. Louis, as an impossible dream. In New York, however, this housing has proved not only functional but also essential to the maintenance of social diversity and to the viability of countless neighborhoods. Without subsidized housing, many sections, especially low-income areas, from Long Island City to East Harlem, might look more like decaying parts of Detroit or Philadelphia rather than the vibrant places that they are today.

Especially in the 1960s and 1970s, when landlords neglected private housing en masse in low-income neighborhoods, it was subsidized below-market complexes

0.7: Community center, NYCHA's Hammel Houses (1955), Brooklyn, 2014

that kept neighborhoods afloat where the market could not. Although the city in effect went bankrupt in 1975, its recovery in the long term was aided immensely by these investments in housing. Recent research even suggests that, contrary to stereotype, certain types of below-market housing can contribute to higher resale values in nearby market-rate housing. In this and other ways, affordable housing offers a concrete, often immediate, financial return to the city.[10]

Meanwhile, with the reversal of New York's fortunes since the 1980s, subsidized housing—where it resisted the temptation to go private (or market-rate)—has ensured a degree of social diversity in gentrifying areas that the market alone would not have been able to preserve, especially as incomes for most workers remained stagnant. From Chelsea and the East Village in Manhattan, to Williamsburg and Brownstone Brooklyn, subsidized rentals and cooperatives remain today among the last bulwarks of an economically mixed city center.

This volume critically evaluates the city's first century of below-market housing from a long-term perspective with the aim of securing more resources for a second. We use the term "below-market subsidized" here quite deliberately. "Affordable" is in wide use today, and for this reason we included it in our title. But it is a comparative term that can be stretched to include many kinds of housing. Much of today's "affordable" housing is far too expensive for working families let alone the very poor; at the same time, everything in some sense is affordable to someone, even the priciest Manhattan apartments. Moreover, "affordable housing" in many parts of the United States has come to connote specific kinds of shallow subsidies and complexes targeting "workforce" families—a term with racial overtones employed to delineate teachers and firefighters from those in more precarious circumstances. We therefore use "below-market" in this book more frequently than "affordable" because it better captures the real goal of New York City housing reformers yesterday and today: to build housing that rents or sells at submarket rates to a wide range of households thanks to government subsidies for construction and/or operations. We should also distinguish here between this type of housing and "market-rate" subsidized, like luxury condos with tax abatements, and below-market "unsubsidized," like rent-stabilized apartments.

Support for below-market subsidized housing is crucial at a time when funding for it is at risk. While arguably more necessary today than ever in New York and, increasingly, other large, expensive cities like Los Angeles and the San Francisco Bay Area, provisions have grown weaker and the system vulnerable, owing in large part to circumstances beyond any city's control. For several decades beginning with the New Deal, New York housing reformers convinced the rest of the nation to support their efforts. But there were disastrous consequences as other places applied the logic of interventions tailored to dense, centralized cities like New York. Support quickly faded. Witness the failure of Pruitt-Igoe, a high-rise complex whose chief design goal was to remake St. Louis in Manhattan's image, but which was quickly abandoned by its tenants and managers and razed, in part, on national television in 1972.

By the 1970s the declining reputation of many projects and growing national political conservatism brought the era of federal public housing to an end. Replacement programs like tax credits, which have been enormously successful nationally—and produced more units of below-market subsidized housing since 1986 than any other program over the previous hundred years—struggle against the high cost of land and construction in New York. More importantly, most of today's programs allocate funds to states on a per capita basis, thus penalizing places like New York with their greater needs and capabilities. Meanwhile, the city has been fighting a war of attrition as public housing subsidies decline and privately owned below-market complexes convert to market-rate after their subsidies expire.[11]

As in earlier eras, proposals to remedy New York City's special housing problems abound. Mayor Bill de Blasio, like Mayor Michael Bloomberg before him, is working aggressively to preserve apartments that are poised to exit subsidy and other rent-restriction programs; his administration has proposed to use billions in city capital funds and city-secured bonds to build new apartments. De Blasio's most provocative proposal is to expand inclusionary zoning, which, following rent-stabilization and -control, shifts some of the burden of subsidy to landlords and market-rate co-tenants. Activists influenced by neoliberal economists like Edward Glaeser argue that the high cost of housing is caused by land-use regulation, including zoning and historic preservation, and that the answer, naturally, is deregulation, ignoring the fact that New York's extreme housing inequality predates the regulation of land use by generations. Yet others, following this same logic, have argued that the housing needs of the city can be better met through a "making room" strategy of building tiny units—so-called microapartments—for the growing number of small middle-class households.[12]

This book, by showcasing inspiring communities, programs, and leaders over the past century, urges New York to think bigger. We believe that the only way to achieve truly equitable, and durable, housing outcomes in the city is, as housing leaders like Mary Simkhovitch realized a century ago, deep public subsidies for production and maintenance of low- and middle-income housing. We hope to marshal new resources for maintenance and production of subsidized housing by showing how most efforts in New York City have been a success—even when mundane in design—by providing quality accommodation for millions of city dwellers over decades of dramatic urban change. Through historic precedent and examination of some of today's more recent examples, we seek to remind a new generation, including politicians in Albany and Washington, D.C., that the housing question in a big expensive city like New York demands big solutions: large-scale funding, and even large-scale complexes, however out of fashion both might be. We hope that our work inspires citizens and leaders alike to pursue them.

Affordable Housing in New York is not the first book to explore housing in New York City with an eye to influencing future action. Yet while there are many studies of below-market housing in New York, our humanistic, longitudinal, large-scale approach fills several gaps in the literature. One is for a single survey. Much writing addresses the city's leading role in the creation of affordable housing: from tenement reform to the National Housing Acts of 1937 and 1949 that created public housing. Other work investigates specific leaders, policies, and themes. Nicholas Dagen Bloom, for example, has previously published a history of the New York City Housing Authority and Matthew Gordon Lasner has written about nonspeculative cooperative ownership as part of a national movement toward co-op and condominium living in the twentieth century. No single title, however, has explored the entire sweep of the city's below-market subsidized housing, much less from a long-term, ground-up perspective that examines housing in its social and neighborhood contexts.

The closest example is Richard Plunz's unparalleled *A History of Housing in New York City* (1990).[13] That book, however, focuses chiefly on architecture, site planning, and other innovations in physical form, as well as on the many shortcomings of postwar Modernism, rather than on long-term results. We imagine our volume as a complement. Form, including site planning, is a crucial part of our story. And our three galleries look specifically at the design of typical units over time. But equally important is how the architecture and planning has fared socially. The experience of residents and communities, we believe, must be accounted for in assessing design outcomes and history. This focus has been central to recent scholarship reevaluating postwar below-market housing in Europe but it remains underexamined in the United States (fig. 0.8). *Affordable Housing in New York* begins to correct this.[14]

0.8: Ordinary life at NYCHA's Ralph J. Rangel Houses (originally Colonial Park Houses, 1951), Manhattan, 2014

0.9: Family at Stuyvesant Town, by Michael Evans, 1973

Conceived by historians, this book trains a humanistic lens on discussions usually dominated by designers, social scientists, and policy analysts. To share the stories of New York City's below-market subsidized housing and draw attention to its remarkable achievement, this volume revisits nearly three dozen projects, some familiar, like Sunnyside Gardens (1928), Stuyvesant Town (1949), and Starrett City (1976), and some more obscure, like the West Village Houses (1974), Twin Parks (1976), and Riverbend (1968). We present them with a fresh eye, using a combination of new and historic news reports and other previously published accounts; original and previously published interviews with tenants, owners, and managers; long-term social data; and original and archival photographs (fig. 0.9). To help us, we invited more than two-dozen colleagues—including leading social and political historians, architectural historians, architects, and urban planners as well as many up-and-coming voices—to do the same. Together, we tell an alternative story about below-market subsidized housing in the United States.

The book is divided into six roughly chronological chapters that track the changing patterns in New York's below-market housing. Each of these chapters, in turn, contains a range of elements that provide opportunities for reflection and analysis: introductory essays and a conclusion by the book's editors survey major programs, leadership, and trends in each era. Case studies of representative communities offer long-term analysis of their design, financing, management, and social history. Short sketches of a few key figures and programs provide more detail and explanation. And images, including historic and contemporary photographs (many never before published), add visual data and suggest a sense of place.

Each case study begins with a summary of key characteristics including the original name of the complex; the year or years of completion, number of units, and borough; the primary initial sponsor or developer; the general program at time of opening (public housing, homeownership, private rental, limited-equity co-op), and the chief architects. We have also included in the three galleries photographs of scale models of ten, two-bedroom apartments from various eras, paired with floor plans, that provide a revealing look inside apartments and the minds of their designers and sponsors. The side-by-side comparative views they offer illustrate in concrete form evolving standards for quality in below-market housing. Models were constructed by students at the New York Institute of Technology School of Architecture under the direction of Matthias Altwicker. Eduard Hueber of Archphoto photographed them. To offer a yet richer sense of daily life in below-market housing today, visual sociologist David Schalliol contributed more than six dozen original photographs taken in the fall of 2014. Twenty-seven of them are presented in a photo essay following this introduction.

None of these elements is meant to be comprehensive or encyclopedic. But we believe that, in concert, they reveal both the quality that New York's housing leaders built into these communities and the value that residents still find in them.

Affordable Housing in New York

Photographs by David Schalliol

Fall 2014

0.10: Co-op City

0.11: Dunbar Apartments

0.12: Co-op City

0.13: Boulevard Gardens

0.14: Williamsburg Houses

0.15: Ravenswood Houses

0.16: Co-op City

0.17: Queensview

0.18: Dunbar Apartments

0.19: Co-op City

0.20: Eastwood

0.21: El Jardin de Selene, Melrose Commons

My Spirit Is with you Always
CONTRALOR
¡MÁS CLARO
NO CANTA
UN GALLO!
WELCOME

25

0.22: El Jardin de Selene, Melrose Commons

0.23: Ralph J. Rangel Houses

0.24: Co-op City

0.25: Harlem River Houses

0.26: Queensbridge Houses

0.27: Ralph J. Rangel Houses

0.28: Rochdale Village

AINBOW shop

0.29: Rochdale Village

0.30: Queensbridge

0.31: Ralph J. Rangel Houses

0.32: Ravenswood Houses

0.33: Markham Gardens

0.34: 74 W. 92nd St., West Side Urban Renewal Area

0.35: Amsterdam Houses

0.36: Eastwood

1

Below-market Subsidized Housing Begins

On May 10, 1926, New York State governor Alfred E. Smith (1919–20; 1923–28) signed into law a housing act that revolutionized the traditional relationship between government and urban housing in the United States. Before then, the public sector had mostly steered clear of subsidizing—let alone financing, building, or owning—housing. Cities and states had long regulated housing for health and safety, and New York State had passed a series of landmark tenement laws between 1867 and 1901 that elevated minimum standards. Such laws did nothing, however, to bridge the gap between the low wages of most city dwellers and the high cost of building and maintaining quality housing. By contrast, many Western European nations by the 1920s offered subsidized (below-market interest rate) loans to low-profit (limited-dividend) developers for worker housing, and authorized cities to condemn slums or buy inexpensive farmland at the urban edge for high-quality, low-cost complexes. Even in the largest, most progressive U.S. cities such as New York, however, public sentiment had remained firmly opposed to such possibilities—at least until 1926.

The 1926 act ran against the grain of urban housing reform in the United States. Most Americans in the 1920s still understood responsibility for "constructive" efforts in below-market housing to rest firmly with private philanthropy, by which was generally meant investors—many of whom were, in fact, well-to-do philanthropists—willing to accept limited profits, or "dividends," in order to offer tenants below-market rents. Several such projects had been built. In New York, the first were those of Alfred Tredway White in the 1870s, and the City and Suburban Homes Company after the turn of the century (fig. 1.1). Unfortunately, this model proved to be as limited as were the dividends, and it was neither alluring to investors on a wide scale nor especially effective at producing alternatives to slum housing except for a lucky few.

 1.1: Riverside Buildings (1890), Brooklyn, n.d.

And even the lucky few often bristled against the institutional look of projects and the strict house rules. As the *New York Times* admitted, "Philanthropy, pure and simple, will never greatly improve the housing of the people. The problem is too vast." By 1910, forty years of philanthropic building experiments had yielded units for just 3,588 families in a city with hundreds of thousands of tenement apartments. City and Suburban Homes, the city's most prolific limited-dividend developer, had still produced only a total of fifteen thousand units by the 1920s.[1]

Reformers did, however, pour energy into tenement house reform in the nineteenth and twentieth centuries, believing that regulating market housing ("restrictive" efforts) was the surest way to improved living standards. Their efforts culminated in New York State's Tenement House Act of 1901 that mandated in new construction amenities such as individual bathrooms for every apartment, larger courtyards, and that every room have a window. The law also required that owners update "old-law" tenements (adding basic indoor plumbing, for instance) and created a more powerful Tenement House agency to enforce laws. The higher-quality "new law" tenements that resulted from the legislation were built by the thousands in rapidly developing sections of the city including northern Manhattan and parts of Brooklyn, the Bronx, and, to a lesser degree, Queens. The 1901 law's attack on existing old-law tenements, however, proved far less successful. The Tenement House Department forced the addition of indoor toilets and windows, but the law had grandfathered in most existing deficiencies in order to gain sufficient political support. Moreover, enforcement proved time-consuming, machine politicians interfered, funding was inadequate, and business interests whittled away at the department's power. Hundreds of thousands of families thus continued to live in rooms that even then were considered substandard and dangerous. The only real chance for relief for most was to move out: out of the neighborhood, if not out of the city entirely.

The seeds of change lay in crisis. World War I, like all big wars, led to a great deal of inflation. In the centers of war production—such as New York City, with its many manufacturers and great port; Washington, D.C., with its government workers; and Camden, New Jersey, with its large shipyards—rising prices combined with surging populations and scarcity of labor and materials to generate an unprecedented pressure on the housing market. Vacancies fell to near zero. Rents rose. With encouragement of leftists, tenants began to organize, accusing their landlords of profiteering. Many leaders came to see the situation as an emergency.[2]

One response was rent control. In the fall of 1919, following the lead of much of Western Europe, the nation's first rent-control law was introduced covering Washington, D.C. After much debate and many failed bills, New York State followed suit in the fall of 1920 (while the war had ended quickly, the worst of the housing crisis did not subside until 1922). Another response was public stimuli for construction. Several states and local governments in the United States had already experimented with public financing or construction of housing for "wage earners," beginning with Massachusetts in 1911. Most of these efforts, however, were directed at encouraging workers to move out of cities into the countryside. Hardly any housing was produced—just a dozen houses in Massachusetts by 1919, for example.[3] Reformer Edith Elmer Wood, however, had been arguing for years for the need for state subsidies like those in Europe to house the urban poor, concluding that on its own the private market was fundamentally incapable of housing workers in decent conditions (fig. 1.2). She defended her thesis in a series of books beginning with *The Housing of the Unskilled Wage Earner: America's Next Problem*, published in 1919. Several

1.2: Below-market housing, Netherlands, from E. E. Wood, *Housing Progress in Western Europe* (1923)

other reformers now came to agree.[4] Believing that rent control was only a temporary balm, they argued for a more aggressive, proactive approach.

Wood had first become interested in housing while living in Washington, D.C., where, as in New York, building codes and philanthropy preoccupied reformers. She quickly came to see these prescriptions as insufficient. Slums, she concluded, were the only way private enterprise could house the poor in cities, and thus the only remedy was government aid. In 1914 she drafted a bill for government low-interest loans for limited-dividend companies in Washington. It failed. Hoping to acquire more expertise and authority, she moved to New York and enrolled in a social-work program, then the PhD program in political economy at Columbia University. Through coursework there she met many of New York's leading housing activists, including Lawrence Veiller and Robert De Forest. Veiller and De Forest had been key champions of the 1901 law and the attempt to enforce higher standards in "old-law" tenements. Her conviction that their restrictive measures could never suffice only hardened.[5]

During the war Wood met a new group of reformers receptive to her constructive approach: architects designing emergency wartime housing for the federal government. Chief among them was Clarence S. Stein. Born in Buffalo, Stein had been reared from age eight in progressive middle-class circles in Manhattan, attending the Society for Ethical Culture's Workingman's School. He trained professionally at Columbia and the École des Beaux-Arts in Paris, and then returned to New York in his late twenties to work for Bertram Goodhue designing, among many projects, the company town of Tyrone, New Mexico, for the Phelps Dodge mining company.

Wartime convinced him and several of his associates not only that Wood's assessment of the private market was correct but also that better housing required comprehensive development and single, nonspeculative ownership. The best way to do this, he came to believe, was government.[6]

Stein's vision encompassed both economic and aesthetic concerns. It was shaped in large part by the success, in his estimation, of several handsome wartime housing complexes his colleagues designed for the federal government in 1918. In anticipation of the war, progressive architects who had seen state-sponsored wartime housing in Britain convinced federal officials to sponsor a similar program in the United States. Congress agreed on condition that the projects be sold after the war. These new communities, both here and abroad, deeply impressed Stein and convinced him that private development, and the typical American street grid, were wasteful, adding expenses better used to improve quality and lower costs. He believed, moreover, that to achieve similar high standards in peacetime the government would have to remain involved.

Cost and control of land were not the only considerations. Stein's vision also reflected new ideas about urban design's potential role in city development and reconstruction. The problem with market-based low-income housing was not just dangerous conditions, Stein and other reformers of his era came to believe, but their high density and evident disorder, which Stein characterized as "un-American standards of living."[7] They, by contrast, favored lower densities, with low-rise structures surrounded by ample green space. This emphasis on visual unity and tidiness reflected widespread faith among reformers in the remedial power of order. They did not believe that low-density, visually controlled complexes could alone solve the problems of social inequality and poverty, but they reasoned that design exerted a strong influence on social outcomes. As architects and design critics, the appeal of such a formula is obvious. But this faith in the power of the environment to shape social conditions extended well beyond to allied fields like social work. As a result, the alternative of direct cash assistance to tenants in the form of vouchers for use in quality, private housing (one of the most common forms of housing subsidy in the United States today) was all but ignored by nearly all housing reformers when proposed in the 1930s, and for several decades more. If slums were the problem, what could prove more effective than moving slum dwellers into places that did not look like slums? Critics later found much to dislike in standardized "projects" inspired by these beliefs, but thousands of developments for both the poor and middle class trace their origins to this vision.

When Governor Smith created a State Reconstruction Commission in 1919 to address postwar housing stress, Stein volunteered to serve as secretary of the Housing Committee. The group's recommendations, published in 1920, closely reflected Stein's ideals. They proposed a state housing agency empowered to make loans, and local housing boards permitted to buy land and build housing, noting that low-interest loans for housing had "been developed by almost every other civilized country, excepting America."[8] Although the governor supported the plan, conservatives in the legislature did not. The state passed a law instead allowing cities to exempt any new apartment house from property taxes until 1932.

Both Stein and Wood kept their faith in the potential of state-subsidized housing and even made new trips, separately, to Europe in the early 1920s to learn about progress in the field. Then, in 1923, Stein organized his cohort as a group, the Regional Planning Association of America, and began forming a limited-dividend development company to construct a privately financed demonstration project: Sunnyside Gardens (1928). Although not subsidized by government, the group hoped it would make a powerful argument for the importance of large-scale, controlled development and for uniform design. In 1923 Stein also accepted an assignment from Governor Smith, heading a new Commission of Housing and Regional Planning to determine whether the "emergency" conditions that underpinned the state's rent-control program still existed. Although Stein acknowledged continuing rental shortages and rent control was extended, he took pains to explain that the housing situation was no longer, in fact, the result of the wartime crisis. Rather, he argued like Wood that substandard tenements were fundamental to the centralized, laissez-faire city. And he stressed that the only way to remedy the condition was for government to promote decentralization and reconstruction of existing slums. The tool to achieve both was low-interest loans to limited-dividend groups for construction of high-quality below-market housing.

While anathema in many respects to long-held American ideas about private property and self-reliance, the spirit of reshaping of the city along the lines that Stein and his circle promoted was in the air in 1920s New York. The city most famous for capitalist excess was simultaneously one of the most progressive on urban regulation and public infrastructure. The introduction of zoning in 1916, for instance, curbed the excesses of an unregulated real estate market that allowed new buildings to steal light and air from their neighbors. The ziggurat skyscrapers that followed, stepping politely back from the street and surrounding buildings, directly reflected the power of this all but novel kind of regulation. At the same time New York experienced its first great speculative suburban boom, as publicly subsidized subways (boasting a nickel fare) and electrified commuter railroads zipped hundreds of thousands of families out of the slums to new houses and steam-heated elevator apartments in the other boroughs and beyond. It was in the 1920s, for instance, that the Grand Concourse filled with its signature apartment houses, Jackson Heights pioneered its unique courtyard "garden apartment" cooperatives for white-collar families, and a builder named William Levitt opened shop on Long Island.

Stein's program for housing aligned with Governor Smith's wider progressive (and populist) agenda, which also included women's rights and protections for labor. Smith's upbringing and political career had been shaped by his intimate knowledge, and revulsion with, the substandard housing conditions on the Lower East Side. He and other social reformers had waited patiently for a quarter century to see if the Tenement House Act of 1901 would fulfill its promise of comprehensive slum improvement. Despite progress in new apartment construction in the boroughs, and some retrofitting to old-law tenements, it was clear that the legislation failed to remedy the tenement evil. Well into the 1920s many New Yorkers continued to live in decaying tenements lacking central heat, hot water, and adequate light and air. Tenement fires were all too common. African Americans, in particular, paid outrageous rent on substandard Harlem tenements because of a racially biased housing market.[9]

Year after year Smith supported Stein's proposals to allow the state to authorize cities to issue tax-exempt bonds to raise money to lend to limited-dividend companies for construction of quality housing for workers, especially in designated "congested" areas (slums), where the market seemed unable to generate up-to-date housing. Later iterations of Stein's proposal called, more specifically, for a state housing board to sell the bonds, a state housing bank to make loans covering up to two-thirds of the cost of construction, and state establishment of several limited-dividend housing companies—mimicking a practice pioneered in Europe. The bank would also have powers of eminent domain. According to Smith, the "fact is that the construction of certain types of homes for wage earners of small incomes is unprofitable under the existing system." But with subsidies, he noted, it would be "possible, by limited dividend corporations, to replace in time all dilapidated, disease bearing, crime breeding houses with safe, sanitary and comfortable homes."[10]

As the rental market calmed in 1924 and 1925, Smith took the lull in debate over the housing emergency as an opportunity to press harder for passage of Stein's constructive agenda, presenting a bill in early 1926. It engendered strong opposition from real estate interests. They opposed the idea of taking property and saw the plan for a housing bank as unconstitutional. But after years of struggle over housing, even some conservatives had become convinced that government action beyond rent laws was necessary. In April of that year a somewhat reduced version of the bill—stripped of the bank idea but that otherwise preserved much of Stein's proposal—passed. Formally known as the Limited Dividend Housing Companies Act, the 1926 law provided participating projects twenty years of tax exemptions and permitted municipalities to use eminent domain for site assembly. In exchange, developers had

1.3: Amalgamated Cooperative Apartments, by Wurts Bros., 1928

to agree to limit their profits to a maximum of 6 percent annually. "In approving this bill," said Governor Smith, "I do so with the sincere hope that it may prove the beginning of a lasting movement to wipe out of our State those blots upon civilization, the old, dilapidated, dark, unsanitary, unsafe tenement houses that long since became fit for human habitation and certainly are no place for future citizens of New York to grow in."[11]

The era of government-subsidized below-market housing got off to an auspicious start. The Stein Commission transformed into a permanent State Board of Housing and was given oversight of the new housing program. Trade unions, whose members were frustrated by the high cost of housing in New York City, and who had supported Stein's housing initiative, showed great enthusiasm for the legislation. Well before the law, unions had already begun building on a limited-dividend basis. The results had been bittersweet, however, because costs were simply too high. The new law now promised what one houser called a "new day in housing."[12]

The first project under the law was the Amalgamated Cooperative Apartments in the Bronx, completed in 1927 (fig. 1.3). Developed by the Amalgamated Clothing Workers of America under the direction of Abraham Kazan, the project was a monument to the power of government. While the Amalgamated Cooperative did not require eminent domain for land acquisition (a provision of the law no developer dared touch in the 1920s for fear of political backlash), it proved the potency of the law's tax abatements, which lowered costs to tenants by an average of $2.10 per room per month for a monthly savings of approximately $450 in 2013 dollars on a five-room apartment.[13] Other union projects followed. Among them was the Amalgamated Dwellings (1930) on the Lower East Side. State leaders eager to apply the 1926 law toward redevelopment suggested the project after acquiring the site privately (again

1.4: Amalgamated Dwellings, by Samuel H. Gottscho, 1931

eschewing eminent domain) (fig. 1.4). Unlike the Bronx project, which adopted Tudor revival style in deference to the architectural fashions that defined many suburban neighborhoods in the 1920s, the new downtown Dwellings embraced the Streamline Moderne style, heralding in no uncertain terms a new era for the old neighborhood.

These and other labor housing projects of the 1920s attracted significant attention for their high quality. They were also notable for their distinctive system of ownership: all were limited-equity cooperatives. This plan of co-ownership derived from the international consumers' cooperative movement, which originated in the U.K. in the early nineteenth century to provide goods and services for workers at cost. In the United States, housing co-ops for the elite were pioneered as early as 1881 in Manhattan, but Finnish immigrants in Brooklyn first applied the limited-equity approach to moderate-cost urban housing in 1916 (fig. 1.5). Unlike in a condominium, which dates to the medieval period in Europe but did not appear stateside until 1947, in a housing cooperative, homeowners held shares in a body corporate that retained title to the entire development, with rights to each home conveyed through a document called a proprietary lease. As in any other corporation, shares were divided in proportion to the size of investment (square footage) and could be sold freely on the open market. The limited-equity format used by the Finns, Kazan, and others on the left was amended to suit progressive political ends: not only were projects heavily leveraged, often with funds lent by the unions, so as to minimize down payments (hence the "limited equity"), but also votes in co-op elections were distributed on a basis of one per household rather than one per share, tenant incomes could be restricted (and were under the New York State law), and private profits from resales were prohibited.

Kazan, like many in his Jewish immigrant milieu, believed that a housing cooperative structured this way could create an alternative model of socialist cooperation

1.5: Alku I and II (1916, 1917), Sunset Park, Brooklyn, 2010

within the capitalist system. In 1924, he had attempted his first cooperative, working in collaboration with architect Andrew J. Thomas. Thomas had designed many market-rate co-ops in Jackson Heights, Queens, and believed the model could be applied to worker housing; he sought Kazan's employer, the International Ladies Garment Workers Union (and, later, the Amalgamated) as partners. Their collaboration in the Bronx failed financially and another investor completed the building. But it inspired Kazan to try again in 1927 with the Amalgamated Cooperative Apartments. With the help of state aid it succeeded. Kazan went on to became the most prolific builder of limited-equity cooperatives in the United States after World War II.[14]

Despite the aesthetic and financial success of the Amalgamated and other projects, the 1926 law was only marginally more productive than plain old philanthropy-and-five-percent. This is evident in the comparable success of John D. Rockefeller, Jr.'s 1920s projects like the Paul Laurence Dunbar Apartments (1926), in Harlem, which he developed for African American families. Like all of Rockefeller's projects, Dunbar did not take advantage of the Stein tax exemptions. Indeed, Rockefeller undertook the housing, in part, to disprove Stein's thesis that government subsidies for housing were necessary. To lower costs, which were not much different from the Amalgamated's, he relied only on construction economies and the limited-equity ownership model of ownership. While Dunbar later ran into major financial problems, so dire that the complex required government funds to survive, the short-term results impressed many.

This success, like the rather modest impact of the 1926 law, was not lost on Stein and other housing reformers. But it hardened their resolve that the only way to achieve very low-cost, up-to-date housing, whether built by municipalities or by limited-dividend operators, was not just tax exemptions or eminent domain but

1.6: Boulevard Gardens (1935), 1940

long-term, low-interest loans covering most of the cost of construction. These types of loans—whose efficacy was being proven all over Europe—later became key elements of U.S. public housing legislation as it developed in the 1930s and 1940s.

When the nation's housing market plunged into crisis in 1929 for the second time in a generation, New York's housers made their case again. And not just to Albany but to federal officials now desperate for ideas that would stimulate the economy. Early on in the Great Depression, President Herbert Hoover's Reconstruction Finance Corporation made federal money available for limited dividends, albeit mainly as a means to stimulate construction. Under this program department-store heir Nathan Straus, Jr., who later served as the administrator of the federal public housing program, built Hillside Homes (1935) in the Bronx, designed by Stein, while mainstream developer Fred French, desperate for work, built Knickerbocker Village (1934) on the Lower East Side. Momentum continued to build with a new Democratic administration. In his first months in office, President Franklin D. Roosevelt launched the Public Works Administration, which had a dedicated Housing Division led by an old colleague of Stein, Robert D. Kohn. Through that program Congress continued to finance limited-dividend projects, such as Boulevard Gardens (1935) in Queens (fig. 1.6). But housing reformers, led in part by Wood and in part by a young protégé of Stein named Catherine Bauer, dreamed bigger. With support from national trade unions, an increasingly desperate American public began to come around to the idea. The call for public housing would soon grow too loud to ignore.

Tenements

The most common type of residence in New York City in the late nineteenth and early twentieth centuries was the tenement. "Tenement" is an old English word. But it was also a legal term, codified by New York State in 1867 to refer to any building housing more than three families living independently and cooking on the premises and, twenty years later, any building housing three or more households, period.[15] This definition was quite sweeping and at first made no distinction between cramped buildings with tiny sets of rooms lacking amenities, and those with well-equipped apartments for the affluent.[16] In common parlance, however, a tenement came to be understood as a speculatively built, multiple dwelling for the poor, set on a narrow lot, housing many families with little light and air and few of the amenities, such as running water, gas, and private toilets (fig. 1.7).

The form that tenements took and the character of the city's tenement neighborhoods was determined by a variety of factors, including the limited size and narrow dimensions of typical New York City lots, the desire of speculative builders to maximize profits, the succession of laws that regulated the size and shape of buildings, and the extraordinary influx of poor European immigrants to New York willing to abide poor conditions, at least briefly upon arrival.[17] As poor immigrants began flooding into New York in the 1830s, older single-family row houses were subdivided for six or more households. Owners soon realized that they could make even more money by replacing houses with purpose-built structures containing twenty or more apartments. The result was the beginning of the tenement as a housing type. By the 1860s neighborhoods closest to the commercial center of Lower Manhattan, notably the Lower East Side, were being transformed by such buildings. As the Citizens' Council of the City of New York noted in 1866 in the first report to examine housing conditions in the city, for the poor and working class, "a degree of crowding has been attained which by itself has become a subject of sanitary inquiry and public concern."[18] Conditions were exacerbated in the late 1860s and 1870s by the construction of scores of new tenements each year, not only on the Lower East Side but in

1.7: Tenements model, Tenement House Exhibition, 1900

Greenwich Village, on the blocks close to the East River as far north as East Harlem and along the Hudson River up to Columbus Circle.

German and Irish immigrants built large numbers of these early tenements. Architects were also generally immigrants. Most buildings were brick with simple façade details in the Italianate and Neo-Greco styles, since cornices, lintels, and other elements in these styles were available at local building yards. Buildings extended deep into the lot, although some were shallower with rear structures behind a small courtyard. They typically had four apartments of two or three rooms per floor, with stores on the ground floor or in a raised basement. Little if any light or air reached the majority of rooms, and there was no access to water, in spite of the fact that water lines had been laid beneath the streets. Privies, generally connected to the sewer system, and a water pump were located in the yard. Design was virtually unregulated. An 1862 state act established what would become the Department of Buildings and mandated certain minimal structural standards, as well as fire escapes; the Tenement House Act of 1867 required a toilet or privy for every twenty families, minimum ceiling heights, and a few other requirements that were frequently ignored. Rather, speculative builders erected tenements with as many rentable apartments as possible.

Density and the resulting unsanitary conditions increased through the 1870s. Reformers advocated for a law that would address these conditions, especially in regard to providing light and air and toilet facilities. The result of this campaign was the New York State Tenement Act of 1879. The tenements erected by the thousands under this regulation, later referred to as "old-law" tenements, still occupied twenty-five-foot-wide lots and still stretched deeply into the lot, but every room had to open onto the street, a yard, or an air shaft, and one toilet was required for every two families. The most common form for tenements erected under the 1879 law was the "dumbbell," so called because of the pinched shape resembling a dumbbell weight that resulted from the addition of shafts at either side of the building. Some architects arranged the air shafts in other ways to meet the requirements of the law, eschewing the dumbbell shafts for multiple rectilinear side shafts or small shafts set in the center of the building. In neighborhoods already filled with tenements, such as the Lower East Side, some surviving small-scale row houses and other buildings were demolished and replaced by tenements erected under the 1879 regulations, but the largest concentrations of old-law tenement construction was in neighborhoods that had not yet been heavily redeveloped with tenements, such as the South Village, or developed at all, including Hell's Kitchen, Yorkville, and East Harlem. Old-law tenements were not much of an improvement over those built earlier, since the small shafts added little light or air to most apartments, and actually served as conduits for noise and smells, and as flues in a fire. As an editorial writer for the *New York Times* noted, if the dumbbell was the best solution to the city's housing problems, then "the problem is unsolvable."[19]

The increase in population density in tenement districts and the increasingly large area of the city filled with these tenements alarmed Progressive reformers and inspired them to press for new restrictive legislation. Growing media attention to the slums, as indicated by the popularity of Jacob Riis's *How the Other Half Lives* (1890), kept the public engaged in the issue (fig. 1.8). Much of developed Manhattan by the turn of the century was packed with tenement buildings. In 1903, 2.3 million

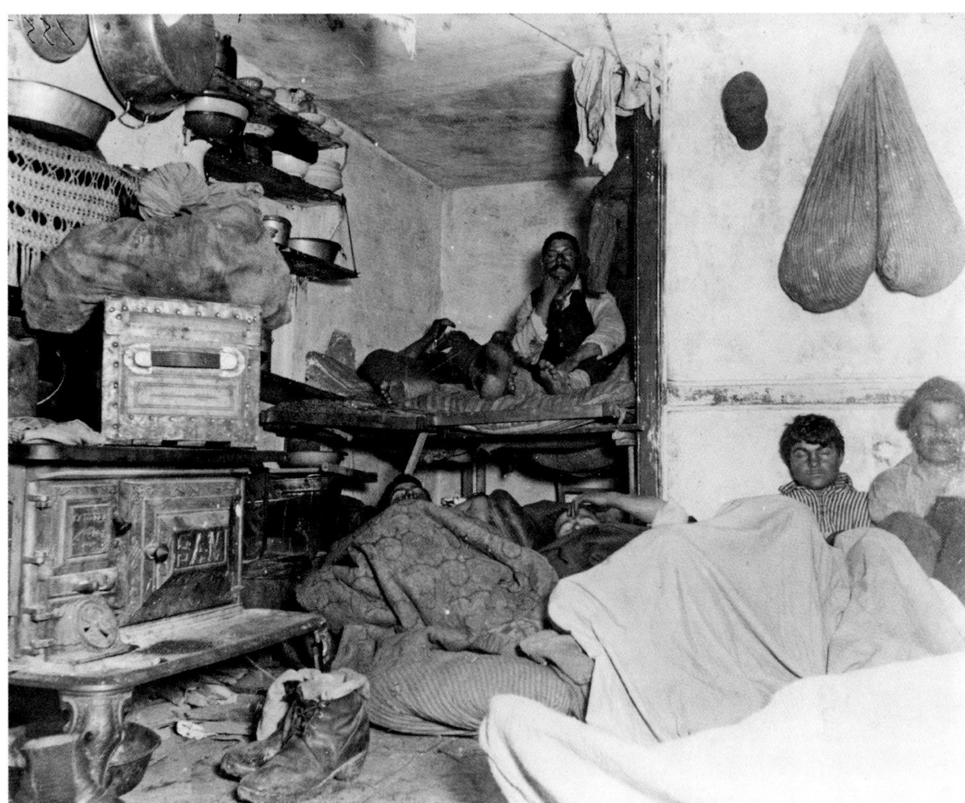

1.8: Lodgers in a crowded Bayard Street tenement, "Five Cents a Spot," by Jacob Riis, ca. 1890

New Yorkers (two-thirds of the city's population) lived in 82,000 tenements, 42,000 of which were in Manhattan. In these Manhattan tenements lived more than 85 percent of the borough: nearly 1.6 million people. Not all tenements were substandard, but even the best reflected an outmoded era's ideas of acceptable housing.[20] The dramatic Tenement House Exhibition staged by Progressives in 1900 included not only major speeches by leading reformers such as Governor Theodore Roosevelt, but also instructive models, plans, photographs, maps, charts and tables of statistics showing the problematic conditions in which so many of New York's citizens lived. Alongside these documents were positioned images of model tenements from all over the world. The cry went out for new legislation, more model tenements, and better management of old ones.[21]

This campaign bore fruit with the passage of the Tenement House Act of 1901, often referred to as the "new law." This act made it impossible for developers to build on single city lots, required larger airshafts and a toilet in every new apartment, and established minimum room sizes. The law also, for the first time, mandated changes to existing buildings, including the addition of lighting, openings between windowless rooms, and one toilet for every two families.

Despite the strenuous objections by the real estate community to what they viewed as significant, unnecessary, and costly improvements, the law was a compromise that had mixed results. Circulation of light and air were greatly improved, but the small light slots added to either the side or rear of buildings in dense Manhattan

1.9: Abandoned tenement, 9–11 Catherine St., Manhattan, by Charles von Urban, 1932

neighborhoods like Harlem were still suboptimal. In areas farther from business districts, where land was less expensive, especially at the northern edge of Manhattan and in the other boroughs, builders erected tenements on much wider plots with more generous light courts that did, indeed, improve conditions for those who could afford the rents and commutes. Although the real estate community argued that the new law was so burdensome that construction of tenements would virtually cease, record numbers of tenements were built after 1901. On the Lower East Side and in other early tenement neighborhoods, the law had a substantial impact, too. After unsuccessfully opposing the toilet requirements all the way to the Supreme Court, many owners chose to build brick and stone or concrete outhouses on their lots; Department of Building records indicate the construction of over one thousand outhouses between about 1903 and 1912.[22] Many other owners took space away from half of the apartments to cut a fireproof ventilation shaft through the building and construct two toilets on each floor, adding water pipes and sinks to apartments as well. In 1934 the law was updated to require the removal of all flammable wood in public halls and stairs. By then, however, so many had moved out of the neighborhood that countless landlords found it more economical to board up their buildings and close shop rather than renovate (fig. 1.9). ANDREW S. DOLKART

City and Suburban Homes Company (1898–1938)

The City and Suburban Homes Company was the largest builder and operator of philanthropic, limited-dividend, "model tenement" apartments in New York City and the nation in the early decades of the twentieth century, eventually owning more than fifteen thousand low-rent apartments in complexes in Manhattan, Brooklyn, and Queens.[23] The company's large-scale operations, high-quality product, and careful methods for selection of tenants set early standards for best practices in model housing, and served as an example for later government-aided efforts. Yet even its leaders ultimately admitted that philanthropic housing was no match for the city's slums.

The company emerged as a Progressive effort to remedy conditions in speculatively built tenements in the late nineteenth century. In 1894 reformers initiated an investigation of the tenement problem that was carried out by the state. This work led to a conference in 1896 sponsored by the Association for Improving the Condition of the Poor, and to the establishment of the Improved Housing Council, which sponsored a competition for the design of a better model tenement. The competition brief required buildings for lots a hundred feet wide, with 30 percent of the site reserved for yards and light courts. The building was to be divided into separate sections, each with its own fireproof stair, thus limiting the number of tenants using a stairway. Apartments were to be two rooms deep with cross ventilation. Each would have its own toilet. The competitors also had to prove that their building could make a 5 percent annual return. The first-place winner was Ernest Flagg, who had previously proposed light-court apartments in an 1894 article in *Scribner's Magazine*.[24] The results of the competition were so promising that the housing council organized the City and Suburban Homes Company to realize them.

1.10: Clark Estate, ca. 1903

Unlike earlier philanthropic efforts such as those of Alfred Tredway White, which were funded in their entirety by a single investor, City and Suburban was planned as a stock company in hope of raising sufficient capital to undertake a large-scale construction program. As in other "philanthropic" housing schemes, including White's, subscribers were promised a modest annual return of 5 percent (later raised to 6 to attract more capital). Excess profits were to go to new construction and maintenance. While the system allowed for investment by people of modest means, shareholders included Astors, Morgans, Pratts, and Rockefellers, many of whom had been involved in housing reform for years. They believed, in conservative fashion, that it was with them and not government that "responsibility" rested for "making good citizens of the tenement population."[25] Elgin R. L. Gould, an economist and a political scientist, who had written the well-regarded book *The Housing of Working People*, was elected president of the company. Gould called overcrowded tenements "little better than a human slaughterhouse" and claimed that they created "poverty, crime, drunkenness, and immorality." To rip these houses down, he argued, "quite accords with other sanitary practices such as pouring bad milk into the gutter and confiscating and destroying decayed articles of food exposed for sale."[26]

In 1896, with a capitalization of one million dollars, planning began on three projects. Flagg designed the Clark Estate, a complex of six tenements on West 68th and 69th Streets between Amsterdam and West End Avenues on land donated by Mrs. Alfred Corning Clark (demolished for Lincoln Towers as part of the Lincoln Square Urban Renewal project) (fig. 1.10). James E. Ware, who won second place in the 1896 competition, designed the first two buildings of what would become the large First Avenue Estate. Percy Griffin, whose design earned third prize, designed a series of houses for the Homewood complex in the New Utrecht neighborhood of Brooklyn

1.11: Homewood, 1897

(fig. 1.11). The First Avenue Estate (1898–1915), on the block bounded by East 64th and 65th Streets and First and York Avenues, eventually came to have fifteen separate buildings, most designed by Ware and the remainder by the company's in-house architect Philip H. Ohm. A few years later the company launched a second large project: The Avenue A (later York Avenue) Estate (1900–1913), on the block bounded by East 78th and 79th Streets, York Avenue, and the East River. This was the company's largest development, providing 1,257 apartments in thirteen buildings, plus the Junior League Hotel for working women, with 336 rooms. The Avenue A Estate buildings were designed by Griffin, Ohm, and Harde & Short, which had won a prize for a model tenement in separate competition,.

City and Suburban's model tenements were six-story walk-ups with small apartments, but each building and unit was well built and carefully configured, affording amenities that contrasted dramatically with conditions in speculative tenements (fig. 1.12). A 1905 City and Suburban publication described a typical unit:

> Every apartment is a complete *home* in itself, with private toilet accommodation wholly within the dwelling. Every room has quiet, light, air, and an abundance of ventilation. Stairways and stair walls are entirely fireproof. . . . Flats have steam heat radiators, private hall, private watercloset, [are] well ventilated [all apartments had cross-ventilation], [have] floors and partitions deafened [*sic*] between dwellings, hot water from boiler room, two porcelain tubs, large sink and drain board, large dresser with shelves, closets and drawers, plaster hanging closets instead of wooden wardrobes, gas range (no rent or deposit to be paid), quarter meter (no deposit to gas company), storage closet in basement. The four-room flats have private baths [baths were later installed in smaller units].[27]

1.12: First Avenue Estate, ca. 1903

City and Suburban's complexes housed a heterogeneous but carefully selected group of working-class New Yorkers. Indeed, the apartments were available to only working, married couples and their children: what, in the nineteenth century, would have been referred to as the "deserving poor." The annual reports frequently listed the nationality of tenants and their occupations. In 1912, for example, residents were of thirty-three nationalities, although unlike in most tenements, the largest number were American born.[28] As would be expected from the location of the two largest projects in Yorkville, a neighborhood largely populated by immigrants from Central Europe, the next largest groups were German and Hungarian immigrants. The City and Suburban complexes were not racially integrated. Nevertheless, the founders were aware of the serious housing needs of the city's Black community and built the Tuskegee (1902) and Hampton (1912) on West 62nd and 63rd Streets in the San Juan Hill neighborhood for Black tenants (both demolished for the Amsterdam Houses). These buildings were designed by Howells & Stokes (I. N. Phelps Stokes was also active in housing reform). The 1912 report also lists 199 occupations for tenants, a cross section of working-class New York, with significant numbers of barbers, bartenders, bakers, carpenters, chauffeurs, cooks, cigar makers, dressmakers, housekeepers, laborers, laundresses, machinists, nurses, painters, porters, and waiters.[29] In many households, both the husband and wife were employed.

City and Suburban Homes was the first of the city's limited-dividend companies to employ the Octavia Hill management methods that had been pioneered in London in the late nineteenth century and are widely viewed as the origins of the modern field of social work. Octavia Hill's model tenements, tightly controlled by the female managers, had long provided inspiration for housing reformers in cities such as New York and Philadelphia. Trained, educated women at City and Suburban Homes thus "[call]on the tenants and collect the rent and report back to the office on the condition of the apartment, the tenant and other matters."[30] Unfortunate tenants who faced a negative report might lose their apartments. A later president of City and Suburban Homes, Allan Robinson, affirmed that when it came to their behavioral standard, "those who do not live up to it will not remain long in our buildings."[31]

City and Suburban continued building model apartment houses after World War I, including one at its Homewood property in Brooklyn designed by prominent reform housing designer Andrew J. Thomas (1919–20) and the Celtic Park Apartments in Woodside Queens (1931–39), with the first unit designed by Ernest Flagg and the remaining five units by Springsteen & Goldhammer, a firm best known for its limited-equity co-ops. City and Suburban also bought several model tenement complexes built by other individuals or foundations. As a business enterprise the operation was successful. The company not only amassed sufficient capital to build, and revenue to return dividends of almost 5 percent between 1899 in 1936, but it also put these funds to work in "careful scientific architectural planning and large-scale production."[32]

As a tool to rebuild more than isolated fragments of the city, however, it was less successful. One problem was scale. As the president of the company, Robinson, admitted in 1917, "if we should increase our capacity tenfold we would be helping only a paltry fraction" of tenement dwellers in the city.[33] A second problem was the depth of funding required to reach a broader clientele. The truly poor lacked the wages necessary to make the philanthropy-and-five-percent model operative. As one of the era's leading architects in the field of model housing, Henry Atterbury Smith, explained in 1912, "The model tenements are too expensive. They are built for the very poor, but the very poor do not live in them. They can't afford it."[34]

City and Suburban continued to operate until it disbanded in 1961. Although several of the small projects, mainly on the West Side, were demolished after World War II, and several on the East Side have been threatened with demolition since the 1980s, most remain intact, home to low- and moderate-income families. They stand as testament to the design, planning, and construction employed by the company over a century ago in meeting its mandate to provide quality housing for working people. ANDREW S. DOLKART

Paul Laurence Dunbar Apartments (1926, 511 units, Manhattan)

Sponsor: private philanthropist (John D. Rockefeller, Jr.)
Program: limited-equity co-op
Architect: Andrew Jackson Thomas

The Paul Laurence Dunbar Apartments set new standards for urban housing by offering well-built apartments at modest prices to African Americans (fig. 1.13). In

1.13: Dunbar Apartments, ca. 1931

the decades to come, however, the Harlem complex revealed the limits of private philanthropy. Like many similar developments, the Dunbar Apartments faced significant challenges maintaining its financial footing, absent government subsidies, as the city's economy and social landscape changed.

Dunbar Apartments was one of half a dozen large-scale housing complexes created by John D. Rockefeller, Jr., in and around New York City in the 1920s. Rockefeller initiated Dunbar Apartments after he was approached by the New York Urban League about the dearth of responsible landlords and high-quality housing for "reputable" families in Harlem. A staunch conservative, he pursued projects like Dunbar in part as an argument against mounting calls by reformers like Clarence Stein for state intervention in housing. For this reason he refused tax abatements that Dunbar qualified for under the 1926 state housing law. He nevertheless achieved lower prices and better conditions than the market. After equity down payments of $50 a room, payable by installment over three years, Dunbar cost about $14.50 per month per room in maintenance, which covered taxes, upkeep, and utilities. In practice this meant $250 down for a five-room apartment with $72.50 a month in maintenance ($10,500 and $3,000 in 2013 dollars).[35]

A major goal for Dunbar was to create an environment less susceptible to social and physical decay than ordinary speculative housing. To help do this, architect Andrew J. Thomas's design emphasized control, surveillance, and intimacy, despite the complex's vast and unprecedented size: 511 apartments arranged in six buildings (later increased to 536 by dividing up some units). Thomas, who had pioneered a new apartment-complex type in the late 1910s at Jackson Heights that came to known for several years as simply "garden apartment," did this in two ways. First, he broke up the block into multiple buildings served by separate entryways, each leading to an enclosed stairwell. Typically only two or three units shared a landing at each floor. Second, he reversed the orientation of buildings so that entries faced the landscaped (and patrolled) garden court rather than the street, creating a cloistered effect

1.14: Dunbar Apartments, entryways from courtyard, by Dynecourt Mahon, 1979

recalling a college quadrangle (fig. 1.14). Access to the court was through eight archways. This feature, which tenants continue to appreciate today, helped distinguish Dunbar from surrounding tenements.

Rockefeller's desire for control was also evident in Dunbar's governance. Unlike market-rate co-ops (or, in later eras, condominiums) where tenant-owners have complete control over their buildings, Rockefeller remained in charge of Dunbar. In this respect he followed the precedent of early co-ownership schemes devised by middle-class reformers to house working-class tenants in Britain in the nineteenth century. Rockefeller effected his paternalism by retaining preferred shares of stock in Dunbar's cooperative corporation, with plans to retire them only once the tenants had repaid all construction loans, after thirty years. In practice he kept a tight grip by imposing rules at whim and selecting property managers who reported directly to his office. At Dunbar this meant no private resales, no playing on lawns, no taking in boarders, and a Harvard-educated resident manager who, despite being African American, saw the owners more as wards than clients.

1.15: Dunbar Apartments, living room, by Dynecourt Mahon, 1979

Notwithstanding concerns that management was "autocratic," for years "Dunbar Gardens," as some called it, was among the best housing open to African Americans in the United States.[36] Dunbar became an important center of Black life, attracting many distinguished tenants at a time when racial discrimination in housing left African Americans with few options for high-quality accommodation. In addition to well-laid-out apartments with up-to-date kitchens and bathrooms, Dunbar offered a nursery, recreation room, playground, and private security (fig. 1.15). The most frequent occupation among tenants was clerks, but it was also home to many Black notables, including W.E.B. DuBois, Paul Robeson, Bojangles (Bill Robinson), and A. Philip Randolph. In the early years median household income was $1,800 a year ($75,000 in 2013 dollars), although a study by NYCHA in 1937 found 70 percent of tenants eligible for public housing.[37] Retail tenants included a large Madam C. J. Walker salon billed in ads as "the race's finest beauty shoppe," and the Dunbar National Bank, set up by Rockefeller to serve, and employ, African Americans. By 1932, after five years in operation, more than three-quarters of Dunbar's original families were still in residence. Many remained for the rest of their lives.

Like many co-ops, however, Dunbar did not survive the Depression. It suffered a comparatively modest vacancy rate but many owners fell behind on maintenance payments and the project began operating at a deep loss. To maintain cash flow Rockefeller began allowing new tenants to rent rather than buy. Eventually he foreclosed on it, buying it back at auction to operate as a rental. Meanwhile, when the first New Deal funds became available for public housing, in 1935, he realized his argument against state intervention in housing was lost and began divesting himself of all his housing. A plan was devised to sell an unbuilt Harlem parcel (where an addition to Dunbar had been planned) to NYCHA along with Dunbar for conversion to low-income public housing. Many at NYCHA and in Dunbar supported the idea, but

1.16: Photographs by Edward Lettau from Edward Wakin and Edward Lettau, *At the Edge of Harlem* (1965)

Rockefeller ended up selling to an investment group comprised of several of his associates, retaining the mortgage. In 1942 he agreed to a second sale, to the New York Society of the Methodist-Episcopal Church, on condition that any operating profits be used to minister to the city's African American community.[38]

Dunbar's community life remained remarkably stable throughout. The Dunbar Housewives' League, established in 1931, continued to sponsor Harlem's Own Cooperative, Inc., a consumers' cooperative for at-cost sale of dairy, and by the late thirties had organized a powerful Tenants' League. Meanwhile, the Methodists maintained high standards with plenty of heat, hot water, and fresh paint, and the complex continued to be described in the press as "swanky." After World War II its many five- and six-room apartments made it a hub of Black middle-class life, complete with Boy Scout troops.[39] In a 1965 book about the Black struggle to escape the ghetto, Edward Wakin and photographer Edward Lettau presented Dunbar as an island apart from the distressed neighborhood. Called *At the Edge of Harlem*, the book, which followed a companion TV documentary, explored the life of one second-generation Dunbar couple, the Crearys, and their six children. Wakin described them as "middle-class holdout[s] resisting deprivation" at the "edge of Harlem—both physically and psychologically" (fig. 1.16).[40]

As the building aged and Harlem decayed, Dunbar struggled to keep at bay the ravages of the urban crisis. Already by 1965, reported Wakin, Dunbar had become "more respectable than stylish . . . straining to keep up appearances." As the open-housing movement advanced, many of the more stable tenants, including the Crearys, sought alternatives. "Unlike the downtrodden Negro who has become a well-known statistic," the Crearys, with their Rambler station wagon and weekend trips to suburban parks and supermarkets, "are ready to leave."[41] Meanwhile, with more half of the apartments under rent control and the balance rent stabilized, it was difficult for the owners to make the complex pay while maintaining high standards. In the mid-sixties, after years of losses, the Methodists were forced to sell. Dunbar was bought by the first in a series of speculative operators who also failed to make the place work financially.[42]

In the seventies, Dunbar earned protection through its placement on the city's list of landmarks and on the National Park Service's Register of Historic Places. Yet by the end of the decade another lender had foreclosed and it was run down, with more than a hundred vacancies. The tenants who remained were struggling, with many qualifying for federal Section 8 rent vouchers. To stabilize the building the lender secured city financing for a costly renovation and launched a plan to convert to co-op. Conversion had allowed thousands of buildings in New York and other cities to pay their way while forestalling, even reversing, decay. At Dunbar the plan was to employ a low-cost limited-equity format that required down payments of just $2,000 to $3,000 from exiting tenants ($4,700 to $7,000 in 2013 dollars). The proposal enjoyed the support of the federal government, private lenders, and many tenants. Others, however, resisted and the plan provoked so much controversy that the bank gave up and sold Dunbar to yet another investor in the mid-eighties.[43]

The past three decades have seen many different owners, many schemes for re-financing, more incomplete renovations, and many failed plans for conversion to co-op or condominium. The buildings have also seen more neglect, more crime (drugs, parties, and prostitution in vacant apartments), and more conflict between landlord and tenant. The most recent such struggle was been between residents and Pinnacle Group, which bought Dunbar in 2005. Dunbar still had seventy-four rent-controlled units, with the balance rent stabilized; Pinnacle specialized in renovating down-at-heels complexes in gentrifying areas. In a series of moves perfected at other buildings, Pinnacle enhanced security while trying to evict nearly half the tenants, including anyone behind on rent or whose name was not on his or her lease (typically heirs claiming successor rights). Although very few of the evictions went through, the Dunbar Tenants Association worked with other Pinnacle buildings to voice concerns, launching a class-action lawsuit in 2007 that was settled in the tenants' favor in 2011. By then, however, Pinnacle had defaulted and the complex had been foreclosed on again; it was sold at auction in 2013 to yet another new investor.[44]

Despite these struggles, many tenants are happy and the complex retains a special mystique—what one tenant calls Harlem "renaissance magic."[45] When Pinnacle bought it, the *New York Amsterdam News* reported that the "apartment fortress ha[d] crumbled into a dingy maze" with vermin, graffiti, drug dealing, and broken windows.[46] Today, disruptive households are gone, maintenance requests are handled (at least for new tenants), and the courtyard, thanks to the efforts of many volunteers, is in bloom. Socially, Dunbar has come to house a greater mixture of New Yorkers than ever before, including many Latinos; new immigrants, especially from Africa; and artists, musicians, actors, and students, some of whom are white (whites now make up 7 percent of the larger census tract, up from 1 percent in 2000). Like the many old-guard and second-generation families who remain, they appreciate the low rents—despite recent increases—and the well-laid-out apartments "designed for people."[47] And they love the sense of community, security, and serenity afforded by Thomas's design. As tenant Ramona explains, "The design of the building is phenomenal. We live in a two bedroom that has light, exposure on all four sides. When have you heard of that?" Moreover, "the gardens are so gorgeous" and, in the words of a neighbor, full of "peacefulness."[48]

As yet another tenant, Barbara, explains, "this building has far more of a hold on people than your average apartment building. . . . The greatest thing is that you do know your neighbors and you do stop and chat in the courtyard." The challenge now is to improve the complex without displacing tenants. She, at least, "remain[s] ever optimistic that it will return to its former glory, and not make people homeless in the process."[49] MATTHEW GORDON LASNER

Sunnyside Gardens (1928, 1,202 units, Queens)

Sponsor: private nonprofit (City Housing Corporation)
Program: homeownership, limited-equity co-op, private rental
Architect: Clarence Stein, Henry Wright

Sunnyside Gardens was conceived by a group of architects and critics led by Clarence Stein to demonstrate the redemptive power of nonspeculative real estate development and high-quality suburban design. The low-slung yellow- and red-brick apartment buildings and row houses, now enveloped by plantings and mature trees, set a new standard for low-cost urban housing both in New York and the nation. Not even Sunnyside's financial problems in the 1930s, and loss of some communal space in the decades that followed, erased the idealism that informed its planning.

Frustrated by the banal designs of developer-built housing, concerned that profit motive helped generate slum conditions, and alarmed by inflationary wartime rents in the years surrounding World War I, Stein along with colleagues like the architects Robert Kohn, Charles Whitaker, Henry Wright, and Frederick Ackerman, and design critic Lewis Mumford, became enamored of new architect-designed communities being built in the U.K. by followers of Ebenezer Howard's Garden Cities movement, who believed that poor urban housing conditions had to be addressed, at least in part, through coordinated decentralization. In 1918 Stein and his circle fought successfully to convince Congress to develop similar communities in critical defense areas state-side. Stein continued to advocate for Garden City-style housing developments on a local basis during peacetime. His efforts, after an uphill battle, led eventually to New York's 1926 state housing law allowing tax abatements for limited-dividend projects.[50]

Stein was eager, however, to get building in the 1920s even without state aid. After formalizing his ever-widening salon—which came to include economist Stuart Chase, conservationist Benton MacKaye, real estate developer Alexander M. Bing, and, from time to time, housing activist Edith Elmer Wood—as the Regional Planning Association of America (RPAA), Stein convinced Bing to create a limited-dividend company to develop complexes in advance of government support. They

1.17: Sunnyside Gardens, display advertisement, *New York Times*, September 20, 1925

called the group the City Housing Corporation (CHC). In 1924 they launched a pilot project. The site selected was an inexpensive industrial tract adjacent to a rail yard in Sunnyside, Queens.

As built Sunnyside Gardens represented a best effort given many constraints. One compromise concerned ownership. Although Stein and friends were interested more in design than in progressive political economies—indeed, the evil they discerned in private ownership was mostly framed in terms of limitations on design—they professed a deep interest in following Ebenezer Howard's model of co-ownership. Borrowed by Howard from earlier U.K. low-cost housing experiments, the model, which resembled a limited-equity cooperative, specified that residents not buy their homes (or the land beneath them) but own shares in a paternalistic corporation charged with ensuring that a development not stray from its designer's mission.

The realities of real estate finance and entrenched American ideals of property ownership, however, foiled any possibility of a garden city-type co-partnership scheme for Sunnyside. City Housing tried to sell whole courts to nonspeculative co-operative groups but devoted no resources to cultivating them. And since virtually none existed in New York, none came forward to buy. From almost the start all the houses were sold outright on a fee-simple plan (fig. 1.17). Even most of Sunnyside's apartments failed to sell as co-ops, as few tenants who inquired of Sunnyside

Gardens' apartments in 1924 or 1925 were interested in buying. A first building eventually sold enough units to begin operation as a co-op, but the second could not. Unable to defer revenue any longer, City Housing began renting the apartments out after six months. All future apartments at Sunnyside, and at RPAA's next project, Radburn, New Jersey, were rentals. If Sunnyside was an exercise in idealism for its sponsors, for its tenants it was mostly a real estate opportunity: a chance to own a well-designed home for a modest price.[51] Half of the new residents counted in 1926 relocated from a tenement on the Lower East Side, and in the succeeding decades Sunnyside Gardens remained a popular destination for those fleeing Manhattan's high rents and crowded conditions.[52]

A second compromise concerned design. A truly satisfactory arrangement would have dispensed with the city grid, with its shallow blocks, in favor a more artful arrangement that permitted clusters of buildings grouped around common green spaces. Indeed, Stein and Wright hoped to treat the entire complex not just as a single legal entity through common ownership but also as a single design statement in the form of a superblock that functioned as a self-enclosed campus. This idea was advanced at later projects designed by Stein or his colleagues, such as Chatham Village, outside Pittsburgh, and Colonial Village, outside Washington, D.C. At Sunnyside, however, the city would not consent to a replatting of the grid, forcing Stein and Wright to break up the development among multiple blocks. This compromise forced them to confront the question of how to bridge separate blocks, programmatically and psychologically. It also threatened to unravel the core concept behind the project—the idea, namely, that Sunnyside should function as an indivisible community. To compensate, they devised a scheme of shallow, attached row-type buildings—some for single families, but most for two or three—fronting common grassy malls and surrounding spacious courtyards (fig. 1.18). The complex's apartment houses were likewise shallow in depth and staggered on their blocks to permit similar amounts of open space, which they programmed for play, sport, and relaxation.

Stein and Wright planned the complex to offer a high-quality suburban, yet community oriented, experience. The choice of historical details lent a vaguely Colonial and rustic—and thus perhaps communal—feel. Row houses featured continuous hipped roofs and uninterrupted stringcourses, which together obscured the boundary between where one ended and the next began. Hudson River brick, rather than clapboard, reduced the likelihood that people would paint their houses and rupture the complex's visual unity. Meanwhile, Stein and Wright believed that staggering individual rows of houses along the street—varying their distance from the sidewalk and allowing them to be penetrated by walkways and green alleyways—added variety and intimacy. They integrated footpaths along Sunnyside's east-west axis to link the main streets, creating surprise vistas and semi-public areas for pedestrian circulation. Courtyards never stretched along the full length of a block, to help break down the scale of the complex. Lot lines also blended one into the other, as Stein and Wright used buildings to frame—but never enclose—courtyards, which helped make open areas feel more inviting. Informal, meandering pathways and public areas interrupted the orthogonal streetscape.

1.18: Sunnyside Gardens, courtyard, 2014

Plantings, bushes, lawns, and trees became integral elements, engendering feelings of safety and sympathy for nature.

To protect their careful planning in the absence of joint community ownership, City Housing created forty-year easements on common areas, and wrote restrictions into all deeds. In a given courtyard, lot lines extended to the center of each space, but only about half that amount could be put to private use. These communal spaces survived the foreclosure of more than half the homes during the Great Depression. But when the easements expired in the 1960s some homeowners responded by building fences that ran to the center of the courtyard spaces. Others built aboveground pools and backyard sheds, further reducing accessibility. Some residents, meanwhile, carved out parking spaces from their front yards. By 1982 just six of fifteen original common spaces remained. Some homeowners lacked the income for common space upkeep, while others, particularly newcomers, simply wanted more private space and cared little for the original planning concepts.[53] These changes raised the question of whether Sunnyside was an experiment in social justice and community as its originators claimed, or merely a new approach to development.

Below-market Subsidized Housing Begins

1.19: Phipps Garden Apartments, rental brochure, ca. 1931

Throughout, Sunnyside remained a beloved space. "Sunnyside is almost like being in a little village," explained Lorraine Wallnik, a retired nurse and thirty-year resident, in the early 1980s. "It's really a warm feeling here, even with the growth and change."[54] As another resident put it more recently, "we feel as if we're living in a tree house."[55] At the behest of residents, the City Planning Commission designated Sunnyside and the adjacent philanthropic Phipps Houses, added in 1931 (fig. 1.19), as a Special Planned Community Preservation District in 1974, although it was not landmarked for another thirty years. In the interim the complex evolved socially, attracting new-immigrant families from Southeast Asia, Turkey, the Middle East, and Eastern Europe, as well as many young professionals with children. As one homeowner notes, "it's wonderful for kids. There are roses growing on the patio, trees and grass just out the front door" (fig. 1.20).[56]

Unresolved tensions between the communal and private visions, however, have torn at the complex. In 2007 these came to the fore as residents divided over landmarking, with bitter debates about property rights, the effect of historic designation on maintenance costs and resale prices, and the complex's architectural merits. As one opponent asked, "Why does someone live in Queens?" His answer might have disappointed Stein: "A house is a place to live in. It may look nice, but most of the houses in Queens are not glorious and extravagant. There's a promise you feel you got, a promise that this was your property."[57] Many others, however, supported the preservation, and the Landmarks Preservation Commission approved landmark status in 2007. No effort, however, has been made to rehabilitate the most radical of Stein's and Wright's intentions: for communal, nonspeculative ownership. To the contrary, many residents fear that landmarking will only increase resale values, bringing to an end, once and for all, the era of Sunnyside Gardens as below-market housing. NADER VOSSOUGHIAN AND MATTHEW GORDON LASNER

1.20: Sunnyside Gardens, enclosed entries, 2014

Amalgamated Cooperative Apartments (1927, 303 units, Bronx)

Sponsor: union (Amalgamated Clothing Workers of America)
Program: limited-equity co-op
Architect: Springsteen & Goldhammer

New York City's system of labor-sponsored, limited-equity cooperatives all but began with an imposing Tudor-style complex in the Bronx, the Amalgamated Cooperative Apartments. Created by Abraham Kazan of the Amalgamated Clothing Workers of America and assisted by the state housing act of 1926, it set a new standard for worker housing in New York City. Unionized workers at Amalgamated, thanks to collective enterprise and state subsidies, experienced immediate social mobility as they exchanged tenements for new garden apartments that they owned and governed.

During the housing crisis of the late 1910s and early 1920s—and following the success of worker housing co-ops in Sunset Park's Finntown—radicalized Jewish workers in East Side tenements and middle-class housing reformers like Clarence Stein became interested in harnessing consumers' cooperative, nonspeculative enterprise—and union money—to produce higher-quality worker housing. One of the chief advocates for this model was Abraham Kazan. As an office boy for the International Ladies Garment Workers Union (ILGWU) Kazan had spearheaded cooperative purchase of groceries and other supplies. Then he met Andrew J. Thomas. Thomas was a progressive housing architect who had designed several innovative market-rate garden-apartment co-ops at Jackson Heights in the early 1920s. Convinced the model could be adapted for workers, he approached the ILGWU in

1.21: Amalgamated Cooperative Apartments, courtyard, 2014

1924 about sponsoring a project. Kazan had left the union for the Amalgamated Clothing Workers of America, where he headed the group's credit union and led other efforts in banking, insurance, and health care that leveraged the modest resources of members into powerful institutions. ILGWU turned to him for advice.

Under Kazan's and Thomas's lead, IGLWU, the Amalgamated, and two other unions launched what they expected to be the first union-built, limited-equity apartment house in the United States. Unfortunately, the project, the Thomas Garden Apartments on the Grand Concourse (1927), faltered due to disagreement among the sponsors and soon ran out of money. To complete it, Thomas called on John D. Rockefeller, Jr., with whom he had collaborated on other low-cost housing projects, for help. This alienated Kazan, who disliked Rockefeller's conservative politics, and he resolved to undertake his next project exclusively under the auspices of the Amalgamated.[58]

For this next project Kazan and the Amalgamated's leader Sydney Hillman imagined a very different kind of building. Rather than a conventional apartment house in a built-up section like the Grand Concourse, where structures sat cheek-by-jowl, they selected a large, leafy site on Van Cortlandt Park South. To design it they commissioned Herman J. Jessor, a young associate at the firm Springsteen & Goldhammer, whose politics were firmly to the left of Thomas's and who perhaps better understood the specific goals of the union. For the site, Jessor imagined six Tudor Revival buildings enclosing a spacious landscaped courtyard (fig. 1.21; see also fig. 1.3). Because deed restrictions on the all-but-suburban site prohibited multifamily construction, a compromise was reached to exclude elevators, limiting the buildings to five stories. For financing, Kazan employed money from the union's credit union and secured a $1.2 million mortgage from the Metropolitan Life Insurance Company. Sales prices for the apartments were set at a rather steep $500 per room ($22,000 in 2013 dollars, or $110,000 for a two-bedroom apartment), but the *Jewish Daily Forward* agreed to lend money to families with insufficient savings.

To aid their project—and the housing cause—union leaders including Hillman lobbied Governor Alfred E. Smith for the Stein Commission's housing bill. Even without the most controversial sections the law promised important savings. Smith shared a widespread Progressive antipathy for the slums and had, for some years, sought to apply state funds to model housing concepts. He and Hillman had a long history of collaboration, dating back to reforms introduced in response to the devastating Triangle Shirtwaist Factory fire in 1911, when Hillman was a union activist and Smith speaker of the State Assembly. Once the bill was passed, Amalgamated Cooperative Apartments, already under way, became the first to benefit. Combined with efficient operations and collective self-management (rather than hiring a paid management company), the tax breaks resulted in monthly charges that were about 25 percent less than rents in comparable apartments.

Jessor's buildings were high quality yet simple. Exteriors were clad in multicolored Holland brick, and bathrooms in ceramic tiles. Kitchens included space for meals (fig. 1.22). Floors were of wood parquet, and closets ample. The perimeter-block with spacious interior garden court helped circulate light and air. It was a world away from the workaday city. "With parks and open space on three sides," noted Kazan, "this development, after two to three years, looked like a group of buildings set in the middle of a large park and gave the impression of a college campus."[59] It was a monumental achievement, prompting Louis Pink to argue that, "The needle trades are no longer sweated and starving. They are well-organized, well-paid and powerful." They also, he noted, "provide an outlet for radical idealism in constructive endeavor."[60] Kazan built additions in 1929 and in 1931–32, more than doubling its size, and again after World War II. Several other Jewish and union groups built similar complexes in the Bronx, some with aid of the 1926 housing law, some without.

1.22: Amalgamated Cooperative Apartments, kitchen, by Wurts Bros., 1929

Life at the Amalgamated Cooperative Apartments was, by design—and with constant encouragement of "Brother Kazan"—intensely communal. Generous community facilities, which tenant-owners were expected to help run and

1.23: Amalgamated Cooperative Apartments, community room, 2014

were modeled on settlement house services, included a club room, library, nursery, kindergarten, and day camp, as well as classes in dancing, nutrition, and current events (fig. 1.23, fig. 1.24). To transport older children to school, Kazan bought a school bus. The complex also included a cooperative laundry service and grocery story. All the tenants were part of a left-wing Jewish world that emphasized both communalism and unionism. As architect Daniel Libeskind, who grew up in the Amalgamated Cooperative Apartments, recalls, it "wasn't just the architecture, which was very simple, but thoughtful. . . . It was also an ethical idea. We formed a community in the real American sense."[61]

The Great Depression hit the Amalgamated Cooperative Apartments and other limited-equities hard. Only three complexes, including the Amalgamated and its sister project in Manhattan, the Amalgamated Dwellings, escaped foreclosure and conversion to bank-owned rentals. The Amalgamated complexes survived because of Kazan's indefatigable efforts. He jostled with utility companies for "fairer" rates and took Works Progress Administration support for theater, cultural, and educational programming. He also allowed renters, took cash from the union, and cut programming. His tenacity in the face of the nation's worst economic crisis not only secured the project's limited-equity status but also instilled a great deal of public faith in him, leading to many new opportunities after World War II.

Although the Amalgamated Cooperative Apartments survived the 1930s, changing tastes and rising expectations for quality in housing prompted Kazan to retire five of the original buildings after World War II, replacing them with new Jessor-designed towers of the type he began to perfect at Co-op Village (1950–1956) on the Lower East Side. The new buildings increased capacity and offered elevators, balconies, parking, and other features attractive to a new generation. Several of the

1.24: Amalgamated Cooperative Apartments, kindergarten, by Wurts Bros., 1929

original buildings remain, however. So, too, do the limited-equity restrictions. So while the Bronx has seen its ups and downs, the co-op on the edge of the park has proved remarkably stable. Today, owners maintain a newsletter, a nursery school, day camp, various clubs and groups—and as they have aged in place, programs geared to seniors. Nonunion families of growing ethnic diversity have also moved in alongside aging Jewish pioneers and their descendants, attracted by the leafy spaciousness, comfortable apartments, modest prices, and deep-seated sense of community. RICHARD GREENWALD

Boulevard Gardens (1935, 968 units, Queens)

Sponsor: private developer (Cord Meyer)
Program: private rental
Architect: Theodore H. Engelhardt

Boulevard Gardens in Woodside, Queens, along with Hillside Homes in the Bronx and Knickerbocker Village in Manhattan, reflects the extension of the limited-dividend model under the early New Deal before the introduction of public housing and the Federal Housing Administration's Rental Housing Division. With their enduring popularity and high-quality design, these PWA (federal Public Works Administration) developments serve as a link between experiments like Sunnyside

BOULEVARD GARDENS . . .

QUEENS, N. Y. C.

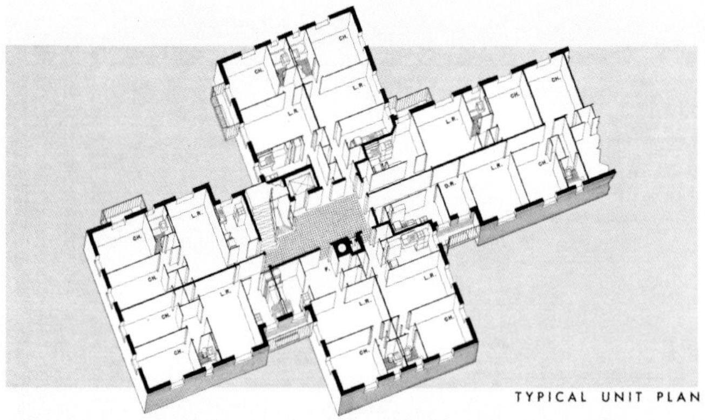

GENERAL VIEW

22

1.25: Boulevard Gardens from NYCHA, *Construction Cost Analysis: Large Scale, Low Rent Housing, Public, Private, and Limited Dividend* (1946)

Gardens in the 1920s and the mass-built, middle-income garden apartments of the 1940s and 1950s.

The PWA, directed by Secretary of the Interior Harold L. Ickes, announced a first round of grants for housing construction in 1933. The agency's Housing Division offered up to 85 percent of the necessary funds to either limited-dividend corporations—private entities that capped profits at 6 percent—or municipal housing authorities. Of the hundreds of applications, Ickes approved only seven, committing about $11 million for the construction of 3,065 units.[62] One of the accepted applications came from the Cord Meyer Company for Boulevard Gardens (fig. 1.25). The Housing Division lent the builder $3.21 million in November 1933 ($160 million in 2013 dollars). It was completed within two years.[63] With private capital scarce and the housing market uncertain, federal funding was a lifeline for Cord Meyer. The company had been a major force in the growth of Queens since the 1890s, building subdivisions in Elmhurst and Forest Hills, including Forest and Arbor Close (1928), which were

1.26: Boulevard Gardens, courtyard, 2014

two- and three-story Tudor row houses surrounding private courtyards that recalled Sunnyside. Plans for Boulevard Gardens were well under way before the PWA announced its housing program.

Designed by architect Theodore H. Engelhardt and landscape architect Charles N. Lowrie, the eleven-acre complex comprised ten, six-story elevator buildings. The buildings covered less than a quarter of the site, with the remainder given over to generous landscaping and a children's playground. In its site planning, Boulevard Gardens thus followed the precedents of garden apartments at Jackson Heights and the more recent Phipps Apartments. But rather than fit buildings into the street grid, the city allowed Cord Meyer to create a superblock. To accentuate the visual separation from the surrounding houses, the complex set back from the street and rested atop a landscaped berm. The buildings themselves were simple yet elegant, with Colonial Revival accents, strong symmetries, and broad lawns that created the feeling of a college campus (fig. 1.26). Rendered in pale brick with an arched opening leading to the courtyard, ornament was limited chiefly to shutters on the second and fifth floors and neo-Georgian entries, which were placed on the short sides of buildings or at corners, leaving longer façades to face the landscaping uninterrupted.

From the day it opened Boulevard Gardens was a social and financial success. In 1936 the Queens Chamber of Commerce honored the complex in its annual Better Building Competition, despite the organization's long-standing opposition to government housing. Residents, including municipal employees (especially teachers and police officers) and white-collar workers (salesmen, accountants, engineers and brokers, tradesmen), loved it, too. Over eight thousand families applied for the 968 apartments, which rented for an extremely reasonable $11 per room per month ($2,200 in 2013 dollars for a two-bedroom unit). Four-fifths of the units were taken before opening.[64]

While small, every apartment had an up-to-date kitchen and bathroom, and ample light and air. But the basic physical amenities were only part of the draw. Like other limited-dividend efforts before it, it also appealed because it promised a new kind of community that tenants perceived as more stable, and modern, than typical city neighborhoods. Indeed, a "spirit of small town living" developed almost immediately. Residents formed a tenants association and published a newspaper, the *Boulevard Gardens Beacon*. The buildings had sizable meeting rooms and soon hosted over sixty clubs: Boy Scouts and Girl Scouts, an American Legion Post, a men's baseball team, weekly card parties, and a drama club, as well as language and arts classes. In keeping with the reform spirit of the place a full-time recreational advisor was on hand.[65]

In the 1930s the state housing board closely regulated Boulevard Gardens, both evicting problem tenants and issuing "diplomas of prosperity" to families moving out because their incomes had grown too high (income ceilings were set at five time annual rents).[66] In 1941, as market rents across the city began to rise with the coming of World War II, the company converted the complex to market-rate by refinancing with a private loan.[67] Ironically, federal rent controls came just two years later, freezing rents at 1942 levels. Thanks to these controls, Boulevard Gardens remained below-market until 1987. That year new owners converted it to a market-rate co-op, responding to rising demand for homeownership opportunities and perhaps in pursuit of greater profits than allowed under rent laws. Despite the project's age and modest appointments, about two hundred tenants bought and stayed. Under New York State's noneviction plan, formulated during a great wave of co-op conversions in the early 1970s, tenants of rent-regulated apartments were allowed to remain indefinitely. As they were vacated, the sponsor renovated to make units "feel new," installing upgraded kitchens and baths, new windows, and wall-to-wall carpeting. With sky-high resale prices even in moderate-income neighborhoods like Woodside, today only Boulevard Gardens' quality construction and collegiate site planning betray its below-market subsidized origins.[68] JEFFREY A. KROESSLER

Mary Kingsbury Simkhovitch (1867–1951)

Mary Simkhovitch played a key role over half a century of activism (ca. 1900–1950), transforming the Progressive Era movement for settlement houses and tenement regulation into a local and national movement for tenement destruction and public housing construction. Her journey from regulation to promotion of permanent, government-created and -operated public housing reflected a common response among reformers to the persistence of substandard, unsanitary tenements in New York City.[69]

Simkhovitch participated in the major Progressive reform movements of the early 1900s, including campaigns for better housing, sanitation, and recreation. As a settlement house leader she and her associates developed gradualist and participatory methods, "working with rather than for our neighbors," that contrasted sharply with public housing management styles she pioneered decades later. This attitude of engagement infused the institutions she founded (with others) including the Association of (now United) Neighborhood Houses of New York (1901) and Greenwich House settlement (1902).[70]

Greenwich House was both a site of cultural and educational activities as well as an organizing space for political initiatives to bring new schools, parks, and other municipal services to the area. Living among the neighbors and participating in both their successes and failures, however, awakened Simkhovitch to the grave issues faced by the working-class families she hoped to help through social and cultural programs. Simkhovitch believed that "congestion" had to be resolved for permanent progress. In the neighborhood around Greenwich House, for instance, she discovered that residents lived at 975 people per acre. She blamed the high death and infant mortality rates primarily on this congestion, because such a crowded population, in unsanitary tenements, tested human psychology, and family life, to the breaking point. She thus championed labor laws, slum clearance, cheap mass transit, zoning regulations, and limited dividend housing, all of which promised, in their own ways, to create better families and neighborhoods.[71]

Despite the city's progress on many of these fronts by the 1920s, the persistence of the tenement slums in the interwar years drew Simkhovitch to more radical solutions. Her confidence in a Progressive extension of government powers to housing related to her admiration for powerful European public planning (she had studied in Vienna) and the ambitious government housing efforts there. But her growing and very vocal support for government-subsidized housing was simply the conclusion she reached as the various Progressive efforts ran their course over the decades, leaving many of the worst slums largely untouched. While she might have once praised the Tenement House Act of 1901 as "a turning point in our social history" because it set such high standards for new housing, by the 1930s she was frustrated that the "old-law tenements have deteriorated still further." She had also lost her faith, if she ever had much, in privately financed limited-dividend companies. Simkhovitch used her growing national profile in the 1920s and 1930s to promote the notion of public housing as an extension of "municipal housekeeping" similar to municipal monopolies in water, education, and sanitation.[72]

Simkhovitch, widely respected for her long-standing integrity and ideals, organized the Public Housing Conference (1931) at Greenwich House with leading housing experts; this group eventually became a national organization, the National Housing Conference, which helped to pass the federal public housing program. She is also credited with pushing Senator Robert F. Wagner in 1933 to include within the PWA the housing division that financed dozens of high-quality complexes nationally, including the public Harlem River Houses (1937) and Williamsburg Houses (1938) in New York. The New York reformers in the White House, Eleanor and Franklin Roosevelt, were also friends of Simkhovitch, a connection that helped immensely when it came time to lobby the president to support of the Housing Act of 1937. Its provisions, drafted by Simkhovitch and Catherine Bauer, created a national low-income housing program for construction, operation, and subsidy (fig. 1.27).

Simkhovitch did not view the dawning public housing era as a temporary jobs program, but as a new kind of "permanent public policy" that would improve housing by replacing slums. She welcomed the legislation that created NYCHA in 1934, for instance, by noting that with "the passage of the Housing Authority bill we have turned a great corner in our social life. For authorities once set up become not an emergency activity only, but an integral part of our city administrative plan." She promised that public housing not only would be "self liquidating" but also would be cost effective by reducing citywide health and crime costs. As an engaged NYCHA board member (serving 1934–48) Simkhovitch revealed a hard-headed commitment to turning NYCHA from an experimental organization into a mass builder with the power to replace the old with modern public neighborhoods. In order to achieve the goal she even, at first, endorsed racial segregation if it meant more public support for the program.[73]

Simkhovitch's values dominated social management of the early housing authority. She was, for instance, the force behind maternal systems of tenant management to ensure that the new neighborhoods preserved the standards that would guarantee better living. To that end she promoted the Octavia Hill method, pioneered in London

1.27: Mary Kingsbury Simkhovitch, dedication of Queensbridge Houses, 1940

in the nineteenth century. In a PWA-funded study in 1933 she and Edith Elmer Wood recommended "a female assistant" look after "protection of tenant health and morals," which included family casework, childcare, recreation, and tenant organization. The document "dismissed any notion of tenant control." Housing assistants in the new NYCHA developments not only collected rent at the door weekly but also played a role in social service referral and other community activities. The system generated so much opposition by residents, however, that after World War II NYCHA switched to monthly rents. The housing assistants remained, however, and many more were added at new projects; even today, they play a major role in NYCHA's rent collection and social work.[74]

Simkhovitch also endorsed the creation of health and community centers in public housing that became a permanent element of the NYCHA system. Greenwich House had pioneered an infant welfare clinic in the early twentieth century, and Simkhovitch successfully had a baby health station installed at First Houses (1936) to ensure the health of the most vulnerable. The New York City Health Department under LaGuardia's rule extended health centers in partnership with public housing. The growing system of NYCHA community centers under her watch also

reflected her retention of Progressive era anxieties about the role of the saloon in working-class city life. While she admitted that it was a natural social space in many tenement neighborhoods, she also believed that saloons were hotbeds of alcoholism, sensuality, venereal disease, violence, and corruption that disrupted families and neighborhoods. In new public housing, this moral redirection took place in alcohol-free community center activities such as kindergartens, craft shops, and nonpartisan civic gatherings. One looked in vain for bars, and commercial activity of most kinds. To run these community centers, the housing authority partnered with the settlement houses, including Simkhovitch's United Neighborhood Houses, which together are still running programs in twenty-three complexes today.
NICHOLAS DAGEN BLOOM

2

Public Neighborhoods

New York City's daring housing projects of the 1930s, such as Harlem River Houses (1937) and Queensbridge Houses (1940), stood out both for their austere red-brick geometries and for their sweeping rejection of New York's long-standing dependence on the private sector, and tenements in particular, to house millions of people (fig. 2.1). Buoyed by the failure of the housing market during the Great Depression, and emboldened by the promising results of New York State's 1926 housing law, reformers like Mary Simkhovitch, Catherine Bauer, and Mayor Fiorello LaGuardia demanded that federal officials, many of whom had roots in New York's reform tradition, demonstrate their commitment to New York City, to progressive government, and to working-class Americans by bringing the federal government into the local, low-cost housing business. With the support of New York New Dealers such as Senator Robert F. Wagner and President Franklin D. Roosevelt, these reformers secured federal subsidies to create large, working-class complexes constructed, owned, and managed by the government.[1]

In fighting for this system, New York advocates repeated time and again in speeches and letters that only government sponsorship, with its strong financial and legal powers, could permanently provide working families with decent housing in cities and transform tenement slums into healthy, up-to-date neighborhoods. Words were not, however, enough to create a housing program. Reformers had to resolve several internal conflicts regarding the scope of public housing; lobby for national, and then state, enabling legislation; devise legal methods for use of eminent domain in housing; determine standards for architecture, construction, and site planning; and establish systems for tenant selection and project management. New York City and, in particular, leaders associated with the New York City Housing Authority

2.1: Harlem River Houses, left, with Dunbar Apartments, right, 1937

(NYCHA), were able to accomplish every one of these ambitious goals in the 1930s. Even in its earliest years, NYCHA distinguished itself from other cities' housing authorities by building large, high-quality developments; by gaining widespread popular and political acceptance of public housing; by building public housing complexes for middle-income families using locally funded programs; by providing a range of community facilities; and, eventually, by tenanting housing complexes on an interracial basis.

2.2: Children in a New York City slum, by Arnold Eagle, 1935

Just as the housing emergency after World War I had catalyzed the first serious effort to subsidize urban housing in the United States, it was the crisis of the Great Depression of the 1930s that generated sufficient public support for a permanent, peacetime public housing program, both in New York and nationally. Housing conditions as a whole had improved substantially in most U.S. cities, including New York, in the second half of the 1920s. Indeed, the Depression was precipitated in part by a huge oversupply of new market-rate housing, especially apartments. Nevertheless, New York City alone still counted nearly 65,000 old-law tenement buildings in 1936 (down from 87,000 in 1909) containing 517,831 apartments housing two million people (fig. 2.2). Not all of these old tenements were bad, but the sheer volume of buildings constructed to the lower standards of an earlier age was worrisome. Other cities faced a similar situation. None was as densely populated as New York, but they also harbored vast slums. Reformers, city officials, and journalists across the nation continued to blame slums for a range of social disorders only some of which, in fact, were a product of poor housing conditions alone: "It is to the slum that the criminologist traces the bulk of crime. To the slum the social worker looks for delinquency; health agencies for much rickets, cardiac trouble, pernicious anemia; and to schools in the slums for great mental deficiency."[2]

As the national economy collapsed in the early 1930s and with it urban housing markets, housing became an acceptable arena for federal relief efforts. Early attention in the Hoover administration focused on conservative approaches that aided private homeowners, landlords, and developers. President Herbert Hoover, for instance, convened a President's Conference on Home Building and Home Ownership, and restricted direct activity in housing to the financing of a handful of limited-dividend apartment complexes. But housing activists, mainly from New York City, turned their attention to Washington to plead their case for more: a true system of public housing modeled on the example of Western Europe.

Concerned Americans in the 1920s and 1930s had their pick of books on the topic of European housing progress. Edith Elmer Wood had been studying housing abroad since before World War I and published *Housing Progress in Western Europe* in 1923. Louis Pink, a major force in city and state housing policy, included many European examples in his *A New Day for Housing* in 1928. Catherine Bauer, a young protégé of Stein and Lewis Mumford—and the figure who deserves the most credit for marshaling national support for federal public housing legislation thanks to her tireless campaigning—revisited the topic in her widely read 1934 book *Modern Housing*. In it, she estimated that 16 percent of families in Britain, Germany, Belgium, Holland, Sweden, and Austria already lived in "modern housing," by which she meant not necessarily Modernist, with avant-garde architecture, but up-to-date, well-planned housing built by municipalities or by limited-dividend or cooperative groups with long-term, low-interest, government loans. In Britain alone municipalities would complete one million houses and apartments by 1938. Some on the right even came to admire this model. In 1937 Herbert U. Nelson, secretary of the National Association of Real Estate Boards, published his own study, *New Homes for Old Countries*, in which he spoke of the positive effects of low-interest, long-life mortgages.[3] Housers made generous use of these European examples in their speeches and essays. Mary Simkhovitch, who would become a member of NYCHA's board of directors, put it, "This business of trying to improve conditions in old-law tenements is all right. . . . But we ought to do what they did in Vienna."[4] Mayor LaGuardia, too, used foreign examples as points of comparison: "Vienna, Berlin, Liverpool and other European cities have done more to improve housing than any American city."[5] The precedent was clear, at least to activists: government housing had the potential to change cities, and the lives of the urban masses, for the better.

Despite the persistence of tenements, deepening poverty, widespread support for government relief generally, and a successful exhibit at the Museum of Modern Art in 1934 called, cheekily, *America Can't Have Housing*, much of the country remained

2.3: *America Can't Have Housing*, MoMA, 1934

indifferent or hostile to the idea of public housing. (fig. 2.3) Convincing them to support housing legislation consumed much of reformers' activities in the early and mid-1930s. Even in New York City there was disagreement over the proper scope of public housing. There were property owners and conservatives like John D. Rockefeller, Jr., who disliked the idea of government housing of any type. There were the slum-clearers: leaders drawn mainly from the settlement house movement who argued that the chief aim of public housing ought to be rebuilding the slums to reduce urban congestion. They formed a group in 1932 at Greenwich House called the Public Housing Conference, under the watchful eye of that institution's leader, Mary Simkhovitch. Other members included socialist Norman Thomas, Henry Street Settlement founder Lillian Wald, and Fiorello LaGuardia, who at the time was a U.S. Congressman. They demanded a program "with powers to supervise slum clearance" and build replacement housing.[6] Then there were the "modern housers." Led by Catherine Bauer, they argued that money spent on land acquisition and slum clearance was a waste and that rebuilding slums would do little to advance the goal of creating a truly modern city. Following the lead of Europe and experiments like Sunnyside Gardens, they believed money should be used to build new communities on inexpensive land at the urban edge.[7]

Despite their difference in strategy, and unlike the situation in most other U.S. cities, virtually all New Yorkers in positions of power agreed that public housing of some kind was necessary. Local labor leaders, bolstered by a public willing to take to the streets for rent strikes and other anti-capitalist actions, vocally advocated for public housing, pushing elected leaders into action. B. Charney Vladeck, one of

New York's socialist labor leaders and a future NYCHA board member claimed "there could be no adequate rehousing in the country until a time when the 'hold' of the real estate interests on urban America 'is completely broken.'" Union members joined in a massive rally in 1934 demanding that the city "recognize housing construction and maintenance as a 'public enterprise' in the same category as transportation and education."[8] Many left-wing Jewish neighborhood activists backed public housing as a tool to rebuild their tenement neighborhoods and create a socialist utopia. As if to aid the cause, the papers regularly featured stories on fires and similarly hazardous conditions in tenements. Establishment organizations reflecting progressive opinion—including the Welfare Council of New York, the New York League of Women Voters, and the Women's City Club—also lent their substantial voices to the movement.

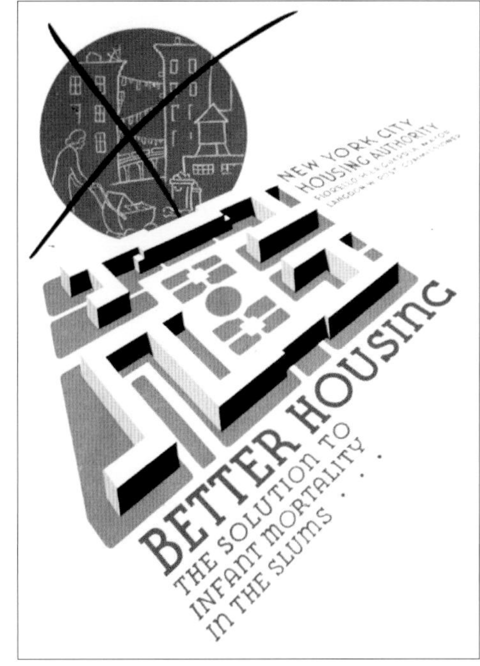

2.4: NYCHA poster, by Anthony Velonis, Federal Art Project, ca. 1936

To overcome any residual resistance on the part of weakened real estate interests, reformers emphasized the practical consequences of public housing. For instance, public housing was most frequently justified as an extension of the public health function of the city government (fig. 2.4, fig. 2.5). Even more common was to frame public housing as a jobs program that would revive the moribund construction industry, or a strategy for liberating valuable urban land near the city's business districts for higher and best uses, or for buying landlords out of decaying properties that had lost much of their resale value. Wealthy tenement owners like Bernard Baruch and Vincent Astor, for instance, came to support public housing as a way to divest their holdings at a decent price. Other property owners dreamed that their tenants might be moved out to new developments, allowing them to convert tenement land to commercial use, which they anticipated would be more lucrative.[9]

2.5: NYCHA poster, by Benjamin Sheer, Federal Art Project, 1936

Legislative progress toward public housing for New York City unfolded simultaneously on two fronts: local and national. Locally, Simkhovitch and her allies at the Public Housing Conference advocated for expansion of the 1926 state housing law, calling for creation of a housing agency empowered to buy land and build. An independent authority, reformers believed, would avoid the problems of patronage by resting power in a technical elite who could be trusted to make impartial decisions on tax exemption, debt, eminent domain, housing design, construction contracts, and tenancy. When the reformers failed in Albany in 1933, they turned their attention to Washington. Congress included provisions for housing programs in the National Industrial Recovery Act, supervised by the new Public Works Administration (PWA), as a direct result of New York lobbying. New York lawyer Ira S. Robbins, in fact, wrote housing into the PWA's mandate at the request of Simkhovitch. The agency's Housing Division was put under the lead of architect Robert D. Kohn, an old ally of Clarence Stein. Although understaffed, the Division immediately set about instructing cities and civic groups how to set up limited-dividend providers to apply for funding. Unfortunately, few of the proposals were well conceived. To accelerate production, a new policy was introduced in the spring of 1934: for the Division to undertake construction directly. This stumbled, too, however. In 1935 the courts ruled that the federal government could not use eminent domain in this way, forcing it to focus on "modern housing"-type projects that would leave the tenements untouched, which concerned slum-clearance advocates like Simkhovitch.

The solution was the municipal housing authority. New York City was the pioneer. Simkhovitch had previously failed to create a housing agency in New York but then Fiorello LaGuardia came to power. As a mayoral candidate in 1933 he condemned slums and the machine politicians who flourished there. In office, he made public housing a priority, predicting that low-cost "housing would become exclusively a function of government." To critics, he claimed that the new housing "will be in competition not with real estate, but with disease and poverty."[10] Immediately he took up the cause of Simkhovitch's agency, advocating in Albany for a new bill written by Robbins and fellow attorney Charles Abrams. It passed in 1934, allowing for the creation of the nation's first housing authority: NYCHA. Overnight it became a national model. It pointed the direction for decentralization of powers in subsequent public housing legislation. More important, its legal structure supported the flow of federal dollars into a municipal agency with broad powers in a way that the courts would not object to. LaGuardia appointed Langdon Post, a long-time housing reformer, as chair, and Simkhovitch, Vladeck, and Pink to the board of directors. Post was simultaneously appointed Tenement House commissioner with powers to enforce building codes, which were tightened.[11] Tenements that did not comply, including many that given the Depression had come to be owned by lenders, were targeted for condemnation. Owners of an astonishing forty thousand apartments abandoned them rather than comply with the law, leaving behind boarded-up shells (see fig. 1.9). Between 1934 and 1936 Post demolished eleven hundred old-law buildings.[12]

NYCHA wasted no time planning replacement housing. Its initial project was called First Houses (1936). Although modest in scale and ambition it represented a monumental achievement. Developed with funds from the Federal Emergency Relief Organization (FERO) and built by labor provided by the Works Progress

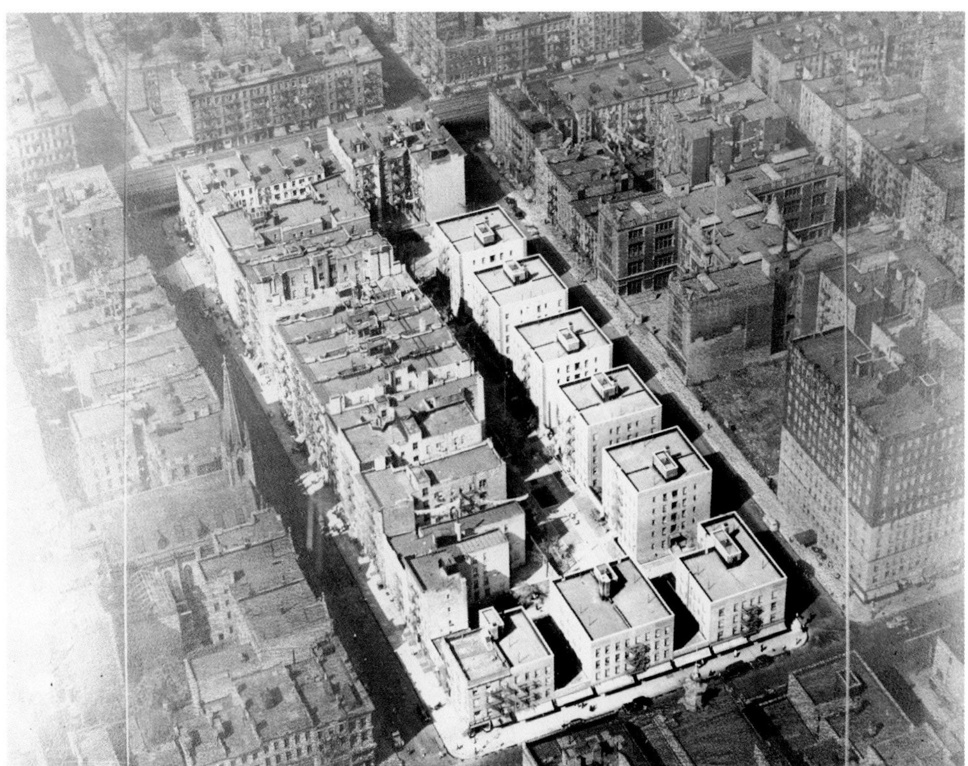

2.6: First Houses, ca. 1936

Administration (WPA), it was the first government-built and -owned complex in the United States erected since World War I, and the first intended for permanent operation as public low-income housing. FERO, unlike the PWA, was not authorized to finance low-cost housing. As a result, NYCHA pitched First Houses as a radical renovation. In late 1934 the agency persuaded Vincent Astor to sell most of what became the site: a group of four- and five-story tenements on East Third Street and Avenue A. To complete the parcel NYCHA used eminent domain to take two other buildings. The owner sued NYCHA and lost, laying the groundwork for broader use of eminent domain in housing both in New York and nationally. The "renovation," which razed every third building and the rear third of remaining ones, introduced new façades, windows, layouts, plumbing, wiring, kitchens, bathrooms, and roofs. Suspiciously little original material remained (fig. 2.6). On the avenue, new one-story shops were added where buildings had been razed, and at the enlarged rear courtyard a shared green space was created, complete with play space (fig. 2.7, fig. 2.8). The complex's 123 reconfigured apartments rented for just

2.7: First Houses, retail space, 2014

2.8: First Houses, from NYCHA, *Annual Report* (1944)

over $6 per room per month ($1,200 in 2013 dollars for a five-room unit).[13] Chairman Post claimed that First Houses, unlike limited-dividend housing, were "the first dwellings which are predicated upon the philosophy that sunshine, space and air are minimum housing requirements to which every American is entitled."[14]

Although a milestone, all those involved eagerly awaited funds to undertake new construction. Help arrived as PWA overcame its initial setbacks and began channeling funds to housing authorities. NYCHA was the first and largest beneficiary, receiving funds to produce two landmark projects: Harlem River Houses in Harlem, completed in 1937, and the Williamsburg Houses in Brooklyn, a year later. Even more so than First Houses these projects demonstrated the singular, transformative power of government subsidies for housing. Critics at the time did, however, raise concerns about the high costs of construction, racial segregation (Harlem River was for Black families and Williamsburg for white), and the fact that, of the two, only Williamsburg replaced existing tenements. Many critics on the left also faulted administrators for using such high standards of selection at Williamsburg Houses that they failed to rehouse site tenants in large numbers.

While all these projects were under way, the cause of public housing continued to advance in Washington. Simkhovitch and Catherine Bauer produced a series of competing bills (sponsored by their ally Senator Wagner) in 1935, 1936, and 1937 until at last the stasis broke: the Housing Act of 1937 included a section offering long-term, low-interest loans for public housing. Bauer rallied the necessary political support. It was Simkhovitch's vision of slum clearance, however, that defined the final bill. The legislation also included many compromises demanded by real estate interests worried that a broader program of "modern housing" would undercut private development. One was an equivalent-elimination clause mandating destruction of one unit of substandard housing for every new unit built. Others included low income ceilings for tenants, tight limits on construction costs (a response, in part, to the high unit costs at PWA projects such as Harlem River Houses), and local control over planning and site selection—which, in practice, ensured that nearly all public housing concentrated in existing slums rather than in new garden cities. Legislators also prohibited subsidies to go to limited-dividend and cooperative groups, much to the chagrin of housers like Abraham Kazan. The rationale was that FHA's Rental Housing Division (1935), which made market-rate loans, already mandated its projects be set up on a limited-dividend basis. These and other provisions put public housing on a long-term path toward becoming inner-city poverty housing. It also meant conservative cities like Los Angeles, and virtually all suburban counties, could forgo public housing with impunity.

The new permanent federal public housing system, housed in a new United States Housing Authority, was put under the control of New Yorker and veteran houser Nathan Straus, Jr., the developer of the RFC's Hillside Homes and a member of the NYCHA board. Sensing a change in the political winds and dissatisfied with NYCHA's productivity, shortly after the law passed Mayor LaGuardia replaced Post as chairman with Alfred Rheinstein, a local builder. Rheinstein vowed "to clear as much of our 17 square miles of slums" as possible, and quickly.[15] He immediately began planning much larger projects than had been possible under the PWA, including Red Hook Houses (1939, 2,545 units) and Queensbridge Houses (1940, 3,149 units).

Rheinstein was ruthlessly efficient, besting already parsimonious federal cost requirements by squeezing contractors, building taller (six stories with elevators rather than the walk-ups at Harlem River and Williamsburg), and stamping identical buildings across whole complexes. He achieved additional economies with small rooms, casting pipes into floors, using concrete floors as ceilings of the apartments below, dispensing with doors on most closets, and replacing ceiling lights with sidelights. Of equal importance was Rheinstein's decision to follow the precedent of Harlem River Houses and to site projects not on slum land in Manhattan, which could be expensive and controversial, but on industrial sites in outer sections. To make these sites appealing Rheinstein included ample green space for recreation—so much, in fact, that some critics wished less attention had been paid to open space and more on the apartments. The Red Hook buildings, noted the Building Trades Employers Association, were "surrounded by far more recreational space that can ever be practical" and "the government renters would prefer more living, and less play room."[16] Interior space, however, was more expensive than open space.[17] Projects also included community services, such as health centers and community centers, often staffed by volunteers from neighborhood settlement houses.

NYCHA in these early years experimented with alternative designs and unconventional financing strategies. Clason Point Gardens (1941), a low-rise garden apartment, resembled FHA-insured complexes for middle-class families (fig. 2.9). NYCHA pioneered more flexibility in site and resident selection after 1938 when at the behest of Robert Moses Albany created new public housing programs for both the state and the city (fig. 2.10). The state program, like ones set up in a few other places including

2.9: Clason Point Gardens, from NYCHA, "Clason Point Gardens, Bronx" (1942)

Massachusetts, resembled the federal program, simply adding more funds to the pot. The city program was different. It much more closely followed the "modern housing" programs of Western Europe, with more generous cost limits and income ceilings. It also differed in its source of funding; rather than cash grants from general budgets, it allowed municipalities to establish an occupancy tax on renters to subsidize construction and operations. In practice NYCHA used the city program to develop complexes with higher-quality apartments for slightly higher income groups and, sometimes, on more expensive sites. Indeed, it was only through the city program that NYCHA was able to undertake its first new-build project on an East Side slum site, the Vladeck Houses, which opened in 1940. This short-lived city program, while small in scale, became the model for a much larger city-funded program after World War II.

Federal—State—City
It Takes All Three

Each level of government, municipal, state and federal, has contributed substantially to New York City's public housing program, which now includes 92 completed and occupied projects with 56 additional in various stages of negotiation, planning or construction. The completed and occupied developments accommodate 109,278 families, and the 56 in work will bring the figure up to 148,672.

Of the total program, the municipal government's financial aid accounts for 39 projects, the State's 47, and the federal government's 62.

Although the several government assistance programs are generally similar, they vary in many details, the net effect of which is to broaden the scope of the service which the Housing Authority is enabled to render.

Jefferson Houses, 112th Street and First Avenue, for 1,493 low-income families, developed under the federal program.

2.10: "Federal–State–City: It Takes All Three," from NYCHA, "Twenty-five Years of Public Housing: 1935–1960" (1960)

Between the federal, state, and city programs, NYCHA set a pace far in excess of the old limited-dividend companies. Some reformers worried about the large scale of the new complexes. Clarence Stein, for instance, criticized NYCHA's "massed, regimented apartment houses."[18] Others criticized NYCHA for the rigorous selection standards that made it difficult for all but a few site tenants to move back to new public housing. But for the most part the press, housing experts, and powerful figures like Mayor LaGuardia drowned out the critiques. By 1942 NYCHA had completed a dozen projects with 13,180 apartments, with many more in the planning stages (fig. 2.11).[19]

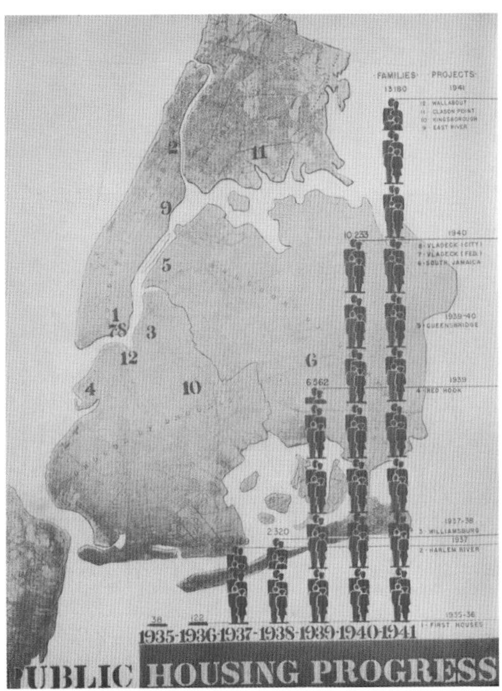

2.11: Public housing progress diagram, 1935–41, from NYCHA, "Wallabout Houses: A Defense Project for Navy Families" (1942)

New York also distinguished itself in effective management. The major reason was that public housing was far more important in New York. Most city governments pursued public housing half-heartedly. Despite the existence of slums, most big-city urban housing markets offered more and better choices to the poor and working class than New York's. Opposition to the ethos of public housing was often so strong that programs were compromised, or in extreme cases like Los Angeles, cancelled. In many places local politics allowed public housing to be used to ulterior ends. In Chicago, for instance, politicians used public housing both for political patronage and to contain the growing African American population. In New York, by contrast, the tight housing market, lingering tenement problem, and strong tenants' movement convinced most leaders that public housing was essential. Managers thus did all they could to maintain projects and ensure they did not become slums in their own right. To do this NYCHA installed a new cadre of civil servants who replicated management practices perfected by market-rate real estate firms. At the eleven-hundred-unit Kingsborough Houses (1941), for instance, NYCHA placed a staff of thirty-six, including fourteen porters to clean stair halls and public spaces daily. Meanwhile, the unemployment crisis allowed NYCHA to recruit high-quality administrators and project staff, tested through the civil service. This hands-on approach, still maintained by NYCHA today, contrasted sharply with the frequently corrupt and slipshod maintenance programs implemented in many other cities.[20]

Effective management extended beyond staff. Despite reformers' frequent declarations that sanitary, modern housing alone had the power to transform slum dwellers, NYCHA chose its early tenants carefully (fig. 2.12). Even the most progressive reformers understood that poverty carried with it many problems that could make for troublesome tenants. In the 1930s they took pains to convince Congress to allow for a very broad system of public housing that would allow a mixture of families of various income levels. The ideal client was the working poor and the

2.12: Williamsburg Houses, family of six in living room, 1938

so-called submerged middle class: young families, or families experiencing short-term hardships, who might use public housing temporarily on their way to private housing. Only once the public housing system was stable and successful, they argued, should the government turn its attention to the neediest. Congress had little of this, however, and insisted that public money for public housing go to the poor.[21]

Still, NYCHA, like other housing authorities, worked to create the best mixture of tenants possible, a task made easier by the pinched situation of so many New York families during the Great Depression. In selecting from among the hundreds of applicants for each apartment, NYCHA considered factors such as income, family status, employment, present accommodations, rent habits, and social background in order to find those most likely to pay their rents and treat the complexes with respect. NYCHA staff also visited every applicant's current home to evaluate living habits and judge their need for new housing. Tenants thus included a high number of breadwinners from skilled labor fields, moving in from old-law tenements.[22] Relief (welfare) tenancy was low: between 5 to 8 percent of families at the PWA developments. And while this rose at federal projects under the 1937 law, such as Queensbridge and Red Hook Houses (both over 20 percent), the higher-income levels targeted for city-funded projects such as Vladeck Houses offered NYCHA a chance to demonstrate the desirability of public housing as it was in Europe: permanent homes rather than as simply a temporary way station to a better life. This ambitious vision was all but unique to New York in the United States.

2.13: Harlem River Houses, music class at preschool, 1938

Leaving little to chance, NYCHA also made it a priority to inoculate its families against a re-creation of slum conditions, physically and socially (fig. 2.13). Furniture was fumigated before move-in. Managers instructed the new tenants in the use of modern appliances and the building's various systems such as trash chutes and laundry rooms. Boarders were prohibited and apartments were designed to discourage them. Female housing assistants, in techniques borrowed from

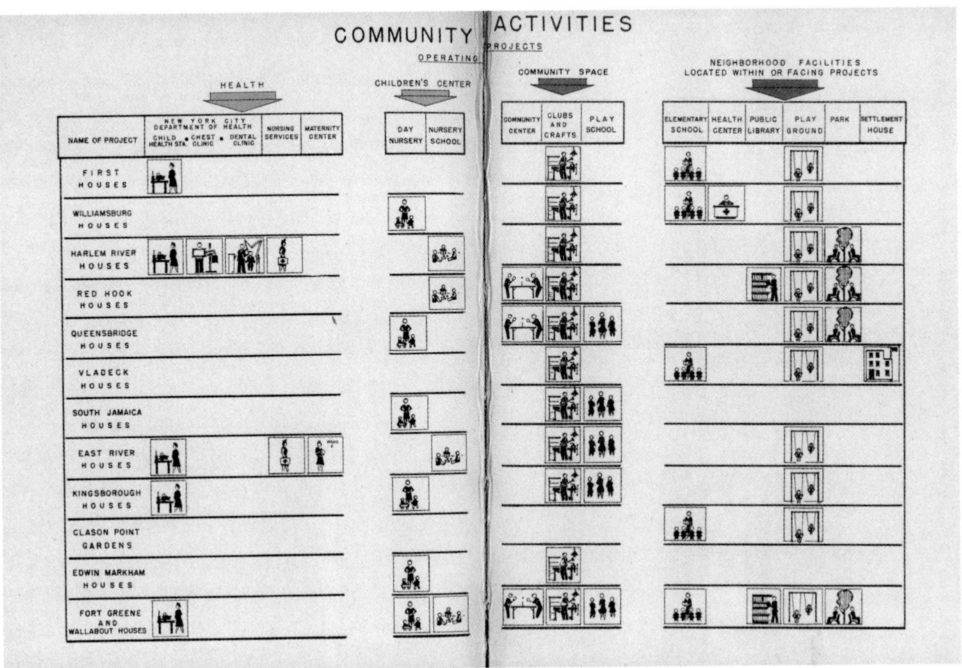

2.14: Community Activities diagram, from NYCHA, *Annual Report* (1944)

the Octavia Hill system of "friendly visitors" pioneered in London in the nineteenth century, collected rent weekly at the door and checked up to make sure the rules were being followed. In essence on-site social workers, they also referred problem families to social services, helped with interior decoration, and promoted community activities (fig. 2.14). Only during World War II, in response to tenant complaints, were tenants permitted to pay rents on a monthly basis and at the management office.[23]

Although New York City was a pioneer in prohibiting racial segregation in housing, in the early years of NYCHA the agency sought not only to cull the "deserving poor" but also to police racial divisions. Pushing racial integration, leaders worried, would alienate many white families and undermine public support. Following custom in the private housing market, NYCHA operated Williamsburg Houses for white families and Harlem River for Black, even though administrators permitted token integration of each. Only in 1939 after a complaint by the National Association for the Advancement of Colored People (NAACP) and the passage of a new state antidiscrimination law did NYCHA promise, and deliver in new projects such as South Jamaica Houses (1940), racially integrated communities. At the same time, NYCHA continued to insist that it had a right to remain sensitive to "existing community patterns." NYCHA maintained this policy into the postwar period even as the percentage of tenants of color increased dramatically.[24] But by then, New York already possessed more public housing—better maintained, governed, and tenanted—than any other American city.

Fiorello LaGuardia (1882–1947)

Through determined leadership and tireless resolve, Mayor Fiorello LaGuardia (1934–45) spearheaded New York's pioneering program of public housing during the Great Depression, marshaling considerable political resources to realize an audacious idea (fig. 2.15). To establish a municipal authority to provide public housing for New York's working poor LaGuardia dramatized the problem of slums with statistical data and vivid anecdotes; underscored the civic, social, and economic benefits of clearance and redevelopment; and effectively lobbied legislators at the city, state, and federal levels for financial support. In twelve years in office the mayor not only oversaw the completion of fourteen projects with 16,815 apartments but also embedded into liberalism the notion that decent housing was a basic responsibility of government.[25]

LaGuardia's interest in public housing preceded his mayoralty. As president of the Board of Aldermen in 1920 he roused fellow members to appeal to the Board of Estimate to approve housing on city property at Jamaica Bay and other sites for New Yorkers of modest income. Against the backdrop of the first red scare, critics charged that the idea was un-American and violated the state's constitution. The proposal withered and died. Undeterred, LaGuardia remained an outspoken advocate for housing reform. As a congressman representing the ethnically diverse slum of East Harlem from 1923 to 1933, he often lambasted rapacious landlords and became a champion of rent control. Elected mayor in 1933, LaGuardia moved quickly to implement his bold ideas on all fronts, including bridges, tunnels, reservoirs, parks, sewers, highways, and airports. He prioritized public housing. "There is nothing," he told a crowd of ten thousand in a Lower East Side park early in his term, "that I consider of greater importance at present than the vast program of housing for the City of New York."[26] Steeped in Progressive Era environmentalist thought, LaGuardia argued that slums bred poverty, crime, and sickness, accentuating the high rates of tuberculosis in overcrowded tenement districts.

At the outset of his tenure, a spate of fires broke out in old-law tenements with fatal results, tragically illustrating the unsafe conditions. Reform legislation had led to improvements in buildings, but upgrades meant expensive renovations and higher rents—certainly higher than tenants could pay, or than just about any New Yorker was willing to pay for a slum tenement, however retrofitted. Buildings emptied, and by 1933, 20 percent of old-law apartments were vacant. Numerous landlords, facing tax arrears, abandoned their properties. Deteriorating neighborhoods and depressed land values only intensified LaGuardia's resolve that private enterprise could not solve the housing problem. The antidote, he contended, was "decent, modern, cheerful housing, with a window in every room and a bit

2.15: Fiorello LaGuardia at East River Houses groundbreaking, 1940

of sunshine in every window."[27] For proof LaGuardia pointed to successful models of social housing in Europe.[28]

Prodded by the mayor and a coalition of housing reformers, trade unions, and even commercial builders starved for contracts, the state legislature passed a bill in January 1934 authorizing the creation of municipal housing authorities. In his first month in office the mayor sprung to action, stirred by twenty-five million dollars in funds earmarked by PWA for housing in New York. He launched the New York City Housing Authority (NYCHA) and appointed its five directors to a board. The quasi-autonomous authority had numerous prerogatives, including the powers to sell bonds and condemn land through eminent domain.

To the frustration of the mayor, NYCHA struggled to build at first, hindered by lack of funds and negotiations with PWA over project management. NYCHA's initial development, First Houses was partly a renovation project. At the dedication LaGuardia belittled critics concerned by the high costs of construction by obstinately celebrating the entire enterprise of public housing. The project represented a physical manifestation of a progressive concept and, in a symbolic sense, a monument to New York liberalism. While thankful to President Roosevelt for support through the PWA, LaGuardia petitioned for bolder legislation. The mayor was ubiquitous in Washington and testified repeatedly in Congress in 1937 in favor of a permanent public housing program. Once the federal program was passed, he set his sights on Albany, deploying his lobbying skills—and Robert Moses—to establish city and state public housing programs the following year.

After the mayor replaced Langdon Post as the chair of NYCHA with businessmen like Alfred Rheinstein (a professional builder) and Gerard Swope (a former president of General Electric), the city blazed trails, completing complexes faster and at a larger scale than any other city nationally. Public housing was central to the LaGuardia administration's drive to modernize New York City. Bold and visionary, but not without shortcomings—especially in thinking about the costs of displacement—it expanded the parameters of liberal ideology. In combination with other programs that drew federal funds to New York, public housing helped transform it, in the words of historian Thomas Kessner, into the "New Deal City."[29] STEPHEN PETRUS

Charles Abrams (1901–70)

During his long and varied career as a Greenwich Village landlord, attorney, writer, and activist for low-cost housing and racial integration, Charles Abrams was often at the center of debates over the best way to build and tenant below-market subsidized dwellings. Inspired by his experience as a child in the Williamsburg slums and his legal training, Abrams left private law practice in the 1930s to join the movement for public housing full time.[30]

Abrams, who was born in Poland, demonstrated his mastery of housing law by drafting, with Ira S. Robbins and Carl Stern, the New York State Municipal Housing Authorities Law of 1933. This law created, for the first time in the United States, a way for municipalities to build, own, and manage housing through the device of an authority. It represented a critical turn in housing from the emphasis on lowering

2.16: Charles Abrams at Cooper Square Association, Manhattan, 1961

costs through limited-dividends to low-cost housing. This new strategy was a crucial distinction given the failure of philanthropic projects and union co-ops to crack the problem of bringing the cost of good city housing into line with wages for unskilled urban workers. The law was also innovative in allowing authority-owned property to be exempt from property taxes and for the authorities to issue securities, which offered them some autonomy.

Even more important, the law gave authorities power of eminent domain, arguing that slum clearance and public housing constituted a genuine "public purpose."[31] Abrams successfully defended this extension of government power between 1934 and 1936 in a watershed Supreme Court case, *New York City Housing Authority v. Muller,* in which property owner Andrew Muller argued that the city violated the state and federal constitutions in taking his property for the construction of First Houses. Abrams persuaded the court that slum clearance and the creation of more low-cost housing was in fact a "large-scale" effort benefiting the public broadly.[32] Although housers like Catherine Bauer questioned the utility of slum clearance, for Mary Simkhovitch and others focused on rebuilding crowded tenement districts it was central to public housing's agenda. In practice, perhaps only one-third of NYCHA's eventual 180,000 units could have been built without eminent domain. As the agency's chairman Langdon Post recalled, "If Abrams hadn't pressed the Muller case and won it, there would be no public housing today."[33] Between 1934 and 1937 Abrams served as a consultant to NYCHA and as an unpaid member of the mayor's Committee on Slum Clearance; after 1937 he served as a consultant to the federal government on public housing.

From public housing Abrams' interest shifted to broader concerns about distribution of, and equal access to, decent shelter (fig. 2.16). Of special concern were racial barriers, and Abrams served as president of the National Committee Against Discrimination in Housing. In *Revolution in Land* (1939) and *The Future of Housing* (1946) he began articulating these arguments. Abrams targeted the Metropolitan Life Insurance Company in particular, taking a pro bono case representing three African American applicants rejected at Stuyvesant Town. He lost the case, *Dorsey v. Stuyvesant Town* (1947), but such high-profile legal struggles eventually yielded action by the city council and state legislature barring racial discrimination in publicly funded housing. In the late 1940s and 1950s he became a columnist at the then left-leaning *New York Post* and in 1955 published his landmark attack on bias in housing, *Forbidden Neighbors: A Study of Prejudice in Housing.*

In his later career Abrams became active in the international housing movement through the United Nations and he taught variously at the New School, MIT, Harvard, and Columbia, where he served as director of the urban planning program. Throughout, he remained committed to bettering life in New York, serving as New

York State Rent Administrator and as chairman of the New York State Commission Against Discrimination (SCAD). As leader of SCAD he made sure properties insured by FHA—whom he long attacked—and the U.S. Department of Veterans Affairs (VA) were included in New York State's law against discrimination. And while always a champion of public housing, he often critiqued NYCHA for withholding apartments from minority applicants in the 1950s to maintain racial balance in developments experiencing white flight and, especially, for the displacement caused by slum clearance—a great irony given it was he who had first figured out how to imbue NYCHA with the power of eminent domain. NANCY H. KWAK

Harlem River Houses (1937, 577 units, Manhattan)

Sponsor: NYCHA (PWA)
Program: public housing
Architect: Archibald Manning Brown, others

Harlem River Houses was the first publicly built and owned housing complex completed in New York City. It is most notable for its design, unique among low-income public housing complexes in New York, which represented a bridge between the garden-type courtyard complexes of the limited-dividend era and the more forward-looking Modernist designs that soon came to be associated with big-city public housing and slum clearance (fig. 2.17). It was also remarkable for its generous amenities—not least because it was built for African American families, who received unequal access to public services—and suggests a path that New York City housers might have taken were it not for the strict cost limits imposed by the permanent

2.17: Harlem River Houses, 1936

public housing programs introduced by Washington in 1937 and Albany in 1938. As it stands, Harlem River Houses remains an isolated experiment in the generous use of government funds to create high-quality communities at very low rentals.

For decades New York City's growing Black population endured some of the worst living conditions in the city because of a segregated, and thus especially constricted, housing market. African Americans suffered from higher mortality rates than rest of city while landlords exploited prejudice to charge higher rents for lower-quality dwellings. Despite this need, the first NYCHA projects planned, First Houses and Williamsburg Houses, were intended for whites. Things only began to change after a riot in Harlem in 1935 focused attention on the fact that the city had not devoted attention to its African American citizens. Harlem River Houses—developed on land bought from John D. Rockefeller, Jr., which the philanthropist had previously imagined for an extension of the Dunbar Apartments (1926)—thus emerged as an opportunity for Mayor Fiorello LaGuardia, who aimed to burnish his image with the Black community without challenging the city's underlying segregation.[34]

Design of Harlem River Houses was given by NYCHA to establishment architect Archibald Manning Brown and his team, which included John Louis Wilson, the first African American licensed architect in New York City. They did not intend for the project to make a major break with tradition. Rather, they used generous federal funds to improve upon it by introducing moderately lower building heights (four and five stories rather than five and six), and more open space (fig. 2.18). Building density, indeed, was about half that of the neighboring Dunbar Apartments, covering just 28 percent of the site, an astonishingly low figure for high-cost Manhattan. Population density was similarly reduced. But the overall effect of the perimeter blocks with their limited openings, outward facing retail, and courtyard facing stairhall entries, continued to recall a college quadrangle, much as limited-dividends had done. As in earlier projects, the primary feeling was of cloistered spaciousness, and the message conveyed by the design was disapproval of the street as a social space.

The design had some grace notes that endeared it to critics and tenants alike. The individual buildings did not block the sky or create a menacing skyline; Art Deco rustication along the base of the red brick buildings as well as sculptural elements designed by Heinz Warnecke added visual interest. Naturally lit stairhalls featured just four apartments per landing in an effort to engender feelings of community. The landscape designer Michael Rapuano, known for his work on many of Robert Moses's parks and parkways, cleverly subdivided the cobblestone-paved courtyards for intensive use including playgrounds and wading pools. Interiors featured soundproof tiles, tiled bathrooms,

2.18: Harlem River Houses, 2014

plaster walls, metal trim, and bronze hardware. Extra generous federal subsidies, which absorbed 45 percent of the construction costs, yielded apartments renting at an average of $7 per room per month ($1,200 in 2013 dollars for a five-room unit), although standard subsidies under PWA would have meant rentals twice as high for such a well-equipped project. As NYCHA administrators admitted, "The houses were built without specific relation to construction cost to the rent paying ability of the prospective tenants."[35]

Harlem River opened in 1937 with 577 apartments for families picked from over eleven thousand applicants—a volume reflecting both the dire circumstance of the Depression, but also the depth of housing privation in the African American community. To select tenants, NYCHA employed a point system favoring the employed, those with savings, good references, and an otherwise unblemished social record. Lodgers and extended families were prohibited. Black leaders encouraged NYCHA to screen this way because they believed that having model tenants would make a model project, and thus bolster support for more public housing in Harlem. Income was capped at five times the annual rents and while the majority of tenants were unskilled there were also large numbers of clerks and semi-skilled workers such as porters. Average household income was $1,340 ($47,000) and the share of tenants on public relief only about 5 percent. NYCHA, as in the other early developments, nevertheless collected rents at the door weekly (a practice disbanded in 1946 thanks to significant tenant resistance).[36]

Tenants—and the media—praised Harlem River Houses' design, especially the social life of the courtyards and the ability to observe their goings on from the apartments upstairs. They also celebrated the complex's social services, including a nursery, library, and summer school, and its active tenants (see fig. 2.13). Things were far from perfect, however. As in every public housing complex in the country, the share of tenants on public assistance rose, although in this case to only a very modest 10 percent by the 1970s. Crime, too, became a problem as the city and neighborhood suffered disinvestment.[37] Even in the worst years of the urban crisis, however, a sense of community kept fear at bay for many. As one tenant proclaimed in 1975, "I'm known here, and I know the crooks here, so I'm safer" than elsewhere.[38]

Harlem River has aged gracefully despite these setbacks and remains a stable, and popular, community. In 2012, it was home to 1,003 residents—about half the number as in 1937, owing to the rise in smaller households, including many seniors. Indeed, while 51 percent of households had at least one working member, 42 percent were headed by retirees (18 percent also included someone with a disability.) Average income of families was $23,000. Crime was down substantially from earlier highs. Racially, it became more diverse, although it was still all of color: 69 percent Black, 28 percent Hispanic, and 2 percent Asian American.

Harlem River Houses reflects the best of early public housing in the United States and affirms the convictions of early housers who believed that quality design and construction were key ingredients in generating value for tenants, and in encouraging long-term upkeep. Good design and a working tenancy alone, however, cannot secure the project's future. Its capital needs are extensive—and made more complicated by its status as a city historic landmark. Renovation of roofs and top-floor apartments started in 2014, but NYCHA estimates the complex needs seventy-one million dollars in renovations over the next fifteen years if it is not to fall into ruin in the coming decades.[39] NICHOLAS DAGEN BLOOM

Williamsburg Houses (1938, 1,622 units, Brooklyn)

Sponsor: NYCHA (PWA)
Program: public housing
Architect: Richmond Shreve, William Lescaze

Like the Harlem River Houses, Williamsburg Houses, which was the largest and most expensive of all the nation's PWA housing developments, was built with comparatively little reference to cost. As a result its apartments achieved a degree of spaciousness and attention to detail rarely replicated in American public housing (fig. 2.19). While singular in this respect, Williamsburg's Modernist site planning proved influential. Williamsburg, unlike Harlem River, rejected prevailing garden-apartment models in which buildings enclosed space in favor of serial repetition of geometric objects in space, heralding a rapid embrace by U.S. housers of tower-in-the-park arrangements (fig. 2.20).[40]

Head architect Richmond Shreve, best remembered for his design of the Empire State Building, tapped Swiss architect William Lescaze to design the site plan and exteriors. Lescaze had trained in Zurich, emigrated to the United States in 1920, and become the lead proponent of European Modernism on the East Coast. He was not a

2.19: Williamsburg Houses, living room, 1937

2.20: Williamsburg Houses, ca. 1938

houser and lacked understanding of the deep social context for Modernism as it had emerged in the 1920s in progressive cities like Vienna, Amsterdam, Frankfurt, and Berlin, but he kept abreast of the latest styles. This talent for "modernism as publicity," in the words of one historian, was on full display in his Philadelphia Savings Fund Society tower (1932) and his 1931 proposal to the State Board of Housing for the unbuilt Chrystie-Forsyth Houses on the Lower East Side. NYCHA, which had imagined Williamsburg as a testing ground for Modernist planning ideas from the start, selected him to advance this agenda.

Before joining the project, NYCHA had already decided the site's sixteen blocks of old-law tenements would be redeveloped as six superblocks (these were later reduced to twelve and four) (fig. 2.21). Through a design competition written by Frederick Ackerman, an old associate of Clarence Stein, it was also decided that the project would comprise twenty virtually identical four-story buildings. Freestanding apartment houses in the park had a long history in the United States apart from European experiments. Lescaze's contribution was to make the complex look modern. To do this, he pivoted the buildings fifteen degrees away from the street to suggest (falsely, as it turned out) *Zeilenbau* planning, which oriented buildings to the

2.21: Tenements, Ten Eyck St., razed for Williamsburg Houses, 1935

sun to maximize heat gain in winter. He also introduced staggered crossbars, some bridging parallel wings, some truncated, swapping, in essence, U- and C-plans for H-, I-, and T-plans that recalled proposals by the Swiss provocateur Le Corbusier. At the façades, Lescaze brought concrete floor plates to the surface and made them obvious by leaving them exposed.[41] In a nod to the popular Streamline Moderne style of the era, entryways and stairwell exteriors featured stainless-steel marquees and blue-tile facings. Williamsburg also helped introduce another shift: retail. The project included stores, although rents were often higher than in run-down buildings nearby and many spaces sat empty. This lackluster performance, along with new limits on retail development in the federal program and opposition by real estate interests to the idea of city-owned commercial space convinced NYCHA to dispense with most retail in the future.[42]

Critics like Lewis Mumford recognized Lescaze's application of Modernism as superficial. Other NYCHA projects of the 1930s—including Red Hook and Queensbridge—shared none of Williamsburg Houses' professed inclination toward European approaches. In other respects, however, Williamsburg signaled a new chapter in U.S. low-income housing design. For like Red Hook, Queensbridge, and later NYCHA projects—and unlike Harlem River Houses—Williamsburg rejected the street, and street life, not just by turning inward to enclosed courtyards but also by obliterating most streets altogether through the creation of superblocks, and efforts to limit outdoor public space to playgrounds and pathways (fig. 2.22).

If Lescaze's contributions to Williamsburg Houses were controversial and largely symbolic, the project excelled in other arenas. Residents enjoyed use of numerous craft and meeting rooms in the project's basement level. Interiors, meanwhile, which were designed by other NYCHA architects, were well planned and built to high specifications, reflecting reformers' hope that public housing in America would offer long-term, quality, permanent dwellings for working-class urban families. While the concrete stairwells that led to apartments lent an unfortunate institutional feel, they were redeemed by their outside-facing windows and by the fact that each landing served just three or four apartments. The apartments themselves were compact and efficient, but included market-rate-type finishes like wood floors, modern and commodious kitchens-and-living-room areas, and oversize casement windows, some of which wrapped around building corners to spill light into the bedrooms from two angles. Adding to tenants' comfort were modern amenities such as a central heating plant, hot and cold running water, private bathrooms with tubs, and appliances such as refrigerators.

Williamsburg's high quality, along with its low height and density, created publicity problems. Many objected to the idea of low-rent homes for the few being built at the high cost of $2,260 per room ($400,000 in 2013 dollars for a five-room apartment), only to be subsidized by the federal government to reach their intended clientele. As

2.22: Williamsburg Houses, lawn maintenance, 1939

in other NYCHA projects of the era, staff carefully selected tenants to ensure proper income, good housekeeping, and social order. In all, over twenty thousand families applied. Top incomes were capped at $2,184 per year ($75,000). Very few of the original site tenants who had lived in the three hundred old-law tenements that were replaced chose, or were chosen, to live in the project. Of thirteen hundred families displaced, 439 applied, and 341 ended up moving in. Many reporters criticized NYCHA for accepting such a low number of site tenants.[43]

Williamsburg housed only one Black family when it opened, reflecting NYCHA's unwillingness to challenge neighborhood racial divisions. A state law banning discrimination in public housing in 1939, and greater demand for housing by people of color citywide eventually changed the complex to minority-majority, although the pace of change was slow compared to other NYCHA developments. By 1954, for instance, there were 397 Black families along with a small number of Puerto Ricans; even in 1969 white families (mostly seniors) were still in the majority. By the late 1970s, however, it was entirely minority, with the Puerto Rican population (646 families) comprising the largest share. Reflecting larger changes in the population of public housing the number of families on welfare increased significantly, from just 14 percent in 1969 to 25 percent in 1977.[44] The development also suffered a wave of crime in the 1970s, although in contrast to stereotypes of public housing, crime fell dramatically after 1990. In the first four months of 2013 and 2014, for instance, there were no murders or rapes, although there were 140 "index crimes," such as robbery, assault, burglary, and larceny.[45]

Like other aging low-income housing projects, a major concern today is deferred maintenance. A $70 million renovation in the late 1990s returned the exterior to almost original condition and in 2003 the city built a multimillion-dollar community center designed by architects PKSB, with basketball court, kitchen, stage, and multipurpose spaces (see fig. 7.4). But decades of wear and tear on the residential buildings require continual capital investment. Already budget shortfalls have forced NYCHA to turn to a nonprofit group, St. Nick's Alliance, to run the new community center.

These problems aside, Williamsburg remains a healthy and by-and-large happy place to live. Hemmed in by higher-income development, residents pay much lower rents than their neighbors in private housing. Many residents express a great loyalty toward, and appreciation for, their community. Julio Cruz, who moved in from NYCHA's Red Hook Houses describes it as "a nice place to live." His concerns are mostly prosaic. "It's not so drug-infested here. The surrounding neighborhood is good. Even the service is better over here." But he and his partner, Edna Maldonado, also appreciate the generous design. They like the layout of their two-bedroom unit because they can go from both bedrooms to either the bathroom or the kitchen without going through the living room, making it easier to host extended family or guests. Eloina Santiago, meanwhile, is thankful for the opportunity for upward mobility that Williamsburg has given her family. She moved in forty-five years ago, fresh off the plane from Puerto Rico, and reared her family there. She feels lucky to have had such a "good place" to do so. Her children grew up to be a real estate agent, a teacher, and a naval officer. Despite the usual grumblings about noisy neighbors, housing authority rules, and crowded city living, the original sense of promise that launched the PWA housing program seems more than just a memory. "We're poor," Cruz says, "but we live well."[46] SAMUEL ZIPP AND NICHOLAS DAGEN BLOOM

Queensbridge Houses and East River Houses

(1940, 3,149 units, Queens; 1941, 1,170 units, Manhattan)

Sponsor: NYCHA (federal)
Program: public housing
Architect: Queensbridge: William F. R. Ballard, Henry S. Churchill; East River: Vorhees, Walker, Foley & Smith, Alfred Easton Poor, C. W. Schlusing

Queensbridge and East River Houses have the hallmarks of the brick-barracks approach to public housing yet also represent creative responses to the constraints of the Housing Act of 1937 (fig. 2.23). They reflect NYCHA's commitment to reordering urban living through design and to long-term maintenance of quality housing for low-income New Yorkers, despite many challenges.

The federal U.S. Housing Authority (USHA), which administered the 1937 law, favored housing on vacant land with low land costs. NYCHA, by contrast, preferred locations where the target population worked and lived, and consequently where the price of land was higher. For example, land costs at Sunnyside, Queens, were 50¢ per square foot; in Manhattan, they could be $10. NYCHA threaded this issue by locating Queensbridge and East River on industrial sites that were centrally located

2.23: Queensbridge Houses, from NYCHA, *Annual Report* (1944)

but moderately priced, and that avoided the expense of tenant relocation. These developments thus established NYCHA's strategy of replacing antiquated industrial uses with public housing along the shores of the East River—long before it was desirable to have East River views. Queensbridge and East River also challenged federal guidelines about tenant eligibility and building height in order to adjust normative USHA rules to the high-cost, high-density conditions of New York City.

Queensbridge Houses, which was (and today remains) the largest public housing complex in the United States, was located in Long Island City, Queens, close to the industrial waterfront and next to the Queensboro Bridge. The site afforded dramatic views of this imposing structure as well as the East River and the Manhattan skyline, but urban scenography did not account for its selection. While close to Manhattan, it was sparsely developed, minimizing residential relocation and keeping land costs just below the USHA ceiling of $1.50 per square foot ($53 in 2013 dollars). Bounded by Queens Plaza North, Vernon Boulevard, 40th Avenue, and 21st Street, the 49.5-acre site was organized into six superblocks with twenty-six, six-story apartment buildings and two community buildings. Initially, the development's 3,149 apartments housed a population of over ten thousand.[47]

NYCHA began planning Queensbridge in 1934, but the project stalled when funding was diverted to emergency relief. It was restarted after USHA funds became available, but NYCHA was obliged to make significant changes to meet the new stringent spending limits. The projects built by the Public Works Administration between 1933 and 1937 were lavish by comparison. The cost per room at Queensbridge was about half that of the PWA-funded Harlem River Houses (1937). In 1938 Alfred Rheinstein, chairman of NYCHA, announced a 66 percent cut in the Queensbridge Houses budget: in effect, federal funds were sufficient to cover only a third of the units as originally planned. Several cost-cutting changes were made to avoid scaling back the project. Closet doors were eliminated at an estimated savings of $250,000. Basements were eliminated and the buildings were set on concrete piles. Concrete slabs between units became floors and ceilings, whitewashed to look like plaster. The elevators stopped only on alternating floors, a feature not well-received by residents and eventually changed. These measures shaved the cost of Queensbridge to $1,044 per room ($36,000 today)—even less than the USHA standard of $1,250 ($43,000).[48]

The original site plan developed in 1936 by Frederick Ackerman and William F. R. Ballard with the Technical Division of NYCHA had arranged the buildings in an orthogonal pattern to create many small courtyards. Ackerman and Ballard published the site plan and underlying research in a 1937 publication, "A Note on Site & Unit Planning," which considered environmental qualities, such as daylight illumination, solar heat gain, and wind velocity, in different building configurations and compared costs of various layouts at different density levels. After the hiatus, Ballard was named chief architect of Queensbridge and established a new arrangement. Ballard was assisted by associate architect Henry S. Churchill.[49]

Ballard's team replaced the bar buildings with an innovative Y-plan, which they argued improved daylight illumination and privacy by creating more building façade. The Y-shaped structures were combined in chains of two, three, or more buildings and placed around the perimeter of superblocks, forming many odd angles along the street edge and a large open areas within. Significantly, the Queensbridge

2.24: Mural by Philip Guston, community center, Queensbridge Houses, by Steve Nessen, 2012

Houses did not rise above six stories. Taller buildings would have reduced average room costs and yielded greater per capita economies. One explanation is that city building regulations would have required a second fire exit stair for buildings of seven or more stories. Of equal importance, Queensbridge reflects USHA's bias in favor of low densities. The quantity of dwelling units, let alone their quality, was a secondary consideration.

The two community buildings provided a variety of social services, including a public library, a clinic operated by the city's health department, a privately operated nursery and nursery school, and a community center with gym and social rooms. Benefiting from the Federal Art Program, the community center was embellished with artwork, most notably a mural by Philip Guston (fig. 2.24). Another community asset was Queensbridge Park, a splendid waterfront space provided through a joint venture of NYCHA and the city's Department of Parks. NYCHA provided the land—approximately fifteen acres between Vernon Boulevard and the East River, in addition to a perpendicular strip beside and beneath the Queensboro Bridge ramp where tennis courts and playgrounds were planned—and Parks designed and operated it.

Construction started in September 1938 and the buildings were dedicated on May 4, 1940. Tenant selection was a source of tension between NYCHA and the USHA because the federal government objected to the city's limits on relief families. NYCHA yielded to federal pressure, lifting the cap from 5 to 8 percent at the PWA projects to 20 to 30 percent at the USHA projects. "We are getting into a different group of tenants at Queensbridge," a NYCHA official observed.[50] At the start, Queensbridge was also a white project: in 1941, it had 3,097 white families and just 52 African American ones. Early tenants of Queensbridge were delighted with their new homes despite the economies reflected in them. A reporter discovered that "of the hundreds of persons we spoke to, not a single one expressed any desire to return to his former abode." One mother, who left behind a Brooklyn tenement, celebrated that at Queensbridge, "We have five-and-a-half rooms, all of them bright and sunny—and a bathroom all to ourselves. We pay $5.70 [$185 in 2013 dollars] a week for them—and that includes gas and electricity, too. The kids sleep better and seem healthier." Many, however, also expressed a desire to own their home when better times returned and eventually left.[51] Yet despite the white flight, interracial friendships were common, and tenants, one former resident remembers, "looked out for everyone else's children."[52]

The East River Houses, in what was then Italian East Harlem, was a much smaller project than Queensbridge and suggests the adjustments required when dealing with Manhattan's high land costs. The site covered nearly twelve acres, about 75 percent fewer than Queensbridge, and the complex had about one-third of the number of apartments. Land coverage remained low (22 percent), but population densities were considerably higher. Three city blocks were merged to form a superblock running from First Avenue to the FDR Drive between East 102nd and 105th Streets. The area, which was in Mayor LaGuardia's home district, was dominated by dilapidated commercial structures: wholesale stores, warehouses, manufacturing buildings, and garages.

The powerhouse New York firm of Vorhees, Walker, Foley & Smith designed the development, with Alfred Easton Poor and C. W. Schlusing as associate architects. In a first site plan the buildings were laid out in parallel ranges diagonally oriented to the Manhattan grid: ten rows with a break in the two middle rows to form a central court. In the final plan, the straight rows were replaced by a more lively arrangement of zigzag structures (still ten in number) that more effectively bounded the open areas. These small, irregularly shaped interstitial spaces were filled with playgrounds, parking lots, and pathways connecting to the surrounding streets. In contrast to Queensbridge's constant six-story height, the East River buildings are six, ten, and eleven stories tall, rising in height from the southeast to the northwest to optimize views of the river. Height kept land coverage and room costs low while increasing density. Despite the project's economies, it also accommodated a nursery school, health center, and social rooms (fig. 2.25). Additionally, NYCHA reserved an acre along the FDR Drive for a playground built at the expense of the Works Progress Administration and operated by the Parks Department.

The groundbreaking on March 2, 1940, exposed rifts between the USHA and NYCHA on site selection, land costs, and density. Manhattan Borough President Stanley Isaacs posited that "the East River Houses would emphasize the fallacy of building modern homes for low-income groups in outer city areas." In response, Nathan Straus, head of the USHA, criticized the density of the project: "Fifty families on an acre is far too many. This project is going to have more than eighty families on an acre" (in fact, it was nearly one hundred).[53] To the chagrin of federal officials, East River Houses established a high-rise pattern that NYCHA would pursue for decades to come to manage Manhattan's high land costs while complying with federal guidelines for open space.

More than fourteen thousand families applied to live in the East River Houses. Tenants were means tested and NYCHA established a rent-differential plan with three tiers per apartment depending on ability to pay. About a quarter of the units were reserved for those in the lowest income bracket. This system served NYCHA's

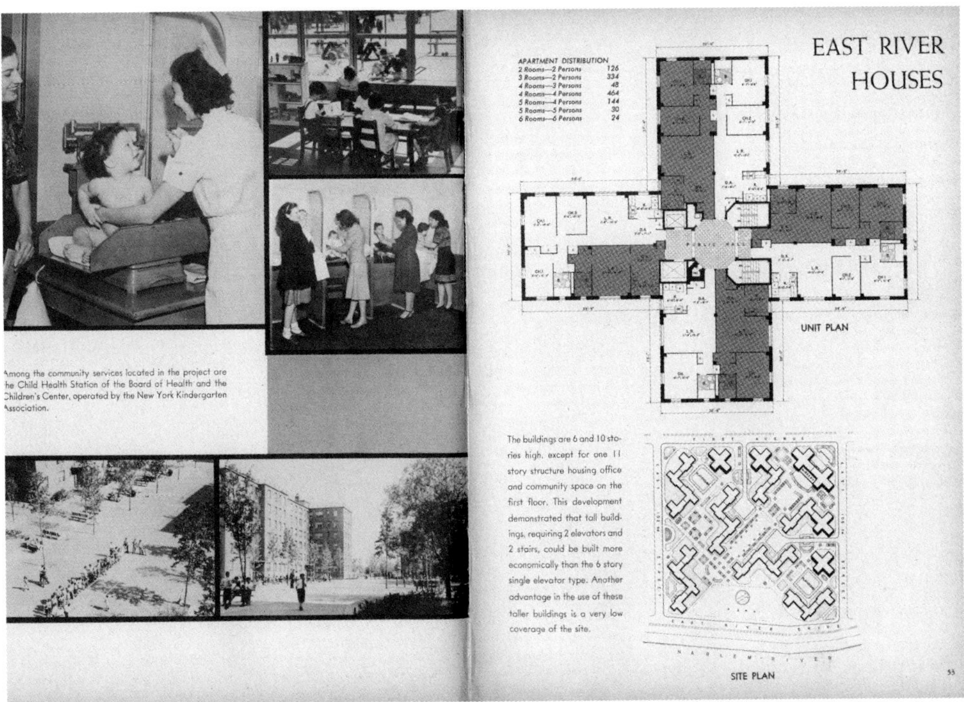

2.25: East River Houses, from NYCHA, *Annual Report* (1944)

strategy of mixing welfare families with the working poor so that rents could cover maintenance costs. As Rheinstein explained, "we think it is harmful to the whole movement of housing if we collect such low rents that the taxpayer will be called upon to make further contributions."[54] Like Queensbridge, the initial population of the East River Houses was largely white: 1,044 white families and 126 African American.

Socially, both projects transformed in the postwar decades. The welfare cohort remained relatively stable. At Queensbridge, for example, 19 percent of families were on relief in 1969 (by 1978 it climbed to 25 percent before falling to 22 percent in 2005). Ethnically, however, both experienced dramatic change, with most white families leaving within a generation. By 1969, 63 percent of tenants at Queensbridge were African American and 16 percent Puerto Rican while at East River just under half were African American and more than 40 percent Puerto Rican.[55] Both complexes also suffered rising rates of crime. In the 1970s and 1980s Queensbridge, in particular, developed a reputation for gang activities, and by 1990 there were half again as many felonies per capita as in NYCHA developments overall. Crack cocaine was an issue of particular concern, forcing many families to live in fear after dark.

Much has improved since then.[56] Like in the rest of the city, crime subsided significantly. More important, faced with growing tenant concerns about quality of life, NYCHA invested tens millions of dollars to repair buildings, redesign grounds, and maintain order, including a $32 million modernization program at Queensbridge.[57] Today both projects are fully occupied and their leafy courtyards remain busy social hubs. The radical break with New York's tenement past and the power of federal aid in public housing are very much still on view.
HILARY BALLON

Amsterdam Houses (1948, 1,048 units, Manhattan)

Sponsor: NYCHA (federal)
Program: public housing
Architect: Grosvenor Atterbury, Harvey Wiley Corbett, Arthur C. Holden

Amsterdam Houses, a slum-clearance project in the historically Black Upper West Side neighborhood of San Juan Hill (now Lincoln Square), reflects the complicated racial politics that came to define NYCHA's site-selection policies after World War II (fig. 2.26). Now encircled by wealthy neighbors, the complex also reflects the challenges and opportunities for public housing residents in today's era of gentrification.

By the time Mayor LaGuardia declared "Farewell to the Slums!" at the site in 1940, the San Juan Hill had already busied a generation of housers. Reformers Carolyn and Olivia Stokes, for instance, used family money in 1902 to help the City and Suburban Homes Company build low-cost, high-quality housing for African Americans there. Still, a 1934 survey declared the quarter to be the city's worst slum. Once Harlem opened to African Americans, by the 1920s, its newer, better housing had pulled north those Black families who could afford it, leaving San Juan Hill, the city's second largest Black community, more desperate and violent.[58]

NYCHA's new vision for the community was not color-blind. Although integrated as required by state law after 1939, the city clearly intended it for Black families: the neighborhood was more than three-quarters African American, with many African American businesses, too (fig. 2.27). While some welcomed the opportunity for new housing others argued the plan was less about slum clearance than maintaining slum boundaries. That said, in an inversion of familiar patterns, the project in its early years became overwhelmingly white. Although announced in 1940, construction was delayed until after World War II, when preferential admissions for veterans allowed many whites to get apartments while African Americans languished on the waiting list. Among initial tenants, only 23 percent were Black and only 4 percent were displaced site tenants.[59] Meanwhile, to not antagonize whites in adjacent areas who feared an influx of slum-dwellers, NYCHA helped move site families to hastily rehabilitated apartments in Harlem.[60]

2.26: Amsterdam Houses site, ca. 1940

In its physical form Amsterdam Houses retains elements of the interwar garden apartment, but also embraces aspects of Modernism (fig. 2.28). The inward-facing scheme concentrates open spaces along a symmetrical tree-lined axis and respects the Manhattan street grid in its pedestrian circulation. Ten of the thirteen buildings rise six stories, and thus did not represent a radical departure from the scale of the tenement neighborhood that it replaced. The complex does, however, sit on a superblock, and buildings cover less than a third of the

2.27: Store razed for Amsterdam Houses, 1941

2.28: Amsterdam Houses, courtyard, 1949

site. Three cruciform towers on Tenth Avenue rise thirteen stories, clad in unadorned red brick, a look that quickly came to define public housing.

Amsterdam's apartments reflected a profound step toward decency over what the market provided previously. Where once stood tenements with nine out of ten units lacking heat, half without hot water, and nearly all sharing a hall toilet, now stood up-to-date structures, built to last, with the amenities necessary for a dignified life. Henrietta Edwards, who moved into her apartment in 1951, said, "It was heaven to me. My children had a room and I had a room and we were surrounded by beautiful parks." Edwards believed that the "healthy" environment made it possible for two of her children to go college even as many of her friends' families fell apart.[61] Three playgrounds were designed for different stages of childhood, a progressive idea at the time; all remain busy today. More than five thousand square feet of the complex's ground floor space hosted a nursery, a clinic, a gymnasium, and offices for the United Neighborhood Houses' Lincoln Square Community Center. Tenants in the 1960s, for example, took classes in money management and child-care, with a free clinic for maternal care and family planning. The authority's independent and largely non-white police force also provided a deeply appreciated form of community policing at Amsterdam Houses and other developments that helped maintain low crime rates.

Growing populations of color and vibrant community institutions helped make the complex what the *New York Times* called a rare "object lesson" in racial integration in the 1950s and 1960s. Amsterdam Houses resident Hortense Vidal recalled six decades later that the development was "like paradise" where "people of all races got along."[62] That moment of integrated housing, however, passed quickly. The late 1950s saw an exodus of nearly half the white families, replaced almost entirely by African Americans and Latinos. The loosening of eligibility restrictions in the late 1960s meant that a third of Amsterdam Houses tenants would pay rent with a welfare check by 1972.[63]

The neighborhood around Amsterdam Houses began to gentrify in the 1960s and 1970s, especially with the opening of Lincoln Center and new middle-income and market-rate buildings that were also part of the Lincoln Square Urban Renewal Area just to the north, which attracted many young professionals. Soon Amsterdam Houses found itself a low-rent island in a high-rent sea—as would be one out of every three NYCHA complexes by the early twenty-first century (see fig. 0.35).[64] Perhaps because of these changes so many of Amsterdam's older residents have stayed put that more than 70 percent of heads of households are now over sixty-two. (That said, this pattern is not unique: more than 40 percent of NYCHA developments are now NORCs, or naturally occurring retirement communities.[65])

In contrast to other cities, where well-located public housing like Cabrini-Green in Chicago and Techwood in Atlanta has often been targeted for redevelopment, Amsterdam's tenants remain committed to it—so much that they have inspired a campaign by neighborhood preservationists to have the complex designated a historic landmark, which surely, in their minds, it already is. FRITZ UMBACH

Model Gallery I: Pre-World War II

Efforts at below-market housing before World War II focused on creating a superior physical alternative to market-built tenements. Sponsors emphasized large, outside-facing windows on two or more exposures to increase the amount of light and allow for cross-ventilation, a crucial comfort before air conditioning. Units also included all up-to-date conveniences, including private bathrooms and kitchens, electricity, hot and cold running water, and central heating.

Architects designed apartment interiors to advance Progressive Era social goals of using the physical environment to improve the moral character of poor and working class tenants. Privacy was a key value. Careful tenant selection and on-site management ensured families were "right sized" for units, with particular attention to ensuring children and parents had separate sleeping quarters. At the same time, apartments—with approximately just five hundred to eight hundred square feet for a unit with two bedrooms—accommodated only the nuclear family, with no space for unrelated lodgers.

In a further nod to middle-class mores, plans stressed separation of the basic functions of living, sleeping, bodily care, and cooking, with small spaces of transition between them, such as foyers. Living rooms in many apartments also served double duty as family gathering places and links between functional zones. Another new feature was closet space, which encouraged tidiness and visual order while recognizing the rise of America's consumer culture, which allowed even poor families to amass personal and household goods. Access to units was organized around small stairwells and landings. These spaces created relatively private common areas shared by just a few families, rather than long, anonymous internal corridors characteristic of later eras.

Dunbar Apartments

1926; 2BR = 560 square feet

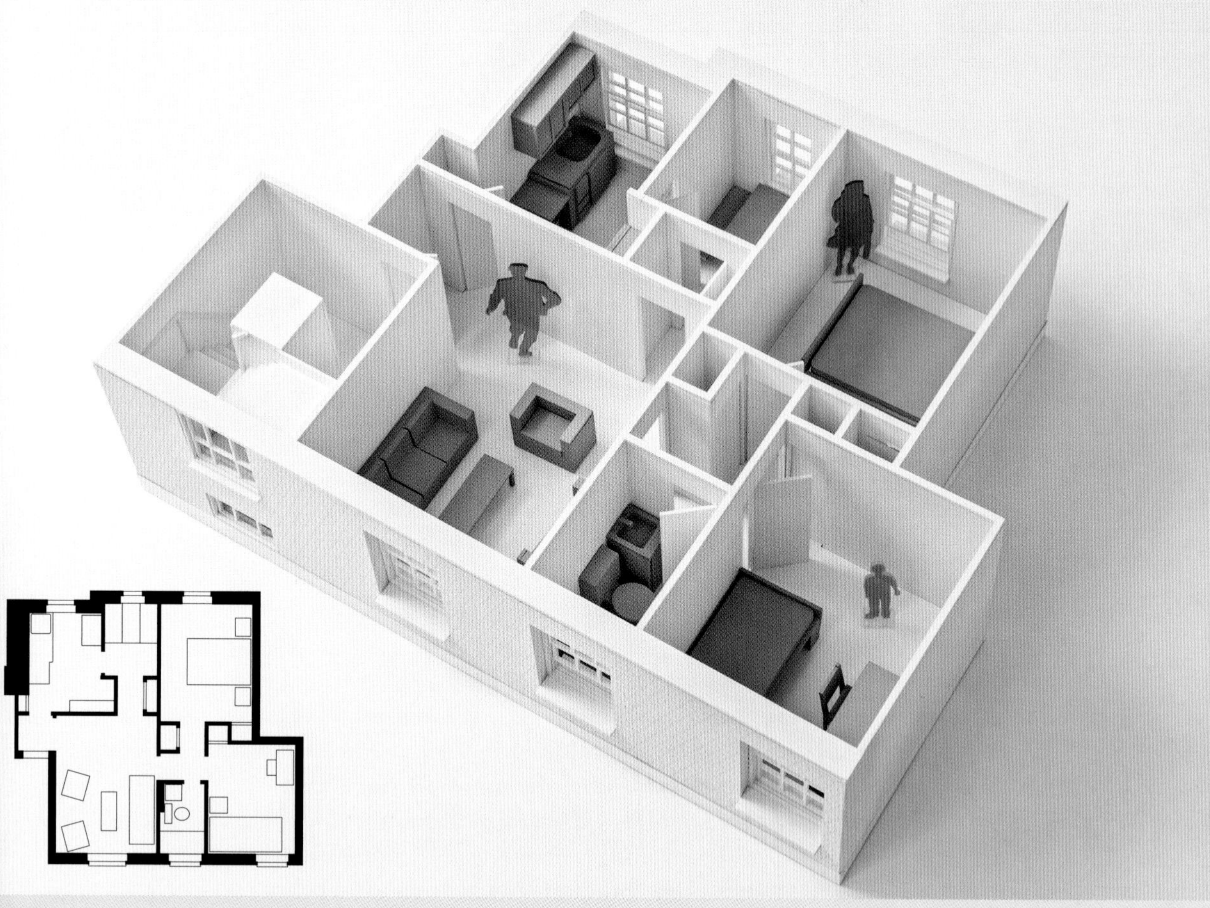

Dunbar Apartments aimed to illustrate that high-quality, below-market housing could be constructed on a limited-profit basis by the private sector without government aid. Each apartment featured three transition zones, one at the entry to the unit, one between the living room and the bedrooms, and the third between the living room and the dining area. This configuration, while reducing living space, added a formal, middle-class feeling to an otherwise small unit, reflecting the architect's experience designing market-rate housing. The small but separate dining area, and decorative treatments like crown moldings, were a further nod to market-rate apartments. Generously proportioned windows faced the street on one side and the complex's landscaped courtyard on the other, enhancing the sense of spaciousness.

Sunnyside Gardens

1924–28; 2BR = 780 square feet

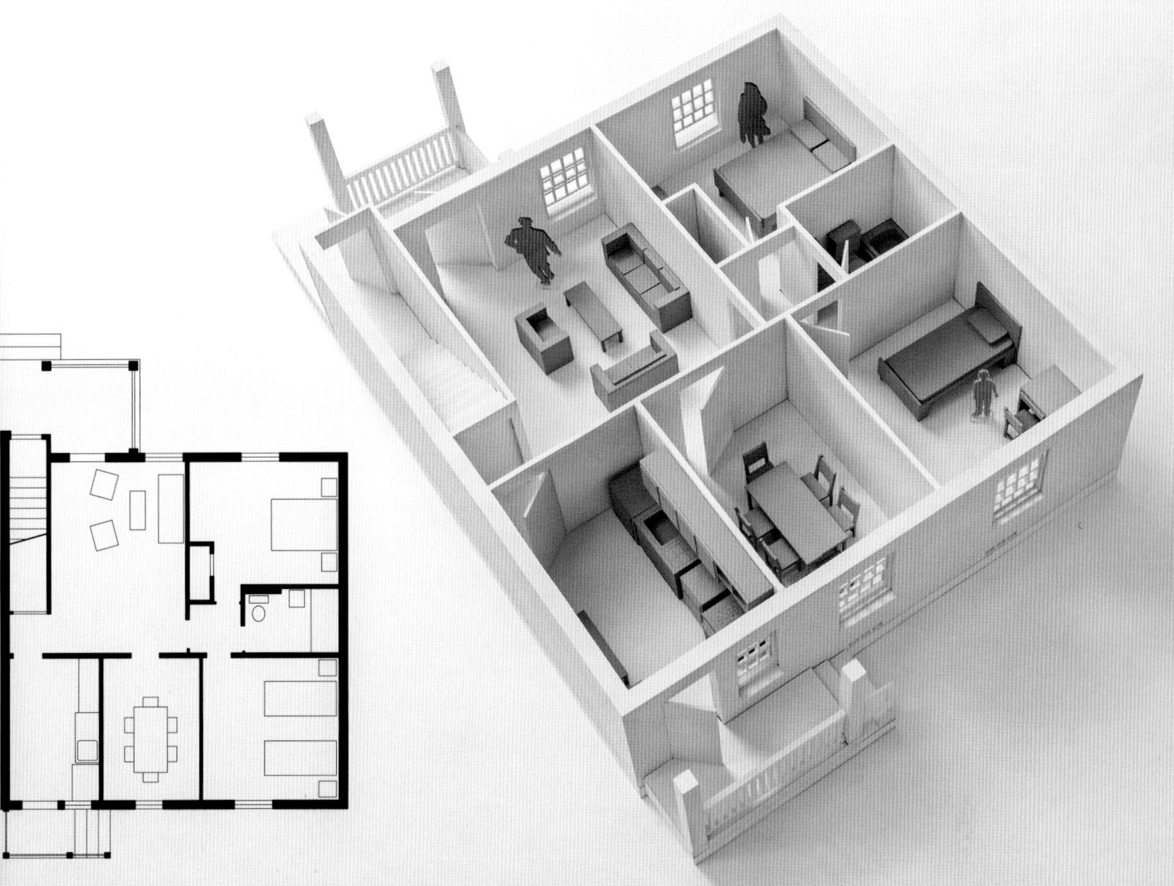

The designers of Sunnyside Gardens had as a goal the integration of urban family life with natural surroundings. Units such as this one, on the first floor of a two-unit row house, took advantage of green space at front and back, with large windows facing common gardens. A unique element was front and rear porches that served as exterior foyers, and which many owners later enclosed. Placement of kitchens on the garden side was intended to give mothers visual control of the back gardens, where children were expected to play—in contrast to tenement districts, where play happened on the street. In a nod to middle-class norms, apartments included dining rooms, although many tenants used them as third bedrooms. The relatively generous floor area reflected the middle-class orientation of Sunnyside's sponsors as well as the low cost of land at the formerly industrial site.

Williamsburg Houses
1938; 2BR = 620 square feet

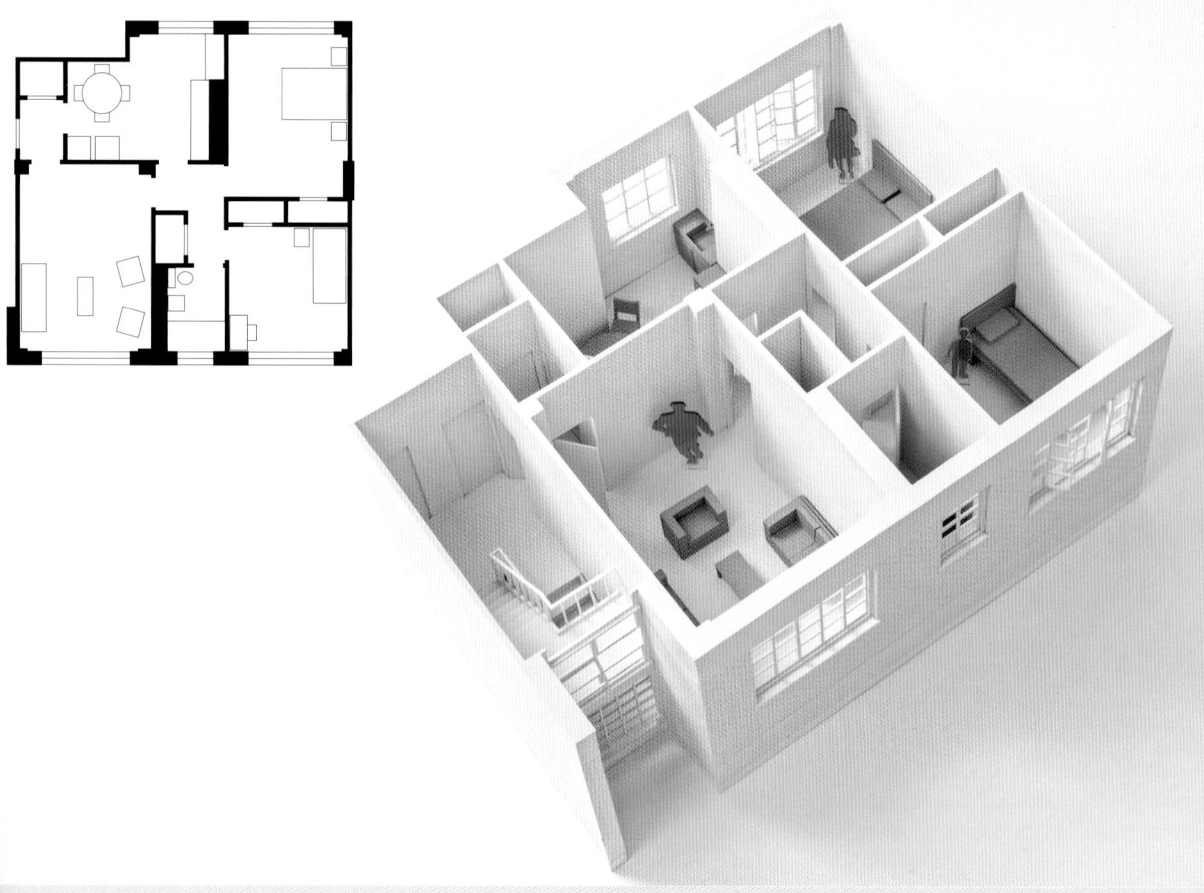

The designers of Williamsburg Houses benefited from budgets and artistic freedom that would rarely be granted to designers of later public housing complexes. Its concrete stairwells may have felt institutional but they were redeemed by their outside-facing windows and by the fact that each landing served just three or four apartments. The apartments themselves were compact and efficient yet included finishes like wood floors, commodious kitchens and living-room areas, and large casement windows, some of which wrapped around building corners to spill light into the bedrooms. Adding to comfort were up-to-date amenities such as a central heating and refrigerators. With its compact rooms arranged off of a central foyer, Williamsburg adopted a streamlined plan that followed German *Existenzminimum*. The layout included a combined living-dining area, rejecting the emphasis on specialized rooms found in market-rate housing. The large windows and low site coverage created interior spaces dramatically brighter and better ventilated than the tenements the project replaced.

Queensbridge Houses

1940; 2BR = 580 square feet

Queensbridge Houses reflected new economies in the public housing program driven by federal cost limits in the Housing Act of 1937 and embarrassing publicity related to high costs of projects like Williamsburg Houses. The concrete slabs between units became floors and ceilings, with the ceilings whitewashed to look like plaster; cheaper sidelights replaced overhead light fixtures. Curtains replaced closet doors. The difficult trade-offs between market standards and restricted costs are also evident in the layout. The entry opens directly onto a generous L-shaped space for living and dining with a separate kitchen. At the back of this space a hallway leads to bedrooms and, at the far end, the bathroom. The arrangement of the interiors as a long series of rooms, as in a railroad-style plan, reduced livable space, although the designers added some functionality to the corridor by lining it with built-in storage. The potential benefits of cross-ventilation promised by the interior plan were also compromised, by placing only private spaces (the larger bedroom and the bath) along the second exposure.

MATTHIAS ALTWICKER, MATTHEW GORDON LASNER, AND NICHOLAS DAGEN BLOOM

3

Public Housing Towers

The differences between public housing in New York City and other American cities became more extreme in the postwar era. A few cities, such as Chicago, St. Louis, Newark, Baltimore, and Atlanta, also pursued public housing aggressively, remaking many of their disadvantaged neighborhoods, especially those that were predominantly African American. But the New York City Housing Authority (NYCHA), under the guidance of Robert Moses, erected vast phalanxes of complexes across the city, in every borough, transforming urban living and countless neighborhoods, Black, white, and industrial, for hundreds of thousands (fig. 3.1).

3.1: Lillian Wald Houses, Jacob Riis Houses, and Stuyvesant Town, ca. 1949

The gap between New York and other American cities grew even wider when buildings opened. While in most cities public housing quickly suffered serious social and physical problems, in New York the decay was far less pronounced. Just as New York had been more committed to the promise of public housing in the interwar period, after the war the city committed itself to maintaining its developments over time, physically as well as socially, through daily maintenance, continued commitment to careful tenant selection, and vigorous policing, sometimes conducted in partnership

3.2: NYCHA Youth Patrol, Kingsborough Houses, Brooklyn, by L. Marinoff, 1969

with residents (fig. 3.2). A large housing project like St. Louis's notorious Pruitt-Igoe had been rendered nearly unlivable within ten years of opening in 1954 but nearly all of NYCHA's housing remained fully rented and decently maintained.[1]

The immediate justification for New York's robust postwar public housing program was a run on apartments. By 1945 New York had entirely shaken off its Depression Era gloom. It hummed with financial, industrial, and mercantile activity. Wartime industries had, however, jammed city dwellers into every available apartment, no matter how squalid.[2] In 1945, for instance, of 2,255,850 dwellings in New York, only two thousand were vacant. Even many abandoned tenements filled back up. Nationwide restrictions on materials during the war brought construction—both public and private—to a halt except in war emergency areas. With demobilization things grew so dire that NYCHA set up Quonset huts on city land for veterans and their families. Only rent control kept chaos at bay. Initiated by the federal Office of Price Administration in critical defense areas in 1942 and extended to New York City a year later, it remained in place until the early 1950s, when Washington determined the wartime emergency to be over. Under pressure from leftist tenants groups, however, New York state and then city extended it.[3]

Meanwhile, voters impatient for better housing gave political leaders the tail winds they needed to launch a massive new effort in public housing. City leaders were near unanimous in agreeing that more public housing and slum clearance were essential to reconversion. Veterans, they believed, deserved up-to-date homes, not slums, even if many tenement dwellers would have to be displaced in the short term. Amid greenery and sunlight, public housing would allow a modern, healthy working class to prosper. Construction firms would benefit. Employers would too.

Robert Moses was essential to realizing this vision. During the 1930s and early 1940s Moses spent a great deal of energy painting NYCHA leaders as incompetent amateurs. This all changed when Mayor LaGuardia placed postwar planning in Moses's hands during the war. LaGuardia's successor, Mayor William O'Dwyer, elected in 1945 on a populist platform strongly supportive of public housing and other public works, collaborated with Moses to launch record numbers of housing developments and other public improvements. Moses's support came with a price, however: control. Moses achieved this not by taking over the agency, but by having close allies installed, including Thomas Farrell, appointed chairman in 1947, and Philip Cruise, appointed chairman in 1950. At the same time, he and his allies forced out older housers like Mary Simkhovitch. Chairman of the Mayor's Committee on Slum Clearance and the city construction coordinator, Moses assumed power over all the city's capital activities, including public housing site selection. Through these tactics Moses played a major role in NYCHA's direction (fig. 3.3).

Moses was not a houser by background, temperament, or politics. But he believed public housing, and lots of it, was essential to modernizing a city that in the atomic age seemed hopelessly antiquated. Moses was open about his position: "it is hardly necessary to tell you that I am not a rabid houser," but "private capital slum clearance requires public housing to take care of displaced tenants of the lowest incomes."[4] Moses's beautifully illustrated reports for Title I clearance projects always included a statement by a NYCHA chairman estimating the "percentage of site families eligible for relocation to public housing." These estimates could range as high as 60 percent of tenants at Harlem sites to 15 percent at Greenwich Village's Washington Square South. Moses also appreciated that NYCHA was a relatively efficient civil-service public authority, of a type he preferred. NYCHA, powerful enough to override objections of elected officials and local residents, could fulfill its mission with great speed. Not wanting to interfere with the work of agency staff who, by this time, had earned a good reputation for their construction and management skills, he mostly left them alone. Instead, he magnified the agency's size without altering its planning, design, or management style (fig. 3.4).[5]

3.3: Robert Moses, second from right, and NYCHA Chairman Thomas Farrell (right), Parkside Houses, Bronx, 1950

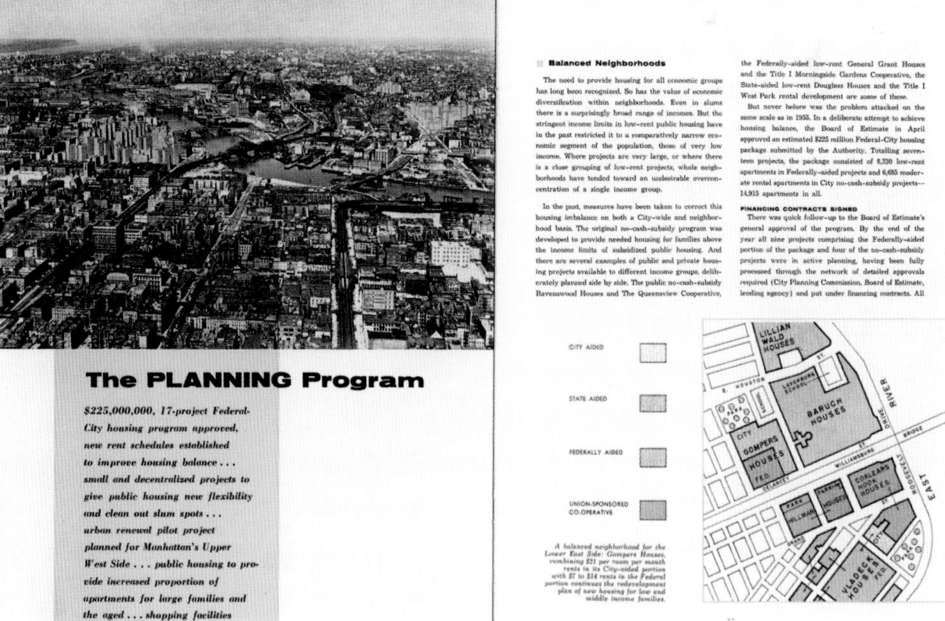

The PLANNING Program

$225,000,000, 17-project Federal-City housing program approved, new rent schedules established to improve housing balance . . . small and decentralized projects to give public housing new flexibility and clean out slum spots . . . urban renewal pilot project planned for Manhattan's Upper West Side . . . public housing to provide increased proportion of apartments for large families and the aged . . . shopping facilities to be provided.

Balanced Neighborhoods

The need to provide housing for all economic groups has long been recognized. So has the value of economic diversification within neighborhoods. Even in slums there is a surprisingly broad range of incomes. But the stringent income limits in low-rent public housing have in the past restricted it to a comparatively narrow economic segment of the population, those of very low income. Where projects are very large, or where there is a close grouping of low-rent projects, whole neighborhoods have tended toward an undesirable overconcentration of a single income group.

In the past, measures have been taken to correct this housing imbalance on both a City-wide and neighborhood basis. The original no-cash-subsidy program was developed to provide needed housing for families above the income limits of subsidized public housing. And there are several examples of public and private housing projects available to different income groups, deliberately planned side by side. The public no-cash-subsidy Ravenswood Houses and The Queensview Cooperative, the Federally-aided low-rent General Grant Houses and the Title I Morningside Gardens Cooperative, the State-aided low-rent Douglass Houses and the Title I West Park rental development are some of these.

But never before was the problem attacked on the same scale as in 1955. In a deliberate attempt to achieve housing balance, the Board of Estimate in April approved an estimated $225 million Federal-City housing package submitted by the Authority. Totalling seventeen projects, the package consisted of 8,230 low-rent apartments in Federally-aided projects and 6,685 moderate rental apartments in City no-cash-subsidy projects—14,915 apartments in all.

FINANCING CONTRACTS SIGNED

There was quick follow-up to the Board of Estimate's general approval of the program. By the end of the year all nine projects comprising the Federally-aided portion of the package and four of the no-cash-subsidy projects were in active planning, having been fully processed through the network of detailed approvals required (City Planning Commission, Board of Estimate, lending agency) and put under financing contracts. All

A balanced neighborhood for the Lower East Side: Gompers Houses, combining $21 per room per month rents in its City-aided portion with $7 to $14 rents in the Federal portion continues the redevelopment plan of new housing for low and middle income families.

3.4: "The Planning Program," from NYCHA, *Annual Report* (1955)

Much of the new construction in the 1940s was paid for with the city and state public housing programs, since federal appropriations from the 1937 Housing Act had expired and Congress did not agree on a new bill until 1949. Both the city and state programs, which had emerged in response to pressure from city leaders, expanded in the late 1940s to fill the federal gap. The city program, which had produced only four developments by 1947, grew significantly after being restructured in 1948. By 1960 it had produced 36,000 units. These "no-cash subsidy" projects, as the city referred to them, remained distinct from federal and state-funded projects. Most were built on low-cost city-owned land with favorable financing backed by NYCHA bonds. Rents were higher but they covered operating and finance costs. Many of them—such as Ravenswood Houses (1951), Pomonok Houses (1952), and Woodside Houses (1949)—were built to high standards comparable to the Federal Housing Administration's, and were surrounded by acres of open space. Some remain very desirable to this day. The state program, by contrast, worked more like the federal one. Projects like the Johnson Houses (1948) had a similar lower-income user in mind and lacked the nicer touches of the city projects. By 1955 the state program included forty-eight developments with nearly 52,000 units.

Combined with the federal program, which revived in 1949, the city and state efforts allowed bulldozers to roll through the slums in the 1950s, effecting the kind of rapid, dramatic change only imagined by reformers of other eras, before and since. By 1955 87,963 new apartments had been built, housing a population of 335,000 people that was already larger than all of St. Paul, Minnesota. By 1959 NYCHA had completed or placed in the pipeline an astounding 148,583 units (fig. 3.5).

Because NYCHA never mastered the difficult job of relocation, the organization found itself vulnerable to criticism, even from those who once had supported slum clearance. Public housing originated in a Depression Era city with many vacant apartments available to those displaced from their tenement apartments in the name

3.5: Architects with plans for NYCHA complexes, n.d. (early 1960s)

3.6: "Site-Clearance; Building on Slums," from NYCHA, "Housing: Public Housing, Slum Clearance, Quasi-Public Housing, F.H.A. Housing, January 1946–July 1949" (1949)

of progress. Moreover, many early projects, such as Queensbridge Houses (1940), rose on nearly vacant or outmoded industrial sites. The situation changed in the late 1940s and the 1950s. The city was crowded again as a result of the war and the postwar boom. And as the immediate postwar housing crisis faded in the early 1950s, Puerto Rican and African American migration kept the market tight. That so much housing was being razed simultaneously for all the other redevelopment projects of the Moses era (roads, bridges, urban renewal) compounded the problem. Little was done by way of aid in relocation for residents and business owners.

The fact that public housing increasingly often displaced site tenants (growing numbers of whom were people of color), and scattered them with only haphazard assistance, soon became a humanitarian and public relations embarrassment (fig. 3.6). By 1957, for instance, the housing authority had rehoused only 18 percent of the site tenants it had displaced. Worse yet, displaced tenants faced an ever-decreasing range of options—especially those who were ineligible for NYCHA apartments. For them, clearance resulted in a net loss of affordable units. To compensate, tenants and landlords made do the old-fashioned way, carving up houses and apartments into small sets of rooms, in the process creating what, in effect, were new slums. One former NYCHA administrator speculated that most former site tenants were now relegated to single-room occupancy hotels (SROs); to be sure, for every tenement cleared in the 1950s, two or three new rooming houses seemed to emerge nearby.[6]

To cope Moses launched a program of construction on vacant city-owned land. As someone more interested in redevelopment than in providing the less advantaged with good housing, he had long decried this approach. But as concerns about displacement mounted, he relented.[7] To accomplish the task he relied on the state and city programs, which lacked the equivalent elimination requirements of the federal one.[8] It worked. By 1961 NYCHA had built fifty-two projects (out of a total of one hundred fifty projects) on more than a thousand acres of vacant "wasteland."[9]

3.7: Frederick Douglass Houses (1958)

Physically, the housing of the Moses era continued NYCHA's tradition, established before World War II, of simple, durable, red-brick towers on green campuses (fig. 3.7). While the origins of this format are often traced to the avant-garde Modernist provocations of Swiss designer Le Corbusier in the 1920s and 1930s, the freestanding high-rise had a broader, deeper history in the United States. As early as the 1910s American architects had begun experimenting with such designs, and in the 1920s it became a standard type in luxury apartments and hotels, especially in resort areas like Long Beach, California, and Miami. Closer to home, freestanding towers appeared in suburban centers, such as Fairmont Park, in Philadelphia, and Scarsdale, in Westchester County, New York. While aware of Le Corbusier, NYCHA designers in the 1930s and 1940s determined this form to be well-suited to the city's needs for more mundane reasons. After experimenting with a range of ideas and building types, the tower-in-the-park was proved to efficient, cost-effective, and practical. And it delivered what was so lacking in slums—open space safe from auto traffic, fresh air, and sunlight—better than any other system. To nearly everyone, it represented a logical next step in the progression away from the tenements, after the courtyard apartments of the 1920s. Moreover, in the age of the automobile, and as pictured in the colorful renderings created by firms working for NYCHA, towers in the park looked as modern as tenements looked retrograde.[10]

Which is not to say that the brick tower block was without flaws. In practice the act of erasure was often too potent, taking with it not just darkness, overcrowding, and poor hygiene, but the identity of entire neighborhoods. Sections of East Harlem, Brownsville, and the Lower East Side, once defined by their squalid collections of tenements and chaotic street life, reemerged as orderly, quiet superblocks of manicured high-rises where nothing much seemed to happen. By design, as in suburbia,

3.8: NYCHA playground (unidentified), Bronx

life was quietly engineered to take place inside the home or in a supervised community center (which NYCHA continued to build in large numbers), rather than out in public. For a time NYCHA police even ticketed tenants for walking on lawns. Out-of-door activities were limited, at least officially, to quiet contemplation on benches or to designated play spaces (fig. 3.8).

This change suited most tenants just fine. But as the towers and open spaces grew larger over the 1950s and 1960s, something was lost. NYCHA's repetitive X-, T-, and Y-plan towers and slabs, with their red-brick exteriors and small windows generated a monotonous "project look" that lacked the visual variety of older neighborhoods. To outside observers like Jane Jacobs the uniformity could seem stultifying. Meanwhile, underprogrammed open spaces proved difficult to police as the city's crime rate, and the number of children in NYCHA developments, increased. Within buildings problems also arose as the number of floors doubled and tripled, often reaching twenty stories or more. As managers found out, such very tall buildings presented unique challenges because of insufficient vertical circulation (too few, too slow, or too temperamental elevators) and greater anonymity.[11]

Despite these challenges, NYCHA offered low- and moderate-income families far better housing, at very modest rents, than were available on the market. The interiors were not luxurious. Finishes were simple, inexpensive, and durable: concrete block and asphalt tile. Until 1958 federal and state complexes did not include showers. City-sponsored projects, by contrast, did, along with closet doors, toilet seat covers, and faster elevators. Everywhere apartment layouts were efficient, and all rooms had fresh air and sunlight. And some initial economies, such as the lack of closet doors, were eventually remedied. The large, civil-service-selected site staff maintained buildings and grounds impeccably.

NYCHA's great postwar construction program had a dramatic effect not just on the quality of housing and the physical form of the city, but on its social geography. Much public housing under Moses was built in areas of crowded tenements, now increasingly filled with Black and Latino families. The long-term migration of African Americans from the rural South to New York and other larger northern cities was complemented beginning in the late 1940s by a large wave of Puerto Ricans seeking a better life. Despite the high hopes of migrants and white liberals, the *Times* admitted: "segregation has confined the Negro people to a Black ghetto, shutting them out from normal interchange with their fellow Americans."[12] Many sections of the outer boroughs, meanwhile, remained almost entirely white. Residents there fiercely resisted efforts to introduce public housing, except middle-income, city-sponsored projects (fig. 3.9).[13] The result was that NYCHA's developments came, by the late 1950s, to comprise something of a "second ghetto": new communities now officially segregated by income, and mostly by race, built atop

3.9: Protest during groundbreaking at Woodside Houses, Queens, 1948

the old slums. This became more acute as the postwar housing shortage subsided. Despite NYCHA's aggressive programs to create and maintain racially integrated developments, white tenants quickly moved out to take advantage of new market-rate housing opportunities—many underwritten by different federal policies. Even the city-funded projects began a steady, if slower, transition to minority-majority tenancies. This process of segregation was never as complete as in cities like Chicago, where a primary purpose of public housing was to contain African Americans.[14] But the net effect was that by 1965, 88,445 public housing units could be found in just seven areas: the Lower East Side, the Upper West Side, East and Central Harlem, Bedford Stuyvesant, Brownsville, Coney Island, and the South Bronx.[15]

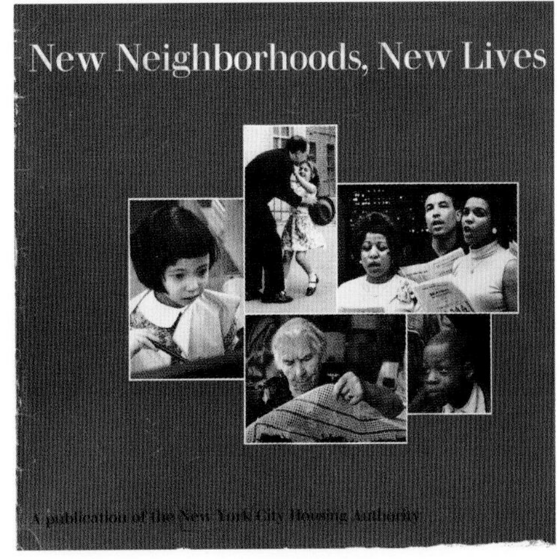

3.10: NYCHA, *New Neighborhoods, New Lives* (1964)

Although in retrospect this concentration of low-income below-market housing now appears as one of many social failings of postwar urban planning, at first the rebuilding was considered by many an unequivocal good and a boon to areas that had suffered the most under laissez-faire market conditions (fig. 3.10). In 1946 in East Harlem, for instance, the combination of public reconstruction, including public housing, was considered essential by the *New York Times* for transforming it into one of the city's more "attractive neighborhoods." Blocks of East 101st Street between First and Second Avenues were once called "Misery Street" for their "dark and grimy stretch of decayed rookeries, of broken and cracked sidewalks covered with overflowing refuse barrels."[16] Populist political leaders such as East Harlem city councilman Vito Marcantonio funneled voters' rage over these conditions into the vast housing program.

While these powerful interventions were welcomed, they also generated many challenges. By the 1960s, after 160 acres of East Harlem had been cleared to make way for brick towers housing over sixty thousand tenants, the limits of design-based solutions became clear: new housing alone did little to address larger issues. Meanwhile, clearance continued to take a high social and economic toll. Large numbers of African Americans and Puerto Ricans, especially, were displaced, sometimes multiple times, and consistently low percentages of site tenants ended up in the new public housing.[17]

Critiques of New York's public housing grew loud by the late 1950s and 1960s, even among many ardent supporters. Architecture critic Lewis Mumford wrote it was "a pathological remedy" that might ultimately exchange "slums for super slums."[18] Catherine Bauer in a landmark article entitled "The Dreary Deadlock of Public Housing," distinguished her own long-standing idea for "modern housing," serving a broad spectrum of working- and middle-class Americans in new developments modeled on Sunnyside Gardens, from the reality of institutional looking,

3.11: Moving day, family with six children, from NYCHA, *New Neighborhoods, New Lives* (1964)

city-center projects common in the 1950s. Manhattan Borough President Hulan Jack, a leading spokesman for New York's Black community, was yet more direct: he believed NYCHA designers had gone too far in their fetish for open space, pointing out that market-rate buildings covering three-quarter of their sites were perfectly healthy.[19] Even Robert Moses complained to NYCHA Chairman Philip Cruise of the "monotonous sameness and institutional character."[20]

In response, NYCHA began introducing a "new look," including additional variations of building heights within developments, faster elevators, more extensive use of glazed brick both on exteriors and in hallways, and even exterior decorative color panels. The agency also included larger apartments that had been in short supply for families (fig. 3.11). Here and there a store was included, and an occasional church or other outstanding building on site was preserved. Serial brick towers, however, more or less continued to roll off the NYCHA assembly line.

More pointed critique flowed from neighborhoods being rebuilt, especially with regard to lack of retail space. In East Harlem alone NYCHA displaced two thousand businesses by the late 1950s, yet by 1965 the city counted only 170 stores across all of its 150 public housing developments. Worse yet, many of the retail spaces, which were expensive to rent, struggled for commercial tenants. This situation made life inconvenient for residents, who also suffered from lack of social spaces that traditionally occupied storefronts, like saloons and small churches. NYCHA, like housing reformers of earlier eras, encouraged tenants to use free time to other improving ends (fig. 3.12). Perhaps the one saving grace was inadvertent: in an era of rising commercial vacancy rates generally, NYCHA resident populations helped sustain nearby shopping areas that escaped the wrecking ball like East 116th Street.[21]

Although public housing in the 1950s enjoyed a degree of public support in New York unparalleled in the United States, NYCHA soon found itself at the center of a reappraisal of Moses's power and influence. Even though NYCHA was prolific, the chorus of skeptics grew ever louder. Mayor Wagner, responding to growing concerns about management issues, design, and Moses's cynical methods, reorganized NYCHA's board in 1958 and purged the Moses men. The new chairman, William Reid, worked to restore faith in public housing as a tool of urban reconstruction. Under Reid's lead, the agency no longer simply acquiesced to Moses's requests for taking more site tenants. And NYCHA began shifting away from mega-projects to smaller-scale efforts of five hundred to a thousand units on "vest pocket" sites, which inserted developments into neighborhoods without eliminating streets to create superblocks. By 1962, 32 percent of NYCHA's developments under way were of this type. Exemplary of this strategy was the Robert Fulton Houses (1965) in Chelsea designed by long-time NYCHA architects

Brown & Guenther, which placed six mid-rises and three towers, along with a community center and playgrounds, on just small portions of four blocks in Manhattan's Chelsea, allowing the warehouses and auto-body shops that occupied the remainder of the blocks, along with the internal streets, to stay.

3.12: Ravenswood Houses, 2014

Another arena in which NYCHA was successful was in maintaining a sustainable tenant mixture. In federal projects, Washington forced NYCHA, like all housing authorities, to evict higher-income tenants. But by the 1950s and 1960s New York's housing managers began to resist and federal officials began to show more leniency, recognizing that projects populated only by the very poor would prove more difficult to sustain financially and socially. NYCHA administrators thus raised income ceilings to keep as much of its working-class tenancy as possible. And when NYCHA managers had to move such tenants out, they worked to relocate them to projects financed under the city's public housing program. Many beneficiaries of this strategy were African American and Puerto Rican families who were stably employed but still unable to compete for, or outright excluded from, private housing despite anti-discrimination laws. NYCHA thus had a much lower share of tenants on public assistance in the 1950s and the 1960s than other cities. This difference was also a product of continued enforcement of strict standards for screening that frowned upon anyone on welfare, unmarried mothers, and those with a host of other social characteristics (twenty-one in total) deemed unacceptable by NYCHA staff.[22] The low welfare rates were also partly attributable to NYCHA's higher ratio of smaller apartments, many of which catered to seniors, than in a city such as Chicago or St. Louis where large, poor families concentrated in public housing.

Despite high standards, the city's faltering industrial economy and the pressures of displacement from site relocation eventually forced NYCHA to accept many welfare tenants and "multi-problem" families. In response, the agency tried to limit welfare concentration and created its own housing police (1952). Even so, projects—especially high-rise projects designed for family living by the carefully selected working poor—were vulnerable to the disruptive forces of even just a few troubled families. Reporter Harrison Salisbury presented many harrowing tales of such problems in a series in the *Times*, later published as a book, *The Shook Up Generation*, on life in new NYCHA developments. A former leader of the Chicago Housing Authority, Elizabeth Wood, also reported in the late 1950s on growing antisocial behavior in New York public housing complexes by so-called problem families.[23] Even Mayor Robert F. Wagner, Jr., who never lost his faith in public housing, acknowledged "once

3.13: NYCHA publicity photograph, ca. 1972

upon a time, we thought if we could just bulldoze the slums of the shiny new public housing for low-income people, all social problems involving these people would virtually disappear. That has turned out to be not so."[24]

Race complicated the picture in ways that made it difficult for many outsiders to evaluate the situation objectively. New York stands alone in the United States in the degree to which it opened and managed racially integrated housing developments in the 1940s and 1950s. NYCHA initially tenanted all postwar developments on an integrated basis and made genuine efforts to maintain racial balance (fig. 3.13). NYCHA tenancy as a whole, however, had become majority-minority by the late 1950s, and the white exodus accelerated in the 1960s and 1970s. Many white families claimed racial intimidation by new neighbors as the primary cause for leaving, but just as influential were high-quality housing options open to whites in surrounding neighborhoods and the suburbs. By the 1970s most remaining white families were in the "no-cash subsidy" city-financed projects. The growing concentration of Black families system wide, even if carefully selected and upwardly mobile, gave public housing a "ghetto" reputation at the first signs of social disorder. Nevertheless, many residents remember the 1950s and early 1960s as a remarkably ordered, and still racially integrated, time.[25]

Maintaining quality of life in public housing thereafter became more challenging. Urban America experienced a great deal of distress in the 1960s, and NYCHA and its tenants were not immune. Social problems like violent crime, vandalism, and drugs began to intrude. Reid and later chairmen benefited from a long tradition of dedicated on-site staff that continued to care for floors, elevators, grounds, and other important systems. With generous city aid the housing police expanded from a few officers in 1952 to more than a thousand by 1966. They practiced community policing (issuing many quality of life tickets) and spent most of their time conducting internal vertical patrols. There was no equivalent force in the country despite frequent tough talk from mayors and police commissioners about public housing safety. Police in some cities, in fact, rarely ventured into public housing. Social dysfunction nevertheless took a heavy toll in New York.[26]

The 1960s also saw another great change for NYCHA: after years of break-neck clearance and construction, production began to slow. There were many reasons for this. An inflationary economy by the late 1960s made building prohibitively expensive at the same that the income of potential tenants was in decline. Meanwhile, as John Lindsay discovered during his terms as mayor, new, better design came with impossibly high costs. NYCHA's Amsterdam Addition (1973) in Manhattan, for instance, was praised for looking virtually indistinguishable from market-rate housing. But it cost $47,484 per unit ($230,000 in 2013 dollars). At that price NYCHA could have bought all the prospective tenants market-rate co-ops, or rambling ranch houses

3.14: City Line Houses scatter site project (1976), East New York, Brooklyn, rendering, 1973

in the suburbs. Between 1965 and 1970, even with new federal Model Cities Program funds, NYCHA developed only six thousand units. Under a separate federal "turn-key" program, which had private builders develop public housing and then "turn keys" over to housing authorities, another ten thousand units were added in the early 1970s. Unfortunately, residents and managers often discovered that they were being given keys to poorly constructed units.[27]

Shifting political winds also affected NYCHA. As early as 1963 Mayor Wagner, for instance, noted that a "false and distorted picture" was driving "growing resistance to the construction of public housing projects" in the city.[28] Republican Governor Nelson Rockefeller (1959–73) also expressed doubts about public housing, announcing in 1963 that his administration was trying "to get the government out of low-cost housing."[29]Although he later reversed this position and supported public housing, the state and city programs all but ended in the 1960s as voters statewide, and even many within the city limits, resisted additional appropriations.

Washington's commitment wavered, too. After a burst of new funding under President Johnson's Great Society program and a limited number of innovative projects launched under Model Cities and new "scatter site" programs, funds dried up (fig. 3.14). In 1973, with the nation in financial crisis thanks to rampant inflation, President Nixon placed a moratorium on new funds for public housing, all but terminating the forty-year-old program, never to be restored. Growing concerns about the quality of life in public housing, and the ascendance of a new conservatism meant few protested.

Postwar New York stands out in the history of American public housing. It built far more of it than any other U.S. city. By the late 1960s NYCHA managed one in five units nationwide: 157 developments housing one in every sixteen New York City families. New York's housing also fared much better. Elsewhere, once wartime housing shortages passed public housing typically became a site of last resort for those unable to navigate, or excluded from, the private housing market. Housing projects from Washington, D.C., to San Francisco were placed in stigmatized locations, underfunded, and then poorly kept up. Within a generation, most were seen as unsalvageable. In New York, by contrast, public housing remained well-maintained, in demand, and essential to the city's vitality.

Robert F. Wagner, Jr. (1910–91)

Mayor Robert F. Wagner, Jr. (1954–65), presided over the most prolific era for production of below-market housing in New York City's history. Under his lead NYCHA completed the bulk of the large-scale red-brick towers that still define many sections of the city. But it was also during his administration that public housing and urban renewal moved away from replacing neighborhoods with monolithic projects on superblocks to improving them with smaller-scale, better-integrated redevelopment.

Wagner was a lifelong New Deal liberal and the son of the "father" of federal public housing, Senator Robert F. Wagner, with a deep and consistent interest in improving the quality of housing in the city. By the time he became mayor he had already served as a state assemblyman, Manhattan borough president, chairman of the City Planning Commission, and commissioner of the city's Department of Housing and Building, where in 1947 he took a strong stand against segregated housing. As state assemblyman and as planning commissioner he had called for New York City to pursue the most ambitious public housing and urban renewal programs possible. He believed, in fact, that low-income public housing ought to be understood as a fundamental part of the American way of life: a controversial position to take during McCarthy era when many in the United States were rethinking their commitment to a progressive political economy.

During Wagner's twelve years as mayor, NYCHA opened 123,000 units of low-income public housing: a feat never equaled again in New York or any other city in the United States (fig. 3.15). While much of the boom can be traced to Robert Moses's

3.15: Robert F. Wagner, Jr., groundbreaking Luna Park Houses, Brooklyn, 1958

ambitious redevelopment plans, Wagner was a strong supporter of the program in his own right. The enormous productivity also had much to do with the larger political climate. "During the years I was Mayor," he later reflected, "I am glad to say that the federal government was headed by presidents who believed in federally aided housing and public housing. The governors of New York State were also supporters." At the same time it was only through his local advocacy that such extraordinary quantities were built. His main regret was only that even this stock of new housing never truly met the city's needs, especially given the rapid loss of inexpensive units in the private market as the city cleared slums for highways, parks, and other redevelopment.[30]

Despite his humanitarian vision, for some time Wagner supported Moses's use of federal funds for wholesale clearance, including many homes of poor people of color, to make space for a variety of new land uses, including public housing but also middle-income apartments and limited-equity cooperatives developed by trade unions and housing reformers. Among Wagner's greatest achievements in housing was, in fact, drafting the state's Mitchell-Lama bill in 1954, which dramatically expanded the city's and state's ability to subsidize middle-income housing, both in and outside of slum clearance areas. To further the goals of stabilizing the city and retaining the middle the class, Wagner also encouraged the proliferation of privately financed middle-income complexes insured by the Federal Housing Administration. In other ways, too, Moses remained Wagner's primary partner in housing. The mayor retained Moses as chair of the Committee on Slum Clearance, which directed Title I Urban Renewal efforts, and he invited Moses's allies at NYCHA, such as Chairman Phillip Cruise, to retain their leadership roles.

Over time, however, the relationship between the mayor and Moses became strained. Wagner avoided confrontation at first. But after a scandal at the Housing Authority in 1957 the mayor replaced Cruise with his own appointee, William Reid. It was under Reid that NYCHA pursued a greater number of smaller-scale projects. Similarly, when scandal emerged at Title I Urban Renewal projects sponsored by Moses like Manhattantown on the Upper West Side early in Wagner's tenure, the mayor launched a major independent investigation. Its findings empowered Wagner to replace the Committee on Slum Clearance—and Moses—with the new Housing and Redevelopment Board, in 1960.

In accord with evolving priorities in Washington and practices in other cities, the new board, ably led by Milton Mollen, shifted emphasis from large-scale clearance planned with little community input to more creative and flexible models emphasizing rehabilitation as much as demolition. Wagner's interest in moving from the large-scale to the small, and from wholesale to piecemeal was informed to a large degree by a growing awareness, both in New York and other cities, of the limitations of the Modernist logic of redevelopment and its many human complications. Wagner laid this vision out at the dedication of the first rehabilitated brownstone in the West Side Urban Renewal Area, in 1962: "Our basic aim in the present program is to do everything possible to stop deterioration, remove spots of blight, and revitalize this entire area as a residential area for all the varied elements which now make up this teeming multi-cultural and cosmopolitan neighborhood. But the bulldozer approach, or anything like it, is out."[31] STEVEN LEVINE

Jacob Riis Houses (1949, 1,768 units, Manhattan)

Sponsor: NYCHA (federal, city)
Program: public housing
Architect: James McKenzie, Sidney Strauss, Walker & Gillette

The Jacob Riis Houses is representative of the public housing complexes deployed by Robert Moses after World War II to redevelop wholesale the slums of the Lower East Side (fig. 3.16). Moses and NYCHA officials believed that they were on the side of the angels as they replaced old industrial sites and tenements with up-to-date housing blocks surrounded by green lawns. But the cumulative impact of Riis with the other neighborhood complexes—Vladeck (1940), Wald (1949), Smith (1953), LaGuardia Houses (1957), Baruch (1959), along with tens of thousands of middle-income units in projects like Co-op Village (1950–1956) and Stuyvesant Town (1949)—led many to question the social and aesthetic consequences of reconstruction.[32]

The fact that few site tenants secured apartments in Riis Houses immediately complicated the claims of urban improvement. Sections of the future Riis site included massive gas tanks, but NYCHA also cleared many tenements. The official goal of aiding tenement dwellers through public housing remained in place, but residents of condemned apartments in the area likely had a different view: only 15 percent of the displaced returned. Postwar veteran preferences, and strict behavioral and income requirements, made it unlikely that site tenants would comprise the majority of public housing dwellers at Riis or in any of NYCHA's postwar projects. Applicants' current housing conditions were a factor in tenant selection, and many Riis families came from tenements in other parts of the city, but the replacement of both buildings and people by public housing became controversial, especially as the pace of clearance accelerated.

The financing of the Riis Houses reflects the city's eagerness to build public housing despite limited federal support. Funding came from multiple sources. To build to a higher standard than federal cost limits allowed the city contributed cash generated through the sale of bonds. The city also created a separate city-financed section of the complex, although both sections were arranged in a single ensemble with a mixture of six-, thirteen-, and fourteen-story towers. The buildings covered just one-fifth of the site, but the height allowed the development as a whole to achieve a high population density. Height came at a high construction cost, but thanks to the subsidies, tenants, at least in the federal section, paid an average rent of just $27 a month ($425 in 2013 dollars), including gas, electric, and heat. Maximum household income was set at $2,880 ($45,000). More than thirteen thousand families applied for apartments. Veterans were given preference.[33] Early tenants were thrilled with the up-to-date accommodations. But as new housing opportunities opened, especially for white families, many left, and the white population declined from 90 percent to 70 percent in just the first five years. By the late 1960s whites comprised just 15 percent of tenants, while over 60 percent was Puerto Rican, reflecting the changing complexion of the Lower East Side.[34]

As the ethnic and racial make-up of the buildings changed, so too did requirements for entry. At first, new tenants of color had to meet the same strict requirements

3.16: Jacob Riis Houses, 2014

as earlier white families. Over time, however, a combination of political pressure from Washington and market pressure—shaped by larger social and economic changes in the neighborhood and city, including deindustrialization and displacement for other redevelopment schemes—demanded more relaxed standards. One result was growing numbers of families on public assistance. These demographic shifts were accompanied by new tensions between ethnic and racial groups at Riis in the 1950s and 1960s, especially among a growing cohort of disaffected youth. After NYCHA transferred the city-funded section to federal management in 1972 in order to receive federal operating subsidies, the problem grew worse. Riis in the 1970s experienced growing numbers of rule violations, disputes among tenants, and assaults, many of which were committed by residents.[35] Serious crime escalated, too, as junkies on Avenue D robbed residents and then sold the loot on nearby tenement streets. Addicts, from both inside and outside the development, frequently targeted the elderly.[36]

Tenant patrols, senior programs, and after-school programs staffed by settlement houses attempted to preserve order. The housing police performed vertical patrols. A more unique response was for NYCHA to redesign Riis's outdoor areas. With funding from the Astor Foundation, the agency hired the celebrated landscape architect M. Paul Friedberg, whose award-winning design for the interior courtyard introduced abstract sculptures, rugged planters, cobblestone mounds, fountains, and pools of water (fig. 3.17). The renovation, Friedberg noted, created a "permissive

3.17: Model of M. Paul Friedberg design for Riis Houses, ca. 1960

plan . . . a continuous play experience" that contrasted with the "keep off the grass" rules that were quickly becoming outmoded. Although the landscaping as a whole has been refreshed a number of times since the 1960s, elements of this landscape plan still remain visible.[37]

Despite the new landscape, the neighborhood's collapsing social scene took a serious toll. The share of families on welfare, for instance, more than doubled between

1968 and 1978, to over a third.[38] Crackdowns on crime by the NYPD under Mayor Koch also did not improve conditions. There was extensive graffiti and other vandalism; elevators smelled of urine: Riis had many of the stereotyped hallmarks of run-down U.S. public housing. In the mid-1980s, however, NYCHA initiated a major reform of the on-site management. The staff of seventy had become complacent; some were corrupt. An energetic new manager, Bill Russo, replaced many personnel, while revamping landscapes and enforcing the daily tasks of caretakers.[39] Despite continuing drug-related crime and other social disorder, life at Riis improved as a result.

Today, Riis has recovered. And after half a century, it is playing a new role in the life of the neighborhood. No longer just an oasis for betterment, it now serves as an island of permanent, below-market rents in an area that has rapidly gentrified. When built, rents in the project were comparable to that of the surrounding tenements; the great benefit was superior accommodations: the "enchantment of having a real, gleaming white bathtub, in a bathroom right in their own home."[40] Today, market rents in the neighborhood run several times the current average rent in the project of $457. About half of families are employed, 10 percent are on public assistance, and another 20 percent are on disability insurance. Average household income is $24,000, or about 28 percent of the city average. Without Riis Houses, virtually all of these families would have to leave the neighborhood.[41]

The persistence of Riis and other low-income developments in similar neighborhoods, especially in Manhattan and close-in sections of Brooklyn, raises provocative questions for the conventional wisdom about public housing. In most U.S. cities, replacement of public housing with mixed-income units is considered an essential strategy for improving not just neighborhoods, but also the lives of public housing tenants. Riis's current residents would disagree that they must leave so that the neighborhood can thrive. NICHOLAS DAGEN BLOOM

Johnson Houses (1948, 1,310 units, Manhattan)

Sponsor: NYCHA (state)
Program: public housing
Architect: Julian Whittlesey, Harry Prince, Robert J. Riley

The James Weldon Johnson Houses were built with New York State public housing funds between 1945 and 1948 as part of a postwar neighborhood redevelopment program that eventually gave East Harlem one of the largest concentrations of high-rise below-market housing in the nation. Johnson has gone through many phases: welcomed in the 1940s, then criticized in the 1950s and 1960s for its contribution, along with nearby projects, to wiping out neighborhood vitality, it is today fiercely defended by resident activists and local leaders. In partnership with NYCHA administrators these residents have fought for millions in renovations and upgrades so that Johnson Houses will continue to serve as quality low-income housing in a rapidly gentrifying district.

To develop the project in the 1940s the city acquired nearly a thousand tenement apartments, displacing 880 families.[42] The design of the new buildings reflected a pragmatic, no-frills NYCHA Modernism, with virtually identical fireproof Hudson

3.18: Johnson Houses, 1949

River–brick towers in connected six- and fourteen-story cruciform layouts set in an open, twelve-acre superblock of grassy fields studded by trees (fig. 3.18). Cost considerations meant flourishes were few—rents averaged at just $37 a month to start ($600 in 2013 dollars)—but the architects made innovative use of glass block for illuminating internal stairwells and corridors and included an experimental playground designed by NYCHA staff that featured rugged climbing structures in imaginative shapes, such as airplanes. A community center was also built, staffed by the Union Settlement Association. Unlike later slab types, with long double-loaded corridors, at Johnson small elevator landings gave access to the apartments, each serving eight units.[43] NYCHA tenanted the project on an interracial basis, with 58 percent of apartments going to African American families, 25 percent to Puerto Rican, and 16 percent to white. Veterans were given preference. Maximum income limits were somewhat higher than in federally financed projects but lower than those built through the city's program.[44]

Despite the fact that NYCHA maintained rigorous screening mechanisms and the share of tenants on public assistance remained low (at least by comparison with public housing in other U.S. cities), mounting social disorder meant that the quality of life in Johnson Houses suffered by the 1960s. Tenants endured, and sometimes committed, growing numbers of assaults on the grounds, in elevators, and in lobbies. NYCHA, meanwhile, noted rising numbers of rule infractions and disputes among residents. In response, the agency deployed private guards to complement the vertical patrols of its own housing police.[45] NYCHA nevertheless kept dysfunction at bay. A long-time manager recalls how challenging it was to do so. "The caretakers who are sort of the forgotten soldiers of this fight. . . . start out on a Monday . . . straightening out the place, and by Thursday or Friday, the development looks good and really nice. Then of course we got bombed on the weekends. . . . So that Monday morning the work had to begin again almost from scratch."[46] The situation only grew more challenging in the 1970s as very poor, distressed, young families came to predominate. By 1975 more than half of all residents were under age twenty-one and the share of families on welfare reached 40 percent. Johnson, in these years, had many characteristics in common with distressed public housing developments in other cities.[47]

Johnson survived these difficult decades, and an escalating drug trade that ravaged much of East Harlem, through the hard work of its large staff, as well as heavy policing and vigorous tenant activism. Resident Ethel Velez, a longtime tenant leader at both Johnson Houses and for NYCHA projects citywide, fought hard for the complex, securing extra funds from the city for security and renovation. Today, twenty-one caretakers, often recruited from among residents as part of a NYCHA program to raise tenant incomes, clean on a fixed weekly schedule. Five full-time maintenance workers also remain on site, as well as a team of elevator technicians (who also serve nearby developments). Two full-time housing assistants chase after late rents and keep an eye on social issues. Velez praises the staff, while also worrying it has become stretched as a result of budget cuts and what she considers to be poor leadership at NYCHA's central offices.[48] Nevertheless, glass-block walls still brighten the hallways, and elevators are relatively new; the roof, parapet, and top-floor apartments of all the high-rises have also been recently renovated.

Johnson Houses landscapes have also evolved. Some years ago, as part of a systemwide overhaul, designers added benches and playgrounds in configurations designed to maximize sociability and casual surveillance of building entrances. In addition, thick steel fencing around planted areas replaced chain link. The greatest change has been the addition, after over a decade of construction, of a large new community center, built as part of an initiative by the city's commissioner of the Department of Design and Construction, David Burney, to bring contemporary design to NYCHA. The glassy center, designed by architect Peter John Locascio and after many construction delays, brightens one side of the whole complex, provides definition for open spaces that had been poorly used, and includes an indoor basketball court, childcare center, and other community amenities. The center is largely subsidized by city funds and provides senior, after-school, sports, and dance programs; it is run by a local nonprofit, SCAN, that is part of the United Neighborhood Houses.

Today, Johnson Houses, like virtually all NYCHA complexes, houses far fewer tenants than it once did thanks to shrinking family sizes and the growth of the elderly population; this population, however, is much poorer (although less so than it was in the 1970s). The most recent data show 3,084 residents and an average rent of $475 a month, making a Johnson Houses apartment cheaper to rent today than when it first opened in 1948 (adjusting for inflation). The complex continues to skew

3.19: Johnson Houses, 2014

young: half of residents are still under age twenty-one, including many who live with their grandparents or other relatives. Fifty-five percent of tenants are working families and the share on public assistance has fallen by more than half from its peak, to 17 percent. Median household income, however, is extremely low: just 22 percent of the city average, or about $19,000. Because of the deep poverty of many tenants, made worse by the recent economic recession, in 2012 Johnson Houses experienced an approximate 11 percent rent delinquency rate and five families had to be evicted.[49] Meanwhile, the police are a constant presence and, under Mayor Bloomberg, practiced controversial "stop and frisk" tactics, including one major sweep that led to the arrest of many residents. Overall, however, crime is down sharply since the 1980s. For unlike high-rise public in many U.S. cities, Johnson Houses, as a result of very hard work on the part of both staff and residents, remains a viable, if fragile, place to live (fig. 3.19).[50] NICHOLAS DAGEN BLOOM

Ravenswood Houses (1951, 2,166 units, Queens)

Sponsor: NYCHA (city)
Program: public housing
Architect: Frederick G. Frost

Ravenswood Houses in Long Island City, Queens, is a large, city-funded, public housing development, originally built for moderate-income, and mostly white, tenants. Despite its urban, industrial location, Ravenswood's broad lawns, heavy tree cover, and moderate building heights lend the complex an almost pastoral air (fig. 3.20). Like other city-sponsored developments now folded into the federal public housing system, such as Woodside and Pomonok Houses, it has resegregated

3.20: Ravenswood Houses, 2014

to a minority-majority tenancy, but its history of long-term racial integration, and enduring popularity with residents, challenges stereotypical public housing narratives.[51]

Ravenswood was built in the early 1950s adjacent to the Queensview limited-equity co-op to cater to a similar, if slightly lower, income group: those too well off to qualify for low-income public housing financed by the federal government or New York State, but without the resources to pay for high-quality market-rate housing in the city. Rents averaged $70 a month in 1952 ($900 in 2013 dollars), and maximum income levels were set at $4,900 ($64,000). Like many city-funded public housing complexes—and middle-income co-ops—Ravenswood appeared at first glance no different from ordinary low-income private housing. The apartments were arranged in thirty-one virtually identical six- and seven-story red-brick slabs on a superblock site plan, with the buildings placed on a north-south axis, staggered to create a sense of enclosure from the industrial neighborhood beyond. Landscaped gardens included playgrounds; entries were clad in inexpensive glazed brick. Interiors, however, were built to higher specifications. Living rooms of fifteen by seventeen feet, for instance, compared favorably to those in market-rate housing. Common amenities included playgrounds and a branch library (fig. 3.21).[52]

Initially, tenants were mainly working-class Irish and Italian families. Unlike public housing in most other U.S. cities, however, Ravenswood was racially integrated: 11 percent of original tenants were African American, a typical ratio for city-financed developments after World War II. Over time the balance shifted, but as late as 1978

3.21: Ravenswood Houses, library, 1952

48 percent of the complex was white. Meanwhile, the number of tenants receiving public assistance, and crime rates, remained low.[53]

The process of "federalization" in the 1970s (transferring city and state projects to the federal program), pursued in order to gain annual operating and capital subsidies, flattened out many policy differences between city-financed projects and other NYCHA developments. By the 1980s admissions standards had been relaxed, and crime and quality of life complaints such as littering and noise increased. Nevertheless, Ravenswood remained a stable, healthy community, maintaining its reputation as one of NYCHA's "prestigious" projects. Reporting in 1984, the *New York Times* observed, "tenants of many races say there is a neighborliness in the project that would be rare in any community." Another resident claimed, "I wouldn't move out for anything." Meanwhile, the head of the residents' association suggested that residents "take better care of their apartments" than at other NYCHA developments, while a strong "community atmosphere" and an engaged population, including tenant patrols, contributed to the continuing feeling that Ravenswood remained a good place to live.[54]

Today Ravenswood is relatively peaceful despite being the largest development with a single management office in the NYCHA system. The complex houses 4,334 residents at an average monthly rental of just $462 in a neighborhood that is increasingly expensive. Many long-term, and even some original, tenants remain (about one in five tenants are elderly). Despite the fact that there are very few big apartments,

3.22: Ravenswood Houses, 2014

however, Ravenswood remains a family development, with one in four residents under age twenty-one (fig. 3.22). Although no longer reserved for moderate-income families, over half of households have paid employment and average income is $26,000; fewer than 10 percent of families are on public assistance. Nevertheless, the complex's four housing assistants devote many days per month in court dealing with residents behind on rent, and despite their best efforts, management still must write off about approximately 10 percent of rents every year. Maintaining such a large development also requires an on-site staff of sixty-four, including twenty-eight caretakers and nine maintenance workers.[55]A police precinct station located directly in the development aids in the maintenance of order.

The long-term history of Ravenswood demonstrates that public housing, despite its stereotyped portrait in both academe and the media, has no essential quality; rather, developments like Ravenswood have been shaped by specific choices in design, management, and tenancy. NICHOLAS DAGEN BLOOM

ideal
FOOD BASKET

4

Stabilizing the Middle

Many reformers and civic leaders beginning in the early twentieth century believed that New York City ought to have below-market subsidized housing not just for the poor but also for moderate-income families. A shared faith in the power of government to make city living more pleasant for middle-class households—a special concern after World War II as Americans began leaving cities en masse for suburbia—gave postwar New York the largest system of private affordable housing anywhere outside Western Europe. The old limited-dividend model of low-cost rentals and limited-equity cooperatives became supercharged after the war thanks to a mixture of private effort, the Federal Housing Administration's multifamily programs, and city and state efforts promoted by leaders such as Robert Moses, Governor Nelson Rockefeller, and Mayor Robert F. Wagner, Jr.

Middle-class families had long struggled to house themselves well in New York City, and Manhattan in particular, with its high population densities, cramped quarters, and extreme land values. The earliest effort to address the problem, back in the mid-nineteenth century, focused on perfecting the apartment house building type, which unlike a tenement was designed for the privacy and comfort of middle-class and well-to-do families. The owner-occupied apartment in the form of market-rate cooperatives, which promised to correct frustrations with renting and to lower expenses by eliminating the landlord's profit, followed. Lack of mortgage financing, however, meant buyers generally had to pay all cash, limiting this option to the affluent. In the 1910s and 1920s, well paid, often unionized skilled laborers, mostly Finns in Sunset Park and Eastern European Jews on the Lower East Side, improved upon this model with the limited-equity format and restrictions on resales. Later, income restrictions were added to the formula. Experiments like these nevertheless served a very small share of the city's population; most New Yorkers survived as best they could in the city's highly competitive rental market, where low vacancy rates left landlords with more power than tenants.

Meanwhile, millions left the city center. As early as the late nineteenth century the outer boroughs and suburban counties were growing far faster in absolute numbers than Manhattan. People moved out because housing at the periphery was much cheaper, allowing them to acquire much more of it. Even then leaders speculated that only the very wealthy and the poor seemed likely to remain in the city center.[1] By way of action, some reformers in the 1920s and 1930s imagined a public system of housing also encompassing a broad middle segment, financed by below-market government loans to limited-dividend providers. This idea was colored by mistrust of the profit motive and the conviction that developer-built housing was of poor quality, but it also recognized a deeper truth: even middle-class wages could not support the cost of up-to-date "American" housing in a large, highly centralized city. Outside New York, most Americans were skeptical. In a major defeat for so-called middle-income housing, Congress limited public housing in the Housing Act of 1937 to low-cost, publicly owned and managed housing projects.[2]

The New Deal, however, quietly opened another door for subsidized middle-income housing. As early as 1934 the National Housing Act included provisions for moderate-cost multifamily housing and in 1935 the Federal Housing Administration (FHA) launched a Rental Housing Division whose purpose was to help limited-dividend companies secure favorable financing for rent-restricted apartments and limited-equity co-ops. Catherine Bauer, champion of "modern housing," felt the program insufficient. She disliked FHA, which was dominated by lenders. More important, loans were made at market interest rates, rather than below-market ones. Nevertheless the program had a substantial impact, producing more limited-dividend housing in the U.S. in its first five years than all previous efforts combined: 291 complexes with 32,617 units in thirty-eight states. The first was completed in the fall of 1935, outside of Washington, D.C. New York City's first, Garden Bay Manor in East Elmhurst, followed three years later (fig. 4.1). Within a decade, FHA was insuring limited-dividend rentals and co-ops across the city (see fig. 0.4).[3]

During and after World War II amid the huge wartime housing shortage there was a surge in interest in the below-market middle-income idea, locally as well as nationally. Housing liberals, confident that the New Deal trend toward more public expenditure in housing would continue, resumed the fight to expand "public housing" to middle-income groups, by which they meant extension of below-market-interest-rate loans to limited-dividends and limited-equity cooperatives. Even some on the right, including national real estate interests, supported the idea, believing such housing might neutralize demand for public housing, which they saw as a greater threat. Most Republicans, and even some Democrats, however, continued to resist, arguing that FHA already covered this group. Indeed, half of the houses and apartments built with FHA-insured loans were occupied by the "forgotten middle" invoked by activists: households earning between $2,000 and $4,000 a year ($31,000 to $63,000 in 2013 dollars). The problem, skeptics pointed out, was not that FHA could not cater to such families, but that subsidies were not deep enough to cater to them in expensive areas, including central areas of large cities like New York. To create special

YOUR first impression of Garden Bay Manor is that you have entered a fascinating new world. Against a background of brilliant blue skies and golden sunshine, mingling with the shining waters of the bay, a new kind of garden community spreads in picturesque fashion over the acres of charming landscape.

Although a colony of ultra modern apartments, the manor buildings are graceful, rambling, artistic structures, having all the characteristics of private suburban homes. Winding walks lead across broad lawns to porticoed doorways. Shrubs, vines and hedges cluster about the porches and dot the greens.

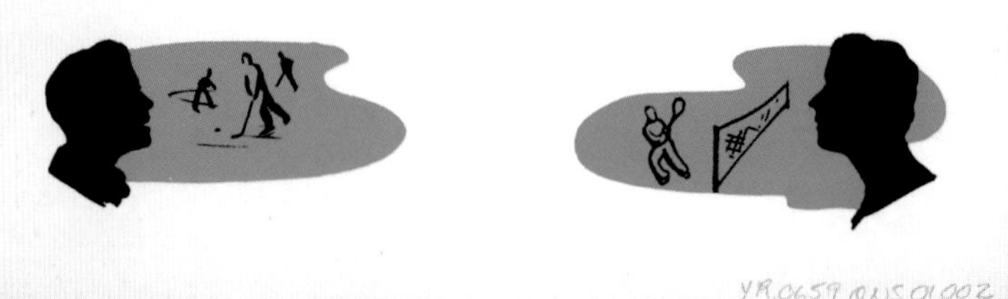

4.1: Garden Bay Manor, rental brochure, ca. 1938

subsidies for this purpose was, they argued, poor use of resources. The measure for limited dividends was thus also stripped from the postwar public housing bill when it went forward in 1949. And when President Truman immediately launched a separate Middle-income Housing bill, it too failed.[4]

As a compromise Congress expanded FHA's limited-dividend program by creating a dedicated office for limited-equity co-ops in 1950. Under these and other FHA multifamily provisions New York City saw a flood of new federally aided limited-dividend and limited-equity construction, with 62,357 apartments alone completed between 1948 and 1956. Among the largest projects were Park City (Rego Park, 5,097 rentals, 1956); Bay Terrace (Bayside, 3,700 co-ops, 1956–66); Vanderveer Estate (today: Flatbush Gardens, Brooklyn, 2,496 rentals, 1952); Electchester (Flushing, 2,225 co-ops,

FHA project in Queens County for 2,904 families.

GLEN OAKS VILLAGE

4.2: Glen Oaks Village, from NYCHA, "Housing: Public Housing, Slum Clearance, Quasi-Public Housing, F.H.A. Housing, January 1946–July 1949" (1949)

1954), which was developed by an electrical workers' union; and Glen Oaks (Bellerose, 2,904 rentals, 1949) (fig. 4.2). As housing liberals feared, however, prices could go only so low without below-market-rate loans, tax abatements, and grants for land acquisition. As a result, the great bulk of this housing in New York City (83 percent) appeared in Queens, which still had hundreds of acres of inexpensive undeveloped land after World War II. (An equal number were also built in northern New Jersey, Long Island, and Westchester County.) At least some examples, however, could be found in all five boroughs.[5]

4.3: Parkchester, ca. 1941

One promising avenue for a more expansive middle-income program was to rely on large insurance companies to build. The Metropolitan Life Insurance Company had developed Parkchester (1942) in the Bronx before the war with more than twelve thousand units in 171 brick mid-rises (fig. 4.3). Equitable Life Assurance Society followed with the Clinton Hill Apartments (1943) in Brooklyn. After the war, Robert Moses leaned heavily on the firms to build more. Met Life built three additional complexes, Riverton (1948), Stuyvesant Town (1949), and Peter Cooper Village (1949), all in Manhattan, and New York Life built Fresh Meadows (1949) in Queens and Manhattan House (1951) on the Upper East Side. By the early 1950s, however, insurance companies came to fear that the middle class was not long for the city, bringing into doubt the wisdom of new investment. They withdrew from the market.[6]

Another way forward was through trade unions. Having proved himself not only a capable builder but also a talented manager—during the Depression, none of his buildings failed financially—Moses turned to Abraham Kazan after the war to undertake middle-income housing. As with the Met Life projects, Moses hoped to see Kazan build on slum-clearance sites. After selecting a parcel on the Lower East Side he asked Kazan to develop what came to be called the Hillman Houses (1950), arranging for a favorable loan from a large insurance company and an extended property tax abatement. Moses was so pleased with the results that after passage of the 1949 Housing Act, with its Title I provisions for urban redevelopment offering federal grants for buying and clearing slum land, he invited Kazan to develop a parcel in the city's first federal renewal area, Corlears Hook. Sensing great opportunity, he also encouraged Kazan to incorporate a new group called the United Housing Foundation (UHF). The UHF went on to develop tens of thousands of limited-equity co-ops on Title I sites and elsewhere in the city, including Seward Park Housing (1960; which, along with East River Houses at Corlears Hook [1956] and Hillman Houses came to constitute Co-op Village), Penn Station South (1962), Rochdale Village (1963), and Co-op City (1968–73) (fig. 4.4). Similar groups developed several others, such as Morningside Gardens (1957), Chatham Green (1962), and Chatham Towers (1965).[7]

CORLEARS HOOK

4.4: Co-op Village

Moses partnered with groups like insurance companies and the UHF because they were reliably able to build on a large scale. With the success of postwar suburban subdivisions like Long Island's Levittown (1947–51), it seemed to Moses and other keen observers that the city was becoming an anachronism. To remain relevant, they concluded, cities needed modern universities, hospitals, cultural centers, and highways, as well as up-to-date housing that could compete with suburbia for the affections of working- and middle-class families in terms of equipment, size, and price. As Clarence Davies, chairman of the city's Housing and Redevelopment Board, put it, such housing, especially middle-income developments, "can be our answer to the flight to the suburbs."[8]

Through FHA, Title I, Moses, and the UHF, New York City developed the nation's largest below-market subsidized middle-income housing program in the 1950s, with no rival in the United States in terms of scale and impact—or financial commitment. Also unique among U.S. cities, New York fought successfully for state approval to introduce separate state and local subsidy programs for middle-income housing with passage of the Limited-Profit Housing Companies Law of 1955. At core this law offered what Clarence Stein had proposed back in the 1920s: long-term, below-market-interest-rate loans for privately developed housing intended for working- and middle-class households. The 1926 law, which did not provide below-market loans, had generated several notable projects after the war, including Bell Park Gardens (1950) and Queensview (1950). Queensview, a co-op developed by Louis Pink and other reformers with 728 units in Long Island City, also made use of Robert Moses's Redevelopment Companies Law (1942), which offered developers eminent domain and twenty-five-year property tax exemptions in exchange for rent and sales restrictions. To better compete on price and quality with the emerging suburbs, and create more enticements for developers to enter the below-market field, Mayor Wagner's office drafted the new law in 1954. Moses promoted it. Newly elected Democratic governor Averell Harriman signed it in 1955 as a symbol of his commitment to housing. It quickly came to be known as Mitchell-Lama after its sponsors in the state legislature, Republican state senator MacNeil Mitchell from Manhattan's East side and Alfred Lama, a Democratic state assemblyman and professional architect from Brownsville.[9]

The package of subsidies under Mitchell-Lama was the most ambitious program of its kind in U.S. history. Under the law, which funded a state program and also empowered cities to set up their own, qualifying projects received low-interest mortgages for 90 to 95 percent of the total cost plus long-term local tax abatements covering 40 to 100 percent of a project's value. Cash to subsidize the loans was generated through sale of bonds approved of by voters. Developers' profits were restricted to six percent. The low profits—and limits on rents and resale prices— initially made developers skeptical and few adopted the program until 1957, when a new provision allowed landlords and cooperatives to buy out of the system after thirty-five years. The Rockefeller administration reduced the buy-out option further to just fifteen years, in 1959. These more generous terms removed the final impediment to widespread use.[10]

Unions and other nonprofit operators, which had a vested interest in making the program a success, constructed the initial round of projects. Most were in the outer boroughs where land costs were comparatively low. The first two projects in Manhattan were undertaken by Brown & Guenther, progressive architects who had previously designed NYCHA projects and Queensview and who had helped draft the 1955 law. Both were built on undeveloped land in Inwood. As program provisions relaxed and early projects proved a safe investment, more developers, including commercial operators, began to participate. By the time the program ran out of cash and ended in the early 1970s it had generated 140,000 units, almost evenly split between rentals and cooperatives (fig. 4.5). Mitchell-Lama's single best client was the

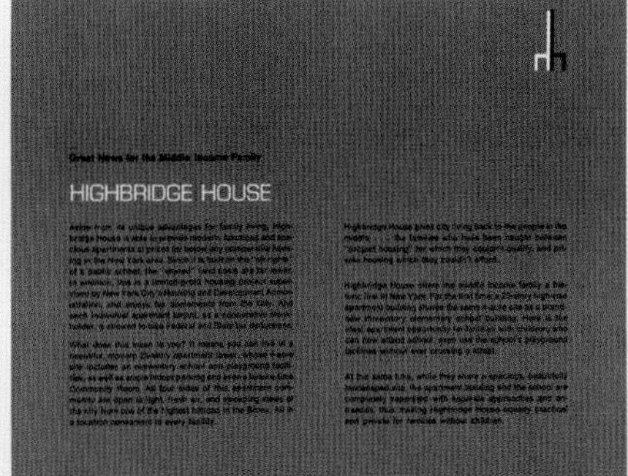

4.5: Highbridge House, rental brochure, ca. 1965

UHF, which by 1968 commanded half of New York State's investment in low-interest mortgage financing (mostly Mitchell-Lama). Skeptics insinuated that Mitchell-Lama tax abatements were gifts to well-connected developers and, later, that they contributed to the city's financial crisis in 1975. Proponents countered that within a few years the new buildings would return more in taxes than the dilapidated, frequently tax delinquent, ones they often replaced.[11] The program proved so compelling that as early as 1961 FHA introduced its own version, and a second one in 1968. These FHA programs helped finance an additional 32,000 units in New York City by the mid-1970s, and 40,000 more in the late 1970s and 1980s.[12]

Physically, middle-income projects took a variety of forms. Several Mitchell-Lamas embraced experimental designs, such as at Independence Plaza in Lower Manhattan (1974), with its large courtyards and futuristic ziggurat profile. The most visible and stereotyped projects, however, were the large-scale high-rise campuses designed by architect Herman Jessor for the UHF (fig. 4.6). Projects like Penn South,

4.6: Rochdale Village, Co-op Village, Amalgamated-Warbasse Houses, and Penn Station South, from Co-op City prospectus, 1965

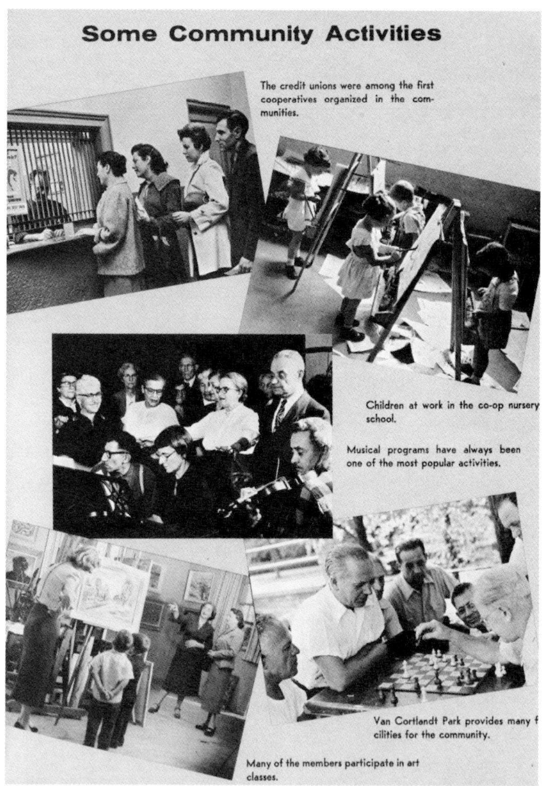

4.7: "Some Community Activities," from UHF, "30 Years of Amalgamated Cooperative Housing, 1927–1957"

4.8: College View Cooperative Apartments, prospectus, ca. 1954

4.9: 1270 Fifth Avenue, prospectus, ca. 1957

Rochdale Village, and Co-op City relied on serial repetition of nearly identical high-rises to achieve their economies. The last, with 15,372 units, was the largest owner-occupied apartment complex in the United States. Like all UHF projects and many Mitchell-Lamas, it shared a utilitarian sensibility with NYCHA's low-income housing, with exteriors clad in plain brick. Mitchell-Lamas and other UHF projects were much better equipped, however: many were meticulously planned for maximum functionality and offered more rooms, more bathrooms, better appliances, larger windows, and, in many projects, private balconies. Community facilities were also more generous (fig. 4.7).

FHA projects also varied physically. Some were modernistic freestanding elevator buildings like The Knolls (1952) in Riverdale and The Carlyle (1960) in Flushing. Others, like College View (1954) in Kew Gardens, updated the 1920s tradition of the mid-rise perimeter block building (fig. 4.8). Yet others were more conventional city buildings, such as 1270 Fifth Avenue (1957) in Manhattan (fig. 4.9). The most common, however, were the "garden apartments," which proliferated between the late 1940s and mid-1950s. These comprised dozens, sometimes hundreds, of small two- or three-story modern Colonial Revival buildings on spacious green campuses. The format had been developed by FHA in the mid-1930s at a time when elevator buildings were begging for tenants in most U.S. cities, having been overbuilt in the 1920s. The new format drew heavily on Sunnyside Gardens and later examples also designed by Clarence Stein and Henry Wright, such as Chatham Village outside Pittsburgh.[13]

FHA-type garden apartments came to define much of Queens in the postwar era, beginning with projects like Bell Park Gardens. Yet larger were Marine Terrace (1948), Deepdale Gardens (1952), Clearview Gardens (1952), Electchester, and Bay Terrace. Among the most expansive was Glen Oaks Village, with 2,904 rental apartments on 112 acres in Bellerose built by the Gross-Morton Company. Mostly tenanted by white, second-generation immigrants, especially Jews, these low-slung complexes were favored by FHA because they were cheap to construct and appealed to postwar sensibilities that regarded older, higher-density neighborhoods as outmoded. Moreover, while there were tensions from time to time with surrounding single-family neighborhoods, most neighboring homeowners objected little, even as they fought plans for low-income housing. The fact that many FHA complexes were owner-occupied and most of the residents were white helped minimize opposition.[14]

The record of achievement of the middle-income programs in fulfilling their social mandate was uneven. FHA fared the weakest. In helping to blanket many parts of the city with new apartments built to high standards, it offered middle-income

New Yorkers a crucial source of new housing and an appealing alternative to suburbia. These complexes have also shown remarkable staying power, despite some neglect in the 1970s and 1980s. But especially in the co-ops, FHA failed to police its own policies. Except in instances like Bell Park Gardens, where the state also had a financial stake in the project and kept a seat on the board, resale restrictions were left in the hands of tenants who mostly ignored them, both because the rules were cumbersome and because homeowners wanted to profit through appreciation of resale values. Mitchell-Lama and most other federal programs allowed no such lapses.[15]

The UHF generated a unique set of problems. One difficulty concerned slum clearance. Projects built in redevelopment areas sold well in Manhattan but struggled in gritty sections of Brooklyn and Queens. Meanwhile, as opposition to clearance mounted, abuses surrounding displacement came to light, tarnishing the reputation of projects like Penn South in Chelsea. As a new generation of leaders rediscovered the charms of brownstone and tenement neighborhoods with their many small shops, such displacement became untenable. Mounting concerns about federally aided Title I projects under the direction of Robert Moses, which included not just housing but convention centers, universities, hospitals, and opera houses, led Mayor Wagner to strip Moses of his redevelopment powers in 1960. Still facing pressure to build big, the UHF turned to inexpensive undeveloped land at the far fringes of the city. These projects, however, produced their own issues as tenants suffered isolation only partially remedied by extensive community facilities. Critics also accused these developments of harming the rest of city by siphoning off middle-class whites from declining neighborhoods thus hastening their decline. This critique was especially loud in the case of Co-op City—something of an irony given that the complex is now

4.10: Co-op City, shopping center, 2014

the nation's largest cooperative enterprise (fifty thousand residents) run by people of color (fig. 4.10).

Yet more challenges followed. Architecture critics and even some political leaders disparaged the utilitarian designs. Steep inflation coupled with the fact that many tenants were older and living on fixed pensions meant they were ill-equipped to support themselves financially. Expenses were rising quickly. But having been promised inexpensive "nonprofit" housing, residents refused to pay higher monthly maintenance charges. By the 1970s, as a result, many UHF projects had "poorly managed buildings, dirty hallways, uncut grass and poor security services."[16] Only after long, divisive rent strikes, additional state and federal subsidies (both in the form of deeper tax abatements and new financing), and, eventually, introduction of federal Section 8 housing choice vouchers, which were intended for rentals but came to be permitted in limited-equity co-ops, did many communities stabilize.

As the city's finances collapsed in the 1970s, such a massive system of below-market middle-income housing appeared to many critics as the height of ill-considered government overreach. The financial struggles of many complexes, along with their bland architecture and passé site planning, convinced many critics that middle-income housing was better left to private developers. Kazan defended subsidies to the end, reminding critics that "each [UHF] project was the biggest and the

4.11: Rochdale Village, living room, 2014

first in its field at the time, featuring low prices and rents, and luxuries such as elevators, central air-conditioning, parquet floors, balconies and gardens" (fig. 4.11).[17] In a city hemorrhaging population and struggling to maintain basic services, however, middle-income housing became a much lower priority.

Kazan's defense has gained standing in the decades since. As their subsidized mortgages and tax abatements have expired beginning in the 1980s, many complexes have abandoned their limited-dividend and -equity formats to take advantage of an improving real estate market. Despite these losses to privatization, New York City's network of middle-income housing still represents a tremendous, if imperfect, achievement. In an era when a wide margin of U.S. families had been able to house themselves to a decent standard without direct government aid, New York's robust middle-income system stands out for anchoring a city in turmoil. Today, this housing has taken on a role few could have foreseen even a generation ago: a crucial brake on the forces of gentrification. Even a project that had notorious financial problems like Co-op City is now not only stable but, in hindsight, exemplary, with large apartments, vibrant shopping areas, and well-landscaped grounds, all at very modest prices.

Stuyvesant Town (1949, 8,755 units, Manhattan)

Sponsor: private insurance company (Metropolitan Life)
Program: private rental
Architect: Gilmore Clark, Irwin Clavan, H. F. Richardson, George Gore, Andrew Eken

Stuyvesant Town was the product of an enormous financial commitment on the part of the Metropolitan Life Insurance Company to build islands of middle-class domesticity in American cities in the 1930s and 1940s. Following best thinking in urban land use at the time, Robert Moses believed that only "great reservoirs of private capital," backed by government power and subsidy, could stop the spread of slums and blight, and provide housing for the middle classes not served by public housing or by the private market.[18] The best partners, Moses felt, were companies, like insurance companies, which had both a stake in city life and ample funds to invest in the city's civic and social infrastructure.

Insurance companies had a fiduciary interest in the communities in which they issued policies—a better urban environment meant healthier people and thus a more financially robust insurer—and some had been involved with housing reform since the Progressive Era. To be sure, several had already developed urban housing projects for middle-income families in the 1920s, including the Met Life's Metropolitan Houses (today Cosmopolitan Houses) in Queens. Luckily for Moses and Mayor Fiorello LaGuardia (1934–45), Frederick Ecker, the head of Met Life, New York's largest insurance firm, had been considering making a new investment in New York, provided that he could secure public assistance—something that other patrician housing reformers had long abhorred, but that in the inflationary wartime climate of the early 1940s and in the wake of the New Deal seemed both increasingly inevitable, and necessary. Ecker's search for a balance between profits and social concerns aligned neatly with Moses's pragmatic planning ambitions; together they forged an unprecedented mechanism for public support of private reuse of urban land claimed through eminent domain. With LaGuardia's blessing, they entered into negotiations in late 1942, setting their sights on the redevelopment of the rundown Gas House District on the Lower East Side (fig. 4.12).[19]

4.12: Stuyvesant Town, aerial view, 1952

Assembling the site presented a great challenge. To facilitate this Moses ushered through Albany a new housing law, the Hampton-Mitchell Redevelopment Companies Act of 1942, which enabled the city to use its powers of eminent domain not just for state-built and -owned public housing but also for private projects deemed by the city to serve a "public purpose."[20] In early 1943, the city and Met Life signed an agreement for redevelopment of a "blighted" area between East 14th and 20th Streets, and First Avenue and Avenue C. By the terms of the agreement, Met Life would buy up as much of the site as it could and the city would acquire the rest through eminent domain and sell it to the company at cost. The city also agreed to close internal streets, give the land to the company, and to maintain property taxes for twenty-five years at the value of the site before redevelopment. Met Life, in return, agreed to limit rents to the submarket rate of $14 per month per room ($1,100 in 2013 dollars for a five-room unit) for the first five years. Actual construction was to be paid for entirely by the company. Mayor LaGuardia announced the plan on the radio that April.[21]

Under the terms of the 1942 law Met Life was obligated to make no provisions for rehousing displaced tenants or businesses, although the company accepted responsibility for doing so. Despite an extensive relocation effort by realtor James Felt for Met Life, the outlook for the eleven thousand residents displaced was not, in the end, very positive. Only 3 percent of households had incomes sufficient for Stuyvesant Town and only 22 percent were eligible for public housing—not that eligibility guaranteed an apartment. While Felt believed that about two-thirds of the displaced found better housing, mostly in nearby neighborhoods, hundreds of other families forced out were not better off and he admitted that "by forcing people from one slum area into another, the basic ills of most urban low-rent housing will merely be shifted to a different location."[22]

In keeping with contemporary fashions in planning—and in line with Met Life's other projects around the city and country, including Parkchester, Peter Cooper Village, and Riverton in New York; Park La Brea in Los Angeles; and Parkmerced in San Francisco—Stuyvesant Town featured thirty-five, twelve- and thirteen-story towers set in a park-like superblock of sixty-one acres offering, according to a press release, "an atmosphere of trees and paths such as many suburbs do not possess" (fig. 4.13). Construction proceeded quickly: clearance began soon after the close of World War II and the first families moved in in August 1947. It was fully occupied less than two years later. The completed project included 8,755 apartments of one, two, and three bedrooms, with a population of just over twenty-four thousand. The buildings covered 25 percent of the land (down from about 70 percent before redevelopment), leaving the rest for lawns, pathways, and playgrounds. A moderate amount of retail space was included in storefronts facing out toward the surrounding neighborhood. This separation of shops reflected the latest ideas about functional zoning.[23]

Met Life's Board of Design, led by Irwin Clavan and Empire State Building architect Richmond Shreve, emphasized a no-frills approach, not dissimilar to that being employed in public housing. Like many of NYCHA's projects, Stuyvesant Town was composed of simplified brick boxes, nondescript, and unadorned at their base and roofline, with blank façades broken only by regular rows of single windows. Each building was composed of from one to five standardized "core units"—various

4.13: Stuyvesant Town, lawns, 2014

groupings of crosses and L-shapes—that joined in a number of different combinations and footprints. To ensure circulation of sufficient air and, especially, sunlight, each building was placed at least sixty feet from every other, and most apartments were given multiple exposures.[24] Inside, the apartments compared favorably with other mass-produced homes of the era, both urban and, perhaps of equal importance in the late 1940s, suburban. Typical Stuyvesant Town living rooms (approximately 215 square feet) and bedrooms (140 to 180 square feet), for instance, were larger that those in many new suburban tracts.[25]

Of course, Stuyvesant Town was not merely a set of buildings but an intensely controversial political and cultural space. Residents and business owners protested the clearing of the Gas House District, but their objections fell on deaf ears so great was the anticipation for new modern apartments in the midst of a devastating, and highly publicized, postwar housing shortage. For its part, the company gave veterans preference. But its other tenancy policies were far less generous. It permitted only stable married couples in its family apartments and encouraged its new tenants to hew to middle-class norms of propriety. More notoriously it restricted the project to whites, prompting great critique by civil rights groups and tenants alike. After a major battle on the part of activists against Met Life, officials reversed the policy in 1950. Many liberals also came to object to the Met Life's use of eminent domain and slum clearance for private profit, as well as the complex's high density and visual and social aloofness from the surrounding neighborhood.[26]

Stuyvesant Town began in controversy but quickly settled down into a comfortable domesticity that has endured, more or less uninterrupted, into the twenty-first

4.14: Stuyvesant Town, couple, by Fred R. Conrad, 1984

century (fig. 4.14). Both then and now tenants appreciated the controlled, verdant character and the high-quality maintenance, thanks to an on-site staff of about 250. For decades it maintained long waiting lists despite widespread criticism of its bland design and prohibitions on air conditioners and pets. The sense of enclosure, further enhanced by Met Life's private security patrols, became especially appealing during the depths of the urban crisis in the 1970s, when crime rates in the complex remained far lower than in surrounding areas.[27]

When the complex's tax abatements expired in 1974, the city government negotiated a ten-year extension and transferred the apartments into the recently introduced rent-stabilization program, where most of them remain today. Market realities began to intrude only in the early 2000s, when Metropolitan Life renovated, including lush new gardens designed by San Francisco landscape architect Peter Walker; introduced market rents for new tenants; and cracked down on unauthorized subletting of rent-restricted units. The company also built new stores and restaurants, brought in a farmer's market, and opened a seasonal ice skating rink as part of a strategy to attract new residents and add vitality to the complex's extensive open spaces (fig. 4.15). Things grew more tumultuous after the company sold the complex in 2006. The new owners, who overestimated the pace of turnover and, in turn, their ability to decontrol rents and charge market rates, paid a greatly inflated price. Despite aggressive tactics to uproot rent-protect tenants, they soon became insolvent. Efforts by tenants

4.15: Stuyvesant Town, cafe, 2014

to preserve socioeconomic diversity and, in particular, disputes over rent increases, found their way into the courts. Some tenants proposed buying the complex on a co-operative or condominium basis.[28]

Given the recent changes—and the gentrification of the neighborhood—Stuyvesant Town has lost much of its original middle-class character. Tenants today are less likely to be young families with children than couples with no children or young professionals living in roommate groups. But at least for now it still offers the same promise of a wholesome, tranquil, affordable environment, with which Met Life first launched the project in the 1940s. As a young mother, squeezed into a one-bedroom rent-stabilized apartment with her child and husband reports, "We found a village in Manhattan," she said. "We love it. We are so, so vested in this community."[29]

SAMUEL ZIPP AND NICHOLAS DAGEN BLOOM

Bell Park Gardens (1950, 800 units, Queens)

Sponsor: NYS Division of Housing, private co-op
(United Veterans Mutual Housing)
Program: limited-equity co-op
Architect: William M. Dowling

Bell Park Gardens is a large-scale garden-apartment complex in Bayside, Queens, with more than eight hundred units in thirty-nine, two-story clapboard and red-brick

4.16: Bell Park Gardens, ca. 1949

buildings (fig. 4.16). The project was conceived of by a consortium of civic leaders under the guidance of New York State's Housing Division to offer young veterans and their families an up-to-date, leafy alternative to other kinds of available city housing. It was organized as a limited-equity co-op open exclusively to veterans and their families, and financed with loans insured by FHA. Most of the original population of twenty-something GI Joes dissipated long ago, but Bell Park Gardens continues to thrive as a low-cost oasis for working families, especially families with children.

In every sense Bell Park Gardens is a hybrid. It is an apartment complex in New York City, yet in many crucial respects it looks, feels, and functions as "suburban" (fig. 4.17). As one recent transplant from Kew Gardens, jokes, "we call it the 'burbs." His wife, who grew up in Manhattan, is yet more blunt: "It's like country here."[30] Physically, it is defined by its forty-acre campus of shade trees, grassy courtyards, and surface parking more so than its buildings. Socially, tenants come, and stay, for distance from city "problems" and, above all else, what they see as "extremely good" public schools.[31] Life for most homeowners is intensely focused on the rearing of children.

Bell Park Garden's conception, design, and organization reflect a mixture of housing-reform optimism and FHA pragmatism. Historically, housing reformers had been concerned with the living conditions of the very poor. Over time, however,

4.17: Bell Park Gardens, prospectus, ca. 1948

attention turned to a broader range of households, including those whom housing activists came to call middle-income. This was an elastic category they invented to describe families too financially secure to merit publicly owned units but nevertheless unable to afford well-equipped apartments or houses in up-to-date neighborhoods. The most robust of the new programs created to cater to this group was FHA's "rental" housing program, which also supported owned complexes. FHA and the federal government are not widely thought of in connection with middle-income apartments. The best known federal housing programs targeted the low-income working poor (public housing) and working- and lower-middle-class suburban families (FHA's small-house program). Yet thanks to support from progressive reformers, mainly from New York City, FHA also leant great support between the 1930s and 1960s to alternative community types, including limited-dividend rental housing and limited-equity cooperatives.[32]

Bell Park Gardens' physical form strongly reflects its mixed heritage. Since the first philanthropic housing experiments, reformers had embraced decentralization. For decades this meant mid-rise courtyard buildings in places like the far East Side, Brooklyn, and the Bronx. With improved transit, mass automobile ownership, and the popularization of suburban living in the 1910s and 1920s, reformers pioneered new kinds of low-density complexes with ample green space for privacy and recreation, and units clustered in small buildings of only two or three stories. When FHA's Rental Housing Division got under way in 1935, its staff, who were drawn from progressive

158 4.18: Bell Park Gardens, groundbreaking, 1948

housing circles, embraced this model and established it as a national standard for multiple-family housing in areas where land costs were low enough to make it feasible. Bell Park Gardens' design by William M. Dowling was exemplary of this idea.

If its physical form emphasized privacy and its Colonial Revival architectural style spoke to conservatism, the organization of Bell Park Gardens as a limited-equity co-op betrayed an equally strong commitment to communalism (fig. 4.18). The idea for the project originated in an effort by New York State's housing commissioner Herman Stichman after World War II to heed reformers' long-standing call to build subsidized housing for middle-income families in New York City. To build it, the state worked with the Foreign Legion of Brooklyn and Queens and labor groups to create a sponsoring corporation, United Veterans Mutual Housing, which operated as a nonprofit. The limited-equity model, which union leaders had embraced for decades, promised to ensure long-term affordability by restricting profits, resale prices, and income levels. Selling the units to tenants, mostly in advance of construction, had several further advantages: it provided the sponsoring group with the capital FHA required of it, it offered prospective tenants the promise of homeownership (a first, and welcome change, for nearly all), and it promised the state a longer return on its efforts since it was widely believed in housing circles that owner-occupied communities enjoyed greater stability, and thus longevity, than rented ones. Thanks to the low cost of land in eastern Queens, the construction economies of the FHA-type garden-apartment design, and favorable financial arrangements including abatements on city property taxes, maintenance charges that covered utilities, upkeep, administration, and capital reserves ran just $14 per room per month ($1,050 in 2013 dollars for a typical two-bedroom unit). At $6,000 to $7,000 ($70,000 to $82,000), average income fell halfway between that of families living in rental apartments and those buying single-family houses.

Life in Bell Park Gardens was also characterized by a tension between privacy and community. Well before groundbreaking Commissioner Stichman cultivated an active group of prospective families who fought with the contractor for better fixtures and appliances and formed committees to negotiate favorable contracts for everything from laundry equipment to health insurance for the homeowners. After moving in, in 1949 and 1950, the "cooperators" set out to create community with equal vigor. They asked the city for a new elementary school and visits from a mobile library, established a credit union, and operated an eight-week summer camp that more than four hundred community children attended. They also organized group outings to Manhattan museums, Long Island restaurants, and Catskills resorts; staged blood drives; and engaged in lively debates about how to racially integrate the complex.

At the same time Bell Park Gardeners could be as focused on nuclear-family domesticity as in any stereotypical sitcom suburb. Tenants were mainly second-generation Jews reared in "old" neighborhoods in Brooklyn, Manhattan, and the Bronx who chose Bell Park Gardens for a new and different experience, one that they perceived as being more "American." Fathers endured long commutes (ninety minutes to Manhattan by a combination of bus and train), children spent most of their free time outside playing games, and mothers—who generally left the paid workforce upon moving to Bayside—customized their apartments and prepared TV dinners. Summer evenings and weekends meant family barbecues. A yearbook for the complex for 1950–51 describes residents as "participating and trying to live cooperatively almost twenty-four hours a day . . . [with] car pools in the morning, the mutual baby-sitting at night, the kids' playing and fighting, the preservation of lawns and shrubs, the care of garbage areas, the building meetings, committee meetings and the Community Council."[33] As Arnold Holzer, developer of several similar complexes observed in the *New York Times* in 1954, "The two-story garden cooperatives have become the answer to suburban housing for the 'intermediate' family—those with growing children who want the advantages of country life but not the responsibilities, maintenance problems and work that go along with private home ownership."[34]

With the passing of time and changing of tastes, life at Bell Park Gardens transformed. The most fundamental shift was that it became comparatively less appealing to young families. In the 1950s and 1960s the complex had as many as two thousand children, with nonstop activity on lawns and playgrounds. By the late 1970s and 1980s the complex was much quieter. Just 15 percent of original owners remained, all in their fifties and sixties. Thanks to low maintenance charges many could afford to own apartments in Florida, too, and were gone half the year. Some new tenants were younger families. Most, however, were at similar stages of life: couples in their forties, fifties, and sixties (fig. 4.19). Summer camps were replaced by senior centers.[35] One reason for this shift was demographic: after the post–World War II baby boom the number of children everywhere fell dramatically. Another was white flight: by the 1970s more families who could afford to buy co-ops were

4.19: Bell Park Gardens, 2009

leaving the city. Of equal importance were changing preferences. Whereas many middle-income families after World War II relished living in a low-rise complex far from city services and transit (Bell Park Gardens is served by bus but is a considerable distance from subway and commuter rail), by the 1970s there was, among families who cared to remain in the city and could afford to own an apartment, a renewed interest in older central neighborhoods.

Another determinative factor was rising standards for quality in housing. To younger generations, Bell Park Gardens (and comparable garden apartment projects) seemed outmoded. As one child of the complex recalls, even in a larger, two-story unit there was "just enough space to walk from couch to television and refrigerator without tripping over a jigsaw puzzle in progress."[36] Single-family communities like Levittown, with houses even smaller than some apartments at Bell Park Gardens, could better resist this fate, as homeowners made updates and, more crucially, additions. The physical realities of multifamily and the social realities of co-ownership, where inertia made change a challenge, meant this was much more difficult at Bell Park. Prices remained reasonable: as late as 1976 two-bedroom units cost $6,000 down with about $140 in monthly maintenance ($22,000 and $500 in 2013 dollars). Younger families buying apartments in eastern Queens nevertheless gravitated to more up-to-date projects like new "townhouse" complexes.

A second significant change at Bell Park Gardens was that after original loans were paid off, in the mid-1980s, the complex went private. Formal ties to the state housing division ended, freeing the community to establish its own maintenance charges and resale policies. In practice this meant abandoning the limited-equity format and centralized resales, allowing tenants to sell their units to whomever they chose (not just veterans), for whatever they could get—although subject to a considerable "flip tax" fee of 20 percent of the sales price, paid by the seller. The board introduced this levy to discourage turnover and speculation, to allow the whole complex to benefit from market-rate resales, and, perhaps most importantly, to shift the burden of upkeep away from continuing owners, many of whom were seniors living on pensions, to sellers. Although resale prices rose after the switch to market-rate, from approximately $25,000 to $150,000 (both figures in 2013 dollars), effectively they were unchanged since buyers became eligible for mortgages. Prices today remain approximately the same, adjusted for inflation.[37]

Although in certain respects old fashioned, Bell Park Gardens is today enjoying a third act, as a new-immigrant enclave. In the 1980s and 1990s the complex grew more diverse in terms of race and ethnicity, while remaining older in age. Since the millennium, however, average age has fallen and household size has grown for the first time in decades. The reason is a substantial influx of younger families, mainly first-generation Chinese and Korean immigrants. As Main Street Flushing emerged as a major center for Asian American life, Bell Park, five miles east but connected by limited-stop public buses, became a bedroom satellite. Today, about half of the homeowners, like half the larger census tract, are East Asian. Despite the half-century gap—and the withdrawal of the complex from state affordable housing programs nearly a quarter-century ago—these families choose Bell Park Gardens for the same reasons the original Bell Parkers did: a "very affordable" environment, according to one tenant, that is well maintained, safe for children, with good schools.[38] Another long-time owner put it, when she moved in six decades ago, "what they were looking for is a place to raise their children where they were not only able to afford the dwellings but where their children would get a good education." And today? "The people moving in now are also very, very interested in their children's education. And so it's worked out nicely."[39] MATTHEW GORDON LASNER

Queensview (1950, 728 units, Queens)

Sponsor: NYS Division of Housing, private co-op
(Joint Queensview Housing Enterprise)
Program: limited-equity co-op
Architect: Brown & Guenther

Queensview is a high-rise co-op apartment complex in Long Island City developed by an ad hoc group of housing reformers under New York State's Redevelopment Companies Law, which signaled the growing interest among city leaders in subsidizing centrally located private housing for the "forgotten middle": families too well off to qualify for public housing but unable to afford up-to-date market-rate housing (fig. 4.20).[40] Intended primarily for returning veterans and their families, complete with playgrounds, playrooms, and storage for strollers and bicycles, Queensview's fourteen towers-in-the-park operated as a sort of vertical subdivision: of the city yet also apart from it thanks to its ownership, superblock design, and spacious lawns. Although the area has changed dramatically since the 1940s, Queensview remains a low-cost oasis and a reminder that with sufficient resources the city and state can nurture durable below-market housing.[41]

4.20: Queensview, display advertisement, *New York Times*, August 4, 1949

As New York became more "American" following passage of federal quotas on foreign immigration in 1924, the city's collective expectations for quality in housing rose. Increasingly this meant large-scale, multiple-building housing complexes offering more privacy and open space than traditional city housing types. One of the great limitations of the city, however, was the challenge of assembling sufficiently large tracts of land to build. Well-capitalized philanthropic bodies like the City and Suburban Homes Company and Clarence Stein's City Housing Corporation had led the way with demonstration projects, but most development continued on an incremental lot-by-lot basis. The introduction of federal aid for public housing empowered the city to adopt modern site-planning. To encourage the trend further the state passed the Redevelopment Companies Law in 1942.

Although tenants and city leaders, especially Robert Moses, were enthusiastic about additional state support for middle-income complexes, developers and lenders were wary. Investors like the Metropolitan Life Insurance Company, which

4.21: Queensview, construction site, n.d.

developed Stuyvesant Town, believed that even the most competitive projects could not counter larger forces of decentralization that would, they feared, inevitably draw tenants to the suburbs. Queensview challenged this lack of faith. To entice further investment by insurance companies Moses proposed a series of smaller projects, including one called Ravenswood for an industrial site in Long Island City that was home to a few small houses but otherwise unimproved (fig. 4.21). He presented it to Mutual of New York Life Insurance, whose directors included Louis Pink, one of the city's leading long-time advocates for subsidized housing. Pink, however, was unable to convince Mutual that the project was safe. Company executives were especially skittish about Long Island City, which they regarded as a "wilted and withering locale." When they declined, Pink devised a plan for a smaller project on 10.3 acres bounded by 33rd Road, Crescent Street, 34th Avenue, and 21st Street, recruiting fellow housing reformers, including Gerard Swope, former chair of NYCHA, and Mary Simkhovitch, to form a nonprofit development company, Joint Queensview Housing Enterprise. As a consolation, Mutual agreed to serve as primary lender. The remainder of the site was given to NYCHA for the Ravenswood Houses.[42]

In many respects the project is a quintessential example of mid-twentieth-century Modernist planning. The architects given the commission were welfare-state technocrats George D. Brown, Jr., and Bernard Guenther. Brown had previously worked on a variety of subsidized housing projects, including for NYCHA, and had become a protégé of Pink. More immediately both designers worked at the New York State

4.22: Queensview, 2014

Division of Housing, which administered statewide low-cost housing programs. The two established a private practice when Pink recruited them for Queensview.

The project's physical form set it apart from surrounding areas. Some area homeowners opposed it on these grounds. Its superblock site plan that required closing three streets, its strong geometries, and its ordinary red-brick cladding all recalled NYCHA housing projects (fig. 4.22). The less restricted budget, however, allowed Brown & Guenther to introduce a number of improvements. Units were arranged just four to a floor in point-block towers rather than along long double-loaded corridors, affording each apartment two exposures and, as a result, plenty of fresh air and sunlight. This was enhanced by employing baseboard heating rather than standard radiators, allowing for oversize windows that started low to the floor. Buildings were spaced sufficiently apart to give every window in every building at least five hours of direct sunlight in winter. The apartments featured an off-the-foyer plan, eat-in kitchens, and many closets. To pay for these embellishments Brown & Guenther made the unusual move of eliminating basements, placing offices, playrooms, and mechanical equipment and storage to the first floors, while laundry and outdoor play space went on the roof.

Socially the project was also quite different from NYCHA antecedents. It was organized as a limited-equity co-op for "lower-middle-income" households. Tenants paid about $600 per room down with the balance covered by a blanket mortgage from Mutual; monthly maintenance was approximately $17.75 per room per month ($1.75 more than rentals at the adjacent Ravenswood Houses). In practice this meant about $2,550 down and $76 a month for a typical four-and-a-half-room apartment with two bedrooms ($40,000 and $1,200 in 2013 dollars). Family incomes were capped at $6,990 a year ($110,000).

Sales at Queensview were robust. Large ads were taken out and a model apartment was erected in a Manhattan furniture store, complete with novelties like Eames plywood chairs and a television set. From the start everyone involved insisted that the project be racially integrated. Many observers worried this would derail the project. In fact, as housing activist Charles Abrams recounts, news coverage dramatically accelerated sales, attracting progressive families, mainly Jewish but also Italian and Greek, from places like Greenwich Village, the Upper West Side, and the west Bronx.[43] Many were at the high end of the permitted range of incomes; they opted to pay for upgraded kitchens and bathrooms and convinced the sponsors to replace asphalt tiling with wood parquet flooring. They also demanded two toilets in even the small apartments. All this prompted the well-known architecture critic Frederick Gutheim to note that "many of the individualizing features of single-family houses or more expensive co-operatives had been kept."[44]

Tenant life at Queensview was very political, with factions of liberals and radicals locked in struggle for control of the board. It was also convivial. Many buyers convinced friends to join them in the complex and one group of four friends bought all the units on a single floor. The Queensview Camera Club sponsored an annual Photo Festival, while other "cooperators" formed a synagogue, organized nondenominational holiday parties that drew hundreds of guests, and banded together to block a nuclear power plant proposed for a nearby site. Racial integration went smoothly, although only about twenty African American families bought apartments, in part for financial reasons but in part, too, because families had concerns about living in a predominantly white community. One of the African American homeowners, however, was elected head of the tenants' group. This success was widely praised in housing and civil rights circles, and delegations of housing and redevelopment officials visited Queensview, including from the Soviet Union.[45] Pink's group went on to sponsor an addition with 364 units that opened in 1958 called North Queensview (also referred to as Queensview West), as well as the Kingsview (1957) complex in the Fort Green Title I Urban Renewal Area in Brooklyn. Queensview also helped shape the Mitchell-Lama program. George Brown served as technical advisor in Mayor Robert Wagner's office in the drafting of the bill and Brown & Guenther designed and developed the first Mitchell-Lama building in Manhattan: Inwood Terrace (1959). All employed programming and design elements tested at Queensview.[46]

As in other new middle-class developments, whether Stuyvesant Town or Levittown, life at Queensview was very much focused on child-rearing (fig. 4.23). Initial plans called for 286 one-bedroom apartments, 416 two-bedrooms, and just 26 three-bedrooms, but demand from larger families was so brisk that plans were revised to replace 78 one-bedrooms with an equal number of three-bedrooms.

4.23: Queensview, children, n.d.

4.24: Queensview/North Queensview NORC, 2014

Even before construction was completed, several dozen families organized a nursery school that remains in operation today, and for summers they built and staffed a popular "play center" with the help of the nonprofit Play School Association and the city's Board of Education. Children were expected to get into top city high schools and prestigious colleges and when the time came, many did.[47]

Some families did leave for the suburbs, just as the big insurance companies worried. Most, however, did not. So many stayed that by the 1980s Queensview had become a NORC, or naturally occurring retirement community (fig. 4.24). As one tenant explained, "Nobody wants to leave here except by death." As late as 2000, 60 percent of owners had been in residence since 1960, and half were still original owners. Alongside the nursery school there emerged an active seniors group run with the assistance of Selfhelp Community Services, a citywide nonprofit serving the elderly, which began a special NORC program at the complex.[48]

As tenants aged, they remained faithful not just to their apartments but to the progressive ideals that gave rise to Queensview: what one referred to as "true cooperative living."[49] As in other state-aided co-ops, when city tax abatements expired the complex went "private." At Queensview, however, 93 percent voted for a plan that maintained resale price restrictions. As a former board president explained in 2002, "We decided not to go to open market because we didn't want people who were used to paying $3,000 a month in Manhattan coming over. . . . We wanted to keep it middle income, the way the sponsors did for us." Share prices have, however, been raised multiple times since privatization in order to keep up with inflation and operating costs, and to undertake important deferred maintenance. Today, minimum incomes of $55,000 to $75,000 are required and share prices are yet higher: $10,000, or $210,000 for a one-bedroom and up to $310,000 for a three-bedroom. Unlike in 1950, however, there is no blanket mortgage, so owners are free to secure financing for up to 80 percent. Monthly maintenance runs from under $600 to around $900.[50]

Tenants, who now include many new immigrants from Asia and Eastern Europe as well as growing number of Latinos, continue to love living there, citing the spotless maintenance, the array of social services, and the sense of community. The nine acres of open space are also a strong allure. The tower-in-the-park format has been at odds with best practices in planning and architecture for half a century. The owners cherish it, however, recognizing it as a "luxury" that would be impossible to pay for today, especially in a middle-income project.[51] Queensview's enduring value is perhaps best illustrated by the low rates of turnover: an average of just two families move out each month. The wait list for two-bedrooms can take several years, while the list for three bedrooms is closed. Meanwhile, even many of the new families are, in fact, old: children and grandchildren of original tenants taking over the family apartment or buying into the complex anew.[52] MATTHEW GORDON LASNER

Abraham Kazan (1889–1971)

Abraham Kazan was the founding figure and, for half a century, most prominent proponent of limited-equity cooperative housing in New York City, responsible for developing over forty thousand apartments. The vast high-rise complexes he created, all still in operation—although not necessarily as limited-equities—were not only models of cooperation, but they also maintained large and comparatively stable pockets of working and middle-class life within the city limits in the postwar era.

Kazan was born in Ukraine, about thirty miles from Kiev, where he was raised on an estate his father managed for a czarist general. When he was a teenager, he came to the United States with his family. After a year spent on a Jewish agricultural settlement in southern New Jersey, he moved to New York City, and after a time working in the garment industry became an official in the International Ladies Garment Workers Union. He soon became a committed anarchist, believing that the best way for workers to advance their condition was through the creation of cooperative enterprises. Around 1916 he developed a cooperative grocery store under the union's aegis. When this closed in 1918, he moved to the Amalgamated Clothing Workers Union, where he created a credit union and other cooperative enterprises. While his focus eventually turned to housing, over the course of his career he would open a number of cooperative supermarkets, cooperative power plants, and a few other cooperative enterprises in his housing projects.[53]

His career in cooperative housing got its start in 1924, when the architect Andrew J. Thomas approached the ILGWU about developing an owner-occupied, low-cost apartment complex. Knowing Kazan's interest in the international consumers' cooperative movement, they forwarded him the request. Together, Kazan, Thomas, the IGLWU, the Amalgamated, and two other needle-trades unions bought a site on Mott Avenue (today the Grand Concourse) in the Bronx, and began work on what came to be called the Thomas Garden Apartments (1926). Unfortunately, the project ran out of money during construction and was completed by John D. Rockefeller, Jr. Undeterred, Kazan launched a second project in 1926: the Amalgamated Cooperative

Apartments (1927). The project opened to great fanfare and several additions followed. As a result of this success, state leaders who were eager to clear slums—so eager that they had bought up a substantial site on the Lower East Side using their own funds—invited Kazan to develop a Manhattan project, which became known as the Amalgamated Dwellings (1930).[54]

The Depression and the war halted building any new cooperatives. Kazan used the time to fight to keep the Amalgamated buildings afloat financially, which they did, while virtually all other worker housing co-ops—and many market-rate co-ops—failed, converting to bank-owned rentals. Kazan also fought hard during the Depression for the inclusion of limited-equity co-ops in federal housing legislation. He was adamant that publicly financed housing in which tenants had no equity stake would fail. Rental tenants, he argued, regarded their tenure as temporary and thus cared little about maintenance, leading to quick decay. Low-rent housing, he insisted, should be provided to people "only on condition that they make an effort to improve their own living conditions." Otherwise, he warned, government housing would destroy the "idea of self help." Furthermore, he predicted that the lack of equity stake would lead to "carelessness and destruction of property. Subsidies now needed to lower the cost of housing may be needed to make operation of the project possible."[55] His ideas garnered support from real estate interests, who recognized that Amalgamated-type co-ops might serve as an alternative to government-built and -owned apartments, but Democratic members of Congress resisted, believing that scarce funds should be used to produce housing for those most in need, not workers able to buy apartments, even if limited-equity.[56]

Although his drive to replicate the Amalgamated model nationally through public housing failed, after World War II Kazan found plenty of new opportunities to expand his empire thanks to a long and fruitful relationship with Robert Moses. The two men's politics were quite different, but each recognized in the other a competent, reliable partner. It began in 1945, as Kazan pursued further expansion of his Bronx projects, which required collaboration with Moses. Then, when Moses sought to redevelop a section of the Lower East Side, he called on Kazan. The result was Hillman Houses (1950), named for the Amalgamated's president, Sydney Hillman. Then, in 1949, Moses invited Kazan to establish a citywide group, later incorporated as the United Housing Foundation, that could dedicate itself to redeveloping slums with co-ops. After passage of the National Housing Act of 1949, which included Title I for urban redevelopment, Moses and the UHF pursued two additions to what came to be called Co-op Village: the East River Houses (1956), built as part of the Corlears Hook Urban Renewal Area, and Seward Park Housing (1960), built as part of the Seward Park Urban Renewal Area.

After this extensive building of cooperatives on the Lower East Side, Moses suggested to Kazan that the UHF develop something in a rundown section of Midtown South on the East Side. Preferring a site closer to the Seventh Avenue garment industry, Moses agreed, and in 1958 the city launched the Pennsylvania Station South Urban Renewal Area for the ILGWU Cooperative Houses, more commonly known as Penn South (1962). Kazan and the UHF, however, ran into opposition over use of eminent domain and the increasingly controversial practice of site tenant displacement. Protests had already led to a reduction in the size of the Seward Park

4.25: Twin Pines Village and Co-op City, display advertisement, *New York Times*, November 24, 1968

project. Now they led to bruising fights in Chelsea and, later, cancellation of a project in a proposed Title I area at Cooper Square in Manhattan's East Village. Thereafter, Kazan and the UHF worked exclusively outside of Manhattan, mainly on vacant or largely vacant land: Rochdale Village (1963), built on the site of the former Jamaica Race Track in South Jamaica; Amalgamated Warbasse Houses (1965) in Coney Island; and Twin Pines Village, completed by another developer as Starrett City in 1976, in East New York. The culmination of his career was the gargantuan Co-op City (1968–73), built on a partially landfilled site in the marshes of the northern Bronx, with 15,383 units (fig. 4.25). By the time the first families moved in, however, Kazan had retired. He would not live to see it finished, and would have been distraught to learn that it was the last project completed by the UHF.

Kazan was never without critics, and people of a range of political perspectives disagreed with some aspects of his work. For many, the idea of public subsidies—whether federal grants for the purchase of land under Title I, tax abatements provided under the 1926 and 1955 state housing laws, or below-market-interest-rate Mitchell-Lama loans from the city or state—going to middle-income households was untenable. Others felt Kazan's projects unfairly completed with the work of private developers. Many liberals, meanwhile, found relocation for slum-clearance projects unpalatable, or objected to the serial high-rise designs favored by Kazan and his architect of choice, Herman J. Jessor. As interest in public participation and historic preservation grew, many came to regard Kazan's complexes as models for how not to build. In defiance of his critics Kazan remained committed to the idea of limited-equity co-ops as a tool for providing persons of modest income attractive homes. Architectural critics, he complained, were more interested in superficial appearances than in his complexes' spacious, up-to-date, and thoughtfully designed interiors. Simplicity of design, he added, kept down costs, saving money for things that really mattered. Kazan's broader agenda went beyond housing, however. Although he realized his tenants were interested chiefly in good apartments at cheap prices, he saw limited-equity co-ops as beachheads of a cooperative economy superior to capitalism. At the very least they offered a crucial alternative to the harsh realities of the New York City housing market. PETER EISENSTADT

Penn Station South (1962, 2,820 units, Manhattan)

Sponsor: Title I, UHF, union (ILGWU)
Program: limited-equity co-op
Architect: Herman J. Jessor

Penn Station South is representative of a brief but dramatic era of below-market housing development that combined slum clearance coordinated by Robert Moses, cooperative enterprise spearheaded by Abraham Kazan, city tax abatements, and federal subsidies through the Title I urban renewal program. The joint effect of such powerful forces was a project that switched out tenements for towers in the park and politically engaged residents: a transformation that continues to shape Penn South and the surrounding neighborhood today.

Penn South, officially called the Mutual Redevelopment Houses, was built as part of the Penn Station South Renewal Area. Under Title I of the National Housing Act of 1949, cities could apply for federal money to condemn, buy, and prepare "blighted" real estate for private redevelopment. Kazan was a pioneer in taking on such projects, setting up the United Housing Foundation to serve as a central clearinghouse for housing under the program, and developing housing at seven Title I areas. Penn South began in 1956, when Committee on Slum Clearance chairman Robert Moses had the idea to rebuild four blocks on the East Side. The partner Moses recruited, however, was Abraham Kazan's UHF, which brought it to the attention of the International Ladies Garment Workers Union, whose leaders preferred a walk-to-work site closer to the Seventh Avenue garment district. Moses agreed and helped select a new one: six blocks on the West Side between West 23rd and 29th Streets, and Eighth and Ninth Avenues. Neighbors included rail yards, wholesale warehouses, auto-body shops, and, toward the river, the freight High Line railroad and elevated West Side Highway (fig. 4.26). The area had thinned out considerably since the early twentieth century, when it rivaled the Lower East Side in population density and concentration of poverty, but it was grayer than gayer for the change. The site itself was mostly old-law tenements, boarding houses, and aging lofts, which the *New York Times* characterized as "twenty acres of squalid West Side rookeries." Few outsiders, with the exception of a handful of preservation-oriented architects, thought it worth saving—although residents rallied to defend their tenements, knowing that they lacked the income to qualify for the new apartments.[57]

4.26: Penn Station South, ca. 1962

Penn South was designed by the architect Herman J. Jessor, a Russian émigré who studied at Cooper Union and had specialized in worker housing since designing the Amalgamated Cooperative Apartments in the late 1920s. The idiom was, in accord with best practices in the 1950s, tower-in-the-park Modernism. Normally this would have demanded closing interior streets to create a cloistered superblock, but concerns about access to the shipping piers required all but West 27th Street remain open. To enlarge two of the blocks and calm traffic the city allowed Jessor to bend West 24th and West 28th Streets. A twelve-story elevator hotel and two churches were kept (two other congregations were given new buildings). Penn South also included one- and two-story retail buildings, a heating (and later electricity) plant, a three-story office building, surface and underground parking garage, and a theater and an indoor tennis center that were leased to commercial operators (fig. 4.27).

Jessor arranged the apartments in ten, twenty-two-story towers, rendered in a simple red brick. The project drew heavily from earlier Jessor and Kazan collaborations, although it included some new embellishments, such as central air conditioning. The basic design element was the cruciform plan, with two or three units occupying each quadrant, arranged around a central elevator landing. This plan allowed all but one

4.27: Penn Station South, 2014

or two lines of apartments to have two exposures, improving the flow of natural light and air. Five buildings comprised a single cross and five "double" buildings fused two modules together. Most of the apartments were one- and two-bedrooms, with two three-bedrooms per floor in the double buildings. In a break from the usual emphasis in postwar below-market housing on families with children, and in recognition of the limited appeal of the West Side of Manhattan to younger families at that time, buildings also included studios. (There was so little demand from younger families initially that even some three-bedrooms were given to one-person households at first.) All the apartments were generous in size: studios, which included foyers, kitchens, dining areas, and dressing rooms, had at least 520 square feet, while three bedrooms had nearly 1,250. Half the apartments had balconies.

Penn South targeted a middle-income group too affluent for public housing but unable to afford high-quality housing at market rates in central sections of town. Original sales prices averaged $650 per room down ($5,800 in 2013 dollars), which covered 20 percent of construction costs; many tenants financed these down payments with loans from lenders like the Amalgamated Bank and a new Penn South credit union, thus effectively putting down nothing. Initially monthly maintenance charges were about $24 per room ($220). Without city tax abatements these would have been 25 percent higher, and without the Title I subsidy for the site, yet more. Among the original owners were 300 families displaced by the project and 715 who were members of the ILGWU, although no apartments were specifically reserved for them. Other tenants were mainly civil servants, teachers, professors, artists, and other blue-, pink-, and white-collar types (fig. 4.28). Credited by some for saving Chelsea, Penn South quickly earned a reputation as a desirable, even luxurious

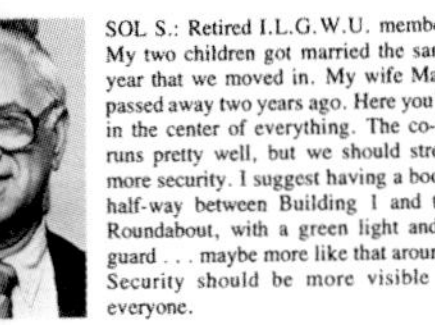

SOL S.: Retired I.L.G.W.U. member. My two children got married the same year that we moved in. My wife Mary passed away two years ago. Here you're in the center of everything. The co-op runs pretty well, but we should stress more security. I suggest having a booth half-way between Building 1 and the Roundabout, with a green light and a guard . . . maybe more like that around. Security should be more visible to everyone.

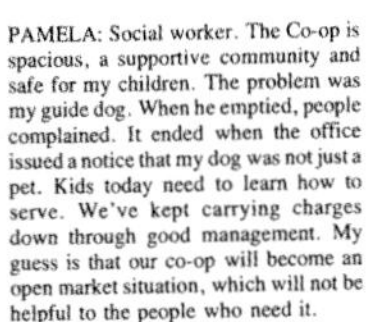

PAMELA: Social worker. The Co-op is spacious, a supportive community and safe for my children. The problem was my guide dog. When he emptied, people complained. It ended when the office issued a notice that my dog was not just a pet. Kids today need to learn how to serve. We've kept carrying charges down through good management. My guess is that our co-op will become an open market situation, which will not be helpful to the people who need it.

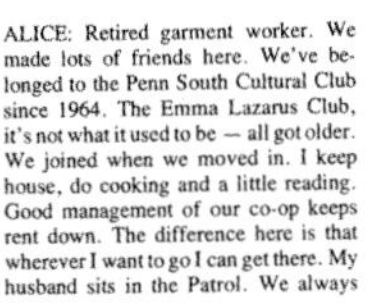

ALICE: Retired garment worker. We made lots of friends here. We've belonged to the Penn South Cultural Club since 1964. The Emma Lazarus Club, it's not what it used to be — all got older. We joined when we moved in. I keep house, do cooking and a little reading. Good management of our co-op keeps rent down. The difference here is that wherever I want to go I can get there. My husband sits in the Patrol. We always vote.

SARAH: Age 8. I was born in Penn South. I have an older brother and sister. First thing I remember is the sandbox and slides. I made friends, Lelia and Monique. We're still good friends. I don't have to go far to get to somebody's house. I met Elliot at nursery school. We take turns sleeping at each other's house. We go to Vermont, but I wouldn't live there. I'd miss Penn South. My Grandpa from Building 8 plays with me; he gives me lots of attention.

SAL: Artist. My first child was a year old, my second was born here. After W.W. II, I was 3½ years in a hospital. We then lived in an illegal loft. We got an apartment here. A beautiful lady next door, if my baby was sick and I had to take the other to school, would babysit and make cookies too. I hope the Board will not let people sell for profit. If a person pays half the rent he'd pay elsewhere, he owes the cooperative some involvement.

MARY S.: Here since 1977. I have two children, 4 and 6. The playground was a place to go when you have small children. We go to museums and movies. We don't spend all our income on rent. Some of our friends do. We've the only playground in Chelsea that is quiet and clean. Most older people enjoy watching the children play. There's a terrific baby-sitting co-op. There are fathers in it, too. We need younger people involved for the future.

MAREA AND BILL: Retired Health Ed Coach/Teacher. I'm active in the Hudson Guild and still feel close to it. We feel lucky here — you can't duplicate it in any part of the city. The services are wonderful, concerned with people. If Marea had not become handicapped, we would have been more active in our co-op. When we see the discipline of children in the playground, we feel this co-op will continue its future on a high level.

FANNY: Retired social worker. Moving here changed my life. I never dreamt I could live in an apartment where I could enjoy the cultural advantages of the City. I always pictured Manhattan as a cold place, but people are friendly and seem to care. Our co-op is well-run, we're fortunate in its Board of Directors, and I hope it is appreciated. I love living here —and wouldn't want to live any other place.

ANN: Retired Nurse. My family didn't want me to move from Harlem. The neighbors here are very nice. I'm one to know, because of ethnic difference. That new Black woman on the top floor, I'll bring her down to Bingo. The 8th Floor lady invites me to go walking, the one with numbers on her arm. You know what's going on here. They put the news under your door almost the same day. On the Lobby Patrol, people stop and talk to you.

ESTELLE: School Administrator. I moved in 4 years ago, long enough to know what's good about Penn South; short enough to know what's terrible out there. The nice thing in our recent mortgage negotiations was the concern that lowest income people would be unable to continue living here. Many deposited money in the Credit Union for loans. This should insure the future of Penn South. I don't think any profiteering suggestion would ever go through.

MARY & BRESCI: Retired teacher and art director: B: I grew up in Chelsea. I had a cold-water flat with a toilet in the yard. When cooperators complain, I laugh inside. Mary holds Xmas Parties for the entire building. We met at the Hudson Guild. M: I thought we could never live with low ceilings because we came from a brownstone. Our daughter lives in Building 2; we look across and see our grandchildren.

DIANA: Retired teacher. When a landlord raises rent, you know he doesn't have to. In a co-op, however, you know it's necessary. If you feel you're paying too much, anyone here will say, "You have the best buy in the city." Only in our co-op can you find tulips, cherry trees and dogwood together. On our Board of Directors, there should be a strong minority, no matter who the majority is. We don't attract children because of our school situation.

FRANCES: Retired psychologist. It's much nicer here than at London Terrace; from where I came. I have some lovely neighbors who, when I was ill, shopped and helped to care for me. There's more friendliness here; you don't feel like transients. When I moved in, it was glorious. You just open your door, and walk into this wonderful city. Co-op literature and minutes make you feel that you know what's going on here.

4.28: Penn Station South, tenants, from Penn South, "Twenty-first Anniversary Journal" (1983)

project for the well-to-do.[58] Tenants were always, however, of modest means. For new tenants there were income ceilings of eight times the annual maintenance (since lowered to seven); existing owners crossing this threshold paid a surcharge. In recent decades many tenants, especially the elderly, have received federally financed Section 8 "rental" vouchers to help pay their maintenance; many also benefit from the city's Senior Citizen Rent Increase Exemption program, introduced in 1970 to aid tenants and owners in many kinds of privately developed subsidized housing.

If young professionals, following the lead of Jane Jacobs, were becoming more vocal about their taste for "diverse" older neighborhoods around the time Penn South was built, the ILGWU crowd—both producers and tenants—did not share their nostalgia. They welcomed the complex's quiet spaciousness, low site coverage, and functional separation of land-uses. As writer Leonard Kriegel, who moved to Penn South in 1962 from a small studio in the neighborhood, notes, "Penn South never lacked the amenities Jane Jacobs thinks of as the glue of a healthy urban community." Moreover, he continued, "what is sterile or totalitarian to some is liberating" to others, especially those who "couldn't afford to view the elevator as incarnate evil."[59] At the dedication ceremony in 1962 attended by President Kennedy, Governor Nelson Rockefeller, and

4.29: President Kennedy, David Dubinsky (president of ILGWU), Robert F. Wagner, Jr., dedication, Penn Station South, by I. D. Ettinger, 1962

Eleanor Roosevelt, Mayor Robert F. Wagner declared Penn South "another milestone on the road to our goal of making New York a slumless city" (fig. 4.29).[60]

Many tenants moved to Penn South from declining sections of the outer boroughs. Manhattan—what some thought of as "the real city"—not only saved them from long commutes, a special concern for older workers, but also permitted them to enjoy urban life in ways they had not done in decades.[61] In this respect Penn South effected a sort of white flight in reverse (for years Penn South was almost entirely white and overwhelmingly Jewish), allowing middle-class families to escape to what one tenant referred to as "a suburban community within New York City."[62] Penn South, even with its greenbelt, security patrols, and fences and cameras, could not counter all the destabilizing forces sweeping through New York City; some early tenants with children ended up moving to the suburbs. But for others, "Moving to Manhattan was a dream come true. For the first time in years I can go out at night."[63] As another owner explained, "We came from the Bronx . . . our life style changed from hell to heaven."[64]

One of the most remarkable things about Penn South was and remains the tenants' politics. As at all owner-occupied complexes subsidized by the city or state from the late 1950s onward, tenant-owners were given mandatory preoccupancy training to generate support for the progressive political economy, encourage feelings of camaraderie, and stimulate participation in project governance. An important message conveyed both here and in attention the complex received from leaders like President Kennedy was that one should think not just about what to get out living in a co-op but what to contribute. Perhaps as a result of this programming Penn South inspired a degree of fealty rare to any community. Owners took particular pride in the role organized labor played in its construction, financing, and public subsidies. "Each day," remarked one owner, "I am thankful to my union, the ILGWU, for thinking of a beautiful place in midst of Manhattan for workers' homes."[65]

Awareness of Penn South's unique status has also manifested in a high degree of volunteerism. Tenants launched Penn South chapters of dozens of social, welfare, and political clubs. During the city's fiscal crisis in 1970s, when the city asked property owners to pay taxes early in return for a discount, Penn South tenants complied but declined the reduction. "We sit in the midst of New York City," explained one owner, "and we wanted to help."[66] As David Smith, a lifelong progressive who was president of the board for decades, put it, "Until now, it's the co-ops that have been receiving various benefits from the city. . . . Now we're giving rather than receiving."[67] Penn South tenants have also voted several times to remain limited-equity: in 1986, extending price and income limits to 2012; in 2001, extending controls to 2022; and in 2010, extending them to 2030. According to Smith the question faced was whether "this development, built by union and public funds and dedicated to working people, [should] be destroyed as a middle-income cooperative" and become a place "where only the well-to-do can live?"[68] Penn South today has a long waiting list—so long it has been closed since 1987, with lotteries for a place held in 1996, 2003, and 2014. But those with sufficient patience pay approximately $40,000 to $110,000 for apartments of two to five and a half rooms, with monthly maintenance of $350 to $1,000.[69]

A decisive factor uniting tenants across the complex's several internal political parties was old age. Many of the first families were older and as early as 1976 half the complex was retired; by the mid-1980s, three-quarters were. In return for remaining limited equity, the city offered to extend tax abatements. Without them, maintenance would have risen by 50 percent, an impossible expense for seniors living on pensions. An additional fear was that market-rate tenants would drive up maintenance even further with expensive demands. "The people coming in," Smith warned dramatically, "will want amenities—carpeting in the hallways, microwave ovens, maybe even gold-plated urinals."[70]

The elderly have dominated life at Penn South in other ways. Concerns about the tremendous numbers of seniors living in a naturally occurring retirement community demanded that the co-op's board introduce services tailored to the elderly. With a grant from the United Jewish Appeal Federation of New York in 1986, Penn South created the Penn South Program for Seniors (PSPS), offering dedicated community rooms for the elderly; opportunities for medical care, home visits, and food delivery; and classes in everything from exercise to the dangers of hoarding. Staffed since the mid-1990s by UJA-Federation agencies Selfhelp Community Services and Jewish Home and Hospital for the Aged, PSPS is now financed by a mixture of private foundations, the co-op, and, thanks to UJA lobbying, the city and state. PSPS has served as a model for NORC programs nationally.[71]

The young, meanwhile, have not been forgotten. For decades Penn South maintained the best playgrounds in Chelsea, and in 1985 a parking area was converted to one of the complex's most popular features, the Penn South Intergeneration Garden, which brings children and seniors together. More recently, the parents group built an indoor play space in one of the complex's many community rooms. And although lawns are off limits to play, families enjoy the campus-like design. As one mother put it, "The gardening, the playgrounds, were a blessing for my children. I never had to worry about hearing [car and truck] brakes."[72] This appeal has brought many second- and third-generation Penn South families to the complex. Unfortunately, there is not room for everyone. Indeed, if there is a problem with Penn South, it is that there is too little of it: tenants of every age wish it were younger, with more children and more "new blood" on the board. Yet perhaps more than any other subsidized housing complex in the country, turnover is minimal thanks to its superior services, management, and location.[73]

Penn South today is surrounded by some of the most expensive real estate in the United States. It would be impossible to create under current housing policies, and the tenants know it. Yet careful stewardship on the part of city leaders and the project's homeowners has ensured long-term affordability. While many complexes like it have abandoned these limits, Penn South has been resolute in its commitment to the commonweal. MATTHEW GORDON LASNER

Rochdale Village (1963, 5,860 units, Queens)

Sponsor: UHF
Program: Mitchell-Lama co-op
Architect: Herman J. Jessor

Rochdale Village reflects the United Housing Foundation's growing scale, formulaic response to site planning and architecture, liberal social values, and search for greener pastures as its center-city clearance projects began to generate significant opposition (fig. 4.30). The project was built on the grounds of the Jamaica Race Track, whose owners started to speak of selling it in 1953, and finally closed it in 1959. Robert Moses was intrigued by the opportunity and generated several ideas, including a UHF middle-income co-op. The site was very large: 170 acres. More important, it had a single owner, few existing buildings, and no tenants requiring relocation. It was, however, in an African American area, South Jamaica, yet most families drawn to UHF projects were Jewish. Would African Americans buy? If so, would Jews buy, too? The unions that typically sponsored UHF projects balked at the proposal, forcing Kazan to turn to the state for $86 million in retirement funds for financing. Remaining support came through the state Mitchell-Lama program. The project, which Kazan named for the industrial city in Britain where in 1844 the international consumers' cooperative movement originated, was announced in 1960.[74]

Architect Herman J. Jessor created a single superblock containing twenty, fourteen-story cruciform-plan towers clad in red brick. Each building was divided into three parts with a separate elevator bank. The apartments were spacious and attractive and many featured balconies with panoramic views. The site plan arranged the buildings into five sections, each with a traffic cul-de-sac providing car access. The complex also contained two shopping centers anchored by cooperative

4.30: Rochdale Village, community garden, 2014

4.31: Rochdale Village, shopping mall no. 2, 2014

supermarkets (fig. 4.31). The larger mall was designed by Los Angeles-based Victor Gruen, one of the originators of the enclosed shopping center in the 1950s. There were also two elementary schools, an intermediate school, a community center with a two-thousand-seat auditorium, and parking lots. Rochdale also had its own power plant, in large part a consequence of Kazan's long-time feud with Con Edison. The facility enabled the UHF to include central air conditioning, an extremely rare amenity, especially in below-market housing.

Rochdale, like all Mitchell-Lama and UHF projects, was targeted to a middle-income clientele, with initial average monthly maintenance of $21 per room a month, with a down payment of $400 per room ($185 and $3,500 in 2013 dollars). (To place these figures in further context, about half of Rochdale's original residents earned more than $7,000, the standard financial demarcation for middle-class status at the time, and half below.[75]) Despite the low prices, however, sales were slow. For the first time in its history, the UHF undertook a major marketing campaign, including ads suggesting "Enjoy Country Living in Rochdale Village."[76] It also opened an on-site sales office. Of those who bought, about 80 percent were white (primarily Jewish) and 20 percent African American (fig. 4.32). The UHF had always placed great emphasis on developing community life through participation in clubs and organizations, and Rochdale was no different. Even before the complex opened, three synagogues had been organized and within a year almost 150 other clubs and organizations had been created, including fraternal, political, musical, sports, and crafting clubs. Among them was a huge array of Jewish organizations, along with what was originally called the Rochdale Village Negro Cultural Society.

Although Rochdale was (and remains) a self-governing cooperative, the UHF controlled the board of directors in its opening years. The board chose the managing

4.32: Rochdale Village, by Sam Falk, 1966

agent, which until the late 1960s was also the UHF. In 1965 residents elected a House Congress consisting of 120 members (two from each of the sixty sections in Rochdale's twenty buildings), which had only advisory powers. Rochdale residents were restless under UHF leadership and wanted to govern directly. In 1969 the first cooperative-wide elections were held. Elections were partisan and often bitter, divided on ideological, although not racial, grounds. There were two main factions, one generally opposed to the UHF (known as the Tenants Council, and in a later incarnation, as the United Shareholders), and one closer to the UHF (the Concerned Cooperators). At first, their politics respectively reflected long-standing priorities and animosities between the "old left" and social democrats, but over time their constituencies broadened. After the demise of the UHF in the early 1970s, the two factions continued to dominate Rochdale politics.

In November 1966 the well-known journalist Harvey Swados wrote an article about Rochdale for the *New York Times* Sunday magazine, "When Black and White Live Together."[77] This aspect was, in Rochdale's early years, its face to the world, one promoted by its residents: an exemplar of integration in housing, education, and the art of living together, whose schools, stores, politics, and organizations were interracial. This image was largely true. Rochdale was not a racial utopia, however, and was never entirely free of racial strife. Schools, crime, and relations with the surrounding community were all matters of contention. But for the most part, these conflicts were contained until the bitter and disastrous citywide teacher's strike of 1968, which divided the complex into pro- and anti- factions, supported, respectively, primarily by more conservative and moderate Jews on the one hand, and African Americans and left-leaning Jews on the other.[78]

The strike shattered the racial comity that had prevailed since Rochdale's opening. One place where this disharmony was felt almost immediately was in the new intermediate school, which opened in 1967. Riven by tension between pro- and anti-strike factions, the school deteriorated and experienced serious discipline problems. In the cooperative as a whole (as indeed, in the city at large) crime was on the rise.

For these and other reasons white families started to leave Rochdale in large numbers in 1969. Efforts were made on a communitywide basis to try to staunch the flow by improving the underlying conditions, but to no avail. By 1974 only 10 percent of residents were white; by the end of the decade the figure was no more than 2 percent. Black families also left in large numbers during this time, but almost all the new arrivals in Rochdale were nonwhite.

There were other changes at Rochdale in the 1970s. the UHF, bruised and battered by a long rent strike at Co-op City, ceased operations. Thanks to the oil crisis of 1973 and Vietnam Era inflation, costs at Rochdale rose, too, necessitating a controversial increase in carrying charges. If Rochdale did not have a crippling rent strike, there were several short rent stoppages and many tenants worried about a possible default. In 1978 the Teamsters Union, which provided maintenance and security, began a long, bitter, and brutal strike, with much vandalism against Rochdale property, assaults (committed by both sides), and even a murder. During the strike, which lasted almost a year, residents discovered the virtues of self-reliance, collecting their own garbage and policing the complex. The strike ended victoriously for the tenants, but it left them in parlous financial condition, owing the state $500,000. Under a "work-out" agreement reached in 1980 the state allowed Rochdale to defer, making their late payments interest-free until 2000. In 1987 a second work-out negotiated with the state gave Rochdale $23 million for repairs.

Long after the strike safety remained a problem at Rochdale, especially during the crack epidemic of the late 1980s. When crime fell in the mid-1990s the project experienced a modest renaissance: repairs were made and there was a general sense that things were improving. Better services, however, have meant higher maintenance charges, which have generated conflict. Modest equity requirements, however, remain, with two-bedroom apartments selling for just $10,800, with a wait time of one to two years. There were extensive discussions about privatization in 2002 but the issue never came to a vote; the tax abatements provided as part of the original subsidies were simply too alluring, and fears about turnover and gentrification too great. Today the complex is the largest owner-occupied Black-majority housing complex in the world, co-op or condominium. Well run and maintained, with a thriving new community garden and plans to renovate the shopping centers, it is, one tenant says after fifty years' residence, "the best place in the world" to live and "a joy to be" in.[79] PETER EISENSTADT

Co-op City (1968–73, 15,382 units, Bronx)

Sponsor: UHF
Program: Mitchell-Lama co-op
Architect: Herman J. Jessor

Co-op City was the final and largest project developed by the United Housing Foundation. It represented the height of the UHF's dream to create a cooperative community that would simultaneously respond to the city's lack of moderate-cost, high-quality housing for middle- and working-class households, while also reshaping society in a "fundamental way." Co-op City included village shopping, parks,

4.33: Co-op City, bike-a-thon, ca. 1977

and educational facilities that built upon both the UHF's long-standing development experience and the postwar new community (or new town) movement to create an entirely new kind of space in New York City.

In 1964, Webb & Knapp, a major developer of urban renewal projects, approached the UHF about buying 415 acres in the northeast Bronx occupied by the company's defunct Freedomland amusement park. With Rochdale Village winding down and encouragement from Robert Moses, who brokered the deal, the UHF agreed to develop the area. It unveiled its plans for a new "city" in early 1965, with 15,382 apartments in a variety of high-rises—33-story towers, 26-story "triple cores," and 22-story chevrons—with a few groups of attached row-type houses. Ample parking would be provided in outlying garages, which was especially crucial given the lack of public transit. Much of the rest of the site was given over to community facilities, shopping malls, and schools, or reserved for open space, including man-made rolling hills and a central greenway (fig. 4.33). The project was financed with a $250 million loan ($1.9 billion in 2013 dollars) arranged through the state's Mitchell-Lama program.

Prospective tenants were generally indifferent to the politics of the international cooperative movement that motivated UHF leadership and determined the project's conditions of ownership and governance. Many, however, looked forward to the opportunity to forge a new community. Even before the first residents took their apartments, in late 1967, the UHF encouraged them to begin building community and they had formed a cooperative nursery school and discussed ideas for a college savings plan and a health-insurance group. Most important were low costs. Initial prices, before Vietnam era inflation, were $450 per room down with projected maintenance charges of about $22 per room per month. In practice this meant a three-bedroom sold for just $2,925 down and $149.50 a month ($22,500 and $1,100 in 2013 dollars). Apartments were spacious and well-equipped with up-to-date amenities like central air conditioning. Many had spectacular views (fig. 4.34). Early tenants loved the place. Although the first families suffered through many years of further construction, few seemed to mind. As one recalled, "The apartment was so spacious and although we were pioneers and had hardships . . . we all had a vision of a bright future." [80]

From the beginning, Co-op City faced critiques. One concerned design. The American Institute of Architects charged that the spirits of Co-op City's residents "would be dampened and deadened by the paucity of their environment." Another line of attack concerned social mixture. Herman Badillo, then commissioner of the Department of Housing Relocation, told Mayor John Lindsay: "Everybody knows

4.34: Co-op City, lifelong resident, by Alan Zale, 1992

that the word 'co-op' is a synonym for 'Jewish housing.' . . . Puerto Ricans and Hispanics don't understand co-ops and don't have the money for co-ops, and neither do blacks."[81] Indeed, in presales Co-op City acted as a magnet for white, largely Jewish, working- and middle-class families in the Bronx. Eleven and seven percent, respectively, of the entire population of the Morris Heights and Highbridge districts made applications. When pressed in 1965 to reserve some units for lower-income families, the UHF resisted, arguing, "subsidizing certain families would tear the cooperative into two separate groups." [82] And when the *Times* reported a year later that the city was thinking of buying space in cooperatives to rent to low-income families, the Co-op City sales office was deluged with calls from worried buyers; some even withdrew their applications despite reassurances that Co-op City was not part of this program. The UHF recognized that "there is no sense in denying that a lot of people are trying to escape from something. They are running, as so many have been running, from changing neighborhoods." [83]

Although the tenets of the cooperative movement proscribed cross-subsidies to accommodate low-income families, the UHF worked hard to integrate Co-op City racially. Officials emphasized, "Co-op City is an open city, open to all people with various backgrounds both racially and ethnically."[84] Black families were prominent in early publicity for the development and the UHF placed ads in the African American and Spanish-language press. The UHF did not publicly discuss the racial make-up but a survey of residents in 1971 found that its population was 70 percent Jewish, 20 percent Black and Puerto Rican, with the remaining 10 percent primarily consisting of other ethnic whites. This diversity was a source of pride for many residents. One early African American resident later reflected, "I never felt a sense of racism. . . . We were all 'haves' not 'have nots.'" An early Jewish resident explained that "Co-op City was a melting pot. We had friends from everywhere, of every skin color."[85]

This is not to suggest there was no conflict. One of the first racial flashpoints was the schools. Co-op City's schools were originally imagined solely for residents. In part, this was a gesture toward Co-op City's size. But it was also recognition of the key role that schools had come to play in New York's racial politics. When a plan was presented in April 1971 to Co-op City's PTA suggesting the possibility of busing in students from NYCHA's low-income Boston Secor Houses, one parent who attended the meeting described the reaction as a "lynch mob in the auditorium."[86] The Department of Education backpedaled, putting forth a compromise plan that would allow minority students to be bused in but would not require children from the development to be bused elsewhere. Some residents of color also resented the development's governance structure, which called for representatives to be elected from each building, a system that was almost guaranteed to result in uniformly white, Jewish representatives.

Another source of conflict at Co-op City concerned age. The UHF—like the Mitchell-Lama program—was interested most in serving young families. Designs included a plan for an "educational park," and ads specifically courted families with school-age children. As in many other UHF co-ops by the 1960s and 1970s, however, the ownership skewed old: even among the first buyers one in five was over age sixty. Tension between elderly residents and their younger, often rowdier neighbors was common, and focused on issues of petty crime, drug use, and loitering.

These racial and generational tensions appeared to the UHF and residents alike to be largely the normal growing pains of any new community. More serious were tensions surrounding project finances. One problem was dramatic cost overruns in construction. Landfill for the swampy site required an additional 300,000 cubic yards of fill above the original estimates. More crucial was inflation. Co-op City coincided with a dramatic period of inflation thanks to the Vietnam conflict and, after 1973, the OPEC crisis. As a result, all the financial facts of the project sold to buyers in 1965 quickly became fictions. Monthly maintenance charges had to double, even triple, to keep the project solvent. These troubles were exacerbated by poor communication between project management and tenants. Although owned collectively by all the tenants on a cooperative basis, the massive size and the UHF's paternalistic by-laws meant that those in charge treated owners more as renters than homeowners.

The result was rebellion. In an attempt to stave off chaos Mayor Lindsay authorized an increase in Co-op City's tax abatement from 50 percent to 80 in 1969. But by 1975 the owners called a "rent" strike. The leader of the strike, Charles Rosen, announced, "This is a militant gesture to guarantee that we are not lost in the legislative shuffle."[87] The strike, which was supported by 80 percent of owners, lasted for thirteen months. In the aftermath control of the development passed from the UHF, which dissolved during the dispute, to a tenant steering committee headed by Rosen, who pledged to return the development to a sound financial footing while also maintaining the community ethos that had inspired the strike. This task would have been a challenge in any situation. It was made even more difficult by rapid demographic change. Starting in the mid-1970s, Co-op City, once the beneficiary of white flight, began to suffer from it. The newly elected management floated a program of racial

4.35: Co-op City, lobby, 2014

quotas. In addition a gifted track was added to the school district. Neither effort halted the exodus. By the mid-1980s Co-op City was majority-minority: 40 percent African American and 15 percent Hispanic. Today, fewer than 10 percent of the population is white, while the rest is approximately 60 percent Black and 27 percent Hispanic.

Ironically, by the mid-1980s Co-op City began to market itself as a community that offered "city living the way it used to be," appropriating a kind of urban nostalgia anathema to its UHF founders. Although residents leaving claimed that "things had changed," new tenants, who were mostly middle-class families of color, spoke in very different terms, with many expressing the same high regard for the tight-knit community as Co-op City's first pioneers. Since the 1980s Co-op City has received hundreds of millions in additional state subsidies, including refinancing on generous terms for its extensive debt. These infusions of capital, made possible by the political sophistication (and sheer size) of the resident population acting through political representatives, allowed for major repairs including the renovation of crumbling parking garages, replacement of elevators and windows, and new landscaping. Since the late 1990s a private management company has overseen day-to-day operations providing high levels of maintenance (fig. 4.35). Commuters speeding by on the highways that divide the complex from the rest of the Bronx have little idea how attractive these spaces between the towers have become. The landscaping has matured enough to break up the vast spaces and soften uniform brick structures. Breezeways

4.36: Co-op City, library, 2014

made possible by pilotis that punch through the base of most towers create arcades that allow for views from one quadrangle to the next, reducing the bulk of the buildings at the ground plane. Community gathering spaces also thrive, chiefly as a result of the density of population and the project's comparative isolation. The neighborhood centers, with their landscaped central areas and community rooms, are alive with people (fig. 4.36). One of the larger shopping centers has also become a magnet for people from surrounding areas.

The physical renovation of the complex has been paralleled by more aggressive resident selection and recruitment by the private management company under direction of the board. New subsidies have come with requirements for the extension of below-market prices but applicants must submit to credit checks and home visits, and Section 8 Housing Choice vouchers are not accepted. Those meeting these requirements then pay from $13,000 down for a one-bedroom unit to $29,000 for a three-bedroom, with installment plans available for well-qualified buyers who lack sufficient cash for a down payment. Income ceilings remain in place, with the maximum for owners of three-bedroom units at $140,000. Monthly maintenance runs from $579 for one-bedrooms to $1,255 for threes. Although Co-op City lacks the long waiting list of other UHF projects that remain limited-equity, such as Penn South in Manhattan, vacancy rates are close to zero.

While different, perhaps, than first envisioned—certainly in terms of race and ethnicity—Co-op City remains true to the aspirations of its creators. Now as then, senior citizens sit on benches and gossip. Now as then, children play in well-manicured playgrounds in the shadows of the towers. And now as then, Co-op City remains a haven for middle and working class New Yorkers in an otherwise expensive city. ANNEMARIE SAMMARTINO

Starrett City (1976, 5,881 units, Brooklyn)

Sponsor: UHF, private developer (Starrett)
Program: Mitchell-Lama rental
Architect: Herman J. Jessor

Starrett City is the largest federally subsidized apartment complex in the country and exemplifies the determination of New York City leaders to leverage private investment for high-quality, low-cost housing in deeply troubled neighborhoods even at a time of severely diminished resources. In spite of the crisis conditions under which it emerged, Starrett became a truly successful experiment in community engineering, suggesting the transformative power of subsidized housing when planned and built to high specifications.

From the ashes of an earlier proposal, Starrett City was conceived of in the mid-1960s by the UHF as Twin Pines Village, a large-scale, limited-equity co-op of forty-six towers designed by the group's architect of choice, Herman J. Jessor (fig. 4.37). Although built on an unoccupied landfill site next to a public mental hospital overlooking Jamaica Bay, what the development avoided in controversies over clearance it faced in addressing anxieties over racial change in the age of white flight. According to the *Times* the very proposal led to a "bloody fight" among housing officials who feared that the project, like Co-op City (1968–73) in the Bronx, would wreak havoc by draining much of the rest of Brooklyn of white families.[88]

4.37: Starrett City, 2014

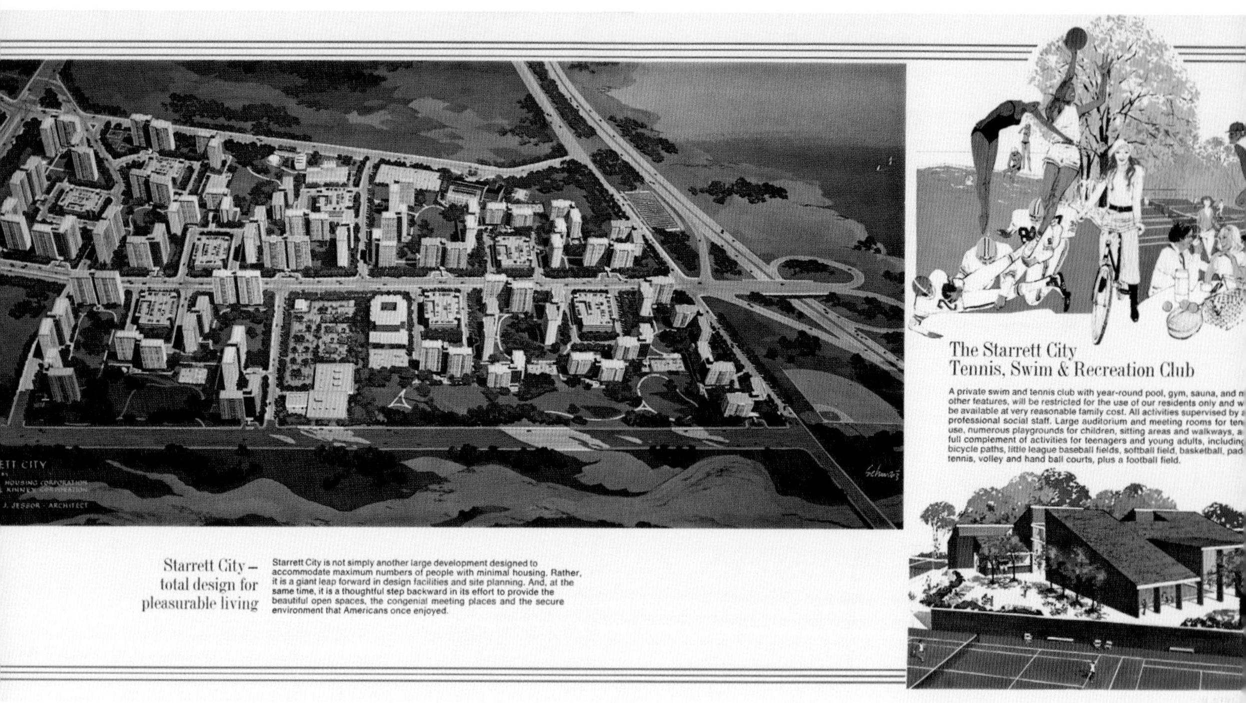

4.38: Starrett City, rental brochure, ca. 1975

While the UHF remained committed, rapidly rising costs for construction, financing, and energy, soon made its leadership skittish, especially in light of tensions surrounding similar issues at Co-op City, where struggles with the homeowners had all but bankrupted the organization. After founder and leader Abraham Kazan died, the UHF abandoned Twin Pines, selling it midway through construction in 1971 to a consortium of investors led by prolific apartment developer Robert Olnick and Kinney Construction. Olnick dispensed with the Twin Pines name, which was the symbol of the international consumers' cooperative movement, in favor of Starrett (fig. 4.38). In 1961 he had bought Starrett Brothers and Eken, one of the city's oldest contractors, and changed the name of his own company to Starrett Housing Corporation. Olnick also jettisoned the owner-occupied format, instead pursuing new subsidies for lower-income rentals, including below-market-interest-rate loans offered by the Federal Housing Administration's Section 236 program and, after 1974, Section 8 project-based funds.[89]

The shift from co-op to subsidized rental generated new controversy. To the north lay East New York, an African American neighborhood suffering tremendous disinvestment and poverty, which Starrett City's general manager watched burn from his construction trailer.[90] To the west was Canarsie, an Italian stronghold, whose homeowners feared an influx of African Americans. To assuage their concerns, management promised city leaders it would reserve 70 percent of the new units for white families.[91] Few came. But rather than rent to Black people, Starrett kept units empty while Black applicants faced long waiting lists.[92] The project remained financially solvent only through special state subsidies. Meanwhile, the owners delayed work on the northern end of the site, which abutted East New York, in favor of sections to the south, opposite from Canarsie and accessible from the Belt Parkway. To further enhance curb appeal, and at the urging of the John Lindsay administration, Jessor's utilitarian towers were dressed up with curving driveways and decorative porticos, while in lobbies Italian stone replaced easy-to-maintain tiles. Within the apartments, luxuries like dishwashers were added, albeit within reason since rental rates had to remain modest, both by virtue of the complex's location and its below-market financing.[93]

The owners, building on the UHF's plans, also aggressively added community amenities, including a recreation center with a gym, tennis courts, and indoor pool; a shopping center; and a first-class medical facility. Land was given to a Jewish congregation for a temple. Meanwhile, city officials introduced express bus service to Manhattan and permitted residents a choice of nearby public schools rather than requiring attendance at the mostly African American schools in the district. Later, on-site elementary and middle schools were added. The project was policed by a private armed security force with the power to make arrests, and safety was further enhanced with cameras and lighting. As a result, Starrett City would have one of the lowest crime rates in the city, despite its location in one of the most crime-ridden precincts.[94]

Meanwhile, the owners had to market the development heavily to recruit the requisite number of white tenants. Advertising started in local newspapers and with mailings. Management then rented a booth at a bridal fair and sponsored an Italian American festival. In 1978, a television ad aired highlighting the diversity of the community's residents, as if to emphasize to white prospects that despite the East New York address and high-rise form, it was not a low-income African American project. Copy described the middle-class neighborhood the owners envisioned: "A totally modern community that recreates the dignity and security of an earlier America."[95] Eventually these strategies worked: by late 1980, Starrett City was, at last, close to full occupancy (97 percent) and near the promised racial quota. Sixty-five percent of tenants were white, 21 percent Black, 9 percent Hispanic, and 5 percent Asian American. For fear of ethnic rivalries developing along territorial lines, management ensured that each floor of each building was racially integrated.[96]

The project's large-scale inward-facing design, extensive dedicated programming, and geographic isolation quickly helped to generate a strong sense of community. Not only did the modern towers in the park, which contrasted with the surrounding neighborhoods, foster a strong identity, but also tenants found little need to leave on a daily basis thanks to the development's extensive services. Further aiding in the community-building process was the fact that many tenants were families with children. As then-project manager Robert Rosenberg recalls, "Within a very short time, tenants, particularly the teenagers and the children, started to really integrate and play with each other and socialize."[97] Tenants also launched an array of religious, ethnic, and secular clubs. Paths and greens were occupied well into the evenings. Children enrolled in Starrett City's numerous after-school programs and applied for college scholarships offered by management.[98] Doors were often left unlocked. In short, Starrett's developers succeeded in creating a remarkably stable community governed by middle-class values despite the very modest incomes of the tenants.

This harmony earned Starrett City accolades. The policies used to achieve it, however, did not. Several lawsuits were filed to put an end to the racial quotas. The NAACP and community civil rights groups brought the first suit in 1978, followed by the U.S. Justice Department in 1984. In 1988 a federal court found Starrett City in violation of the Fair Housing Act and ordered management to abandon the quota system.[99] Taking advantage of a loophole that allowed them to give priority to applicants who were homeless, management got creative, setting up booths in Russian airports to recruit Jewish émigrés. This helped maintain the community's racial integration for many years.[100] Nevertheless, the original quota has now been inverted: today, 56 percent of residents are African American, 29 percent white, 12 percent Hispanic, and 3 percent Asian American.[101] While the project's complexion has changed, its income mix remains largely as it was originally. Sixty percent of residents live in units subsidized by the federal Section 8 program, 20 percent in units covered by Section 236, and 20 percent in units financed and still governed by Mitchell-Lama. Even the Mitchell-Lama tenants, however, earn no more than $10,000 above the maximum eligible income to qualify for Section 8—$61,850 for a three-person family. A majority of households earn below New York City's median income.[102]

Despite a lower-income residential base, Starrett City's substantial rent-rolls and good reputation have made it an appealing investment. In 2007 the complex's developers arranged to sell it to Clipper Equity for $1.3 billion. Such debt could only be managed by increasing rents, prompting concerns that Starrett City would withdraw from its subsidy programs and begin charging market rates. Amid opposition from tenants and local and state politicians, HUD exercised its authority to prevent the sale. In 2009, after Starrett City's owners began taking new bids, New York State governor David Paterson arranged to keep it in the Mitchell-Lama program for an additional thirty years by refinancing its debt.[103]

Although in these respects unchanged, life at Starrett City, whose name officially became Spring Creek Towers in 2002, is quite different from the pioneering days of the 1970s and 1980s. Back then, as at any new development tailored to families rearing children, the project was overwhelmed by energetic new residents eager to build community. Today, by contrast, it is mature, with a mixture of old households and new, at all different stages of life. Programming still runs at capacity, but the emphasis is on delivering services, mostly to youth, rather than building community. The number of resident-led clubs and organizations has declined. Many of the remaining first-generation residents, largely living in buildings now set aside for seniors, claim new tenants do not share their values.[104] Neighbors still sit on park benches, but they seem less likely to share in conversation. After sundown, the complex no longer bustles with outdoor activity. At the same time, Starrett remains true to its original mission of providing high-quality, safe, well-designed housing, attentively managed and maintained, for families at low rents. KARINA MILCHMAN

Model Gallery II: Post-World War II

The gap between low-rent public housing and privately developed below-market middle-income housing widened in the postwar era. To compete with suburban houses for the affections of middle-income families, two-bedroom apartments in private developments expanded in floor area, to as much as eleven hundred square feet. Windows also grew larger. By the late 1950s and 1960s many apartments also included private balconies and second bathrooms. In public housing, by contrast, stricter cost limitations meant units remained compact and windows small; balconies were rare. In other ways, however, both groups followed a similar course. Designers—who were often one and the same firms—employed similar materials, including inexpensive red brick for exteriors and, for interiors, asphalt-tile flooring. They also built much taller than before, replacing mid-rise walk-ups with elevator towers that reflected greater pressures to produce units in volume as well as new fashions in architecture and site planning, and generating new economies of scale. With the advent of air conditioning sponsors of middle-income housing also abandoned floor plans that permitted cross-ventilation in favor of slabs with double-loaded corridors, which allowed each unit just one exposure.

Johnson Houses

1948; 2BR = 700 square feet

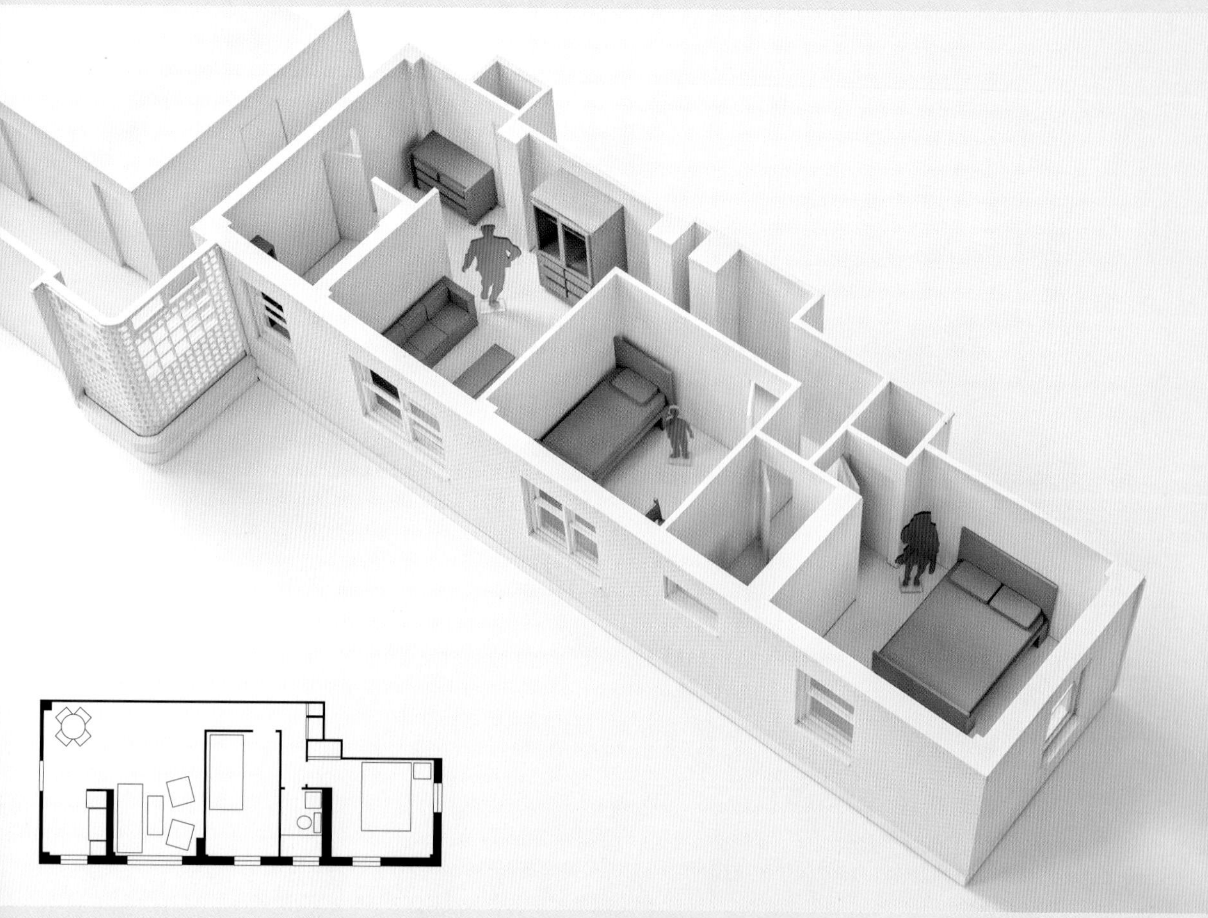

Johnson Houses is a typical NYCHA high-rise development of the postwar era. The architects updated the elongated Queensbridge configuration by moving the bathroom closer to the living room, which made it more accessible to visitors, leaving the master bedroom the only room with a second exposure. In keeping with prewar precedents and as part of the continuing positioning of public housing as the remedy for slums, all of the rooms in the complex still enjoyed ample sunlight. Yet the layout as a whole did not compare well with those of market-rate or middle-income complexes. The foyer and dining area was ill-defined and awkward, since the entry door, kitchen door, and passage to the living room interrupted it. The hallway within the unit was narrow and dark; insufficient cross ventilation made life unpleasant in summer. Families also suffered a lack of storage. Individual rooms, however, were larger than those in Queensbridge, reflecting rising standards for private space, even in low-cost housing.

Penn Station South

1958–62, 3,142 apartments; 2BR = 850 square feet

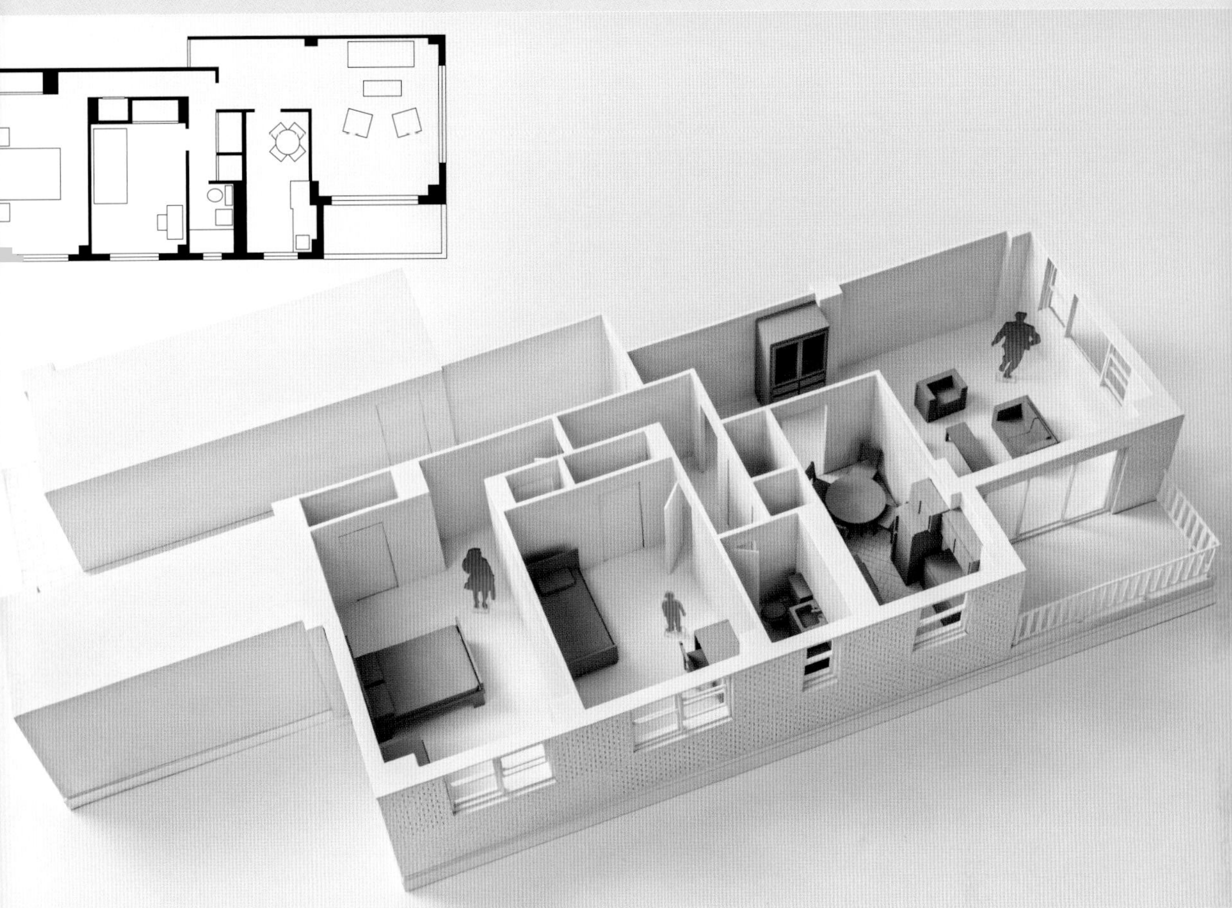

In a bid to prove housing built by and for workers could be as high in quality as that built for profit, the sponsors employed a network of small corridors to create separate zones for private and public use. An oversize foyer doubled as a dining area between the entry and kitchen and the living room, whose dimensions recalled those of some prewar market-rate apartments and accommodated grouped seating and bookcases. The living room also opened to a large balcony through floor-to-ceiling glass doors, offering ample sunlight and fresh air despite the lack of cross ventilation (central air conditioning kept apartments comfortable in summer). Grouping the bathroom and kitchen allowed for efficient distribution of building services, while placing the bathroom off its own small corridor helped further divide private and public zones. Bedrooms were placed down a corridor off the opposite side of the foyer, separated from the living areas by the bathroom and kitchen. MATTHIAS ALTWICKER, MATTHEW GORDON LASNER, AND NICHOLAS BLOOM

5

Housing Reimagined

Postwar New York City developed not only the largest low- and middle-income below-market housing programs in the country but among the greatest number of experimental developments, especially during the administrations of New York's liberal Republican leaders Mayor John Lindsay (1966–73) and Governor Nelson Rockefeller (1959–73). Confronted with a deepening urban crisis—white flight, poverty, and abandonment—but also lingering 1960s-era optimism about the power of the state to remedy inequality, leaders remained committed to the idea that government-subsidized housing was essential to the social and economic health of the city. But following increasingly loud critiques by displaced residents, they recognized that in the rush to build and rebuild in the two decades after World War II, quantity had often become more important than quality. To address these issues, and to ensure future support for below-market subsidized housing, strategies evolved. The result was a new sensitivity to surrounding neighborhoods, a reluctance to displace site residents, and a proliferation of new physical forms and development models (fig. 5.1).

5.1: Twin Parks NW, ca. 1973

The search for innovation in below-market subsidized housing had several roots. As early as the 1940s and 1950s

5.2: Easter Hill Village, ca. 1953

other U.S. cities experimented with redevelopment models quite distinct from New York's. In the Bay Area, planners and architects mixed housing types in redevelopment areas, including mid-rise courtyard buildings and row houses that recalled local vernacular types. Even public housing, like Easter Hill Village (1953) in the East Bay city of Richmond, reflected these ideas. Rather than monolithic towers, the housing authority built clusters of staggered row houses, each with a unique color and trim, many with a front porch and rear yard (fig. 5.2).[1] Chicago, despite its ghastly record in public housing, was also a pioneer in urban redevelopment that responded to human needs. In the late 1940s it established two designations: "blighted" areas targeted for demolition and "conservation" areas, where the city worked to foster incremental improvement including "spot" clearance. Illinois' Urban Community Conservation Act of 1953, which embraced the new approach, served as a partial model for 1954 revisions to the National Housing Act that replaced the federal Slum Clearance and Urban Redevelopment Administration with one for "Urban Renewal," opening the possibility for more sensitive approaches. Many struggling neighborhoods welcomed it as a path to stability without displacement.[2]

In New York, Robert Moses remained dedicated to the totalizing project but by the late 1950s major cracks had appeared in his redevelopment machine. Questions arose about the quality of life in tower block projects, irregularities and delays in Title I redevelopments, and the social and economic costs of relocation for both residents and small businesses. Title I projects like the West Side Urban Renewal Area, announced in 1956, attempted to emulate the Chicago approach with a mixture of selective clearance for new, mixed-income tower blocks, blended with renovation and reconstruction of many of the neighborhood's brownstone row houses and better-built apartment houses (fig. 5.3).

5.3: City of New York, Housing and Redevelopment Board, "West Side Urban Renewal Area: A Summary of the Final Plan," ca. 1959

Jane Jacobs proffered an even more potent and transformative critique of New York's program of housing and urban renewal. A transplant from Pennsylvania charmed by the gaslamp-era ambiance of neighborhoods like Greenwich Village, where she bought a row house, and the street-oriented lifestyles of its remaining working-class inhabitants, she relentlessly attacked the city's below-market subsidized housing programs for violating her idea of the good city. She questioned the notion that blight could be eliminated when it was clear that new slums were still forming, often as a direct result of displacement by aggressive redevelopment programs that pushed slum conditions around without eliminating underlying causes. More fundamentally she questioned the very idea of "slum," arguing that the formulation overlooked many positive attributes of older working-class neighborhoods (fig. 5.4). She also cast doubt upon the

5.4: Street market before clearance for Mayor John F. Hylan Houses, Bushwick, Brooklyn, 1956

value of unchecked planning and progress. The city had a certain order, she argued ("lively and interesting" "continuous" streets; corner stores) and large-scale redevelopment ("concoctions grafted into cities") stood in opposition to it.[3] She targeted tower developments like Morningside Gardens (1957) as exemplary of the flawed logic of urban redevelopment. Her writing also legitimized inchoate concerns that many others harbored about renewal. Though attacked by some for being biased, dismissive, and, at times, wrong, her voice galvanized surging interest in historic preservation and "brownstoning." As one architect and planner wrote, "Jacobs says out loud what many of us have been saying under our bad breaths."[4]

Canadian architect Oscar Newman, writing a few years later, refined these sentiments further, arguing that Modernist planning actually caused dysfunction. Rather than see success in the reconstruction of the city, the stabilization of neighborhoods, and the improvement of material conditions for the poor, Newman discerned failure. Lost with the old tenements, he believed, was the essential vibrancy of city neighborhoods. Where life once poured out of apartments into streets and shops, and neighbors and shopkeepers kept an eye on each other, now stood unimaginative towers set in underprogrammed green spaces. Gone were children playing in traffic. But gone, too, was a sense of community. Where reformers of earlier generations saw triumph in rational planning, postmodern critics, nostalgic for the rapidly vanishing white-ethnic city neighborhood, saw pathology. In his writings, Newman offered a recipe for "defensible space," which, like Jacobs' ideal neighborhood, usually included small-scale, low-rise buildings arranged like row houses, with direct visual connections between each home and the street. He developed a lucrative practice selling this idea, winning commissions throughout North America and beyond to redesign public housing developments, including some of NYCHA's.

Critics of Jacobs and Newman like Columbia University sociologist and urban planner Herbert Gans countered that these approaches represented a "fallacy of physical determinism." Gans excoriated Jacob's view of the city for being shaped by a romantic view of working-class life that ignored both harsher realities and longer-term neighborhood decline. He had even less patience for what he considered to be the "superficial" diversity Jacobs celebrated. Yet the agendas that Jacobs and Newman argued in best-selling books and repeated widely in academic and popular circles proved powerful, and were as widely embraced by left-leaning reformers and right-wing critics as they were by architects and planners.[5]

Evolution of national policies also contributed to experimentation in below-market subsidized housing in the 1960s and 1970s. Social problems in low-rent public housing stemming from entrenched racialized poverty and the decentralization of industrial employment, coupled with underfunding of maintenance and services, took a heavy toll on many projects, especially in other cities that lacked New York's commitment to, and aptitude for, maintenance. By the 1960s "the projects" in most places came to be characterized by crime and dysfunction, serving as warehouses for the chronically poor living on public assistance. For better or worse the very concept of public housing came to be indelibly linked with dilapidated and dangerous towers-in-the-park. Housing authorities and the federal government began to think of these communities as "distressed" and, eventually, unsalvageable. In 1972 St. Louis razed a first section of its sixteen-year-old Pruitt-Igoe high-rises (1956), setting a precedent most big

5.5: Central Brooklyn Model Cities Mobile Homes, Brownsville, by William E. Sauro, 1971

American cities would follow over the next half-century. The one bright spot seemed to be a few recent "vest pocket" complexes, including several built with funds from the Model Cities Program, announced in 1966 as a federal grants program that aimed to put the poor at the helm of renewal efforts in designated zones.

Under President Nixon, HUD attempted to address the problems in public housing in several ways. It encouraged housing authorities to reduce the scale of complexes. It decentralized production through programs like "turnkey" development, which allowed housing authorities to buy new buildings that had been developed privately with federal financing. And it sponsored experimental programs in manufactured housing, including a prefabricated renovation program on the Lower East Side and a trailer park in central Brooklyn (fig. 5.5, fig. 5.6). Further opportunity to reenvision low-income housing came with a federal moratorium on new expenditures in public housing and urban renewal in 1973, introduced as part of range of freezes and price controls Nixon used to address steep inflation. Public housing, in particular, had long been a target of conservative opposition, so the moratorium had political undertones. The Community Development Act of 1974, which replaced the older programs,

5.6: HUD Instant Rehabilitation demonstration project, 533–37 E. 5th St., Manhattan, 1967

substituted direct funding for urban renewal and public housing with block grants that cities could use at their discretion. Section 8 of the bill also made permanent a housing choice voucher program.

The voucher program brought major changes to below-market housing nationally and locally. First discussed in the 1930s and experimented with in the mid-1960s, vouchers helped qualifying households pay for private market-rate housing. Recipients paid a set share of household income (25, and later 30 percent) in rent and the local housing authority covered the balance, within defined limits, using federal grants. The program was popular among liberals and conservatives. On the right it appealed because it wrested control over planning and production of housing from the state and empowered private developers. On the left it appealed to critics who believed public housing caused too much displacement, eliminated too much existing housing, and was inefficient because new construction, especially on clearance sites, was very expensive. The voucher system also appealed to many civil rights advocates because it addressed growing concerns about the concentration of racialized poverty, especially in public housing. In the mid-1960s a group of Black public housing tenants in Chicago had filed suit against the city claiming it had used redevelopment to sequester African Americans. Vouchers were the remedy and the program quickly was expanded to other cities in the run-up to the 1974 law.[6]

Private landlords with empty apartments proved to be reliable partners in the voucher program. So, too, were private builders. Until cancelled by President Reagan in the early 1980s, Section 8 also allowed cities to channel funding to private developers to build dedicated "project-based" complexes that they then rented out on the voucher system. Tens of thousands of apartments were built under the program in New York and other cities. Vouchers also proved an important ingredient in preserving existing buildings, including many below-market middle-income developments that had initially failed to attract tenants. Were it not for vouchers these buildings, including many Mitchell-Lamas, would have ended up in foreclosure.

The decentralized nature of Section 8 tends to leave it out of most accounts of New York City's renaissance since the 1970s. But this oversight fails to acknowledge its crucial role. Although now closed in New York to new applicants because of drastic federal cuts, in 2015 NYCHA still supervised over 91,000 private apartments, owned by more than 29,000 landlords, with over 220,000 residents in its voucher program. The city's Department of Housing Preservation and Development (HPD) supervised an additional 33,000 units. Although most voucher units were in older buildings and poor neighborhoods, residents have rated their apartments and surroundings highly.[7]

Innovation in housing in New York also benefited in this era from a unique entity: the Urban Development Corporation (UDC). Created after urban rioting in 1967 and 1968 by Governor Rockefeller to burnish his humanitarian credentials before a planned run for the presidency, UDC quickly became a primary force for experimentation in housing and community design, making $6 billion ($40 billion in 2013 dollars) available for transformation of slums, mainly through private rebuilding using subsidized mortgages (fig. 5.7).[8] Before fiscal austerity and inflation forced UDC to shut down in the mid-1970s, the agency became a key force in the development of thirty-two projects with approximately 33,000 units. Most were in New York City. Led by Edward J. Logue, the former redevelopment director of New Haven and Boston,

5.7: Ed Logue, right, and Nelson Rockefeller, center, groundbreaking, UDC housing in Buffalo, ca. 1970

the focus was on innovative, mixed-use, and mixed-income subsidized complexes that were large enough to transform their neighborhoods. The state legislature approved of the program, rather symbolically, on the evening of the Rev. Dr. Martin Luther King, Jr.'s funeral in 1968. Rockefeller chose Logue because of his reputation for big thinking and getting things done. The governor bestowed upon the agency power of eminent domain, exemption from local zoning, and the ability to sell bonds to fund its operation, backed by the full faith and credit of the state. Rockefeller left no doubt about his agenda: "We are running a social institution trying to help people."[9]

Mayor John Lindsay, despite misgivings about UDC's broad powers, recognized the agency as a crucial source of funding and invited it to work in designated city urban renewal and Model Cities areas. Lindsay, however, insisted that city agencies plan the developments, acquire the land, relocate the tenants, and demolish the buildings. UDC would then hire architects (with the city's approval), pay legal fees, and build the housing, which would then be sold to private developers or NYCHA.[10] Despite this support and the power to clear neighborhoods, however, most UDC projects rose on empty sites in order to minimize displacement.

Under Logue's leadership UDC emphasized creative design, often partnering with pedigreed architects such as Richard Meier (Twin Park Northeast, 1976), Kenneth Frampton (Marcus Garvey Village, 1976), Philip Johnson (the Roosevelt Island master plan, 1969), Josep Lluís Sert (Eastwood, 1976; Westview, 1976), and John Johansen (Island House, 1975; Rivercross, 1976). Logue's design lieutenant, architect Theodore Liebman, staged architectural competitions, soliciting proposals (unbuilt) from designers like Rem Koolhaas. This emphasis on innovative form was part of an emerging strategy, both in the United States and Europe, to better tailor redevelopment and housing to the needs of the user. By way of research Logue and his staff even spent the night in select UDC projects. The idea was "to give people who were doing the planning a better appreciation of how a project functioned, what people wanted, what it felt like to live there."[11]

The leading example of UDC's approach was Roosevelt Island. Planning and construction of large-scale new communities, or garden cities, began as a tool of urban reform in Europe in the early twentieth century but grew slowly until government entered the picture. By the late 1940s and 1950s updated Modernist versions, now known as new towns, became a hallmark of state-led, social democratic development throughout Western Europe. European planners aimed to rehouse urban workers, reduce social conflict, and contain suburban sprawl by channeling urban growth into planned, multipurpose communities that provided a balanced mixture of social classes, housing, industry, retail, and recreation. In the

United States, by contrast, New Deal experiments with this approach proved controversial and most faltered. After World War II it became clear that without strong centralized government like in Europe, metropolitan development would remain fragmented. But as critiques of incremental suburban development mounted in the 1950s and the scale and capacity of real estate development grew, a new homegrown trend called master-planning emerged, beginning with the Irvine Ranch in Orange County, California, in the late 1950s. In the early 1960s progressive developers James Rouse and Robert E. Simon, sponsors, respectively, of Columbia, Maryland, and Reston, Virginia, imported the model to the East Coast. Although these and other U.S. new towns struggled financially, by the end of the decade the federal government had come to support the idea with a New Communities program; some builders even began to conceive of applying the model to sites in cities. Roosevelt Island was the first in-town project to participate in the HUD program and the most extensively developed.[12]

Welfare Island, as it was once known, had for over a century been a dumping ground for institutions that housed the prisoners and the dangerously ill. The new Roosevelt Island as envisioned by Logue would not only be architecturally innovative but would stand in contrast to the racial and income segregation of both the region as a whole and the below-market subsidized housing of the past. Roosevelt Island would be a socially and economically integrated community of eighteen thousand people who would "live harmoniously and send their children to the same schools."[13] Influenced by the aestheticizing arguments of Jacobs and other critics of Modernism, UDC rejected tall, freestanding towers, landscaped superblocks, and shopping centers with off-street parking in favor of a site plan centering on a shopping street (albeit one with very little traffic, since private cars were prohibited) (fig. 5.8). After decades

5.8: Ed Logue, Roosevelt Island, n.d.

of working to separate children from unregulated street life, Johnson and Burgee placed Main Street at the heart of Roosevelt Island, foreshadowing the neotraditional planning of Battery Park City and the New Urbanism in the 1980s.[14]

Other UDC projects including Twin Parks East and West (1976) in the Bronx and Marcus Garvey Village (1976) in Brooklyn also reimagined the relationship between the home and the street. Targeted to lower-income families, financed with a combination of UDC money and below-market federal loans, and sold upon completion to private operators, they offered poor New Yorkers appealing new housing options. Unfortunately, the social outcomes rarely matched the initial idealism. Moreover, unlike in low-income public projects managed by NYCHA or built under the authority of the Mitchell-Lama program, many developments suffered from lackluster management.[15] Efforts to maintain buildings were undermined by rising costs in an inflationary economy, coupled with stagnant tenant income. Especially challenging were innovative designs that saved money in construction like superbricks, electric heating, and unique windows, but that were expensive to maintain. Cloistered courtyards intended to counter the limitations of sprawling superblock lawns were also a problem, inviting antisocial behaviors. These issues were not unique to UDC but were common to many of the privately built, below-market projects developed with federal aid in this era. From Boston to the Bay Area, in fact, between 20 and 30 percent of such projects ended up being foreclosed upon.

Some of the troubles at UDC complexes were specific, however, and can be traced to Logue's ambitions. Logue's UDC became so aggressive that at one point it had commanded half the funds nationwide in one of the federal government's main below-market housing programs. Logue became notorious for starting three developments when he only had the money in hand for one. Facing the 1973 federal moratorium on housing funds he was left with a dangerous gap between his commitments and actual federal contracts. Nelson Rockefeller's rise to the vice presidency in 1974 also removed Logue's key supporter in Albany. Operating costs in some UDC developments already exceeded tenant incomes; now skeptical financiers forced UDC to pay high interest rates on its growing obligations. In 1975 UDC sank under $1 billion in debt and defaulted on millions of dollars. Logue resigned.[16]

The efforts of UDC and other builders to rethink below-market design represented, in retrospect, a last attempt to salvage the bruised reputation of large-scale, state-subsidized housing in the United States. The results were clearly mixed. As a consequence, the below-market subsidized housing that emerged after the reorganizations of the mid-1970s rarely shared the grand ambitions of Logue and Lindsay. The hold of Modernist planning formulas on large-scale development was broken. In its stead came not new avant-gardes but a retreat to nostalgia: postmodernism in the 1980s and the New Urbanism in the 1990s. Nevertheless, despite the limitations of the experiments of the 1960s and 1970s, in the long term residents came to appreciate the unique apartments and public spaces, which have few equivalents. Today the greatest threat to these distinctive complexes, at least in New York City, may well be their success, as more and more convert to market-rate housing.

West Side Urban Renewal Area (1950s–1980s, Manhattan)

Sponsor: Title I, NYCHA, private nonprofit (Strycker's Bay Neighborhood Council), others
Program: public housing, private rental, limited-equity co-op, homeownership
Architect: various

The West Side Urban Renewal Area (WSURA) marked a significant shift in New York City's approach to housing and redevelopment. Proposed by City Planning Commissioner James Felt in 1955 as an alternative to the dominant model of slum clearance practiced by Robert Moses's Committee on Slum Clearance, the WSURA prescribed instead a combination of targeted redevelopment, residential rehabilitation, and the conservation of the neighborhood's existing housing stock (fig. 5.9). In the terminology of the period, it was a plan for "urban renewal" rather than "urban redevelopment," drawing on the new tools and techniques available through the National Housing Act of 1954.

New York was one of a number of cities reconsidering housing and urban renewal policies in the mid- to late 1950s. Large-scale clearance projects were coming under fire and both planners and politicians had begun to look for alternative approaches that would help them reverse the decline of city neighborhoods without bulldozing them entirely. Some projects, like Society Hill in Philadelphia or Wooster Square in New Haven, emphasized the preservation of historic architecture; others, like Hyde-Park Kenwood in Chicago, focused on citizen participation in the planning process. On the Upper West Side, the city aimed to maintain racial and economic balance in one of New York's diverse neighborhoods though a range of affordable and market-rate housing options.[17]

The WSURA encompassed twenty city blocks stretching from West 87th Street to West 97th Street and from Central Park West to Amsterdam Avenue.[18] This part of the Upper West Side was going through a transition in the 1950s, attracting Black and Puerto Rican families displaced from nearby redevelopment projects while losing middle- and working-class Jewish and Irish residents to the outer boroughs and the suburbs. Upper middle-class professionals continued to move into the well-maintained apartment buildings along Central Park, but much of the rest of the housing stock in the area was deteriorating due to neglect and overcrowding, including the old-law tenements lining Columbus and Amsterdam Avenues and the brownstones on the side streets.

5.9: WSURA, looking north toward W. 88th St., by Fred R. Conrad, 1980

A team of planners, social workers, and economists descended on the urban renewal area in 1956 to assess the feasibility of Felt's idea. The resulting 1958 report, entitled simply *Urban Renewal*, offered a vision of what the neighborhood could become—indeed, what another model of urban renewal in New York might look like. *Urban Renewal* recommended retaining the existing street grid and limiting clearance to sites along Columbus and Amsterdam Avenues, where some of the oldest tenements were located. High-rise housing and public plazas would be constructed here, and most of the brownstones along the side streets were slated for extensive rehabilitation (fig. 5.10). Code enforcement and federally insured loans for rehabilitation would spark reinvestment in the area. In fact, Felt, confident of the catalytic potential of urban renewal, had spoken of the plan as one that required a "minimum of government subsidy."[19]

5.10: WSURA, model, ca. 1961

A range of housing options lay at the heart of the plan. With different types of financing, the report explained, the plan could accommodate everything from low-income public housing to middle-income rentals and limited-equity cooperatives to market-rate, privately financed apartments. This range would help the neighborhood achieve a "racial and economic balance," something that seemed increasingly elusive in a racially and economically segregated city. In keeping with its promise to renew the neighborhood for those who already lived there, *Urban Renewal* recommended meaningful citizen participation in the planning process, the construction of public housing within—rather than adjacent, as was done typically—the Title I renewal area to house relocated families, and phasing redevelopment and rehabilitation to minimize the hardships of displacement and construction.[20]

Shortly after the report's release, Mayor Robert F. Wagner, Jr., established the Urban Renewal Board (URB) to develop a plan and execute the project, with leadership drawn from the City Planning Commission and NYCHA. The URB, which operated concurrently with Robert Moses's Committee on Slum Clearance, worked with a citizens' committee organized for this purpose, the Strycker's Bay Neighborhood Council (SBNC). This group shared the URB's commitment to a racially and economically balanced neighborhood but objected vociferously to the specifics of the Preliminary Plan when it was released in 1959. Despite the city's pledge to renew the neighborhood for existing residents, the breakdown of allocated housing was heavily skewed toward market-rate housing unaffordable to most current residents. Of 7,800 projected new units of housing, only 400 would be low-rent public housing, while 2,400 would be moderate-income units built with public subsidy and a full 5,000 would be market rate. Fifty-eight hundred households faced relocation—a figure almost double initial estimates. Fearing disruption on the scale of one of Moses's traditional slum-clearance projects, the SBNC rethought its mission. Rather than acting as an impartial representative of the area's residents or a pro forma group for consultation, it became an outspoken advocate for the poor and an active force determining the direction of the project. Father Henry Browne, a priest at St. Gregory's

5.11: WSURA, Father Henry J. Browne at SBNC meeting, from City of New York, Housing and Redevelopment Board, "West Side Urban Renewal Area: A Summary of the Final Plan," ca. 1959

Church in the WSURA, emerged as its leader, spearheading a campaign to mitigate the effects of relocation and increase the number of housing units available to both low- and moderate-income residents (fig. 5.11).[21]

During community meetings and public hearings on the Preliminary Plan in 1959 and then again on the Final Plan in 1962, community opposition transformed the city's goals. Facing active opposition, the planning commission promised greater attention to the relocation process for small businesses and altered the proportion of low- and middle-income housing units—first to 600 low-income, 3,600 moderate-income, and 3,600 market rate units, then to 1,000, 4,200, and 2,800, respectively and finally, after a protest over the Final Plan that required Mayor Wagner's intervention, to 2,500, 4,900, and 2,000. Felt's initial plans for market-driven change had given way to a plan that aimed to use a variety of state and federal subsidies to provide an unprecedented range of housing options for West Side residents.

NYCHA was the first to develop new housing in the area. Following the basic idea of the plan, it broke with its superblock design tradition. The area's first redevelopment project, Wise Towers, a 399-unit, nineteen-story set of two towers located midblock on one of the side streets, opened in January 1965. Father Browne and the SBNC also worked with NYCHA to construct what they called "human-scale" housing. The resulting vest-pocket project, one of the city's first, opened in 1965. Known only by its street address, the nine-story, 70-unit brick building faced directly onto one of the side streets, virtually indistinguishable from the surrounding housing. In keeping with the plan's emphasis on brownstone rehabilitation, NYCHA also bought four contiguous row houses and rehabilitated them as a single structure with forty low-income apartments (fig. 5.12). Building on the success of this first project, NYCHA ultimately took over an additional thirty-six tenement rooming houses, converting them to 236 units of public housing.[22]

Much of the WSURA's moderate-income housing was constructed in high-rise buildings along Columbus and Amsterdam Avenues using Mitchell-Lama funds. The limited-dividend sponsorship requirement attracted organizations with strong social agendas that helped develop a culture of cooperative living on the avenues. These sponsors actively sought displaced residents, applicants who favored renewal and racial integration, and families. Indeed, several of the developers opted to build units with three and four bedrooms, intended to appeal to families who might otherwise move to the suburbs. The first of the high-rise housing developments—the Goddard Tower, Strycker's Bay Apartments, RNA House, and Columbus Park Towers limited-equity co-ops—opened in the spring of 1967. Because of their high density and their tight budgets, carefully calculated to yield the lowest possible cost

5.12: WSURA, row houses owned and renovated by NYCHA, 131 W. 92nd St., ca. 1962

per room, they were architecturally modest. At twenty-seven stories, they were also massive, towering over nearby brownstones and prewar elevator buildings.[23]

These first projects set the tone for further development along the avenues. When demand for market-rate housing proved weak, the Housing and Redevelopment Board—the successor to both the mayor's Committee on Slum Clearance and URB—began to amend the plan to redesignate sites for moderate-income housing. By the end of the 1960s almost all of the new development was limited-profit housing, some funded through Mitchell-Lama and some funded through federal programs. Each of these middle-income developments also contained a designated number of "skewed rental" units available to qualified families at public housing rates, further diversifying the housing in the area. Under this program, monthly rentals or maintenance charges for 80 percent of units were "skewed" up so that the remaining apartments could be offered at costs comparable to public housing. This formula was used throughout WSURA until 1970, when it was revised so that 70 percent of units were skewed up and 30 percent down.[24]

Brownstone rehabilitation progressed more slowly. The city, which had initially conceived of the brownstones as a moderate-income housing resource, encouraged tenant-financed renovation achieved by simultaneous conversion of buildings to small cooperative apartment houses. To facilitate the process, the city bought contiguous brownstones and offered groups of three and four for sale as packages. Despite an ambitious demonstration project along West 94th and West 95th Streets and a few experiments by investors, however, the idea failed to gain traction. Ultimately, individual families who negotiated purchase of houses privately carried out the majority of row house rehabilitation in the WSURA.

By the late 1960s and early 1970s the West Side's support for a racially and economically integrated neighborhood had frayed. A decade of city-led redevelopment along Columbus Avenue and private brownstone rehabilitation along the side streets had displaced thousands of low-income residents, and rising construction costs and interest rates made newer subsidized projects significantly more expensive, even at below-market prices. Frustration over displacement and the scarcity of low-income housing sparked a city-wide squatting movement in the spring of 1970. Although squatters in this era occupied buildings from Morningside Heights to the Lower East Side, the movement was centered on the condemned brownstones and tenements of the Upper West Side Title I project. The organizers of a new group called Operation Move-in, including West Side residents, Puerto Rican activists, and anti-poverty workers, selected as their headquarters a condemned old-law tenement on Columbus Avenue slated for public housing known as Site 30. There, they protested the demolition of structurally sound buildings, called for immediate shelter for homeless families rather than further planning or redevelopment, and demanded their inclusion in the city's relocation caseload.[25]

The squatters' movement galvanized a group of brownstone owners, tenants, and small business owners calling themselves the Committee of Neighbors to Insure a Normal Urban Environment (CONTINUE), which was concerned that too much low-income housing would take the neighborhood past a "tipping point" and discourage private investment in a district that was just beginning to turn around. Instead, CONTINUE argued, the city should be building market-rate housing and accommodating a limited number of low-income residents in skewed units within those projects—a new idea at the time. Their suit to halt the construction of public housing on Site 30, the center of the squatters' movement, held up construction on that site until the 1980s.

The Nixon administration's moratorium on the construction of subsidized housing ended the deadlock between CONTINUE and advocates of-low income housing. Yet, as a result, more than a dozen redevelopment parcels were left to languish empty for years. Vendors sold Christmas trees on Site 30, and neighbors established a community garden on a nearby undeveloped site. By the mid-1970s many of the moderate-income buildings in the area dramatically increased monthly payments—some more than doubling—and residents began to stage rent strikes. Meanwhile, market-driven gentrification continued to cause displacement at the southern end of the project.

In 1980 the Reagan administration decided that market-rate construction could begin on all remaining redevelopment sites without any reference to the original public housing commitment, and the project was closed out in 1981. New design guidelines accompanying a fifth amendment to the plan in 1977 introduced more buildings with ground-floor retail and lower densities, aligning with the urban values that Jane Jacobs had advocated in the 1960s. As the West Side gentrified in the late 1980s and 1990s, the final sites were developed, some entirely as market-rate housing, some with a mixture of market-rate and subsidized units.

The WSURA's legacy is complex. Between redevelopment on the avenues and the gentrification of the side streets, the scale of intervention was vast; one observer of the project estimated that thirteen thousand people, one-third of the area's total population, had been displaced between 1960 and 1970. Only a fraction returned. But if the relocation process failed the neighborhood, the project succeeded in other ways. It demonstrated the potential for community groups to guide the development process, the ability of the city to implement a variety of housing programs in a single neighborhood, and the power of activists to gain racial and economic inclusivity. With its high-rise housing on Columbus Avenue, scattered public housing projects, and rehabilitated brownstones, the WSURA retains a remarkably wide array of housing options that blend seamlessly into the rest of neighborhood and that remain popular today.[26] JENNIFER HOCK

Jane Jacobs (1916–2006)

Jane Jacobs was a key figure in postwar debates on public housing and urban renewal, a writer and an activist whose appreciation of older city center neighborhoods helped transform the way we think about urban space. At a time when planners and politicians were eager to rebuild aging cities, Jacobs argued that density and diversity of buildings and people—both signs of obsolescence in the eyes of the postwar planners—were in fact cities' greatest strength. In an era of high rises, superblocks, and expressways, she celebrated the sidewalk and the street as the building blocks of socially and economically viable neighborhoods and urban districts. Her popular writings signaled a new approach to housing and planning that emphasized context, participation, and small-scale, incremental change.[27]

Jacobs is closely associated with New York City, where she lived and worked for more than thirty years (fig. 5.13). A native of Scranton, Pennsylvania, where she got her start in journalism at the age of seventeen, Jacobs moved to New York in 1934 and wrote for several trade magazines before finding a position as an editor at *Architectural Forum* in 1952. Working at the *Forum* at a time when cities were tearing down older neighborhoods for public housing, redevelopment projects, and infrastructure, she found herself increasingly skeptical about the claims that architects and planners made about the value of these new spaces. Projects like Gateway Center in Pittsburgh, Penn Center in Philadelphia, and Stuyvesant Town in New York, not to mention vast tracts of public housing in East Harlem, seemed to establish a monumental formal order at the expense of economic vitality and social life.[28]

5.13: Jane Jacobs, meeting of the Committee to Save the West Village, by Phil Stanziola, 1961

She also encountered the disruption of postwar planning closer to home, in Greenwich Village, where she and her husband, the architect Robert Hyde Jacobs, had owned a house on Hudson Street since 1947. Alongside Village activists, the couple fought plans to open Washington Square to traffic and to widen Hudson Street. To Jacobs, the city's proposals invariably threatened the very things that made her neighborhood appealing: the small scale, the mixture of stores and houses and cars and pedestrians, and the broad expanses of sidewalk that accommodated a multitude of activities. Generations of reformers, including Mary Simkhovitch at Greenwich House, had associated these qualities with slums; Jacobs believed they made a good neighborhood.

Jacobs's *The Death and Life of Great American Cities*, written on a leave of absence from *Architectural Forum* and published in 1961, billed itself as "an attack on current city planning and rebuilding."[29] Planned change, Jacobs argued, was ineffective as a top-down proposition; cities grew best organically, developing a fine-grain complexity and diversity that housing and renewal schemes could not replace. The kind of money that accompanied these programs was "cataclysmic," effecting large-scale, unsustainable change where, instead, neighborhoods needed to grow slowly and incrementally. Criticism of public housing and redevelopment programs was not new, but Jacobs was among the first to attack these liberal programs from the left, arguing that they hurt the very residents that they were intended to help.[30]

Her view of public housing was particularly grim. Drawing on research conducted by social workers in East Harlem, she pointed out that the clearance and assembly of dozens of blocks of tenements had not only displaced tens of thousands of residents, but it also had decimated the local economy by condemning thousands of small businesses. Where an older generation of housers like Simkhovitch believed that modern high-rise housing set in superblocks would form the basis of a new community—and that blight could be stemmed only by creating neighborhoods large enough to stave off future encroachment and eradicating all traces of the old—Jacobs observed extreme income segregation, few local job prospects, and ill-defined common areas that seemed destined to attract crime. She also objected strongly to the way that public housing, developed and managed outside the larger housing market, isolated and stigmatized its inhabitants. "It is wrong to set one part of the population, segregated by income, apart in its own neighborhoods with its own different scheme of community," she wrote. "Separate but equal makes nothing but trouble."[31]

Instead, in a foreshadowing of the housing voucher program that emerged in the late 1960s and 1970s, she proposed a system of portable rent supplements that could be used in a variety of buildings, old and new, as well as a program of new guaranteed-rent apartment buildings that would encourage the construction of new housing by the private sector and privatize the development of low-income housing.

Death and Life was also distinguished from other writing of its era by its clear vision of what planners overlooked in their rush to modernize: the very qualities that made existing neighborhoods and cities work well. Greenwich Village had taught Jacobs the value of short blocks, older buildings, and mixed uses, all of which generated social, economic, and visual diversity. She also emphasized how, in her experience, high densities sustained the city's underlying social order, including neighborly trust. She was critical of Modernism's "doctrine of salvation by bricks": the assumption that new housing would lead to improved social conditions, which she branded paternalistic. She dismissed purely formal, architectural solutions, but her vivid descriptions of the Village's small scale, welcoming storefronts, and bustling sidewalks, and her insistence that social and economic diversity were closely linked to urban form, suggested that nineteenth-century tenements and sidewalks offered an antidote to Modernism.

Written just as the first "brownstoners" were moving into the Upper West Side, Chelsea, and Park Slope, and as popular critiques of postwar suburbia reached the national press, *Death and Life* marked the beginning of a middle-class back-to-the-city movement that continues today. Many of the key concepts behind housing and redevelopment legislation of the 1930s and 1940s had been formulated by previous generations of activists who had watched the middle class depart for the suburbs while immigrants were trapped in substandard housing in working-class districts. To these men and women, only government intervention would reverse the process of slum formation.[32] Writing at a time of economic expansion, Jacobs assumed instead that cities contained the seeds of their own regeneration. In thriving neighborhoods like her own, or Boston's North End, she saw evidence of a spontaneous self-organization that would help aging working-class neighborhoods gradually "unslum" themselves. Like the early brownstoners, she saw the value in old tenements and row houses that could be rehabilitated.

Shortly after the publication of *Death and Life,* Jacobs left her job at *Architectural Forum.* By the early 1960s she had become a public figure in New York, as well known for her activism as her writing. Even as *Death and Life* was in press, the West Village was threatened by an urban renewal designation that Jacobs and her neighbors defeated by demonstrating that the West Village was not, by any measure, a slum. More battles, large and small, followed. She was involved in many 1960s-era protests including those against the Lower Manhattan Expressway, the destruction of Penn Station, and the Vietnam War. With two sons facing the draft in 1968, Jacobs and her family moved to Toronto, where she remained active in local planning politics.[33]

Jacobs's hostility toward the planning profession is very much a product of the 1950s and 1960s, and her unshakeable faith in neighborly trust in public places and the self-regulating, regenerative qualities of cities can seem naïve. Gentrification has eroded the diversity that she observed in successful neighborhoods like Greenwich Village, and racism has concentrated poverty in neighborhoods that are unlikely to spontaneously "unslum." But her ideas remain relevant today. Her advocacy of diversity—a mixture of buildings old and new, a range of uses and activities and schedules, "so many people . . . so close together, and among them . . . so many different tastes, skills, needs, supplies, and bees in their bonnets"—has inspired many, including preservationists, developers, community activists, and policymakers.[34] Her greatest contribution may be her emphasis on participation and local knowledge. In a period obsessed with the abstractions of physical modernization, Jacobs urged her readers to look around rather than accept the advice of experts, a suggestion that still resonates today. JENNIFER HOCK

West Village Houses (1974, 420 units, Manhattan)

Sponsor: private nonprofit (Committee to Save the West Village)
Program: limited-equity co-op (converted to Mitchell-Lama rental 1976)
Architect: Perkins & Will

The West Village Houses were inspired by their association with activist-author Jane Jacobs and became a principled embodiment of the urbanistic ideas she developed in the 1950s and 1960s (fig. 5.14). Residents in the far western portion of Greenwich Village began organizing in 1961 to oppose a fourteen-block urban renewal proposal, entailing the likely demolition of every structure from Hudson Street to the Hudson River and West 11th to Christopher Streets. By 1962 a neighborhood group spearheaded by Jane Jacobs managed to halt the project by applying public and private pressure to the City Planning Commission via the mayor's office, marking one of the first high-profile defeats for the urban renewal order in the United States.

Taking up the idea that the best defense is a good offense, the group followed this unprecedented victory against the city's planning agencies with a counter proposal. In 1962 the ad hoc "Committee to Save the West Village" transformed itself into a permanent community organization that immediately turned its energies toward demonstrating alternative means of meeting housing needs in the neighborhood. Sensitive to accusations of obstructionism, the group announced in its first newsletter, in 1962, the formation of a committee to investigate options for the provision of affordable housing. Jacobs was well-versed in the discourse of architecture and planning; others in the group brought expertise in law, public relations, and city politics. The committee resolved two core principles: planning through "positive consensus," and preventing involuntary displacement.

5.14: West Village Houses, by Meyer Leibowitz, 1974

However forthrightly they set out their terms for the housing, the community could not design or construct it alone. NYCHA or the city's Housing Renewal Board were obvious agencies to undertake such a project, but city officials were not to be allies for this venture—in fact quite the opposite. So, to give initial form to the community's aspirations the group approached Chicago's Perkins and Will, whose location, the group hoped, might make them less wary of challenging New York's urban renewal machine. Ray Matz, one of the firm's designers, engaged the committee in a collaborative design process. The committee organized concerts, lectures, and individual contributions to fund financial analyses, planning surveys, and preliminary plans and sketches by Matz. These were incorporated into a proposal brochure, embellished with an iconic bird accompanying the motto: "not a single person—not a single sparrow—shall be displaced." The materials were released with much fanfare—including a front-page story in the *New York Times*—in May 1963.[35]

The proposal envisioned just over four hundred new units, ranging from one-bedrooms to four-bedroom duplexes, for a mixture of low- and moderate-income residents, along with street-level shops. Provocatively, it was imagined as a low-rise project. The plan avoided dislocation with resourceful opportunism by proposing to use a thin strip seven blocks long on the west side of Washington Street, between Morton and Bank Streets, recently vacated by the New York Central Railroad's elevated freight line. The plan proposed forty-two small structures, reserving one block for a vest-pocket park, incorporating apartments above commercial space in five-story walk-up buildings. Although scaled low, exposed structural concrete and floor-to-ceiling plate-glass windows lent the complex an up-to-date appearance. Matz once boasted that whereas the city's clearance redevelopment sought three hundred units for thirty million dollars, his design would offer more than four hundred units for a third the price via "high-density, low-rise structuring that uses all available living space."[36]

Reception was mixed. The proposal keyed to a nineteenth-century urban vernacular that was long out of fashion in professional planning and design circles. The proposal also became a lightning rod for city leaders' frustrations with mounting neighborhood opposition to urban renewal projects—including the preservation-oriented revolts led by Jacobs and her allies. It is not too surprising, then, that the city agencies produced a damning series of memos, field inspection surveys, and reports attacking the West Villagers' proposal: it was an architectural throwback to old-law tenements that would exceed zoning limits on density; it would be unmarketable without elevators; it constituted, at best, only piecemeal renewal, and financial recklessness at worst. Outside of city government the plan's most vociferous critic was the head of the Citizens Housing and Planning Council, Roger Starr. The community group also counted a number of key partners and patrons. Foremost among them was Mayor Lindsay, who had backed the West Villagers against Mayor Wagner's administration as early as 1961, while he was a U.S. Representative. Once elected mayor, Lindsay eased the city's bureaucratic opposition, beginning with a supportive 1966 memo to his agencies. The Planning Commission finally gave the project a green light in 1969. Approval of the Board of Estimate came a year later.

As first proposed, the $8.5 million plan was backed by the New York State Division of Housing and Community Renewal (financing 90 percent) and the International Longshoremen's Association (10 percent). By the time the West Village housing plan

5.15: West Village Houses, by Meyer Leibowitz, 1974

came before the Board of Estimate seven years later, it had become a $15 million project, with 95 percent loaned by the city under Mitchell-Lama. The developer recruited to sponsor the project was Starrett Housing Corporation. It contributed most of the remaining equity investment (roughly $1 million). Further delays in approval meant costs ballooned to $25 million by 1972, triggering another round of hearings and a redesign that entailed significant deviation: heights rose to six stories, small sash windows replaced plate glass, and exteriors came to be dominated by dark bricks. *New York Times* architecture critic Paul Goldberger decried the result as banal. A ribbon-cutting ceremony was finally held in the summer of 1974, and the apartments—which were planned as co-ops—went on the market (fig. 5.15).[37]

Despite the high hopes of the West Village Committee and attractive, well-priced apartments the project was a financial failure (fig. 5.16). The housing market was in dire straits in 1974, locally and nationally, and after a dramatic boom, collapsed with the OPEC crisis in 1973. Only a handful of units sold before the city's Housing and Development Administration, by then headed by Starr, foreclosed on its $23.9 million mortgage. The project was called a "disaster" and "a financial nightmare of giant proportions for the city" in the press.[38] The city let the complex sit empty for two years until Starr announced, in 1976, that it would convert to rentals and be sold to a private landlord (ultimately Starrett).

5.16: West Village Houses, model apartment, by Don Hogan Charles, 1974

For the next quarter century the project remained an island of moderate rents in an increasingly expensive neighborhood. To capitalize on changes in the Village, however, a new owner announced plans in 2002 to buy the project out of the Mitchell-Lama program. With rents expected to triple, the tenant association proposed an alternative, and two years later it was agreed to convert the building to an income-restricted co-op. Following long-standing law in New York State for conversion of rental buildings to co-op or condominium, tenants not wishing to buy their apartments were allowed

to stay at protected rents. To further defray rents, and owners' maintenance, Mayor Bloomberg's administration, whose New Housing Marketplace Plan prioritized preservation of below-market units, forgave a portion of the project's original debt, extended another portion of the debt on an interest-free basis for thirty years, and froze property taxes for twelve years. Additionally a "flip tax" of 25 percent was introduced, shifting some of the burden of maintenance from tenants to sellers profiting from resales. The conversion went ahead in 2006.[39]
CHRISTOPHER KLEMEK

John Lindsay (1921–2000)

John V. Lindsay was elected mayor in 1965 on the promise of fresh start for a socially and physically troubled city. Integration—fulfilling the vision of an "open city"—and design improvements would make New York City a model of urbanity and democracy in a decentralizing age. For the Lindsay administration, architecture served a politics of visibility—evidence on the ground of a city government actively addressing urban problems and recognizing the humanity of all its citizens. To that end, Lindsay, a liberal Republican who later switched to the Democratic Party, sought to redefine municipal housing policy in contrast to what he characterized as a decades-long focus on simply building as much housing as fast as possible. The alienating model of the tower in the park, too, would have to go. The goal, instead, was to create neighborhoods that were integrated socially and physically, with contextual housing interventions to provide living space for mixed race and income populations. Whereas the incorporation of physical rehabilitation, a mixture of income groups, and attention to relocation and participation in neighborhood planning had been city policy for almost ten years, Lindsay recast it as a philosophy.[40]

The concept of "vest-pocket" housing central to his approach was likewise not a brand new invention. In the late 1950s NYCHA began to develop smaller projects of one to four buildings on vacant land with the goals of creating new housing while integrating neighborhoods and avoiding displacement. Vest-pocket housing gained in symbolism under Lindsay, even if construction did not keep pace with aspirations. The city adopted vest pocket planning for areas in the South Bronx, Central Brooklyn, and Harlem designated for comprehensive redevelopment with funds from President Lyndon Johnson's Model Cities Program (fig. 5.17). These Model Cities plans sought to implement the "maximum feasible participation" required by federal War on Poverty programs, and were developed in consultation with local planning committees at each site. Physically, the new vest pocket developments were characterized by low-rise, infill housing for low and moderate-income residents, creating new units of sound housing without disrupting the scale of the neighborhood. The Betances Houses, completed in Mott Haven in the Bronx in 1973 and 1974, combined rehabilitated tenements and new construction of three-, four-, five-, and six-story buildings and two towers on a series of infill sites. NYCHA planned vest pocket towers at sites in predominantly white neighborhoods in four boroughs, insisting that "scatter site" housing had an important role in achieving economic and racial integration along with solving urgent housing needs. In the

5.17: John Lindsay, groundbreaking, Model Cities Program, Bedford-Stuyvesant, Brooklyn, 1970

highly polarized climate of the late 1960s and early 1970s, some New Yorkers vehemently disagreed. Community opposition stopped or modified numerous projects, most notably in Forest Hills, Queens.

The mayor's Urban Design Group extended the logic of these vest-pocket projects to re-envision neighborhoods as a whole. The group's young Yale-trained architects went to work within the Department of City Planning, in 1966. Seeking a middle way for municipal architecture between advocacy planning and top-down designs, the architect-planners engaged in many difficult rounds of community consultation to draft demonstration neighborhood plans at Twin Parks in the Bronx and Coney Island. These vest pocket plans incorporated mixed-income high-rise housing on scattered sites. The planners emphasized participation, not only in planning phases but by bringing on local organizations to sponsor housing. They also advocated for high-quality architectural design. The final task of housing construction went to the New York State Urban Development Corporation, as Mayor Lindsay and the city struck a deal with Ed Logue and state officials to take over the projects. The UDC maintained an emphasis on good design, hiring young architects to carry out projects for middle-income and elderly housing interspersed throughout the neighborhood at both sites.

The Lindsay administration consistently encouraged experimental projects to deal with housing problems that threatened the image of city as much as the quality of residents' lives. The Housing and Development Administration (HDA), a superagency combining many formerly independent city offices, spearheaded many of these experiments, commissioning prominent architects, building at new waterfront sites, and exploiting technological conceits—in projects like a two-day "instant rehabilitation" of tenements. HDA also promoted research into housing quality, in support of new residential design guidelines that would emphasize not only the character of dwelling units but, crucially, the relationship between housing developments and their urban context. HDA commissioned California landscape architect Lawrence Halprin to survey housing developments and draw up environmental planning principles and guidelines for future projects, emphasizing the utility and quality of their open spaces. Halprin's report, published in 1968 as the influential book *New York, New York*, promoted interweaving of housing with city streets and open spaces, turning the critiques of superblock planning into actual design recommendations.[41]

An HDA-sponsored architectural competition for middle-income housing in Brighton Beach led architects to weigh in on the aesthetics of subsidized housing. Most proposals attempted to impart aesthetic quality to the humble social housing project through allusions to preindustrial housing or the embrace of a technological modernity. But the third-prize entry by Robert Venturi and Denise Scott Brown, a polemical defense of the "ugly and ordinary," was a notable exception. Here and in their writing on other housing experiments in the city, the architects argued that quality and expediency were mutually exclusive. The massive towers of Co-op City (1968–73), for instance, were "almost all right."[42] They certainly delivered more moderate cost housing, faster, than the city's new experiments in neighborhood planning. Indeed, during Lindsay's eight years as Mayor, new housing starts failed to keep up with increasing residential abandonment. In 1973 the city's architectural critics lauded Lindsay's contributions to the built environment. But as the liberal values underpinning these reforms eroded as quickly as the city's economic landscape shifted, the era of design experimentation would be short-lived. MARIANA MOGILEVICH

Riverbend Houses (1968, 628 units, Manhattan)

Sponsor: private developer (HRH)
Program: Mitchell-Lama co-op
Architect: Davis Brody & Associates

The architects, developer, Harlem leaders, and key city officials behind the middle-income Riverbend Houses sought to build a community that overcame balance-sheet minimums typical of mass urban housing. They succeeded. As architecture critic Herbert Muschamp later wrote in the *New York Times*, Riverbend "broke the mold" of subsidized urban housing. "Duplexes in the sky!" trumpeted editorial and advertising copy.[43]

The site for Riverbend along the Harlem River was made available around 1960, when the city's Department of Sanitation vacated a facility there. Within two years developer HRH Construction had bought it. At first the firm considered two towers of fairly conventional design. HRH's Richard Ravitch, in conversation with architect Lew Davis of Davis Brody & Associates, quickly became interested in alternatives. The triangular site, cut by the Harlem River Drive access ramp at East 139th Street, offered interesting possibilities. More important, the architects sought to avoid the on-the-ground spatial experience of conventional housing towers.[44]

View West – City College at sunset.

The Neighborhood

This riverside section of uptown Manhattan benefits from some of the best housing and community facilities in the area. The Riverton Apartments, built and owned by the Metropolitan Life Insurance Company, as well as the recently completed Lenox Terrace and Delano Village developments, are in the immediate vicinity.

The new 800-bed Harlem Hospital, affiliated with the Columbia University College of Physicians and Surgeons, is rising two blocks away. One of the City's great educational institutions, the College (and University) of The City of New York, is only four blocks to the west.

A riverfront park and promenade will be built by the City, from 135th Street to 145th Street.

View South – Fifth Avenue and midtown.

View North – The River and Washington Heights.

RIVERBEND AT A GLANCE

- *624 cooperative apartments all with terraces*
- *Scenic river views*
- *Parking for 250 cars (146 indoors, 104 outdoors)*
- *Air conditioner sleeves and outlets in all living room areas and master bedrooms. Provisions in 2nd and 3rd bedrooms.*
- *Apartment intercom and annunciator system*
- *Master TV antenna system*
- *Eleven cubic feet refrigerators standard in all units except studios*
- *Advanced design, sliding glass windows throughout*
- *Laundries in four convenient locations*
- *On-site local shopping facilities*
- *TV elevator monitors*

SIMPLEX APARTMEN

	Equity Purchase Price	Estimated Monthl Carrying Charge
32–studios	From $950	From $81
280–one bedroom	From $1,425	From $106
112–two bedroom	From $1,750	From $121

DUPLEX APARTMEN

	Equity Purchase Price	Estimated Monthl Carrying Charges
150–two bedroom	From $2,225	From $132
50–three bedroom	From $2,725	From $152

**(Monthly carrying charges do not include utilities)*

Builders of the Best

Riverbend is being built by HRH Construction Corporation, one of the country's largest and most respected builders. With a history tracing back to 1888, their work includes such New York landmarks as the San Remo and Beresford Apartments on Central Park West, among many other outstanding residential and institutional structures in the City. During the past two decades alone, HRH built over 25,000 housing units in New York and many more in Washington, Los Angeles, Philadelphia, San Juan, as well as in Europe and South America.

Urban renewal apartment developments built recently by HRH in Washington, D.C. and San Juan, Puerto Rico have both received first honor awards in a national competition for outstanding planning and design.

PRIDE OF OWNERSHIP

When you subscribe to a Riverbend Cooperative apartment you are buying a share in your community. Along with over 100,000 other New Yorkers who already enjoy the benefits of cooperative apartment ownership you will live among people who care about their homes and environment as much as you do, and who are interested in the best possible day-to-day maintenance of their property. You will also enjoy the income tax benefits that belong to any homeowner, and are entitled to deduct your share of interest and real estate taxes paid by the Cooperative Corporation in calculating your Federal and State income tax returns.

City Aid and City Supervision

Riverbend is being built under the Limited Profit Housing Program of the City of New York. Its development, construction and sales program are supervised by New York City's Housing and Redevelopment Board. Low interest, long term mortgage financing along with 50% tax abatement from the City make the moderate equity payments and carrying charges possible.

APPLICATION INFORMATION

All applicants must be residents of the State of New York and are subject to approval by the Board of Directors of the Housing Company and the Housing and Redevelopment Board of the City of New York. Cooperators must satisfy the income limitations established by Article II of the Private Housing and Finance Law of the State of New York. (Our sales agents will be pleased to explain these requirements to you.)

Applications are submitted to the Housing Company through our sales agents, together with a deposit of $100.00 plus $3.50 to cover the cost of credit investigation. The $3.50 credit investigation fee is not returnable.

After your application has received approval by the Housing Company, you will be required to pay the full amount of the equity for your chosen apartment. In the event an application is withdrawn before it has received final approval, the equity payment deposit of $100.00 will be returned in full. Applicants who withdraw after they have been approved by the Housing and Redevelopment Board will be reimbursed, less a $50.00 resale fee, but not until their apartment has been resold and the new applicant approved.

The estimated monthly carrying charges herein stated reflect a rate of interest based on temporary financing, and is subject to change dependent upon the cost to the City of permanent financing for this development. Such adjustment would then be reflected correspondingly in the monthly carrying charges.

5.18: Riverbend, prospectus, ca. 1967

Davis Brody's new plan proposed to update older perimeter-block arrangements, a form of city building in which the street walls create a public realm and the backs of buildings enclose a private or semi-private one (fig. 5.18). To accomplish this, the firm proposed two towers and five mid-rise buildings grouped as a "connected series of apartment blocks" toward the western and northern edges of the site (Fifth Avenue and East 138th Street), allowing for courtyards, open to the river, in the manner of a traditional urban block. The courtyards were multi-purpose (fig. 5.19). At grade, parking structures were provided; their roofs were designed as community and play spaces. These play areas were reserved for residents, an exclusivity that added to the project's status. In recent years, however, these have fallen into disrepair—largely, one resident reports, because so many tenants have aged in place with a consequent decline in the number of young families.[45]

Even more than its site planning, Riverbend was unusual for including more than two hundred, two-story duplex apartments, stacked four or five units high, in the five mid-rise buildings. This was a core idea of Modernist apartment-house design

5.19: Riverbend, balconies, by Norman McGrath, 1969

but had rarely been used successfully in below-market housing in the United States. Ravitch and Davis confirmed the concept after speaking with potential tenants: Harlem's African American middle class, for whom exodus from the neighborhood was becoming a bittersweet sign of success. The meetings were arranged by Clifford Alexander, Sr., the general manager of the nearby Riverton Houses, which had been developed by Metropolitan Life in 1948. From these consultations one key design idea emerged: a desire to capture the spirit of multistory brownstone living. As Davis recalled, "we wanted to give them the kind of variation in apartment size and orientation that one would find in an established Harlem neighborhood, not the anonymous plans of a typical public housing project." HRH marketed the duplexes as "family apartments," and the "townhouse living" they promised quickly came to carry considerable social value. They sold from $2,225 down with $132 in maintenance ($16,000 and $950 in 2013 dollars) on a limited-equity cooperative plan.[46]

In Davis Brody's plan, apartment entries opened onto busy living room and kitchen areas, with private, more quiet areas, including bedrooms, placed upstairs or down. As in several avant-garde earlier examples from Europe, including Le Corbusier's Unité de Habitation in Marseilles (1947–52) and Alison and Peter Smithson's 1952 Golden Lane Housing proposal for London, the duplexes were arranged just one deep—allowing all of them both east and west exposures—and laid out along outdoor corridors, or galleries.[47] The front door of each unit and a small, low-walled patio were raised three steps up from the gallery, giving the space in front of the unit a distinctly more private sensibility. These front "yards" were, and continue to be, highly customized spaces; some residents use them as summertime sleeping porches, others set up their televisions outside, and still others fill their porches with elaborate gardens. One resident happily notes that the patio made the apartment just like "real" house. Riverbend's two towers, whose elevators also served the duplex buildings, which were attached, were more conventional in plan. But instead of balconies cantilevered beyond the face of the building, which characterized typical middle-income towers of the time, units were given an inset balcony. Residents report that these partially enclosed spaces feel more secure and private, and more integrated into their apartments, than the usual type.

Riverbend also broke with the simple "red-brick prisms" of New York's postwar below-market housing in its assertion of a late Modernist, sometimes called Brutalist, idea of structure and materials—an architecture "without rhetoric."[48] Quite simply, the buildings are made of, and perceived as nothing more than, a concrete frame

5.20: Riverbend, balconies, by Norman McGrath, 1969

with brick infill. The concrete is "board-formed"—that is, it was poured to expose and demonstrate its construction; some of the balconies are made in the same manner and project out from the building line (and also double as fire escapes) (fig. 5.20). In addition, the concrete frame of the building is exposed in the galleries and at the street. The overall effect of the expression of the concrete is sculptural and creates textures and shadows across the faces of the buildings. Even the brick is used in nontraditional ways. Davis Brody created a custom superbrick for the project, 5.5 by 8 inches, about double the size of ordinary bricks. They were laid vertically, instead of horizontally, demonstrating a non-load-bearing role and giving the buildings a unique appearance.[49]

Riverbend's innovative construction methods enabled a unique housing solution but required particular attentiveness to maintenance, creating many challenges for management. For instance, the superbricks, which saved on labor costs, have proven expensive to replicate for repair work. Exterior paving, walls, and public spaces now show considerable signs of wear. Recent patching of the concrete exteriors was done crudely and the building is oddly spotted.[50] Hurricane Sandy, meanwhile, brought floodwaters into the ground floor community and parking spaces. Despite these troubles, Riverbend residents—who include many transit and construction workers, nurses, and police officers—remain committed to their homes. This "composure" in the face of adversity, reports the *Times*, derives from the fact that the tenants are "not averse to a little hardship or to getting their hands dirty carrying out some manual labor. And after decades of living together, they are not shy about pulling together in times of trouble."[51] DAVID SMILEY

Schomburg Plaza (1974, 600 units, Manhattan)

Sponsor: UDC, private nonprofit (Committee for Central Park North)
Program: Mitchell-Lama rental
Architect: Gruzen & Partners, Castro-Blanco, Piscioneri & Feder

Schomburg Plaza was the product of 1960s idealism, including hopes for racial integration, participatory planning, and higher standards of design in below-market housing. The multiple goals, processes, and actors involved reflected the possibilities of urban redevelopment in the post-Moses era, but also its complexity: when Schomburg Plaza opened in 1974 it was only after a decade-long planning process that dramatically reduced the scope of the project and whittled away at the aspirations of the sponsors for an integrated middle-class community in Harlem. Developed by UDC, Schomburg Plaza provided six hundred apartments for low- and moderate-income families. Located at the northeast corner of Central Park, it occupies a full city block, bounded by 110th and 111th Streets and Fifth and Madison Avenues, and consists of twin, thirty-five-story apartment buildings facing the park, a mixed-use building on Madison Avenue combining apartments with shops and social services, and an open-air plaza.

The key drivers of the project were Mamie Phipps Clark and Kenneth B. Clark, pioneering African American psychologists who, in 1946, not long after obtaining their PhDs from Columbia University, founded the Northside Center for Child Development to provide mental health, counseling, and other social services to children.[52] Their studies of the psychological effects of racism on Black children had national impact after the U.S. Supreme Court cited Kenneth Clark's research in the 1954 decision *Brown v. Board of Education* that outlawed school segregation, but Harlem was their urban laboratory and center of operations. The Northside Center was named after its original location in the Dunbar Apartments, but in 1948 it moved to the southern edge of Harlem: 31 West 110th Street, between Fifth and Lenox Avenues. The location suited the Clarks' commitment to serve a mixed population, including white children, and a compatible co-tenant, the New Lincoln School, a progressive, integrated K–12 facility, moved into the building a few months later.

Over the ensuing twenty years the Clarks witnessed the postwar transformation of Harlem as tenement blocks were razed and replaced with public housing. The concentration of public housing in Central and East Harlem fundamentally changed the character of those areas in the 1950s and 1960s.[53] Multi-ethnic neighborhoods were re-sorted on racial and ethnic lines, and became strictly residential, deprived not only of shops but also street frontage as roads were closed to make superblocks. On 110th Street, the Northside Center became virtually walled off by such complexes. Set against the backdrop of Harlem's transformation and increasing segregation, it is remarkable that the Clarks still believed in the regenerative, reform capacity of large-scale redevelopment—a hope commingled with the bitter recognition, as Kenneth Clark put it, that urban renewal projects "designed for the people of a ghetto community exclusively reemphasize the ghetto."[54]

Beginning in late 1964 the Clarks gathered allies to envision the redevelopment of a fifteen-block area in East Harlem, from Fifth to Lexington Avenue between 107th and 112th Streets. As reported in their meeting minutes, the group aimed through "systematic and imaginative planning" to create "an attractive, racially integrated community that would facilitate eventual renewal and a two-way opening up of the larger Harlem area."[55] The group, which convened at the Northside Center, constituted itself as the Committee for Central Park North, elected Mamie Clark as the chair, and engaged an architect, Edgar Tafel, to visualize their ideas. Tafel, a graduate of Frank Lloyd Wright's Taliesin fellowship who was responsible for many community buildings in New York City, reimagined Frawley Circle, the traffic roundabout at the corner of the park, as a spectacular urban plaza. Featuring a grand fountain, the plaza was framed by low-rise, circular buildings on Fifth Avenue, colonnades, and a major entrance to the park: a Beaux-Arts composition that would have made Frawley Circle a monumental counterpart to Columbus Circle at the park's southwest corner.[56] The planning group hoped to attract cultural, educational, and commercial elements to the district, and Tafel's scheme included high-rises for residential, office, and institutional needs, arranged about a reinstated street grid. As far as its efforts with city government, the Committee for Central Park North made no progress: the only outcome of meetings with Mayor Robert Wagner's administration was the renaming of 110th Street as Central Park North in September 1965.[57]

President Johnson's declaration of a war on poverty and announcement, in January 1966, of a Model Cities Program changed the dynamics of the Clarks' initiative. In November that year Mayor Lindsay nominated Milbank-Frawley Circle area as one of the first three sites for the new federal program. HUD approved the city's application in November 1967 and released funds for survey and advanced planning work. The City Planning Commission's survey found that 99 percent of 1,054 residential buildings violated city codes and half were structurally unsound.[58]

The Model Cities area of fifty-four blocks—107th to 125th Streets between Lenox and Park Avenues—encompassed a far larger territory than that originally targeted by the Northside group. The affected population jumped from 4,000 to 45,000. It also changed the racial mixture to two-thirds African American and one-third Puerto Rican. This shift was controversial—"Negro-Latin Feud Hurting Harlem" reported the *New York Times*—and brought the project to a halt. As required by federal guidelines, community groups were established to represent the various interests in the redevelopment process. When elections for the local planning committee resulted in an African American majority, Puerto Ricans contested the results and formed rival community groups, stymieing the planning process. What was at stake, the *Times* reported, was "a much bigger prize—control of the huge Harlem-East Harlem Model Cities area." [59]

With the odds now demographically stacked against Northside's goals for integration, the organization reconsidered its role in the redevelopment project. A new pathway opened when Governor Rockefeller established the Urban Development Corporation in 1968. Recognizing the opportunity presented by UDC, Northside decided to scale back their plan to focus on a single block and approached Ed Logue. It was an easy contact to make: Kenneth Clark was on the Board of Directors of UDC.[60] UDC stepped in as the developer with the newly formed 110th Street Housing Development Corporation as the local co-sponsor.

To balance African American and Puerto Rican involvement Mamie Clark forged a coalition with other neighborhood groups. The groups included La Hermosa

Christian Church, the Omega Psi Phi Fraternity, and the Unity Mission Christian Society.[61] Notwithstanding her efforts, frictions erupted. The Young Lords, an activist group whose offices happened to be on the redevelopment site, protested the project and harassed the development corporation to do more for Puerto Ricans, fearing that the subsidized housing would only serve African Americans. It was in this context that Mamie Clark engineered the renaming of Frawley Plaza after Arturo Schomburg.[62] A Black Puerto Rican, Schomburg was a bibliophile collector and expert on African American and African diasporic history, and he perfectly embodied the harmonious union of the two identities. (The New York Public Library's center for research on Black culture, in Harlem, was also named for Schomburg.) Tensions nevertheless endured, reigniting in 1995 when the circle was renamed for Duke Ellington and a statue of him was placed in it in 1997. Latinos sought equal recognition for Puerto Rican bandleader Tito Puente, who died in 2000, and succeeded in having the eastern half of 110th Street (from First to Fifth Avenues) renamed Tito Puente Way.[63]

By 1970 the program of the new UDC project had taken final shape. It included six hundred apartments ranging from studios to five bedrooms, with rents of $149 to $517 (approximately $650 to $2,300 in 2013 dollars). Smaller units were placed in the towers and larger ones in the Madison Avenue building. The complex also included new facilities for the by-now acclaimed Northside Center and the Cadet Academy of the New York Mission Society, a day care center for seventy-five children, retail space for shops or a supermarket, and a parking garage. Construction was scheduled to begin in February 1971, although legal actions delayed clearance until early 1972.[64] African American management firm Webb-Brooks and Brooker was the rental and managing agent, and under Mamie Clark's guidance the Douglass Urban Corporation, a minority employment agency, was hired to ensure minority employment on the project.[65] The cornerstone ceremony took place on May 17, 1973, the anniversary of *Brown v. Board of Education*, and the completed buildings were dedicated on December 17, 1974, with Mayor Beame presiding. The project was built at a total cost of $25.6 million ($118 million today), with UDC providing seed money and long-term capital financing and New York State providing Mitchell-Lama loans.[66]

Unfortunately the leasing process thwarted the Clarks' goal of integrating middle- and low-income whites, Hispanics, and African Americans. When the first apartments were offered, in 1974, few whites applied. The 110th Street Housing Corporation mounted a publicity campaign, running advertisements in a variety of ethnic papers, including *Il Progresso* and the *Jewish Daily Forward*—as well as the *China Tribune*—but to no effect. The Clarks retrenched, accepted the absence of whites, and embraced a modified goal of balancing Hispanics and African Americans. With about six thousand applications to choose from, this balance was readily achieved.[67]

Architecturally ambitious, Schomburg Plaza looked nothing like most below-market subsidized housing (fig. 5.21). It was jointly designed by Gruzen and Partners, and Castro-Blanco, Piscioneri & Feder Architects. Gruzen and Partners was a mainstay of housing development in postwar New York, and David Castro-Blanco was a Colombian architect active in the Hispanic community; his role was in part a response to demands for Hispanic participation in the project.[68]

5.21: Schomburg Plaza, 2014

Physically Schomburg Plaza is defined by its twin octagonal towers. Alternating sides were recessed with balconies projecting on two of every four floors, creating a banded effect and casting the recessed areas in shadow. (The addition of balconies also allowed greater variety in rents.) Strong three-dimensional forms in the skyline, the complex was shaped to count in the landscape of Central Park. And according to Jordan Gruzen the form was inspired by the grand twin-tower apartment buildings of Central Park West: the El Dorado, San Remo, Majestic, and Century. Whereas the Central Park West towers crown a single mass, however, Schomburg Plaza features two freestanding buildings, which offers every apartment unobstructed views and light. Gruzen and Partners were experimenting at this time with octagonal buildings, and related designs include the UDC-sponsored Seven Pines (1972) in

Yonkers and the Galaxy Towers (1976) in Guttenberg, New Jersey, on the Hudson River shore. The Schomburg towers also related to the octagonal tower typology that Frank Lloyd Wright first developed for an unbuilt New York City project, St. Mark's Towers (1929). Wright argued that the central service core and compact plan that eliminated the need for hallways offered economies, and Gruzen developed a similarly efficient plan with a central core and short U-shaped corridor wrapping around the elevators and providing access to the eight apartments per floor.[69]

The towers were built with poured-in-place concrete with a corduroy treatment, akin to Paul Rudolph's Art and Architecture Building at Yale University (1963). The concrete block was less expensive than brick and a relief from the depressed visual vocabulary of most below-market projects in the city. More than any other factor, the change of building materials kept Schomburg Plaza from being seen as a low-income complex.

As urban design, the buildings poorly define the edge of Ellington Circle, but they serve as a gateway into the block. The space between the towers draws visitors into the site and directs circulation, via a ramp, to the interior plaza located above the parking structure on a second floor level. From there visitors approaching from Fifth Avenue could enter the Northside Center and day care center. Mamie Clark had been dissatisfied by the architect's original plan to place the entrance to the Northside Center on Madison Avenue, facing East Harlem. The addition of a west-facing entrance on the plaza had an important signaling role to Northside's core constituency in Central Harlem. Trellises wrapped around the perimeter of the plaza, creating a sheltered area for seating and giving a needed sense of enclosure to the space, which was used as a play area by the day care center and Northside. There is no sign of other landscaping depicted in original renderings, and the plaza today has an austere appearance but for the trellises.

The Madison Avenue building is a simple rectangular block, reestablishing the traditional street wall in an area dominated by public housing towers divorced from the grid. Moreover unlike the mono-functional projects of East Harlem that created a retail desert, Schomburg Plaza included street-level stores. The original site plan anticipated the closure of 111th Street between Fifth and Madison Avenues to create a pedestrian mall, which was not built. The "111th Street Mall" was planned as a landscaped corridor, with shade trees and sunken areas for games, "theatrics," spray pool, and seating.

Now in its fortieth year, Schomburg Plaza has experienced two traumatic events: a deadly fire in 1987 and departure from the Mitchell-Lama program in 2005. At that time Schomburg Plaza was purchased for $295 million by a private equity firm that opted out of Mitchell-Lama, thereby allowing it to hike rents. Two years later Schomburg Plaza was sold to Urban American Management for triple the amount, $918 million.[70] The buildings were recently renamed The Heritage, shedding the symbolically significant name that saluted the Puerto Rican and African American history of the area. The chapter of Schomburg Plaza's history as low- and moderate-income housing, the hard-won outcome of Mamie and Kenneth Clark's effort to mold urban renewal in the name of integration, seems to have come to an end.

HILARY BALLON

Edward J. Logue (1921–2000)

Edward J. (Ed) Logue arrived in New York in 1968 to head the Urban Development Corporation, New York State's ambitious new renewal operation. Logue believed deeply in the responsibility of government to provide below-market subsidized housing and to keep cities as vibrant communities where people of different ages, classes, and races could live. Logue's social vision is often missed in indiscriminate condemnation of the era's liberal urban renewal project, but his UDC program in New York City, in particular, stands out for its sensitivity to context, social mixture, and architectural inventiveness.[71]

Much in Ed Logue's life before he arrived in New York contributed to his commitment to using public funds and power to make cities viable. He grew up in Philadelphia in the 1930s with a progressive political consciousness shaped by President Franklin D. Roosevelt's New Deal. He attended Yale on scholarship, where his love of cities encouraged him to explore New Haven beyond the college gates. A strike by university maintenance and service workers during his senior year channeled his political commitment toward labor organizing and upon graduation, in 1942, he became chief organizer for the trade union local representing the workers. After serving in World War II, he returned to Yale for law school, where he focused on labor and dabbled in urban questions. After a short stint working as a labor lawyer, he became Labor Secretary to the new governor of Connecticut, liberal Democrat Chester Bowles. When the voters denied Bowles a second term, President Truman appointed him ambassador to the new nation of India and Bowles took Logue along as his special assistant.

The eighteen months that Logue and his wife spent in India were formative. He closely observed the joint efforts of the U.S. State Department and the Ford Foundation to bolster democracy in a Cold War world by linking the modernizing of village infrastructure to land and other social reforms. The link that Logue made throughout his career between improving the built environment and a broader social agenda would date from this experience. Returning to New Haven in 1953, he soon joined the administration of newly elected Democratic reform mayor Richard Lee, serving as his redevelopment administrator at a time when the federal government was making substantial new funds for redevelopment available to cities through Title I. Logue would speak frequently about how he was bringing the "community development" work he had observed in Village India to struggling American cities like New Haven.[72]

From New Haven, Logue went on to Boston in 1961, where another new mayor, John Collins, hired him to head the Boston Redevelopment Authority (BRA). Logue and his staff of seven hundred undertook an ambitious plan to redevelop downtown Boston and some key neighborhoods as part of a citywide turn-around.[73] During his time in Boston, John Lindsay was elected mayor of New York City, and in 1966 he hired Logue to lead a task force to recommend improvements in housing and neighborhoods. "Let There Be Commitment" was the comprehensive report that Logue's commission submitted. Lindsay offered Logue the job of implementing it, but without the extensive powers he enjoyed in Boston, Logue declined.[74] When Boston's Collins announced he would not seek reelection, Logue decided to run for mayor himself. He campaigned for the primary during the summer of 1967 but failed to make it into the final run-off.

Out of a job at the BRA, Logue responded enthusiastically to Governor Nelson Rockefeller's offer of the presidency of UDC, so long as the agency had power of eminent domain, could override local zoning and building codes, and its projects were tax-exempt.[75] UDC under Logue constructed 33,000 units of housing in complexes that integrated seniors and low- and moderate-income tenants with those paying market rate; developed industrial parks and redeveloped downtowns; built three "new towns"—two upstate and the car-free "new town in town" of Roosevelt Island in New York; experimented with low-rise, high-density subsidized housing such as Marcus Garvey Village in Brooklyn; and much more. Sensitive to community objections to the demolition that had accompanied urban renewal in New Haven and Boston, Logue sought to put UDC projects as often as possible on open land.

Another kind of resistance Logue had encountered elsewhere also drove his UDC work, and ultimately undermined it. Frustrated in New Haven and Boston with the exit of middle-class city residents to the suburbs to live and increasingly work, leaving what he saw as an unfair burden of solving social problems to cities, in 1972 Logue introduced a "fair share" plan to build subsidized housing in nine towns in suburban Westchester County, threatening to override local zoning if necessary. His project was met with a ferocious backlash, including the state legislature's and a curtailing of UDC's override powers in villages and towns. That rejection, combined with the loss of protector Governor Rockefeller to the U.S. vice presidency, the growing fiscal crisis in the city and state, and President Nixon's moratorium on housing led UDC to default on bond payments and to lose the confidence of bankers and politicians. In the winter of 1975, faced with mounting opposition, Logue resigned.[76]

Logue got one more opportunity in his career to build subsidized housing in New York City. In 1978, he successfully lobbied to be appointed by Mayor Ed Koch as president of the South Bronx Development Organization (SBDO). Working in a very different political moment—faced first with the limited federal programs under President Jimmy Carter followed by the market-oriented urban policies of President Ronald Reagan—Logue implemented a unique but still ambitious strategy. Charged with developing industrial and employment opportunities as well as badly needed housing in one of the most deprived areas of New York City, in 1982 Logue began developing the SBDO's signature project, Charlotte Gardens (1983–87), an unorthodox development of a hundred prefabricated, ranch-style houses to be sold with below-market-interest-rate mortgages to working-class New Yorkers eager to own their own homes (fig. 5.22). Although he admitted that these conventional suburban dwellings "would not win the architectural awards that I have so enjoyed receiving," Logue judged correctly that new homeowners would provide a stable anchor for revitalizing the South Bronx.[77]

Urban renewal is not popular today, and figures like Logue are often criticized for insensitive interventions in the delicate fabric of the city, demolishing too much of the old, and constructing too much of the new at an inappropriate scale and design. There is much truth in these critiques. But it is also important to remember the many positive aspects of Logue's work. He viewed cities as sites for strengthening American democracy and pushed hard to build affordable housing and for long-term

5.22: Charlotte Gardens, Ed Logue, center left, watching Ed Koch speak, ribbon cutting, n.d.

economic strategies that would provide good jobs for city residents. Roosevelt Island epitomized his vision for communities where people of different ages, classes, and races could live together. And although he recognized the necessity of involving the private sector in urban redevelopment, Logue believed deeply that the public sector needed to lead: "I've always felt [you] can't trust the private sector to protect the public interest."[78] When Logue died he was a controversial figure who nonetheless had devoted his career to ensuring that cities continued to provide homes, and be home, for many Americans.[79] LIZABETH COHEN

Twin Parks (1976, 2,250 units, Bronx)

Sponsor: UDC, NYCHA, others
Program: Mitchell-Lama rental, private rental, public housing
Architect: Richard Meier, Giovanni Pasanella, James Polshek, Skidmore, Owings & Merrill, Prentice & Chan, Ohlhausen

Conceived of in the mid-1960s and completed in the mid-1970s, the Twin Parks portfolio of below-market subsidized housing in the Bronx was part of a broad revision in the city's approach to large-scale housing production. Rethinking policies to accelerate production of below-market housing, the Lindsay administration prioritized the construction of mixed-income, mixed-race housing on vacant or underused infill sites. In particular, the mayor's team turned its attention to a section of the Bronx situated between two parks: Crotona and Bronx. Designated as urban renewal areas in 1967, Twin Parks East and Twin Parks West suffered from disinvestment and

5.23: Twin Parks SW, n.d.

were transforming rapidly from largely Italian American communities into ones of Puerto Ricans and African Americans. The administration hoped that government aid for new housing could help slow the pace of change and staunch the disinvestment (fig. 5.23).

In 1966 a group of five recent architecture and planning graduates initiated a Twin Parks Study that identified underused sites for new construction as well as existing buildings for rehabilitation in two focus areas. Co-financed by the J. M. Kaplan Fund and the Lindsay administration, the plan was developed in close collaboration with the Twin Parks Association, a group of almost fifty local religious organizations whose original goal was to create a total of three thousand units of new or rehabilitated high-quality low-, moderate-, and middle-income apartments. The neighborhood group, which had intended to act as a nonprofit developer, could not secure funding, however, delaying work until 1969, when UDC selected Twin Parks as one of its eight projects in the city. As built, it comprised four subzones: Twin Parks Northwest, Northeast, Southwest, and Southeast. Construction began by 1970 and was completed in 1973.[80]

UDC placed a high priority on physical form and hired emerging architects to experiment with urban design configurations and new unit types for a range of studio to five-bedroom apartments. Richard Meier was commissioned with Twin Parks Northeast. Its three mid- to high-rise buildings were designed around existing structures on three adjacent blocks, articulating existing street walls with arcades, and

5.24: Twin Parks NE, 2014

creating a new, publicly accessible plaza by closing off a block of Grote Street (fig. 5.24). James Polshek designed part of Twin Parks Southeast as a gateway formed by a point tower and a mid-rise block comprising duplex apartments accessed from open-air galleries across private porches. Three nearby buildings originally assigned to Polshek were realized by Skidmore, Owings & Merrill as modular concrete structures with distinctive, repetitive balconies, co-financed through the short-lived Operation Breakthrough, a federal initiative to promote industrialized construction methods.

Prentice & Chan, Ohlhausen, in collaboration with landscape architect Terry Schnadelbach, dealt with two heavily-sloped sites at Twin Parks Northwest, one resolved as a sleek nineteen-floor tower with intricately interlocking one- and two-story units, the other as a five- to ten-story building framing a large, sunken courtyard (fig. 5.25). Giovanni Pasanella was responsible for three UDC buildings as well as NYCHA's Twin Parks West complex, all comprised of split-level floor-through apartments that the architect heralded as an urban alternative to the suburban house. At Twin Parks East, Pasanella designed high-rise towers atop two new public schools.

While the large number of dwellings made the Twin Parks effort a quantitative accomplishment, the variety of sites, programs, and architectural expressions ensured that it was not perceived as a single project. Only at Twin Parks West do the buildings, related through their eight-by-eight-inch brick façades, but distinct in terms of massing and orientation, read as an ensemble; historian Vincent Scully aptly described it as a "flotilla."[81]

The Twin Parks effort was motivated by the desire to bridge the Puerto Rican, Black, and Italian communities. In part, it attempted to do so through quality urban design and the provision of a variety of dwelling types. But the integration program was also formalized through UDC-led leasing that aimed to attract a wide variety

5.25: Twin Parks NW, 1973

of ethnic groups and income levels. Twin Parks plans were predicated on serving a mixture of low- and moderate-class families to "help prevent one income group from overwhelming another," according to a 1967 city report. From the commencement of leasing, however, UDC failed to achieve the envisioned ethnic integration. In theory, the projects were meant to be one-third equal parts white, Black, and Puerto Rican. But initial targeted outreach to white residents yielded limited results. The UDC reserved sixty-nine apartments for "non-minorities" in two of its four developments, but those were difficult to fill; by 1972 even those whites who had agreed to move in were leaving. In mid-1973 Edward Logue agreed in a staff memo that the goal of integrating Twin Parks was largely "hopeless."[82]

On the other hand, the economic integration planned for the buildings, if not the larger neighborhoods, proved more successful. UDC dictated that 30 percent of its units should be affordable to low-income households, and the balance to middle-income.[83] The development still reflects this make up. In 2010 roughly a third of residents had incomes below $20,000, with the balance under $60,000. Furthermore, economic integration did not come at the cost of demand. Leasing records released by the state in 2013 indicate that the wait time for moderate-income family apartments ranged from one to two years for units at Twin Parks Northeast and Southeast, although interest is weaker at Northwest and Southwest.

Design also aimed to integrate a variety of public amenities. All sections included plazas and other public spaces. The Northeast (Meier) and Southeast (Polshek) buildings also incorporated retail, distinguishing them from most postwar below-market housing. Commenting on Twin Parks in 1973, *New York Times* architecture critic Paul

Goldberger noted that the complexes' "massing carefully relates to existing buildings and street patterns . . . set down with immense care in this old neighborhood." The plaza between two of the Meier buildings, in particular, seemed to Goldberger like "a meeting place for neighbors with friendly intentions."[84] At several of the steeply sloping Twin Parks West sites, the architects created pedestrian connections across the escarpment using dramatic stairs and porticos, allowing passers-by to slip underneath the buildings.

Though UDC buildings were planned and developed by the agency, all were owned and managed by private organizations, which exposed them to fiscal uncertainty.[85] By the early 1980s projects supported by New York State's Mitchell-Lama financing, including many of Twin Parks' units, faced considerable financial difficulties. For instance, the Dic-Underhill Investment Group, which managed several of UDC complexes, fell into arrears and had to be rescued by the state. The state could have foreclosed but decided to maintain the buildings' private management because of concerns about losing income-restricted housing and the lack of an alternative government manager. From management's point of view, the restrictions on rent levels made it impossible to cover rising maintenance and energy costs.[86]

Poor management led tenants to grow increasingly dissatisfied with building maintenance. A 2010 review of building violations shows that private ownership at the Southeast and Northwest complexes has continued to produce a significant number of violations (eleven and twenty-seven respectively). By contrast, the buildings under temporary state ownership, Twin Parks Southwest, had only one violation. The Northeast buildings—which suffered 245 violations in 2010—were abandoned by Ocelot Capital after the 2008 recession. With state aid, new owners Omni New York undertook $30 million in improvements financed through federal Low-income Housing Tax Credits as well as public bond measures.[87]

Today, tenants live in fear of rising rents. They campaigned aggressively in the first decade of the millennium to preserve prices by remaining in the Mitchell-Lama program. Meanwhile, in 2013, Governor Andrew Cuomo approved state funding to transfer UDC developments, including Twin Parks, from the vestigial UDC portfolio to the state's Department of Homes and Community Renewal, promising access to tax-exempt bonds and tax credits for upgrades, while extending price restriction for another forty years.

Though affordability has been temporarily addressed, private management has systematically diminished many of the innovative design characteristics of the Twin Parks complexes. At one of the Meier buildings, six floors of windows that lighted and ventilated single-loaded corridors have been replaced with metal panels, allegedly to discourage their use as lookouts for drug dealing. In the community room at roof level, cinderblock walls block views. Access to roof decks is prohibited. Similarly, at the Prentice & Chan, Ohlhausen courtyard building, the ground-floor community room's original large windows have been bricked over, and the gently terraced sitting and playground areas, formerly a stimulating pattern of concrete pavers set in grass, were covered in concrete. While recent changes in ownership and the ongoing influx of capital have resulted in upgrades to interiors, there has been a consistent disregard for the exterior spaces and common amenities.[88] YONAH FREEMARK AND SUSANNE SCHINDLER

Marcus Garvey Village (1976, 625 units, Brooklyn)

Sponsor: UDC
Program: private rental
Architect: Kenneth Frampton, Theodore Liebman

On June 12, 1973, Marcus Garvey Village broke ground in Brownsville, Brooklyn (fig. 5.26). The very same day an exhibition entitled *Another Chance for Housing: Low-Rise Alternatives* opened at the Museum of Modern Art in Manhattan. Both were the product of UDC working in collaboration with The Institute for Architecture and Urban Studies (IAUS), a group of young progressive architects led by Peter Eisenman. Both Marcus Garvey, as an example of theory in practice, and the show offered a "future housing alternative" that its authors claimed would remedy problems typical of below-market housing.[89]

The Marcus Garvey complex occupied twelve acres, bisected by the elevated Livonia Avenue subway, of the fifty-six acre Marcus Garvey Park Village Urban Renewal Area. Nearly a third of the nine thousand households lived in poverty; physical abandonment and decay were rampant. The *New York Times* described the place as "the most devastated neighborhood" in the country. HUD called the renewal project, which was also designated a Model Cities Program area, "of national importance because Brownsville . . . has been a coast-to-coast symbol of physical deterioration of a neighborhood."[90]

The 1968 plan called for rehabilitation or construction of more than thirty-seven hundred apartments and transfer to tenants for refurbishment of one thousand more. As part of the Model Cities Program, the work was to be accomplished by neighborhood-based groups (fig. 5.27). Unfortunately, this provision delayed progress considerably; ground was broken for the first new housing project only after four years, in late 1972. UDC's and IAUS's Marcus Garvey Village, which was the second to begin, followed seven months later. While building high-rises elsewhere, UDC was keen to explore low-rise, high-density designs as an alternative, working with IAUS and other architects to develop several projects, including Marcus Garvey and Elm Street, designed by Werner Seligmann in Ithaca (1972). Presented as viable option for both suburban and urban sites, these experiments were dense enough to support public transportation and civic and commercial amenities, yet provided integrated open spaces and a sense of individual identity.[91] The Village and an unbuilt sister project planned for Staten Island also designed by IAUS were hoped to prove the idea viable.

5.26: Marcus Garvey Village, groundbreaking, Edward J. Logue, center, and Theodore Liebman, right, 1973

Modeled in part on seminal examples of the type in Europe, such as Atelier 5's Siedlung Halen (1961) on the outskirts of Bern, Switzerland, Marcus Garvey Village revived street-focused design principles long out of fashion. It not only

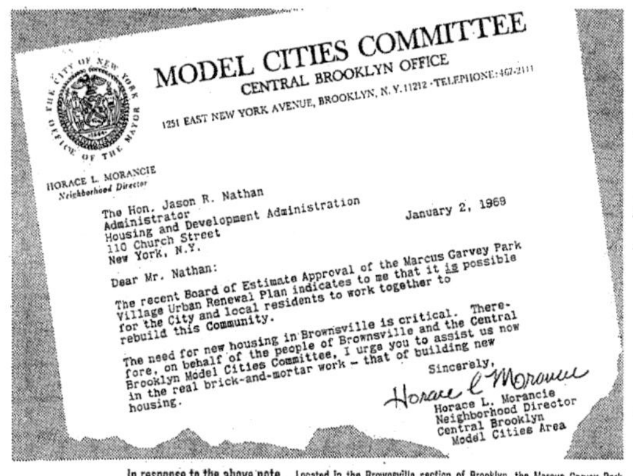

MODEL CITIES COMMITTEE
CENTRAL BROOKLYN OFFICE
1251 EAST NEW YORK AVENUE, BROOKLYN, N. Y. 11212 · TELEPHONE: 467-2111

THE CITY OF NEW YORK · OFFICE OF THE MAYOR

HORACE L. MORANCIE
Neighborhood Director

The Hon. Jason R. Nathan
Administrator
Housing and Development Administration
110 Church Street
New York, N.Y.

January 2, 1969

Dear Mr. Nathan:

The recent Board of Estimate Approval of the Marcus Garvey Park Village Urban Renewal Plan indicates to me that it is possible for the City and local residents to work together to rebuild this Community.

The need for new housing in Brownsville is critical. Therefore, on behalf of the people of Brownsville and the Central Brooklyn Model Cities Committee, I urge you to assist us now in the real brick-and-mortar work – that of building new housing.

Sincerely,

Horace L. Morancie
Neighborhood Director
Central Brooklyn
Model Cities Area

In response to the above note,
The Housing and Development Administration
invites applications from qualified
community organizations interested in
sponsoring moderate-income
housing in the

MARCUS GARVEY PARK VILLAGE

NEIGHBORHOOD DEVELOPMENT PROGRAM IN BROWNSVILLE

Located in the Brownsville section of Brooklyn, the Marcus Garvey Park Village Project is part of a comprehensive housing improvement program for the Central Brooklyn Model Cities Area. Developed through the cooperative efforts of the Community and the City, this project involves the construction of 2,600 new dwelling units and several related community facilities. The new housing will be for families of low and moderate income and will be financed under applicable Federal, State and City programs. In addition, a Home Maintenance Program designed to upgrade about 1,000 apartments, and other programs for the rehabilitation of existing buildings are planned. All of these efforts will generate jobs and business opportunities for local residents in the construction, maintenance, ownership and management of properties.

Using the early action "Vest Pocket" approach to new construction, the plan encompasses 25 sites that can be quickly redeveloped. The City will make sites available at a cost which will permit economic development. Strict standards of architectural design and site planning will be established to assure development of the highest quality.

Redevelopment activities in Marcus Garvey Park Village will lead to ownership by local non-profit sponsoring corporations. Successful applicants for sponsorship will receive assistance from a team of experts in legal requirements, mortgage analysis, formation of a housing company, and related technical matters.

To insure full consideration, letters of interest should be postmarked by January 30. Applications will be accepted only from the officers, director, trustees or other executive heads of non-profit community organizations (community-approved non-profit groups, church groups, labor unions, etc.), and should include a detailed statement of the background and history of the applicant organization as well as a record of its role, interest and achievements in the community. No designation of sponsors will be made without the concurrence of the Central Brooklyn Model Cities Committee and the Neighborhood Director.

The letter of interest should address itself to the following sponsor selection criteria: 1) Community identification, experience and involvement, including information on its membership and financial structure; 2) Demonstrated commitment to work with dedication as a member of a team effort in the Model Cities Program; 3) A proven capacity to maintain a sustained effort over a period of years for community improvement; especially with regard to housing problems. After initial review of the letters of interest, it is anticipated that the Housing and Development Administration will contact groups for further discussion. More detailed information about sites, housing types, costs, etc. will be available at that time.

PLEASE DO NOT TELEPHONE: WRITE TO:

JASON R. NATHAN, Administrator
HOUSING AND DEVELOPMENT ADMINISTRATION
2 LAFAYETTE STREET, NEW YORK, NEW YORK 10007
Attention: Office of Community Development,
Model Cities Program, Room 1603

5.27: Marcus Garvey Park Village Urban Renewal Area, display advertisement, *New York Amsterdam News*, January 11, 1969

maintained all existing streets (and without gates) but incorporated new, fifty-foot-wide pedestrian-only streets that the designers referred to as "mews." The whole was scaled to give the feeling of the nineteenth-century row house district, but with a clean, Modernist aesthetic (fig. 5.28). The result felt at once part of the neighborhood and an enclave; its stoops and mews providing a seamless transition from the street to the internal paths of circulation. The units themselves mimicked traditional row house forms, each exterior door leading to four or fewer apartments. Lower-level units had small, private backyards.

Marcus Garvey presented a clear rhythm of built and open space: blocks had a perimeter of housing at the street's edge and were "interrupted in a syncopated way" by the mews, according to the lead designer with the IAUS, Kenneth Frampton.[92] Six hundred twenty-five, one- to five-bedroom apartments—40 percent of which had three, four, or five bedrooms to cater to families—were arranged in rows, stacked to a uniform four stories, some opening onto the mews, some the street (fig. 5.29). Built in concrete and faced in light brown brick, the housing was set back a hundred feet from the elevated subway, with surface parking for three hundred cars. Despite the low profile, by building on a greater proportion of the site and creating intimate open spaces, the Village achieved a higher density of units per acre than at many towers without reducing the sizes of the apartments.

5.28: Marcus Garvey Village, site plan and rendering, from MoMA, *Another Chance for Housing: Low-rise Alternatives; Brownsville, Brooklyn, Fox Hills, Staten Island* (1973)

While generally lauded, some criticized aspects of the project. Frampton disliked changes made to save costs. As built, for example, yards were pushed almost a full story below the adjoining apartments and were separated from each other by chain-link fencing, resulting in uninviting private spaces that are not well used.[93] Judged in terms of UDC's seven original goals—"sense of community, child supervision, security, maintenance, livability, responsiveness to context, and flexibility"—its record is also blemished. Elements intended to engender safety by cultivating feelings of proprietorship and community have made the Village ideal for drug and gang activity, prompting the current landlord to begin renovations in 2014 that, in addition to interior upgrades and new landscaping and mechanical systems, gated the mews and introduced more security cameras. Yet it is too easy to attribute persistent social and economic difficulties to architecture. Evaluation of the long-term success of the Village, which has recently been rebranded the Marcus Garvey Apartments, must be complicated by an understanding of its larger context. So while high crime, poor maintenance, and persistent poverty at the

5.29: Marcus Garvey Village, mews, 2014

complex are undeniable, we can more convincingly ascribe these problems to chronic neighborhood disinvestment, higher than average rates of crime in Brownsville, and poor management than to design.[94] KAREN KUBEY

Eastwood (1976, 1,003 units, Roosevelt Island)

Sponsor: UDC
Program: Mitchell-Lama rental
Architect: Sert Jackson Associates

In 1969 Edward J. Logue's UDC established a bold agenda for its highest-profile and highest-stakes project, the new town of Roosevelt Island: generating a mixed-income and, more crucially, mixed-race community, free of the white flight and instability so characteristic of urban neighborhoods in New York and nationally in the 1960s. In particular, UDC envisioned a neighborhood of Black and white, as well as young and old, and, rather uniquely, able-bodied and disabled, aiming for a social profile that might otherwise have taken decades to develop. The master plan by Philip Johnson and John Burgee reflected this ambitious agenda. It dispensed with a conventional approach, the Modernist tower-in-the-park, for a more social organization with a main street as a central spine flanked by a series of residential complexes with rear courtyards facing out to the East River and to Manhattan and Queens beyond (see fig. 0.36).[95]

Eastwood was the largest of the four buildings in the first phase of development, housing half the new residents in its 1,003 units, many of which were reserved for disabled and elderly tenants. The design by avant-garde architect Josep Lluis Sert, dean of the Harvard Graduate School of Design, explored many ideas in one single, very large building. Building on ideas from Moisei Ginzburg's Narkomfin Block (1929), it treated corridors as semi-public rights of way, courtyards as common squares, and lobbies as intersections (fig. 5.30).[96] Other buildings on Roosevelt Island, designed by Sert or by John Johansen and Ashok Bhavnani, were also experimental to varying degrees.

5.30: Eastwood, courtyard, 2010

Eastwood, like Roosevelt Island generally, suffered many complications in its early years. Originally Eastwood and the three other first-generation buildings—which for decades were the only ones completed—were scheduled to be part of a second phase. Delays in construction of an aerial tram and subway stop, and complications with the demolition of existing buildings remaining from the defunct City Hospital (closed 1957), demanded a less aggressive production schedule. Other difficulties followed. Between

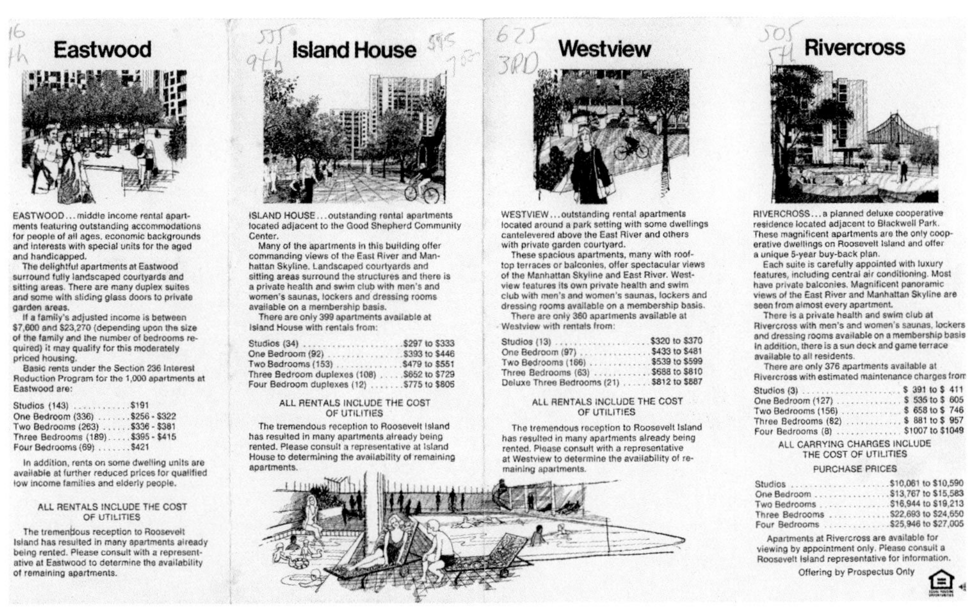

5.31: Roosevelt Island, prospectus, ca. 1975

1970 and 1973 UDC raised $500 million through bonds to support construction. But the project still relied heavily on federal support, especially below-market-interest-rate mortgages from HUD. That program, however, was suspended as part of President Nixon's housing moratorium. By 1975 UDC was all but out of money, requiring emergency loans of $320 million from insurance funds and private banks to remain solvent. In response to these financial difficulties construction slowed and cost-saving adjustments were made at Eastwood, such as elimination of air conditioning. Regrettably, Eastwood's many apartments for disabled tenants were reduced in size, from two bedrooms to one, making in-home caregiving impossible, and thus dramatically undercutting one of UDC's goals.[97]

Eastwood also suffered lukewarm reception in the market. Promotional efforts for Roosevelt Island, which included a Manhattan sales office on 50th Street near Fifth Avenue, were geared to middle-class families attracted to living in a progressive, mixed community knowing that it was just "400 yards east of Sutton Place," one of the Upper East Side's tonier enclaves. The campaign also included stylized brochures, newspapers ads, and limousine service to carry prospective tenants to the site, which before the subway and tram opened could only be done via a bridge from the gritty Ravenswood section of Long Island City (fig. 5.31). Yet while promoted as a "middle-income" complex, like many later Mitchell-Lama complexes and other complexes built using federal below-market-interest-rate mortgages, Eastwood, with simple finishes such as asphalt tile, was really targeted to families of very modest income. As an isolated construction site without transportation and shops, however, Roosevelt Island alienated this clientele, since unlike more affluent households they would be more dependent on local amenities. As the construction wrapped up, half of higher-rent Island House, across the street, was leased, but only 20 percent of lower-cost Eastwood. It would not fill until 1978, after completion of the tram and good word of mouth.[98]

5.32: Eastwood, kitchen, 2014

Weak initial demand does not seem to have been a direct result of the project's unique design, however, which residents embraced. Sert introduced the skip-stop system of vertical circulation not just to save money (as was done in some earlier low-cost housing projects) but to allow a plan giving most units windows facing both east and west (fig. 5.32). Yet more crucial to the life of the building were the corridors, which as a result of the skip-stop system were shared by three stories of occupants. These halls overlooked the courtyards through a ribbon of windows and tenants often congregated along them to observe the activity below. Another unique feature was that on the fourth floor the corridors ran uninterrupted, nearly a quarter of a mile, through the entire complex, which was otherwise divided into eleven separate buildings served by a total of eight entrances and elevator banks. This was especially appreciated by the many tenants who came to have extended family in the complex. Lobbies, like the corridors, were also large and open, with views to both Main Street and the East River. On the inland side, the building extended over the sidewalk, creating an arcaded sidewalk with benches, which became a popular place among the complex's many elderly and disabled tenants (fig. 5.33). On the water side, the building extended over the perimeter road to the shoreline, defining small seating areas that became especially favored by teenagers. The planning and social mixture immediately paid dividends: social groups began to form around caregivers for the disabled or around playgroups for families; sidewalk sales happened regularly to fill the void left by the lack of commercial opportunities. Small businesses serving daily needs of the residents eventually filled in most of the commercial spaces along the covered arcade.[99]

While successful in these respects, UDC's high-risk strategy of using expensive fast-track construction for moderate-rent housing in difficult-to-market areas led to

5.33: Roosevelt Island, Main Street and Eastwood arcade, 2014

a series of difficulties that sapped resident confidence in management. According to Eastwood's owner, Jerome Belson, a long-time lawyer who had helped unions and others develop limited-equity co-ops beginning in the 1950s, cost limits made Eastwood a challenge to run. "You're being given a project [by UDC] with an architect that you didn't select, with a price that you didn't create, with a number of units that you didn't dictate, with the specifications that you didn't set forth, and you're told, come in with a[n unrealistically low] number." Then once open, operating subsidies promised by HUD failed to materialize. "We had no income. The residents were paying their subsidized portion, but the federal government didn't come along for eighteen months before they were able to give us the contract that would make up their portion of the rent. So that every . . . one of the developments that we had, was a failure fiscally from day one."[100] Meanwhile, there were costly construction problems. Failure to install fire stops in walls between apartments, for example, caused a series of multi-unit fires. There were also ongoing problems with water in the masonry walls and parapets, which damaged units. But because two of the three contractors went bankrupt, recovery of funds was impossible. This led Belson to propose a rent increase in the early 1980s. Tenants resisted, leading to a fifteen-month rent strike.[101]

Ongoing tensions between landlord, tenants, and New York State, which continued to oversee UDC's below-market projects after the agency collapsed, led Governor Mario Cuomo in 1986 to create a new governing body called the Roosevelt Island Operating Corporation (RIOC) with responsibility for operation, management, and future development on the island. Unlike UDC, it relied on earned income, outside grants, and an annual state operating subsidy to pay for maintenance and services. Unfortunately, no tenants were placed on the board until revisions to RIOC's by-laws in 2008, which reserved three of the nine seats for residents of the island. Neither creation of RIOC nor the change resolved all conflict, however. One especially bitter, long-term struggle has been over security. Sert's interior corridors as public spaces and the building's twenty-four separate entries left Eastwood vulnerable. Fortifying the building meant either more vertical patrols (and more security officers) or adding internal barriers. The tenants fiercely resisted the latter. Both before and after 2008, however, RIOC refused to hire more security, despite the fact that Eastwood rents would have covered half the cost.[102]

This conflict and others, while frustrating, suggest the deep sense of ownership that many tenants, especially long-term rent-restricted ones, feel toward the complex in spite of their status as renters. Around 2004, amid a citywide wave of Mitchell-Lama privatizations, faculty and students from the Department of Environmental Psychology at the CUNY Graduate Center surveyed Eastwood residents. Eighty-six percent indicated that they felt that RIOC was not meeting its responsibilities and all believed residents should comprise the majority of RIOC's board. The study also revealed anxieties about privatization and displacement. Eight-four percent worried that they were being pushed out by new higher-income residents. As one tenant put it: "We've lived here for 30 years, and we know we are going to have to leave in a year or so. We won't be able to afford it."[103]

Yet perhaps paradoxically, attempts in 2004 by an elected tenant group, Eastwood Building Committee, to pursue a tenant-sponsored co-op conversion faltered. The effort lost in good part because although conversion would have protected tenants, like all conversions it also would cost tenants money in the short term. The landlord, who hoped to hold onto the building and convert it to market-rate rental, launched a misinformation campaign exploiting these anxieties, overstating potential expenses. Fear won and the building went private under a plan that protected the tenancies of current below-market tenants, making Eastwood the only one of the three original Roosevelt Island buildings to not convert to owner-occupancy.[104]

Around this time the project changed hands. The new owner, Urban American Management, immediately grasped the latent value in Eastwood. The company created a new upscale identity, Roosevelt Landings, despite the unconventional design, renovating lobbies and adding bike storage. It also began updating apartments as they are vacated, installing wood-veneer flooring and new kitchen surfaces. The firm also joined a wider campaign by RIOC to update the commercial district in Eastwood's arcade, although the plan remains only partially realized, as much of the new retail activity on Roosevelt Island concentrated in new market-rate buildings located closer to the subway and tram. Since 2007 the share of below-market tenants has fallen from 87 to 58 percent. In the place of older residents on limited incomes have come many college-age students and young families (who enjoy rents still 35 percent less than in Manhattan), testament to wider market pressures, the growing attractiveness of Roosevelt Island as a whole, and the enduring appeal of Sert's unconventional design.[105]

Futher instability has been engendered by efforts to improve energey efficiency. Since opening, power has been included in rental charages. This made sense originally given the incomes of tenants and also that UDC negotiated favorable electricity rates from Con Edison. Unfortunately, this led UDC to choose inexpensive-to-install but inefficient systems like electric baseboard heating. Now that Eastwood pays market rates for power, about half of building costs are for energy. The problem is exaccertabed by large windows, double exposures, and a complicated exterior form. Since buying the complex, Urban American has installed new windows but now also wants to install submeters that would allow it to bill tenants for power. In a protracted battle, where it appears the residents will eventually lose, each apartment will be responsible for energy use. While legal and not uncommon, this outcome will be very difficult for the long-time below-market tenants. Tests have indicated some apartments may face costs as high as $400 to $800 a month, which Urban American might be able to absorb into market rents but would need to pass on to below-market ones. As Eastwood struggles in this way and others to adjust to life after its initial subsidies have expired, its future as a diverse below-market complex appears to be in doubt.[106] MATTHIAS ALTWICKER

Hip Hop and Subsidized Housing

Hip hop is an intensely urban art form that was nurtured in New York City's below-market subsidized housing developments. While housing reformers since the 1930s envisioned closely supervised, wholesome social and cultural activities in community spaces as a substitute for the saloon and other commercial entertainment, hip hop emerged in the 1970s as both a rejection of this middle-class morality and as a grassroots cultural response to the decline of other opportunities in inner-city neighborhoods. Hip hop, in short, was nothing less than urban youth's response to poverty, racism, and the civil rights movement.[107] It provided a powerful vehicle for sharing stories about the urban experience and, for the first time, gave marginalized youth of color, especially African Americans, a platform to tell their stories and to fashion a distinct cultural identity. Hip hop was both a movement in music and style as well as a pointed critique of everyday life in a big city in crisis.

Hip hop's genesis is widely attributed to a 1973 party at General Sedgwick House (1969), a Mitchell-Lama rental building in the West Bronx. Here, in the complex's community room, DJ Kool Herc hosted the first documented party that involved all four elements of hip hop: DJing, MCing, graffiti, and breakdancing.[108] Hip hop is, in many ways, the product of the distinct environment of New York in this era. Characterized by disinvestment and despair but also a generous landscape of subsidized housing and other community spaces, the South Bronx, in particular, proved rich terrain for the nascent movement (fig. 5.34). According to South Bronx rapper Grandmaster Caz:

> The times and the environment played a big part in bringing about hip hop. I think that the [economic] conditions had more to do than anything with hip hop. And it was a physical thing, you know? We played in those burnt out, abandoned lots. We jumped off fire escapes into dirty mattresses in these places. The conditions that we lived in were right in our faces. This was at the forefront of us, so we needed a relief—a coping mechanism.[109]

At the same time hip hop culture was a means for local youth to resist the burning of the Bronx. According to Maria Fernandez of the Urban Youth Collaborative, a New York-based youth organization that promotes justice in urban education, "groups of young people used dance and hip hop as a way of fighting back the attack and neglect of their neighborhoods . . . it allowed them to express their anger and claim territory through that art."[110]

The specific combination of a ravaged urban landscape and many inexpensive-to-use spaces was a key element in hip hop's genesis. Despite widespread disinvestment, places open to young people remained plentiful and at little to no cost: in parks, playgrounds, and recreation centers; in unpoliced streets; in storefront nightclubs; and in the function rooms of public housing and Mitchell-Lama complexes (fig. 5.35). This urban commons allowed growth of an expression that required both spaces to gather and the talents of a diverse range of individuals. Rap, DJing, and breakdancing emerged through technical experimentation and collaboration. At Kool Herc's famous party, the combination of beats scratched from a record player with a greater role for the MC (master of ceremonies) produced the rhythmic spoken word that define "freestyle" rap. That middle-income Mitchell-Lama buildings—home to kids with access to stereo equipment and large record collections—were typically located near low-income public housing, and parties drew kids from both kind of developments facilitated cross-fertilization.[111]

5.34: Party, Bronx River Houses, Tony Tone and Red Alert, by Joe Conzo, 1981

Building courtyards, in particular, produced encounters between young aspiring MCs. In his memoir, *Decoded*, Jay

5.35: Party, Bronx River Houses, Cold Crush Bros., by Joe Conzo, 1981

Z discusses his early exposure to rap in the green spaces at the Marcy Houses in Brooklyn's Bedford-Stuyvesant, where he grew up: "DJs started setting up sound systems in the development courtyards and me and . . . other MCs from around the way would battle one another."[112] Breakdancing moves were similarly developed, compared, and shared in parks, while graffiti styles and techniques spread through the tagging of public walls and urban infrastructure. The four elements of hip hop also came together in large block parties. In the summer, DJs would take power from street lamps to run turntables and speakers. Parks also offered a place to gather, freestyle, play music, and look at the new tags passing by on trains.

These places provided the necessary socio-spatial configurations for hip hop to flourish because they were accessible: one did not need more than two or three dollars to attend parties, and park jams were free to all (fig. 5.36). Both provided a powerful resource for youth to transform, claim, and shape the built environment. According to Orlando Torres, a Bronx-based community organizer,

> Hip hop is an expression of public space. Everything that was being done in those years in the 1970s and the 1980s was in public space. The parties were in public space. The graffiti was in public space. The dancing was in public space. The music started outside at those public housing parties. It was not declaration of 'we want public space'—at that point the space was already there and it was abandoned. What people were saying was: this is ours and we're going to make it beautiful.[113]

In the words of Bonz Malone, a writer who grew up in the Bronx, "for us, it was a way of taking something depressing—something depressed—and making it into something cool."[114]

5.36: Hip Hop Flyer, Leland House Mitchell-Lama complex, 1983

The notoriety of gang tagging and the rise of hard-core "gangsta" rap in the 1990s led many to view hip hop as a menace, while "broken windows" theories of policing, popularized in the 1980s, drove graffiti underground. But although gangs have appropriated some elements of hip hop—many have their own graffiti artists, rappers, and breakdancers—for most, hip hop crews represented an alternative to gang membership. Rap battles, competition between breakdancing crews, and graffiti writers gave youth the opportunity to form identity groups and to build respect in their communities without recourse to violence.

For Afrika Bambaataa hip hop was indeed an answer to the violence of gang conflict in the South Bronx. Being a member of a hip hop "crew" rather than a gang offered protection and a sense of purpose, not to mention a nonviolent means with which to establish a reputation. After a formative trip to Africa, Bambaataa, who had once been a member of the Black Spades gang, formed the Bronx River Organization. It was named for, and based in, the Bronx River Houses, a NYCHA complex in Soundview, where he lived. Along with other prominent DJs, including DJ Kool Herc and Kool DJ Dee, Bambaataa hosted meetings and hip hop parties in the complex's community rooms, hoping to draw kids out of gangs. The organization served as the platform for the Universal Zulu Nation, a group that came to serve a sort of governing body for hip hop, while devoting energy to quelling gang activity. Bonz Malone estimates that Zulu Nation "smashed 40 gangs because of hip hop."[115]

XXL Magazine columnist Brendan Frederick has described hip hop as a "the voice of specific blocks, capturing the distinct tone and timbre of an artist's environment."[116] Life in New York City's below-market subsidized housing, and in particular

5.37: Jay Z at Marcy Houses, "99 Problems," music video, dir. Mark Romanek, 2004

low-income public housing, has thus been carefully documented. The Marcy Houses and the Queensbridge Houses are two especially significant projects in the legacy of hip hop (fig. 5.37). Queensbridge in particular was home to many important artists, as well a site of the "Bridge Wars," a very public rivalry in the 1980s over the provenance of hip hop between the complex's Juice Crew and the South Bronx's Boogie Down Productions. Complexes like these continue to occupy a seminal space in the hip hop imaginary as artists establish childhood homes as cultural landmarks in their rhymes. Place-based references create context for stories rappers tell about their life experiences. As Jay Z writes: "Housing projects are . . . these huge islands built mostly in the middle of nowhere, designed to warehouse lives. People are still people, though, so we turned the projects into real communities, poor or not." Meanwhile, he continues, "even when we could shake off the full weight of those buildings and just try to live, the truth of our lives and struggle was still invisible to the larger country."[117] LILIAN KNORR

6

The Decentralized Network

Commitment to subsidized housing, weak to begin with in the United States, eroded significantly in the 1970s and 1980s, even in New York City. Public housing had become stigmatized by its negative association, only sometimes accurate, with poverty, crime, and drugs. Middle-income complexes like Co-op City (1968–73), which were concentrated in New York City but could also be found in other American cities, muddled through serious financial and management problems. Compounding these challenges were financial straits that threatened cities' ability to manage basic affairs, let alone build new housing. At the same time many of the old rationales for below-market housing, including high rents and housing shortages, dissipated as a result of steep population losses, widespread abandonment, and, in New York, robust rent controls, which were bolstered by a new Vietnam Era rent "stabilization" law, passed in 1969 with support of leftist activists at organizations such as the Metropolitan Council on Housing.

The idea that below-market subsidized housing could stabilize neighborhoods, however, gained a new cogency amid widespread urban disinvestment. Many in New York and other cities worked creatively to cultivate new tools, programs, and agents to fill the voids left by abandonment, arson, and the disappearance of federal, city, and state programs and long-trusted partners like the United Housing Foundation. The result was that from the ashes of the welfare state arose what one expert has characterized as a new "decentralized housing network."[1] At its core were community development corporations, city and state agencies responsible for housing and housing finance, foundations offering technical assistance, and an evolving range of small-scale grants, tax credits, and other inducements offered by the city, state, and federal governments that could be harnessed toward housing. New York, as in earlier eras of housing reform, was a leader.

The wider context for the emergence of the decentralized network was the international urban crisis: deindustrialization and population loss in inner sections of older industrial cities, including New York. Despite the efforts to modernize the city in the 1950s and 1960s through redevelopment, by 1971 New York's suburbs had more than half the metropolitan population and half of its manufacturing, retail jobs, and restaurants.[2] And the trend seemed to be accelerating: between 1969 and 1976 the city lost 600,000 jobs, primarily in manufacturing. And between 1970 and 1980 the city lost a million residents. Left behind were a small elite in gold coast sections of Manhattan and Brownstone Brooklyn, a dwindling number of white middle-class enclaves elsewhere, and a growing working class, mainly of color, with declining occupational prospects.

New York also suffered from some unique problems built up over decades of aggressive government expansion. The city government's large unionized workforce, expensive social welfare programs, and staggering debts drove budgets billions of dollars into the red in the 1970s. Declining property values; loss of tens of thousands of apartments due to abandonment, arson, and demolition; generous tax abatements for below-market and, as a construction stimulus, market-rate housing; and the loss of manufacturing and employment, all made it difficult to pay mounting bills. In 1975 the municipal bond market cut the city off.[3] To rescue what was still America's largest and most important financial center, Governor Hugh Carey created the Municipal Assistance Corporation in 1975, led by financier Felix Rohatyn. Restoration of faith in the city required severe austerity measures, which were carried out by Mayors Abraham Beame (1974–77) and Edward I. Koch (1978–89). The result was higher taxes, higher transit fares, and elimination and reduction of social programs.[4] Maintaining existing below-market housing, let alone a new housing program, seemed all but impossible.

To many, much of the city looked beyond saving. Large sections of the South Bronx, Lower East Side, Harlem, and Brooklyn had transformed beyond recognition since World War II, as second-generation white immigrants left and Black and Puerto Rican families, suffering high rates of unemployment, moved in. Despite substantial public investment in subsidized housing, these neighborhoods suffered from rapid withdrawal of capital. Loans were impossible since banks had redlined these areas as investment risks, making it difficult for even conscientious landlords to improve their buildings.[5] Most owners, meanwhile, claimed with some justification that rent control and rent stabilization, however popular with voters, made it impossible to maintain and heat their buildings. Apartments in these areas may have been cheap to rent, but after decades of deferred maintenance, conditions were often abysmal, leaving tenants reliant on ovens for heat, fire hydrants for water, and, if lucky, the city for coal (fig. 6.1).

6.1: Mobile heating unit, 51½ W. 129th St., Manhattan, by Tyrone Dukes, 1971

As in other U.S. cities in steep decline, many landlords paid "torches"

6.2: Near Bathgate Ave. and E. 173rd St., Bronx, by Mel Rosenthal, ca. 1976–82

to burn down their properties, even while some residents remained. Some speculators bought and burned buildings as part of complicated financial schemes to defraud federal rehabilitation subsidies. Junkies, too, set fires to steal pipes, wire, plumbing fixtures, and architectural elements. Some experts claimed that tenants even set their own apartments on fire to try to get emergency relocation payments and priority placement in public housing. In New York, the cash-strapped city government moved slowly to track down the perpetrators.[5] By the late 1970s, 100,000 apartments had been lost citywide, prompting leaders like city housing administrator Roger Starr to explore the idea of "planned shrinkage."[6] City Hall, meanwhile, had no choice but to raze damaged properties, leaving acres of empty lots (fig. 6.2).

6.3: Tenant placed in charge of her building by the courts, 1086 Kelly St., Bronx, by Edward Hausner, 1969

With few other options, the city settled on a policy of small-scale rehabilitation (fig. 6.3). The city had supported renovation as far back as 1946, when it introduced a tax-abatement program known as "J-51" to encourage landlords to subdivide larger, older apartments into smaller ones as a way to cope with postwar housing shortages. Amended in 1955 and again in the 1970s, it became a critical tool, helping to produce or modernize 675,000 apartments by 1977.[7] The push for rehabilitation accelerated under mayors John Lindsay and Abraham Beame, whose commissioner of housing, Roger Starr, helped steer remaining government subsidies into renovation programs, despite his quip about planned shrinkage.[8]

As the worst of the urban crisis abated in the 1980s, renovation continued to enjoy widespread support. This was a practical strategy given that the city could no longer support large-scale construction. It was also ideological, as a new generation of leaders who, like Jane Jacobs, had more faith in the past than in Modernism assumed power. It was clear to all that chief among the few bright spots in the fatigued city were "brownstoning," loft living, and the conversion of aging apartment houses to cooperatives. These efforts were aided by a 1971 state program encouraging lenders to make mortgage loans for the purchase of individual co-op apartments—a practice they had long resisted—and by two federal laws introduced as part of a class-action settlement out of Chicago to correct redlining: the Home Mortgage Disclosure Act (1975) and the Community Reinvestment Act, or CRA (1977). These laws required lenders to disclose where they made loans (a shaming tactic) and then to increase loan activity in areas in which they took deposits. Under the program lenders like Chemical Bank (now Chase), established a subsidiary, Chemical Community Development, which by the late 1980s made more than $100 million in commitments for housing, primarily renovation of aging apartment buildings in places like Brooklyn's Bedford-Stuyvesant. CRA requirements have remained an important source of financing for housing in underserved urban areas nationally ever since.[9]

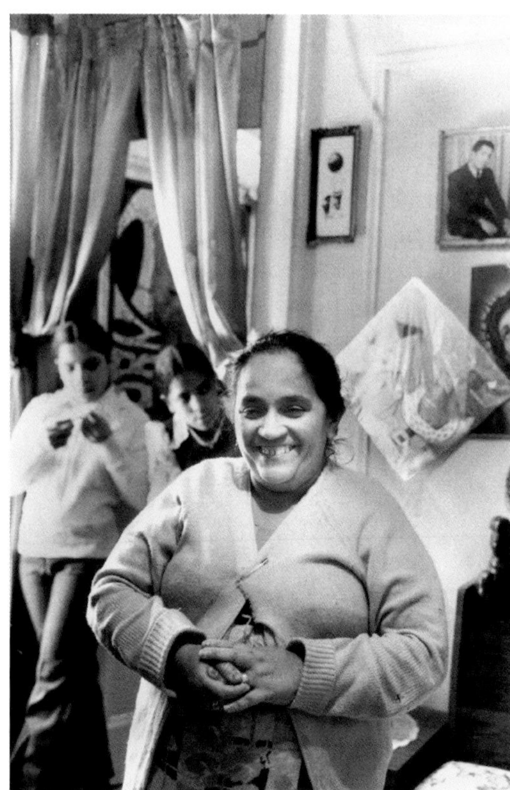

6.4: Tenant at Community Management Program building (for *in rem* properties), operated by Adopt-a-Building, 73–75 Ave. C, Manhattan, by Chester Higgins, Jr., 1978

The numerous tenant activists who worked to save their own buildings also gave form to the decentralized housing network. Among the first efforts in this direction were those of the so-called homesteaders (fig. 6.4). With the aid of new nonprofits like the Urban Homesteading Assistance Board (U-HAB), established in 1973 by former city employees, tenants began converting buildings that had been abandoned by their owners to tenant-led limited-equity co-ops. U-HAB helped groups prepare cost estimates, hire professionals, write grant applications, and work with the city to obtain permissions and loans. With funds from a federal employment the program also trained groups to do much of the renovation work themselves. To aid in this bootstrapping process the

6.5: Mid-Bronx Desperadoes at site of new row houses, Longfellow Ave., Bronx, by Ted Thai, 1996

city began foreclosing on buildings in deep tax arrears that had extensive housing code violations and/or on which the city had already been forced to make emergency repairs, then sold the buildings to the tenants or to other nonprofit operators. This aggressive *in rem* foreclosure program stands in stark contrast to the experience of other U.S. cities, where all too often tax-delinquent properties were allowed to rot beyond repair.[10]

New neighborhood-based community development corporations (CDCs) complemented these efforts by putting city funds and the *in rem* program to work on a larger scale. Among the first CDCs to focus on housing were the Mid-Bronx Desperadoes, established in 1974 by Genevieve S. Brooks and other "desperate" citizens, and the South East Bronx Community Organization (SEBCO), which had been established in 1968 by Father Louis Gigante, a local priest, but which ventured into housing in 1975. Other early CDCs active in housing included Banana Kelly, BUILD (Bronx United in Leveraging Dollars), Fordham Bedford Housing Corporation, South Bronx Churches (affiliated with Nehemiah Houses), and Nos Quedamos, all in the Bronx; the Fifth Avenue Committee in Brooklyn; and Harlem Congregations for Community Improvement in Manhattan. These groups and others undertook larger-scale renovations of tax-delinquent properties. Later many also did new construction (fig. 6.5). SEBCO's first project, for example, rehabilitated nine buildings with 360 units, using funding from project-based Section 8, one of the federal government's post-public-housing programs. Over the next quarter century SEBCO renovated and then developed from scratch more than six thousand apartments in 450 buildings. The group also established subsidiaries for management, maintenance, and security.[11]

The emphasis on self-help and community uplift aligned squarely with growing wariness of the welfare state in the United States. Rather than government intervention the poor now created their own housing, rules, governance, and sense of community. Yet for all the novelty of the decentralized housing network—and the marked social gap between CDC leaders, drawn from their communities, and the middle-class housing reformers of earlier generations—the new system reflected long-held beliefs and adopted long-held practices. Most CDCs, for instance, carefully screened tenants for stable income and good behavior even at the lowest income levels, checking credit and housing histories, and conducting home interviews. The new CDCs also developed social-service programs for their tenants, including those for employment and literacy training, childcare, counseling, and recreation. The goal as in earlier eras remained not just to provide better material conditions but also to offer good housing as a reward for certain behaviors while neglecting the so-called difficult-to-house, including those whose incomes were so low as to require much deeper subsidies.

Critical to the success of CDCs were a range of new larger-scale nonprofits. Outside New York City, privately built below-market housing developed in the 1960s suffered high rates of foreclosure, often due to inexperienced community-led management.[12] The late 1970s and early 1980s saw a proliferation of nonprofits providing professional support for CDCs as they navigated a complex new financial, legal, and managerial landscape. Most of these groups were financed by philanthropists, including the Ford Foundation (Local Initiatives Support Corporation [LISC; 1979]), developer James Rouse (Enterprise Foundation; 1982), and in New York, David Rockefeller (Community Preservation Corporation; 1974, and the New York City Housing Partnership; 1982) (fig. 6.6).

An even more crucial ally was local government. In New York City the chief public partner for CDCs was the Department of Housing Preservation and Development (HPD). Established in 1977 as a successor, most immediately, to the Housing and Development Administration of Mayor Lindsay, HPD was responsible, among other things, for carrying out unfinished urban renewal plans and proposing and managing new ones, despite the demise of federal Title I funds. It also administered federal housing and redevelopment grants with the exception of those for public housing, and managed the sale of *in rem* buildings.

HPD administrators took an active role in the new housing network, conducting housing inventories, prioritizing projects that they anticipated would have the greatest impact on neighborhoods, and managing the tenanting process, which was done increasingly by a combination of screening and lottery. To support these efforts HPD also opened satellite offices in Harlem, the Tremont section of the Bronx, and other distressed sections. Additionally, administrators developed standards for renovation that focused on basic systems such as boilers, roofs, plumbing, and kitchens, which made housing safe but kept capital costs low.[13] Over time the agency also nurtured more specialized firms to assist CDCs in renovating, owning, and managing privately built or renovated "HPD" buildings. They included Lemle and

6.6: David Rockefeller, right, with HPD Commissioner Abraham Biderman on tour of South Bronx, by Neal Boenzi, 1989

Wolff, which began developing the first of seven thousand apartments in 1981, and Grenadier Realty, run by former HPD official Felice Michetti, which by 2015 managed 22,000 below-market units, many for CDCs.[14] Mayor Koch formalized all these initiatives in a $5.1 billion, Ten-year Housing Plan launched in 1986. Running well into the 1990s—through the David Dinkins administration (1990–93) and into that of Rudolph Giuliani (1994–2001)—it helped to restore or build 100,000 apartments.[15] Other divisions of the city, meanwhile, such as the planning commission, partnered with the federal government and private lenders to make loans available for projects approved by HPD. Especially successful were initiatives like the Neighborhood Preservation Program and the New York City Rehabilitation Mortgage Insurance Corporation, both created in 1973.

New York's renewed investment in below-market housing also benefited enormously from—and paralleled—a quiet revolution in housing policy in Washington. In the 1960s and 1970s many Americans began to think of below-market housing as ungovernable, culminating in 1974's Community Development Act. Another watershed moment came in 1986. That year, Congress amended the Internal Revenue Code to permit low-income housing tax credits (LIHTC, and pronounced *lie-tech*). The LIHTC program offered generous tax breaks to businesses willing to invest in below-market housing that met certain requirements. More critically, the credits were transferable, allowing developers to sell them to investors to generate the cash needed to build. In practice tax credits served as a generous source of back-door funds that were all but insulated from attack in Washington because the program was operated by the IRS rather than by HUD. The financial complexity of "packaging" the tax credits required specialized skills that most CDCs did not have, forcing them to turn to LISC, Enterprise, and other experts.[16] But with their help the tax credits created an all but entirely new below-market housing industry that in twenty-five years produced half again as much housing (2.5 million units through 2012) as had been built under forty years of public housing.[17]

Unfortunately for New York the new system showed the city none of the favor that public housing had. Congress allocated LIHTCs on a per capita basis to state housing finance agencies rather than through grants to housing authorities, which under public housing had favored aggressive agencies such as NYCHA. In addition credits did not come with subsidies for construction as for public housing, nor did they cover the cost of site acquisition or clearance. This put high-cost cities like New York at a further disadvantage and required them to use additional subsidies—local, state, and federal—to get projects done. Nevertheless, by 2010 more than 80,000 apartments housing an estimated 210,000 people had been built with the help of LIHTCs in New York City. Factoring in other programs of the 1970s, 1980s and 1990s, the decentralized network of CDCs yielded yet more impressive results. The Bronx, for instance, saw restoration of 36,863 apartments and construction of about 12,700 new ones between 1978 and 1986, while Washington Heights in Northern Manhattan saw rehabilitation of 13,898 apartments by 1993. By 2004 David Rockefeller's New York City Housing Partnership had helped create 18,000 housing units citywide. The Community Preservation Corporation has financed the preservation or development of 147,000 in the region, mostly in New York City.[18]

By design many of these efforts served a broader spectrum of families than public housing. One of the rationales for dismantling public housing at the federal level in 1973 was mounting evidence that concentration of poverty, fomented by the market but reinforced by policy, hindered upward mobility. Voucher programs, in fact, were first tested not to address management problems but to expand tenant opportunities. LIHTCs and other programs that emerged in the 1970s and 1980s were similarly engineered to avoid concentration of those most in need. This flexibility often aligned with local political priorities. Moreover, it helped leaders in New York to fill the gap left not just by the demise of public housing but of middle-income programs like Mitchell-Lama. In practice the decentralized housing network introduced a range of rental tiers with units earmarked for households at income thresholds ranging from between 30 percent to 175 percent of average city income (what HUD refers to as area mean income, or AMI). Mixing of incomes had the additional benefits of broadening political support for below-market subsidized housing and engendering diverse neighborhoods.

If public housing and Mitchell-Lama encouraged bigness, smaller-scale programs like LIHTC helped cement the turn toward smaller-scale approaches designed to revitalize, rather than replace, existing neighborhoods. This shift in approach is perhaps most vivid in efforts in the early 1980s to replace abandoned multistory tenements in the South Bronx with small freestanding houses, in effect bringing suburbia to the city. The example that attracted the most attention was Charlotte Gardens (1983–87). The site was a swath of rubble-strewn lots that had been made infamous when Jimmy Carter stopped there while campaigning for president in 1977. Developed beginning in 1982 by the South Bronx Development Organization—created by Mayor Koch and directed by Edward J. Logue—in partnership with the Mid-Bronx Desperadoes CDC, the development comprised ninety single-family houses (fig. 6.7). Each cost about $80,000 to $110,000 ($180,000 to $230,000) to build but sold for $47,000 to $59,000 ($105,000 to $125,000) with subsidies, including federal grants from U.S. HUD.[19]

6.7: Charlotte Gardens, 2010

Although the clapboard houses were popular with their tenants, many leaders were skeptical of the small-scale approach. In 1987 one deputy mayor proclaimed that single-family "houses cannot be the answer to New York's housing problems."[20] And Bronx Borough President Fernando Ferrer argued that city efforts should "mix density and provide a fabric for the community—not Levittown."[21] A more efficient and sustainable approach that drew inspiration more from Jane Jacobs than Long Island was attached row houses. In 1983 East Brooklyn Congregations with the help of Ira D. Robbins, a retired developer active in civic affairs, and the Industrial Areas Foundation formed a CDC called Nehemiah Housing Development Fund and began building the first of many hundreds of simple, inexpensive row houses in Brownsville and East New York. Projects on this model soon appeared in many other parts of the city, and the format remained in use well into the second decade of the twenty-first century (fig. 6.8,

6.8: Partnership New Homes, Washington Ave. and E. 179th St., Tremont, Bronx, by Grace Madden, 1998

6.9: Homeowners, Nehemiah Houses, Brownsville, Brooklyn, by Sarah Krulwich, 1987

fig. 6.9). By the 1990s many CDCs were also using LIHTCs to develop larger apartment buildings, although not on the scale afforded by postwar policies. Typically, the new CDC apartments complexes were six- to eight story buildings designed to complement their older neighbors (fig. 6.10). These "contextual" multifamily models soon came to dominate.

As the decentralized housing network became more capable and was re-created in places like the Bay Area, where BRIDGE Housing Corporation (formerly the Bay Area Residential Investment and Development Group) became one of the largest providers of below-market housing nationally, the urban crisis began to abate. Earlier booms in market-rate co-op and condominium housing in the 1960s and 1970s foreshadowed a more enduring renaissance of city centers, especially in a global financial center like New York. After decades of below-market housing as a tool for reversing the forces of decentralization, reconcentration announced itself as a powerful market countermovement in the 1980s and 1990s as young professionals and bohemians began to "colonize" run-down neighborhoods. Housers in this context reframed below-market efforts as a bulwark against gentrification. Meanwhile, new immigrants began to return to city neighborhoods with

6.10: Spring Creek Gardens, East New York, Brooklyn, by Nancy Siesel, 1989

6.11 Norfolk Apartments, 108–10 Norfolk St., Manhattan, 2014

the lifting of restrictions on foreign immigration. Although the majority of immigrants now settled in suburbs rather than urban ethnic villages, in New York City burgeoning numbers of families from Asia, Latin America, Africa, and the Caribbean put new pressures on areas like Chinatown, prompting CDCs like Asian Americans for Equality to develop housing for the first time (fig. 6.11).

New York's improving social and economic conditions challenged below-market housing in several ways. One was surging demand. In the 1960s and 1970s many Mitchell-Lama buildings outside Manhattan went begging for tenants until Section 8 vouchers were introduced. Ten years later, by contrast, new HPD buildings received many qualified applicants for every apartment, leading to the introduction of lotteries and waiting lists (fig. 6.12). Another problem was surging costs, especially as the stock of city-owned foreclosed land dried up. Yet another was attrition. Public housing, owned by the city, was permanently low-rent, but other forms of below-market subsidized housing were not. So long as the city was in the economic doldrums there was little threat of this housing going market-rate because, in effect, there was no market. In the 1980s, however, rent and resale restrictions began to expire as market prices began to climb. For a time the city was able to stave off "going private" by offering extensions on tax abatements and low-interest loans for rehabilitation. This strategy, which later came to be called "preservation," was effective only to a point, however, succeeding mainly where large majorities of the tenants lived on fixed incomes, such as at Penn South (1962).

Economic exuberance also presented new opportunities for generating below-market housing. One method was a cross-subsidy program like inclusionary zoning (IZ), where landlords and market-rate tenants helped to subsidize below-market ones. Historically, IZ had been most successful in suburbs being rapidly built up, like Montgomery County, Maryland, adjacent to Washington, D.C. In New York, the idea generated resistance from developers, who claimed

6.12: 15,000 applications for 208 units in Bedford-Stuyvesant, Brooklyn, by Don Hogan Charles, 1984

that passing costs onto market-rate tenants made prices uncompetitive. But as the housing market became more robust, the plan became viable, promising not just more affordable units but a way to advance the social goal of deconcentrating poverty. As introduced in New York, however, the law permitted below-market units to be built off site or in separate sections of a complex, raising questions about the effectiveness of the program in creating social mixture.

In the 1980s the city and state began offering low-interest rate loans and tax abatements for projects in select areas in which one unit of below-market housing was included for every four market-rate units. Early on, most "80/20" buildings were in Manhattan. More recently many also have appeared in gentrified sections of Brooklyn and Queens, especially after the program was expanded to include waterfront areas "upzoned" to encourage their transition from fallow industrial use to high-density residential. Despite its limitations, because IZ shifted much of the burden for construction onto groups often construed as villains in the battle for affordable housing—developers and market-rate tenants—it has attracted disproportionate media attention. Today, indeed, it is often considered to be a system whose capacity is on par with conventional subsidy programs, despite very limited evidence and disappointing early results.

The city's rising fortunes have also inspired other innovations in housing such as the neo-SRO (single-room occupancy) dwelling. Since the nineteenth century, the focus of American housers has been families and, occasionally, the elderly. Yet as flophouses and SROs closed in response to market pressures and community op-

position in the 1960s and 1970s, homelessness became a problem, compounded by the closure of state institutional homes. In the 1980s cities nationwide struggled to modernize and expand their networks of shelters. Housers, meanwhile, pioneered innovative service-oriented neo-SROs called "supportive housing." One of the leaders in this field was Rosanne Haggerty's Common Ground, whose first project was the Times Square, built in the shell of an old Manhattan hotel in 1991. Since then Haggerty and other providers have marshaled city and state fund to build thousands of units (fig. 6.13).[22]

If New York City housers responded with energy and creativity to the retrenchment of the welfare state, it is perhaps a great irony that the decentralized housing network has, in many respects, served other places better. Outside of New York, the decentralized network achieved a degree of efficacy and popularity that public housing and older below-market models never could. Small in scale, often neotraditional in design, and under no compulsion to demonstrate government economies, developers created low- and middle-income housing complexes that blended in with their surroundings. The new approach became so popular, in fact, that many cities chose to replace their public housing with new complexes using a HUD program created to rehabilitate "distressed" sites called HOPE VI (for Homeownership and Opportunity for People Everywhere). Atlanta, which pioneered this practice, knocked down all of its traditional public housing except a few buildings for seniors. Chicago also razed thousands of apartments, including Cabrini-Green, Robert Taylor Homes, and most of the Chicago Housing Authority's other high-rises (see fig. 0.5). While some replacement public housing units were built, redevelopment targeted moderate-income families (using LIHTCs) or market-rate options. Displaced families mainly received

6.13: The Brook (2010), developed by Common Ground, by Michael Moran

vouchers. In these and other cities, the decentralized network ushered in an era of clearance that was in many respects as traumatic as that which characterized public housing to begin with.[23]

In New York things were different. The city preserved nearly all its public housing, spending billions of federal dollars to do so, as well as much of its older middle-income stock. Moreover, the decentralized network, despite limitations, increased the supply of below-market units. Much of it is very high in quality. As the decentralized network grew more sophisticated and its capacities more robust, policy makers began demanding more from designers and developers. Every state, for instance, came to require buildings receiving tax credits to meet exacting LEED (Leadership in Energy and Environmental Design) standards. Via Verde (2012) in the Bronx, which was the product of a major architectural competition, counts among the most innovative and livable apartments houses built in New York in a generation. Architects like SHoP, Magnusson Architecture and Planning, SLCE, Alexander Gorlin, and Meltzer/Mandl also designed thoughtful buildings for ever larger, more sophisticated providers such as Atlantic Development and the Related Companies, and nonprofits like Phipps Houses and the South East Bronx Community Development Corporation. The result was many bright and modern apartments that took pains to enhance, rather than overwhelm, their neighborhoods. Capacity, however, never caught up to demand. And with no new low-income public housing or large-scale middle-income housing, old scourges like excessive rents, unsafe conditions, and overcrowding, were all in evidence by the turn of the twenty-first century.

Urban Homesteading (1970s–)

Politicians did not travel to the South Bronx in the 1970s for inspiration. Like many poorer sections of New York, it had suffered for years from the abandonment and arson that gave the city a reputation for the most severe urban blight in the nation. But in the fall of 1977, after passing through blocks of vacant and fire-ravaged buildings, President Jimmy Carter came upon a site that gave him hope: a six-story, formerly abandoned tenement on Washington Avenue that had been revitalized by dozens of community members and now offered freshly painted, oak-floored apartments and rooftop solar panels.[24] The community members who inspired President Carter called their effort "urban homesteading." The group was just one of hundreds engaged in similar initiatives in 1970s New York (fig. 6.14). Though homesteading emerged initially as a survival strategy among the urban poor, participants and proponents communicated a greater political message: low-income people could themselves help solve the problems of desertion and disinvestment by taking control of abandoned buildings and turning them into owner-occupied housing cooperatives. Their argument would have a profound influence on New York housing in the 1970s and in years beyond.

Abandonment plagued lower-income neighborhoods in the 1960s and 1970s, threatening thousands of residents with homelessness. Vacant tenements lining the streets in the South Bronx, Harlem, Central Brooklyn, and the Lower East Side served as reminders of the depths of New York's economic crisis and its punishing effects on the city's lower classes. Homesteading emerged as a community response to this emergency, which officials seemed to be able to do little to stem. In dozens of buildings, tenants who were mostly African American, Latino, and poor, stayed after their landlords walked away and began to manage their building themselves. In other cases, groups of residents took over and renovated buildings that had already been abandoned.[25] Homesteaders not only alleviated dire housing conditions but also rejected the notion that poorer areas—and the people who lived there—should be written off. They illustrated how low-income New Yorkers "will neither sympathize with nor tolerate," in the words of one supporter, government neglect that strangled "communities by curtailing essential services and accelerating the already disgraceful level of decay in the inner city."[26]

6.14: Tenants assuming management of building, 580 Empire Blvd., Brooklyn, by Barton Silverman, 1972

Early successes in homesteading caught the attention of dozens of

6.15: "Save the Lower East Side," Adopt-a-Building flyer, n.d.

grassroots housing organizations that had begun forming in the late 1960s and early 1970s in low-income, heavily Black and Latino neighborhoods. What brought these grassroots groups together was the desire to improve conditions in, and tenant and community control over, neighborhood housing. Homesteading appealed, one resident noted, because "the process of trying to turn a building into a co-op is one of the people reclaiming the right to make their own decisions about their own needs." New groups like Adopt-a-Building on the Lower East Side, People's Development Corporation in the Bronx, and the citywide U-HAB emerged to help organize homesteaders, provide training, and fight for greater municipal and federal resources for homesteading initiatives (fig. 6.15).[27]

Homesteading found support from across the political spectrum, garnering not just the attention of President Carter and the media but also financing from federal and municipal programs across several administrations. The idea of low-income residents responding to a housing and economic crisis with their own sweat and

6.16: *In rem* building up for possible sale to tenants, 320 W. 53rd St., Manhattan, by William E. Sauro, 1982

labor gave homesteading political currency among both the left and the right. Unfortunately, there was relatively little money to go around in this era and homesteading never received the support necessary to combat the staggering loss of units—about thirty thousand a year by the mid-1970s. Worse yet, some city responses seemed only to deepen the crisis. Toward the end of the 1970s, for instance, the city tried to curtail landlord-abandonment by aggressively seizing tax-delinquent property. But doing so only vastly increased the amount of city-owned, occupied housing, with few avenues to remedy it. The number of city-owned buildings quadrupled between 1976 and the end of 1978 to at least 35,000 tenanted units. Residents of these long-neglected buildings faced among the worst housing conditions in the city. The City of New York became the city's biggest slumlord.[28]

But the powerful statement that homesteading made that all New Yorkers deserved decent housing and a say in its governance proved critical to reshaping policy. Housing activists and many tenants of city-owned buildings began advocating for ownership programs, arguing that since this was housing that the private market had failed, it should remain in the hands of residents not speculators. "There is no choice," they argued, "but to build a new sector for low income residential management and ownership. . . . One that is based on various forms of non-profit and cooperative ownership, and has locally and democratively [*sic*] controlled planning, management and development as its cornerstone."[29]

This grassroots pressure pushed the Koch administration to establish a Department of Alternative Management Program (DAMP) in 1978. DAMP created or vastly expanded several programs activists demanded be at the forefront of the city's response. Community Management, for example, enabled a neighborhood nonprofit housing organization to take over a city-owned building and work toward tenant self-management. The Tenant Interim Lease (TIL) program bypassed nonprofit management, allowing tenants to take ownership as a limited-equity cooperative after having proved, as a tenant group, they could successfully manage a building (fig. 6.16). The city also agreed to contracts with community organizations to help run these programs, including U-HAB, which provided essential technical assistance and training to fledgling TIL co-ops. These programs, especially TIL, vastly expanded the conversion of buildings to co-ownership. They also became a significant part of Koch's unprecedented Ten-year Housing Plan (1986). By the end of the 1980s approximately 350 buildings with 8,500 apartments had been sold to tenants as Housing Development Fund Corporations (HDFCs), New York State's legal designation for such low-income cooperatives.

6.17: 1116 Hoe Ave., tenant-owned building, 2014

Though the crisis of abandonment subsided by the 1990s, the number of HDFCs grew to more than sixteen hundred, with tens of thousands of apartments. Many struggled to survive financially. Even with support of U-HAB, buildings suffered lengthy and complex renovations, poor organization, and all the other challenges of running a complex operation collaboratively, many of which were exacerbated when shareholders were poor, often with limited professional skills. HDFCs nonetheless enriched city life tremendously. They not only provided decent and low-cost housing but helped stabilize and even revitalize their neighborhoods. As one co-op owner on Hoe Avenue in the South Bronx explained when asked why she and her neighbors had worked so hard to renovate their building after their landlord fled, it was to fortify the community: "so that we could join people one to another, so that we could be a neighborhood" (fig. 6.17). Unlike some other kinds of privately developed below-market housing, many of these low-income cooperatives were required to retain resale and income restriction in perpetuity, so when families vacate, new ones could enjoy the same.[30]

Homesteading and co-ownership were not for all; many found it as burdensome as they did empowering. But the driving principal that low-income people deserve good housing over which they have authority served the city well, and should remain a priority. "I feel proud of the fact that we are truly in control of our living space," noted one Harlem co-op resident. "*We* can control how much we pay, and *we* can insure the fact that we will be able to afford to live on the island of Manhattan" in the future.[31]
BENJAMIN HOLTZMAN

Roger Starr (1918–2001)

For half a century Roger Starr was one of the most opinionated voices in New York City housing. As leader of a housing advocacy group, the city's top housing official during the mid-1970s, and a member of the *New York Times* editorial board, Starr occupied a prominent pulpit that allowed him to be an influential, if controversial, advocate. A one-time leftist who came of age in the era of big government, his approach was most notable for its constant reinvention. From the 1940s to the 1990s Starr evolved from a young Trotskyite to an ardent New Deal liberal to a leading neoconservative. In the process, he symbolized the broader transitions that characterized New York in these decades.[32]

Born in New York, Starr embraced the ideas of Leon Trotsky while an undergraduate at Yale, then joined the Army and the U.S. Office of Strategic Services, serving in China and Burma (Myanmar). Upon his return to New York he went to work as a

6.18: Roger Starr and NYCHA Vice Chairman Simeon Golar (right) at panel on economic integration in housing, 1968

writer at CBS News and then as an executive at his father's company, which shipped construction materials. He remained there until 1974. This day job did not eclipse his affection for the legacy of the New Deal, especially in housing. In the early 1950s Starr joined the Citizens Housing and Planning Council (CHPC), a key supporter of the city's urban redevelopment efforts, and became its executive director in 1958. Here he offered enthusiastic support for the tenets of midcentury liberalism.

CHPC was established in 1937 in part to support Robert Moses's reconstruction of the city. Starr maintained the organization's advocacy for government's role in development, especially public housing, to which Starr unrelentingly pushed New York's chief executives to expand their commitment. In the late 1950s, for example, he proposed that Governor Rockefeller not only increase financial support for public housing but also require private developers of state-supported, below-market housing—such as that constructed under the Mitchell-Lama program—to reserve 20 percent of units for the poor. On the twenty-fifth anniversary of the First Houses in 1960, Starr made his position clear: "It is well that the citizens of New York commemorate this anniversary, because the vast program that has followed . . . should be one of the proudest achievements of the American people."[33] He maintained this perspective well into the 1960s (fig. 6.18).

Such orthodoxy belied Starr's intellectual and political curiosity, however. And by the late 1960s his faith in the efficacy of the public sector began to erode in the face of mounting municipal debt and rapid urban decay. By 1970 Starr was calling for a greater private sector role in below-market housing. He began to criticize sacred cows like rent control, aligning himself with landlords who claimed that state-enforced limits made their investments unsustainable and thus, ultimately, did more harm than good. As the city tipped toward fiscal crisis Starr became yet more critical of city-led housing efforts, which he characterized—like many architecture critics—as "blandness in the face of disaster."[34] Starr was hardly alone in his views. In 1973 Mayor Beame appointed him head of the city's Housing and Development Administration (HDA). Starr used this platform to advocate for new approaches that he believed better suited the realities of the 1970s. Once a major supporter of large-scale public housing, he now called for small-scale solutions, such as the three-family house. A lifelong renter, he increasingly embraced the goal of homeownership. He often criticized the very agency he helmed, vowing to dismantle it into smaller departments (a change that took place only in 1977, after his departure). In the meantime, faced with the city's insolvency, the federal moratorium on public housing, and the collapse of Mitchell-Lama, the UHF, and UDC, Starr advocated for modest measures like tax incentives for rehabilitation and, building on the nascent popularity of loft living, conversion of commercial structures into housing, both through expansion of the city's J-51 program.

Starr's most notorious idea, floated in February 1976, was "planned shrinkage." As the city found itself unable to perform its duties, Starr proposed accelerating the abandonment of certain neighborhoods, such as Brownsville and the South Bronx, by cutting support for their rehabilitation and inducing residents to move elsewhere. Public reaction was explosive. One Harlem city councilmember called it "genocidal, racist, inhuman and irresponsible." Starr anticipated such responses. But he had lost faith in the city and believed that other alternatives, like relying on grassroots revitalization efforts, could not succeed. Beame dismissed Starr as HDA's leader within the year.[35]

The controversy did not chasten Starr, who embraced his new role as a provocative public intellectual willing to question inherited policies he believed to be ineffective. In 1977 he joined the *Times*, where his opinion pieces tilted increasingly toward neoconservatism. He attacked rent control, blaming it for the city's burgeoning homelessness problem. He became enamored of law and order. In his 1985 book *The Rise and Fall of New York City*, for instance, he sympathized with the subway vigilantism of Bernhard Goetz and offered harsh critiques of welfare and its recipients. Starr never left his former selves behind entirely: editorials criticized the Reagan administration for underfunding public housing and continued to praise Robert Moses's accomplishments (if not his methods). Yet these moments were rare. Soon Starr left the city itself behind, retiring to the Poconos, where he did not have to bear witness to the collapse of New York he believed was inevitable.

Starr was wrong that New York was in permanent decline. He never lived to see the city in its second Gilded Age, characterized by accelerated private development—an approach that, at least in his later years, he would have approved. Nor did he see the reemergence of "planned shrinkage" as a strategy some offered in response to the foreclosure crisis in cities like Detroit and to the extensive destruction of New Orleans by Hurricane Katrina. But as his thinking transformed, he anticipated many of the directions that below-market housing would take in the late twentieth century. BRIAN GOLDSTEIN

Nehemiah Houses (1982–)

Sponsor: private nonprofit (Nehemiah Development Corporation)
Program: homeownership
Architect: James T. Martino & Associates, Alexander Gorlin, others

The Nehemiah Houses program pioneered an important new strategy for developing below-market housing in New York City. The sponsors, rejecting decades of emphasis on low-cost rental and cooperative apartment houses, proposed that moderate-income New Yorkers become owners of modest attached row houses in order to shore up declining neighborhoods (fig. 6.19). They believed, and correctly so, that pride of ownership would, in time, lead to neighborhood stability, further upgrading, and the building of equity. The project's success beginning in the early 1980s led many others to emulate the Nehemiah model.[36]

In the 1970s and 1980s East Brooklyn was characterized not just by social problems like poverty and crime but also by extensive physical decay: vacant lots, burned-out buildings, decrepit schoolyards, and empty factories. Beleaguered by these conditions, a group of long-time community members, led by several churches, banded together to rebuild. They recruited leaders from the neighborhood. One was Sarah Plowden, who joined the effort when a friend pointed out to her that the area looked "like someone had dropped a bomb" on it.[37] What first started out as a conversation between neighbors soon evolved into a full-scale community-organizing group aided by Saul Alinsky's Industrial Areas Foundation: the East Brooklyn Congregations (EBC; formerly known as the East Brooklyn Churches). The Industrial Areas Foundation is a network of civic groups and religious institutions that facilitates community development and leadership in disadvantaged neighborhoods.

6.19: Nehemiah Houses, 440 Williams Ave., Brownsville, Brooklyn, 2014

One of the issues facing East Brooklyn was abandoned lots, most of which the city owned; the solution proposed was to build for-sale houses. The idea originated with the Rev. Johnny Ray Youngblood, a former pastor of one of the member churches, St. Paul's. He believed, like many housing experts, that ownership empowered people by making them feel that they were part of the community. Ira D. Robbins, a long-time developer, suggested a method of inexpensive serial construction that borrowed from suburban precedents such as Levittown (fig. 6.20). Together, EBC and Robbins launched Nehemiah Houses, named after the story of the Prophet Nehemiah who is credited with rebuilding the walls of Jerusalem.[38]

Since the 1980s four phases of Nehemiah Houses have been built in Brooklyn. In 1982, the first 1,100 houses began construction, in Brownsville, in the Marcus Garvey Park Village Urban Renewal Area (fig. 6.21). Five years later, another 1,100 were started, in East New York. In 1996, 700 more went up in East New York, in the New Lots section. And in 2006, work began on 1,525 units in East New York's Spring Creek. In the late 1980s, South Bronx Churches expanded Nehemiah to that borough (fig. 6.22). As outlined by EBC, the core concepts of the plan centered on homeownership (with financial counseling) and cost-saving innovative construction methods, today in the form of prefabrication. The houses were modest: in the initial phase 18 feet wide, 32 feet deep, with two or three bedrooms and one bathroom in 1,150 square feet, with deep front and rear yards.[39] Designed with input from EBC, security was a priority. Kitchens were placed at the front to facilitate observation of goings-on outside. Houses at corners were given two rather than three bedrooms under the assumption that this might lead to fewer people congregating at block edges, where scrutiny would be weakest.

Low prices were achieved not just through economies in construction but by the layering of multiple moderate subsidies. Partners including the city government and EBC provided no-interest construction loans. The city's Community Preservation Corporation managed a revolving construction fund, with money left over from one project

6.20: Ira D. Robbins at Nehemiah Houses, Mother Gason Blvd., Brownsville, Brooklyn, by Nancy Kaye, 1983

6.21: Nehemiah Houses, Brownsville, Brooklyn, by Sarah Krulwich, 1987

6.22: Rally for Nehemiah Houses, South Bronx, by Dith Pran, 1989

applied to the next. The first houses cost $53,000 to construct ($119,000 in 2013 dollars). But since even this was too much for the target families, who were expected to earn between $20,000 and $40,000 a year, each house received an additional subsidy of $20,000. Half of this was a no-interest loan from the city to be repaid when the house was sold. To cover the balance of $33,000 buyers were given below-market mortgages by the State of New York Mortgage Agency and no-interest second mortgages by the federal government. The city also abated property taxes for twenty years. Monthly costs for new homeowners thus ran around $550 ($1,250 today), making the houses affordable to owners like Carmelia Goffe, who moved in with her three sons in 1984. A retired conductor and tower operator for the Metropolitan Transportation Authority, homeownership seemed like an unobtainable dream for her until Nehemiah.[40]

More recent Nehemiah projects have continued to meet the needs of such families, most of whom are African American or Hispanic, including many city employees (fig. 6.23). In 2000, corrections officer Pat Worthy moved to the Nehemiah New Lots complex. Her three-bedroom, one-and-a-half-bath house with a full basement, backyard, and parking pad cost approximately $110,000, with a down payment of $12,000 and monthly payments of about $600 (equivalent to $145,000, $16,000, and $800 today). An active member of St. Paul's church, Worthy was drawn by the feeling of community but also the allure of owning her own house where she might have a

6.23: Nehemiah Houses, East New York, by Nadia Mian, 2013

6.24: Nehemiah Houses, customized living room, 2014

backyard for her children to play in. Although she liked the design of the Nehemiah houses she also relished the opportunity, as a homeowner, to customize (fig. 6.24). Since moving in she installed new flooring and added an island in her kitchen, as have many Nehemiah owners.[41]

Over time the design of Nehemiah Houses evolved. When Worthy first moved in, the area suffered from issues with illegal dumping, robbery, and petty crime. Today it is safe and "tight-knit": a place where neighbors know one another, there is little turnover, and worries center most on things like traffic violations. Reflecting the reductions in crime, Nehemiah moved kitchens to the back of newer houses. Reflecting new standards for quality in housing, the houses grew by 14 percent, and were given private rather than shared porches. An even more consequential change derived from the shift from serial on-site construction to prefabricated modular, which allowed for a revolutionary change: the scattering of houses on noncontiguous lots without raising costs. At the most recent complex, built on the site of a former landfill at Spring Creek, clusters of houses designed by Alexander Gorlin and manufactured by Monadnock Construction now dot the landscape with their strong, colorful geometries and high stoops (fig. 6.25).[42]

6.25: Nehemiah Houses, Spring Creek, 2014

Demand for Nehemiah Houses in Brooklyn—half of which are reserved for local families—has outstripped supply for decades. To buy a house, one enters a lottery and must meet a variety of income criteria. If selected to buy, one must submit to financial counseling to ensure one understands the responsibility of ownership. HPD manages the lottery and supervises the processing of applications. Acceptable income ranges today are approximately $60,000 to $100,000. Linda Boyce, who has lived in Spring Creek with her husband and son since their house was built in 2009, applied to a lottery back in 1992; her name came up only in 2007. A former administrator for the Department of Social Services, Boyce paid $11,000 down on the $230,000 house. Having rented in a Mitchell-Lama complex for almost thirty years, she loves being an owner. A member of the East Brooklyn Congregations, she adores the new neighborhood and the opportunity to build the kind of community she always dreamed of living in, in part by participating in the Nehemiah Spring Creek homeowner's association. (Nehemiah has set up every project with a mandatory homeowners' association.)[43]

The success of Nehemiah Houses has been built upon its ability to navigate and coordinate property development, while remaining true to its ideals about community, social justice, and homeownership. Mass production, subsidized mortgages, grants, and donated land have been essential tools. But it has been the dedication, commitment, and perseverance of residents who have made Nehemiah Houses, with their well-lit streets and manicured lawns, truly successful. Eastern Brooklyn remains in need of revitalization, but Nehemiah has shown that the city can be rebuilt, one community, one house at a time. NADIA A. MIAN

Abyssinian Development Corporation (1987–)

When congregants left Harlem's famed Abyssinian Baptist Church on Sundays in the mid-1980s they were faced with a harsh reminder of the dire social, economic, and physical trauma that was devastating the neighborhood. The north side of West 138th Street, facing Abyssinian, looked like a losing boxer's teeth. Seven vacant lots pitted the block. Just six of the twenty-two lots claimed any inhabitants. Every other building was vacant, city-owned due to tax foreclosure, or both. These were physical traces of events that ran much deeper. Central Harlem had lost more than forty percent of its population in the decade of the 1970s, its middle class going first. New scourges worsened conditions for those left behind: crack cocaine and the emerging AIDS epidemic.[44]

Mixed with the ever-rising tide of abandonment, these forces created a vicious circle, one whose reality brought a physical and spiritual emergency for its ecclesiastical neighbors. "I can look at 138th Street buildings that were completely filled and now have only forty to fifty percent capacity," Abyssinian's executive minister, Rev. Calvin O. Butts III explained in 1985. He called for a renewed commitment to Harlem by his flock, many of whom had moved elsewhere and returned only on Sundays. The church launched a housing venture to build a hundred-unit apartment building for its elderly members (fig. 6.26). In 1987 volunteers formalized their housing ministry, which soon became the Abyssinian Development Corporation. One of many church-based CDCs to emerge in this era, it became a major force in the construction of below-market subsidized housing on the surrounding blocks.[45]

6.26: Abyssinian Towers, 2014

Abyssinian was at the leading edge of a nationwide movement of CDCs, but this was not the first such movement. Community development corporations had emerged initially in the late 1960s as an outgrowth of both the participatory spirit of the War on Poverty and the demands for "community control" that emanated from the Black Power Movement. Early CDCs, such as the Bedford-Stuyvesant Restoration Corporation in Brooklyn and the Harlem Commonwealth Council, focused especially on commercial ventures and business development, dreams that they fueled with funds obtained from an eager federal government. When such funds dried up in the 1980s with retrenchment, so did their activities. But they gave way to a second wave of

CDCs, whose church sponsors tended to focus on the exigencies of their surrounding communities and on activities that complemented their faith. Preston Washington, a Harlem minister who launched another local CDC, the Harlem Churches for Community Improvement, looked upon his deteriorating neighborhood as "the mission field next door."[46]

Abyssinian Development Corporation and its peers provided social services, encouraged economic development, sponsored drug rehabilitation, and supported teenage mothers and the homeless. But most of all they focused on housing development, a task that they approached with the specific ambition of creating and maintaining an economically integrated community. While income diversification had long been a goal of postwar liberal housers, it acquired a new status in this era through the work of organizations like Abyssinian, who hoped to construct a mixed-income reality on a neighborhood scale. Several factors encouraged this goal. One was the existential crisis that Harlem faced. Despite Harlem's tenuous position, many feared that gentrification was inevitable and that vacant lots would attract speculation. Abyssinian hoped to manage such change through mixed-income housing, listing its early goals as "balancing proposed development" while "preserving existing residents."[47]

Changing sociological thought also shaped Abyssinian's approach. The contemporaneous literature on the "underclass," especially the work of William Julius Wilson, shined a light on the extreme urban poverty that resulted from the suburbanization not just of the middle class but also the African American middle class.

Wilson argued that historically such families had helped to soften the blow of widespread joblessness, and to lessen economic shocks. Their departure brought "social isolation," worsening the problems of poverty for those left behind. Wilson wrote his landmark 1987 book *The Truly Disadvantaged* as an explanation for larger-scale patterns and offered broad, structural solutions. But many, including those occupied with rebuilding Harlem's housing through CDCs, read it as a literal prescription. If the departure of the middle class worsened poverty's effects, they reasoned, then the return of the middle class would help solve those problems. This became a central goal in their work in housing.[48]

The transformed funding context of the early 1980s also shaped Abyssinian's strategy. CDCs like Abyssinian partnered with diverse actors, assembling their assistance in a patchwork of funding. To a large extent, income diversification was intrinsic to the public-private alliance they depended upon. Mayor Koch, for example, had long emphasized mixed-income housing as a development goal in the city. His Ten-year Housing Plan made this a central ambition. But the complex nature of the funding itself also helped contribute to this outcome. A smorgasbord of support enabled and encouraged a range of strategies among CDCs: one source funded development for senior citizens, a second for the homeless, and a third for middle-income residents. Frequently, multiple sources would fuel a single project. Abyssinian's Hattie Dodson Houses (1992), for example, created low-income housing through support from the Enterprise Foundation, LISC, and the city's Department of Housing Preservation and Development. The CDC followed any trail that would enable housing construction, adopting a decided pragmatism in forming alliances in the public and private sectors.[49]

6.27: Astor Row, 58 W. 130th St., 2014

This eagerness to partner with a wide array of backers fueled Abyssinian's work. By the mid-1990s, as its first projects opened to residents, the church had begun to make a marked—if gradual—improvement to its surrounding blocks, building housing for low- and middle-income residents, both owners and renters, usually by rehabilitating existing buildings. The Hattie Dodson Houses offered seventy-one units to low-income tenants; the George W. Lewis Houses (1996) provided forty-two units; and the Lilian Upshur Houses (1994) added sixty-six apartments, one-third for the previously homeless. Across from the church, the Samuel D. Proctor apartments (1991) provided twenty-five units for a range of income levels. Nearby, on the historic stretch of West 130th Street known as Astor Row, Abyssinian partnered in the transformation of two vacant houses (1997) into eight limited-equity cooperative apartments for low- and moderate-income families (fig. 6.27). And on West 131st Street, the CDC tapped funding from the New York City Housing Partnership, among other

6.28: West One Three One Plaza, 2014

sources, to create West One Three One Plaza (1993), a thirty-four-unit middle-income condominium intended to encourage homeownership (fig. 6.28).

West One Three One Plaza exemplified both the strategy of economic integration that the CDC pursued and the benefits—profane and sacred—that it hoped new housing development would bring. Marketing materials directly targeted middle-class families, emphasizing proximity to the subway that connected Harlem to midtown and downtown, and pointing to luxurious features, such as oak cabinets and high ceilings. "Take stock in Harlem," ads encouraged, an appeal that asked buyers to commit their financial resources and grow roots in the community. One of the first residents took a reporter around her home, suggesting the more ineffable benefits that could accrue from such development projects. "I fell in love with it the moment I saw it," she explained. "I knew it had to be mine." Her pride in the rehabilitated unit surfaced throughout the tour. "You should see it when the sunlight comes in in the morning," she said.[50]

Despite the constraints of its context Abyssinian made substantial material improvements in the physical and social lives of the residents it served. Its counterparts did too. Harlem Churches for Community Improvement carried out a mixed-income vision for the Bradhurst neighborhood, a stretch of Harlem north of Abyssinian's area of focus that included the poorest census tract in the city. The two CDCs encompassed nearly half of Harlem north of 125th Street in their activities.[51]

Yet with Abyssinian's success came complicated, sometimes vexing questions. The CDC's efforts to build bridges to diverse funding partners and its emphasis on development largely overshadowed any ambition for broad structural change. Leaders moved away from community organizing as a tactic, for example, and proved politically malleable. These decisions kept money flowing but undermined the idealism that had once motivated the creation of CDCs, lessening the possibility of social and political movements as a strategy for community development. Leaders like Rev. Butts saw their profiles rise on New York's nonprofit stage, but observers often wondered whether all of their decisions and alliances best served their communities. Likewise, while many proponents pointed to economic diversification as an unquestioned good, even a panacea, the prospect of attracting new middle-class residents with market-rate housing worried many who feared that such efforts at deliberate upscaling would go too far. Some gentrification was, of course, precisely the point of mixed-income housing and its social vision. But such fears were not unfounded. Abyssinian's plans in the 2000s to demolish the historic Renaissance Ballroom and build a nineteen-story residential tower with 120 condominiums, 80 percent at market rate, raised the ire of many, who pointed out the CDC's responsibility to its rapidly changing neighborhood. "If you want to branch out into business and moderate-income housing, that's cool," one Harlem tenant advocate said. "But don't forget about the people."[52]

On balance, these paradoxes proved difficult to resolve as Harlem's physical and social transformation accelerated in the new millennium. Where the possibility of large-scale displacement had once seemed remote, the success of groups like Abyssinian in reconstructing Harlem's streets made those fears more likely. Their work in a new era—and the growing pains that followed—raised important questions about the role such organizations would and should take in urban development as places like Harlem began to face challenges in many ways the opposite of those of the 1980s. BRIAN GOLDSTEIN

The Koch Housing Plan (1986–96)

In his 1985 State of the City address, Mayor Edward I. Koch (1978–89) announced one of the most ambitious plans of his political career: a five-year program to spend $4.4 billion ($9.2 billion in 2013 dollars) of city money to build and rehabilitate 100,000 units of low- and moderate-income housing. The idea attracted great enthusiasm, and in 1989 he expanded the program to $5.1 billion ($9.6 billion) and 252,000 units over ten years. Some experts, at first, said that the idea was more aspiration than realistic. Indeed, no one in the administration knew precisely where the money would come from. It was found, however, and the plan launched what became perhaps the largest municipal investment in housing in U.S. history.[53]

The idea for the Koch housing plan emerged in 1984 in response to concerns that while the city's population was in decline, so, too, was the volume of its housing stock, with the result that rents remained uncomfortably steep for many (fig. 6.29). In Koch's

6.29: Ed Koch, center, with Governor Mario Cuomo, left, selecting names for housing lottery, Brooklyn, by Fred R. Conrad, 1983

first term alone the city lost 81,000 apartments to abandonment and fire. Meanwhile, two-thirds of renters were spending more than 35 percent of their income on rent, violating old rules of thumb for housing affordability established back in the 1910s and 1920s. The plan sought to address the imbalance by stimulating production while staving off additional losses. The program quickly advanced, achieving a breathtaking scale and complexity. At its core lay four main goals: reconstruction of all suitable city-owned vacant buildings, renovation of all occupied city-owned buildings, promotion of below-market-interest-rate loans and property-tax abatements to encourage private owners of low- and middle-income housing to renovate, and construction of new units of for-sale housing, especially in the most deeply trouble sections: the South Bronx, Harlem, and central Brooklyn.[54]

Cobbling together the complicated financial package necessary to realize the plan took significant politicking. Most of the funding came directly from the city's capital budget after the state legislature freed up billions of borrowing capacity by creating a separate Municipal Water Finance Authority for an enormous new water main. Additional money came from the Port Authority of New York and New Jersey in lieu of taxes for the World Trade Center and the Battery Park City Authority, which borrowed against anticipated revenues from the World Financial Center, then under construction. The overwhelming share, however, came from new debt the state permitted the New York City Housing Development Corporation to take.[55]

Turning the money into housing was difficult. Some obstacles concerned resistance to new ways of doing things. HPD Commissioner Paul Crotty, for instance, felt it crucial to reorganize the agency if the program were to advance quickly, so he eliminated four of the six deputy commissioners. Meanwhile, Kathryn Wylde, president of the New York City Housing Partnership and politicians such as David

6.30: Katherine Wylde at New Horizon Village, Amboy Street, Brownsville, Brooklyn, by Chester Higgins, Jr., 1986

Dinkins, then borough president of Manhattan, and Representative Charles B. Rangel, of Harlem, complained as HPD began to play a larger role in developer selection.[56] Other challenges simply concerned the complexity of building on a decentralized basis. Complicated financing and regulation, and the need to create effective channels between a hodgepodge of agencies all militated against the will to build.

Progress was mixed for the first two years. An improving economy meant that losses of housing slowed to a trickle, the city started upgrading streets and infrastructure near designated sites, and the administration pushed through Albany approval for wider use of manufactured housing and permission for tax-exempt housing construction corporations. But there were bureaucratic hurdles, especially in disposition of city property. Evidence of impropriety demanded the city set up a high-level committee to value the land for each project, prompting housers like Wylde to complain about the slow pace (fig. 6.30). By 1987, however, building was under way. Annual expenditures on the program reached $62 million, and the city saw a net gain of 37,000 units. By 1990 expenditures reached $340 million.[57]

The Koch program, like those of earlier administrations, emphasized serving a mixture of tenants, racially, socially, and economically. "We definitely wanted to have a mix. We would have neighborhoods where it was working people, it would be just people who were unemployed, etc. . . . So it's a combination that we strove for, including the working poor and a little bit of middle class," recalled one administration official.[58] This goal helped the city engage African American community leaders in tense neighborhoods like Crown Heights, where the Rev. Clarence Norman, for example, promised the mayor "a working meeting, without any confrontations or arguments" in hope of securing "a program that will move toward rebuilding our neighborhood."[59] These goals were further enhanced by the fact that so much of the effort was in small-scale ownership projects.

Today, Koch's initiative is generally viewed as the greatest success of his mayoralty. When the program started the city owned approximately 50,000 units of abandoned housing. By 1993, 42,000 of them were rebuilt or under way. In total between 1987 and 1993 more than 100,000 units were renovated or constructed. This housing did not end homelessness—to the contrary, Koch has been critiqued for his lack of support for SROs. Nor did it reduce citywide rent burdens. But without a doubt it helped to reverse the city's physical and social decay.[60] JONATHAN SOFFER

Asian Americans for Equality (1970s–)

Asian Americans for Equality (AAFE) is a Chinatown-based organization that provides services to the Asian American community in New York City including the development and preservation of affordable housing. Conceived during the struggles of the civil rights movement, it was a pioneer in its use of the Low-income Housing Tax Credit program in the late 1980s and has since grown to become the largest nonprofit developer of below-market housing in the Lower East Side-Chinatown area. Following New York City's rapidly expanding Asian population, it now also serves the immigrant communities in the outer boroughs, with offices in Flushing, Queens, and Sunset Park, Brooklyn. Like San Francisco's Chinatown Community Development Center or the East Bay Asian Local Development Corporation, two of the other nationally recognized community-based organizations serving the nation's fastest growing immigrant group, AAFE acts as a cultural broker for new immigrants and limited English speakers, providing multilingual counseling services and housing programs while advocating on their behalf with landlords, banks, and governmental agencies.[61]

AAFE had its origins in a storefront civil rights organization formed to advocate on behalf of the immigrants who arrived in the city after the 1965 federal Immigration Act relaxed restrictions on foreign immigration. Chinatown, once a tightly knit community centered on a few blocks near Mott and Mulberry Streets, expanded eastward toward the East River, south toward City Hall, and north past Canal Street, which had traditionally divided Chinatown from Little Italy. Just as during previous waves of immigration, housing conditions in the area's nineteenth-century tenements quickly grew overcrowded and deteriorated. Families shared illegally subdivided apartments and slept in shifts. Aging wiring, poor maintenance, and occasional lack of heat and electricity meant that fires were frequent. Unscrupulous landlords took advantage of tenants who were often reluctant to register complaints with city agencies.

In 1974 these young storefront activists united with restaurant and garment factory workers over anti-Asian discrimination at a local construction site. Chinese American workers had been excluded from construction jobs at Confucius Plaza (1977), a federally funded Mitchell-Lama cooperative slated to include community facilities, commercial spaces, and a school. The private construction company had hired no workers from Chinatown, complaining that Asians were "too weak" for construction work. After six months of pickets twenty-seven workers of color were hired, among them two dozen Chinese Americans.[62]

AAFE—initially Asian Americans for Equal Employment, then Asian Americans for Equality—organized formally in the wake of this battle. In the following years they led protests against police brutality in the 1975 Chinatown beating of the engineer Peter Yew and the 1982 death of Vincent Chin, whose murder by laid-off autoworkers in Detroit sparked a wave of pan-ethnic Asian American organizing across the nation. They fought the construction of a prison in Chinatown and the establishment of the Special Manhattan Bridge District, which they feared would encourage gentrification in the area. Given the condition of the area's tenements, however, housing issues were increasingly important. AAFE's volunteers helped residents with applications to public housing, organized tenant groups, ran housing clinics to inform tenants of their rights, and took negligent and predatory landlords to court.

A fatal fire in January 1985 caused AAFE to change direction. The fire, which broke out at 54 Eldridge Street on one of the coldest nights of the year, was sparked by faulty wiring in a building where tenants had been forced to use electric heaters after the landlord shut off heat and hot water. Two tenants were killed and 125 left homeless. Doris Koo, the executive director of AAFE, was called in by the Red Cross to help translate for victims entering the shelter system. An immigrant herself with community organizing experience in Chicago's garment district, Koo had worked with Brooklyn law students to take action against Chinatown's negligent landlords and had seen local housing conditions firsthand. Concerned about the ability of the shelter system to provide for clients with limited English proficiency, frustrated by activists' inability to effect long-term change with landlords, she took a step back. "We can either keep organizing rent strikes and hauling landlords to court," she recalled thinking. "Or we can build housing."[63]

AAFE initially looked for a location for a shelter in the heart of Chinatown, close to the neighborhood's schools and social services, but no buildings were available. Instead, they turned to 176 and 180 Eldridge Street, two city-owned vacant buildings on the Lower East Side scheduled for demolition. When a second fire gutted these buildings, raising the projected costs of rehabilitation, Koo traveled to the Columbia, Maryland, offices of James Rouse's Enterprise Foundation (now Enterprise Community Partners). At the time, Enterprise was involved in a campaign to create the Low-income Housing Tax Credit, which, as enacted in 1986, uses tax incentives to encourage individual and corporate investors to invest in the development and rehabilitation of below-market housing. Koo's personal appeal to Rouse resulted in a partnership with Enterprise that created Equality Houses, the first project in New York City to leverage equity through LIHTCs. Completed in 1989, Equality Houses consisted of two rehabilitated six-story tenements reconfigured to include a variety of units, single rooms through two-bedroom apartments, all made available, according to LIHTC guidelines, to tenants with incomes below 60 percent of the area median income. In keeping with AAFE's concern for immigrants within the city's shelter system, 30 percent of the units in the fifty-nine-unit building were set aside for homeless referrals.

Working primarily with vacant or foreclosed tenements north of Delancey Street, where arson and disinvestment had left century-old tenements uninhabitable, AAFE sought to duplicate the success of Equality Houses in the late 1980s and 1990s. These

6.31: Norfolk Apartments II, 111 Norfolk St., 2014

buildings typically had units so small they were illegal by current standards, but rehabilitation allowed AAFE to work with the existing housing stock and maintain residential density for their clients, who often preferred to stay close to Chinatown's commercial areas, institutions, and services.[64] Through the city's Department of Housing Preservation and Development's LISC/Enterprise Production Program, AAFE created several hundred affordable units in rehabilitated buildings in Chinatown and the Lower East Side. It also embarked on several new-construction projects, including Norfolk Apartments, a seven-story building with two dozen residential units built on a vacant lot in 1999 (see fig.6.11), and Norfolk II, three buildings with forty-one units completed in 2003 (fig. 6.31). New construction allowed AAFE to design handicap-accessible units and units designed for seniors, and to add community spaces and offices for counseling and outreach programs. AAFE remained a presence at these sites even after occupancy, acting as property manager and setting up tenant organizations.

As it added below-market housing development to its advocacy agenda, AAFE strove to act as an intermediary between recent immigrants (and other limited English speakers) and the institutions of New York's housing market. Christopher Kui, who succeeded Koo as executive director of the organization in 1992, has spoken of a myth of self-sufficiency among Asian immigrants that, above and beyond language and cultural barriers, can prevent them from asking for or receiving assistance. AAFE thus positioned itself as a cultural broker for new immigrants, a role that included advocacy on behalf of their clients as well as educational programs and counseling. It sought alternative forms of income verification for potential tenants who were self-employed or who worked in the informal economy, helped tenants file complaints against negligent landlords, and worked with city agencies that lacked Chinese-speaking staff.[65]

AAFE grew quickly in the 1980s and 1990s, spinning off the Downtown Manhattan Community Development Corporation in 1994 to plan and implement its subsidized housing projects, and the Renaissance Economic Development Corporation in 1998 to provide low-interest loans and financial counseling to women- and minority-owned small businesses. By the late 1990s, as well known as a landlord and developer as it was as an advocate for tenants and workers, AAFE even faced charges that it had allied itself with business interests and the political establishment at the expense of its low-income constituency.[66]

By the millennium, as national homeownership rates reached historic peaks, AAFE began to focus on low- and moderate-income ownership. Like many nonprofit housing developers, it saw individual long-term investments in homes and small businesses as a form of asset building, promoting the overall health of low-income and immigrant communities. In 1999 AAFE set up the AAFE Community Development Fund to offer loans and promote homeownership through counseling. In 2000 it worked with Phoenix Builders, a minority-owned construction company, to build Suffolk Homes, a forty-eight-unit condominium on city-owned vacant lots using city and state subsidies available through HPD's Partnership New Homes Program, launched in 1983 in conjunction with David Rockefeller's Housing Partnership Development Corporation (fig. 6.32).[67]

6.32: Suffolk Homes, 130–48 Suffolk St., 2014

The issue of low- and moderate-income homeownership became especially relevant in the emerging "new Chinatowns." Following other post-1965 Asian immigrants who settled in neighborhoods like Woodside (Filipinos), Jackson Heights (South Asians), and Flushing (Koreans), as well as in suburban towns in northern New Jersey and Long Island, many Chinese immigrants went to places like Flushing and Elmhurst in Queens and Sunset Park in Brooklyn. This has been especially true of new arrivals from Taiwan and other parts of China speaking Mandarin or Fujianese (Manhattan's Chinatown had traditionally been home to Cantonese immigrants). Even in these relatively low-density neighborhoods poor housing conditions prevail. In Flushing almost one-quarter of housing units are overcrowded, and many of the new immigrants are living in illegally converted basements and attics.[68]

In 2004 AAFE set up a branch of its affordable homeownership affiliate in Flushing and in 2010 entered Sunset Park. As with tenants in Manhattan, AAFE acts as an intermediary between clients, lenders, and regulatory agencies, working to combat discrimination and establish the credit-worthiness of clients unfamiliar with the U.S. system of mortgage financing and home-buying. It helps potential homeowners who previously paid their rent in cash, who lack credit history, or who have difficulty substantiating transnational incomes or capital available through cultural networks.[69] AAFE's Community Development Fund, a member of the national group NeighborWorks America, secured $300 million in mortgage financing for approximately two thousand homebuyers, while its Community Homes Housing Development Fund began overseeing the purchase and renovation of single- and multi-family homes for low- and moderate-income homebuyers. In the wake of the housing crisis of 2008, AAFE's affiliates also worked to keep homes out of foreclosure.

Manhattan's Chinatown, itself still a magnet for recent immigrants, has been transformed in recent years both by gentrification and the economic devastation that followed the September 11 attacks in 2001. Already faced with the decline of the garment industry, one of its major sources of employment, the area lost nearly eight thousand jobs in the months after 9/11. At the same time, like Chinatowns in Boston and Philadelphia, the area faces gentrification as developers construct new hotels and market-rate housing, and convert old garment factories to spacious residential lofts.[70] In an effort to maintain affordability AAFE now works to preserve existing housing with the HPD's Chinatown/Lower East Side Acquisition Program, which provides subsidies for nonprofit developers like AAFE to buy apartment buildings and convert them to below-market housing. It has also launched a campaign to prevent landlords from neglecting rent-regulated buildings to the point where they need to be demolished.[71] Almost thirty years after the fatal fire at Eldridge Street, AAFE continues to advocate on behalf of residents left homeless after catastrophic fires decimate overcrowded and substandard tenements that often lack heat, smoke detectors, or safe wiring.

Today, AAFE is the largest developer of affordable housing in Lower Manhattan, having preserved or developed eighty-six buildings with more than seven hundred apartments since 1989. The organization has moved far from its radical roots and now has close ties to the city's political establishment and the subsidized-housing industry. It continues to focus its attention on Chinatown and the Lower East Side, where today low-income Latinos comprise a substantial part of their multi-racial clientele. It also works to respond to the needs of the growing Asian American population of all five boroughs—which now stands at more than a million, or about 13 percent of the entire city—demonstrating the importance of culturally competent community-based organizations that are able to act as intermediaries for recent immigrants. JENNIFER HOCK

Hughes House (2011, 55 units, Bronx)

Sponsor: private nonprofit (Urban Pathways)
Program: private rental
Architect: Jonathan Kirschenfeld Architects

Hughes House is a supportive housing residence dedicated to formerly homeless single adults with mental illness and/or addiction disorders. The unassuming brick complex occupies a narrow infill lot in the Tremont section of the Bronx. It was developed and is operated by Urban Pathways, a nonprofit organization dedicated to serving the homeless. Hughes is one example of the recent wave of supportive housing built across the nation, made possible by federal, state, and municipal funding. Supportive housing is permanent housing with integrated, on-site social and medical support for special-needs populations, in particular the formerly homeless, mentally ill, HIV-positive, or people with substance-abuse disorders. It was formalized as a federal program in 1987 through the McKinney-Vento Homeless Assistance Act. New York City today counts twenty-eight thousand units of supportive housing, of which seventeen thousand have been newly constructed, like Hughes, or converted from other uses.[72]

In the 1980s several trajectories created an unprecedented homeless epidemic. First, there was a dramatic reduction in the availability of low-cost private housing due to abandonment and demolition. The loss of single-room occupancy hotels (SROs), due to the perception of this housing as substandard, contributed to the crisis. Studies indicate that in 1950, for instance, New York had 200,000 SRO units; fewer than 40,000 remain today. Second, the loss of working-class jobs in the city created a growing population of the permanently and regularly unemployed who struggled to pay regular rent of any level. Finally, the massive deinstitutionalization of psychiatric patients, due in part to the availability of new drugs, swelled on-street homelessness, as many former patients fell through the cracks or avoided continuing treatment or halfway houses.

In winning over policymakers to pass funding for supportive housing, advocates pointed to pilot projects showing that it was far more cost-effective to provide permanent housing with integrated support services than to have homeless persons cycling from jail to emergency rooms to shelters and back. The fact that many homeless were veterans provided the moral rationale for even small-government proponents to commit to funding a long-term "continuum of care" program. Urban Pathways cites 2011 data comparing per-day, per-person expenses in New York City to make this point: supportive housing costs $44, shelter $74, and jail $168.[73]

Hughes House articulates the twin, interconnected programs of supportive housing in the form of two distinct buildings joined by a courtyard. The two sections are indicative of the dual role of supportive housing: high-quality design and construction, on the one hand, and to step back and become almost imperceptible as highly subsidized special-needs housing, on the other. On Hughes Avenue a two-story front with six double-height vertical window slots cut into dark, reflective brick creates an industrial feel, as if this were a former power substation (fig. 6.33). This is the main entrance leading to a lobby, mail room, and shared dining room at ground level, and offices for caseworkers on the floor above. Along parallel Belmont Avenue, in contrast, the five-story brick façade is punched with identical pairs of double-hung windows, suggesting housing. In this building, each floor accommodates eleven fully handicapped-accessible studios around a double-loaded corridor; each studio is furnished and complete with a full bath and kitchenette.

The New York State Office of Mental Health, the Federal Home Loan Bank of New York, and Low-income Housing Tax Credits covered Hughes House's total development costs of $18 million. The New York State Office of Mental Health funds ongoing operations, including its sixteen permanent staff. With the exception of a cook, a nurse, and a consultant psychiatrist, all work full-time: a program director, directors of social services and operations, four case managers, two maintenance personnel, and five security staff are each on call around the clock. According to Urban Pathways, fifty to fifty-five residents per building, as in Hughes, is ideal for maintaining this level of staffing, which serves residents exclusively (that is, no other clients use the services provided here).[74]

6.33: Hughes House, 2014

The greatest design opportunity in supportive housing is the calibration of private, shared, and public space. Since the individual studios are largely set through city regulations in terms of minimum dimensions (approximately 325 square feet) and the furniture to be provided (twin bed, chair, table for two, TV stand), it is the in-between that distinguishes each complex.[75] At Hughes extensions of the minimum are provided throughout in the form of built-in benches and a daylit lounge on every residential floor. The central shared space is the courtyard, however; it provides the building's anchor, visible upon entering the lobby, but also from the dining room and the elevator landing at every level.[76]

A 2011 study of common spaces in recent supportive housing in New York concludes that whether common spaces are used by residents depends not only on their location within a building but also on management practices. The study points to the lobby as a key place for staff to "gauge the tenants' mood each day and interact casually," but only if management "encourages tenants to 'hang out.'" Where security concerns over congregating in the lobby prevail, that opportunity is lost.[77] Judging from the seating provided in Hughes's lobby, it seems that client and designer agreed on wanting to enable a certain amount of lingering. Judging from a security guard's difficulty in negotiating the coming and going of residents and guests, however, it becomes clear that the real issue at stake in the space of the lobby is the threshold between the controlled interior and the world beyond.

To become a resident of Hughes, individuals need a "level two" approval by the city's Human Resources Administration, indicating a history of severe and persistent mental illness and chronic street homelessness, in addition to an "assisted outpatient treatment (AOT)" order. Most are referred from shelters, psychiatric hospitals, or the justice system. Once accepted, residents sign a yearly occupancy agreement and lease rider, and pay one-third of their income, generally from supplemental security income (SSI), for rent. Over three-quarters of Hughes's residents are male, consistent with the make-up of the on-street homeless population, and range in age between twenty and seventy. Residents are responsible for their own lives, but meet weekly with their case managers; many are enrolled in additional health or educational programs. Medications are stored in a locked room next to the front security desk and are dispensed by staff. While the setup of the studios encourages residents to prepare their own meals, those who cannot or do not want to may eat in the shared dining room. There are no curfews, but visitors need to be signed in and overnight guests are allowed only on weekends after the resident has successfully complied with all building rules for ninety days. Residents are not involved in building management but assist with cleaning of common spaces and are responsible for cleaning their own living spaces. Apart from a monthly "community meeting" of residents, there are no formal meetings or associations; instead, case managers encourage residents to get involved in neighborhood organizations.

In its new construction projects Urban Pathways is moving away from residences for a single target group toward buildings that accommodate a broader mix of backgrounds and needs. But in its focus on the "permanent," how is success measured in supportive housing? To Fred Shack, executive director, it needs to be defined differently for every client. For some long-term homeless, "just getting them inside" and "keeping them inside, one day at a time" is an enormous step toward stabilization. These clients may need the intensive care of a place like Hughes for the rest of their lives and likely will never be able to support themselves financially. Others are ready to live independently after a few months. SUSANNE SCHINDLER

Melrose Commons and Via Verde

(1994–, 3,000+ units; 2012, 222 units, Bronx)

Sponsor: Melrose: HPD, private nonprofit (Nos Quedamos, Phipps Houses), private developer (Procida, Atlantic, L&M), others; Via Verde: HPD, private nonprofit (Phipps Houses), private developer (Rose)
Program: Melrose: private ownership, private rental; Via Verde: private rental, limited-equity co-op
Architect: Melrose: MAP, Hugo S. Subotovksy, Dattner, others; Via Verde: Grimshaw, Dattner

Melrose Commons and the adjacent Bronxchester, home to Via Verde, are post–Title I urban renewal areas in the South Bronx. Their implementation reflects some of today's best practices for the design and development of below-market housing in New York City. Melrose Commons was planned from the bottom up in partnership with community leaders, while Via Verde resulted from a design-driven architectural competition. Both projects incorporate a variety of housing models with the goal of re-creating a mixed-use, mixed-income urban neighborhood, implemented under the auspices of HPD. Melrose Commons is remarkable, in particular, both for its collaborative planning process and for departing from earlier experiments in the South Bronx that had emphasized low-density housing, like Charlotte Gardens. But it also

6.34: Melrose Commons site, by Keith Meyers, 1994

exemplifies the challenges of the decentralized housing network, as CDCs struggle to balance the interests of tenants with the financial imperatives of development.

During the 1960s and 1970s Melrose lost its elevated train along with much of its population. To stem decay the city launched a South Bronx Neighborhood Development Project in the mid-1960s, and shortly thereafter helped develop one-family row houses, under the federal Model Cities program. NYCHA also invested heavily. Nevertheless, by the 1970s more than 70 percent of the district had fallen into city ownership for tax delinquency, and the area's ruins and despair came to serve as the setting for films like *Fort Apache, the Bronx*. By the late 1980s what remained were a few public housing projects, some marginal businesses, and many empty lots, along with a small handful of older buildings that housed a community of mostly Hispanic residents determined to stay (fig. 6.34).[78]

In 1989 the city launched the Bronxchester Urban Renewal Area, and in 1992 it proposed one for Melrose Commons. Low-rise developments, such as Melrose Court (1994), followed (fig. 6.35). Fearing their own displacement and that urban renewal would bring low-density, low-quality housing of the sort recently developed in adjacent areas, residents and business owners organized the We Stay Committee: Comité Nos Quedamos, led by Yolanda Garcia, which requested time and resources to formulate an alternative plan. With the support of Borough President Fernando Ferrer, the city agreed. The Department of City Planning and HPD met with the group weekly and hired design firm Magnusson Architecture and Planning (MAP) to represent the community on an advocacy basis. The final plan contained far more detailed design requirements than typical renewal plans. Its main goal was to maintain the existing street grid, placing mid-rise buildings with ground-floor retail on

6.35: Melrose Court, by Chester Higgins, Jr., 1994

north-south avenues built to a uniform height and up to the street edge, and row houses on side streets. Parking was to be hidden behind buildings or in garages. An earlier proposal for a single, large park was replaced by one for a series of smaller-scale, more manageable open spaces. The plan was approved by the city in 1994 and Nos Quedamos reconstituted itself as a CDC to implement it.[79]

Development proceeded from south to north as HPD disposed of city-owned land. The first projects were modest in scale and relatively low risk: a seniors-only mid-rise and Plaza de los Angeles (2000), a complex of for-sale row houses, each with one apartment for the owner and two units designed to provide rental income. Larger projects, however, had to wait. The city might have organized substantial subsidies but the expectation was for market-oriented developers to propose ideas and prove their economic feasibility.

To encourage this, HPD began offering parcels, sometimes groups of parcels, on a competitive basis. Proposals were evaluated for three things: mixture of units, including those targeting "income levels not otherwise served in the area"; feasibility of financing and developer experience; and community buy-in.[80] Most were won by groups assembled by Nos Quedamos with designs by MAP. Partners included for-profit developers Procida, L&M, and Melrose Associates, a development firm set up by MAP, and later, the established nonprofit Phipps Houses. Taking on private partners, including limited-dividend subsidiaries of for-profit firms, became common in the 1990s and 2000s as CDCs lacked the experience to succeed in developing housing on their own. The results of these RFP (request for proposals) processes included projects like the Orion and Aurora, the area's first condominium buildings, completed in 2008. As confidence in the area rose, the scale of projects increased, necessitating amendments to the urban renewal plan, increasing permissible densities and height limits. The Melrose Common plan was also amended to reintroduce

6.36: Parkview Commons, 2014

several streets that had been initially demapped for a proposed "village center" to its north. Instead, here was built one of the area's largest projects to date: a fourteen-story "vertical campus" for Boricua College together with seven hundred units of housing.

While the Melrose Commons plan was informed by strong goals for physical form, beyond the basic formal requirements design has had little bearing in the awarding of contracts. As MAP partner Magnus Magnusson put it, HPD's model is "to get the most housing for the least subsidy."[81] As a result, much of the housing has followed a single generic formula: double-loaded corridor buildings sixty-five feet deep, up to twelve stories high (fig. 6.36). This approach is not only typical for Melrose, or for below-market housing, but for virtually all new housing built in New York City. It is based on a block-and-plank structural system, with one bearing interior wall made of concrete block supporting pretensioned concrete floor elements. This basic formula is based on the presumed superior economics of the "net to gross": the ratio of rentable or salable living space to common areas for circulation, garbage, or other services. It has produced impressive volumes of below-market housing at Melrose for a range of clienteles, including the formerly homeless, working families, and middle-income households, and has accommodated vital new services and retail in these projects, including chain supermarkets (Foodtown, 2011) and drug stores (Duane Reade, 2013). New projects have also incorporated energy efficiency and healthy materials, key for the reduction of many chronic diseases such as asthma endemic among residents of the South Bronx.

At the same time the HPD formula has limited what the buildings offer in terms of program and aesthetics. Apartment sizes range from studios to three bedrooms only, even though Nos Quedamos had advocated for larger apartments demanded by the extended families common among its Latino constituents. HPD, however, considered these larger units to be a "luxury," and the developers were given no incentive to provide larger units, since HPD subsidies are allocated on a per-unit basis, not according to the apartments' size.[82] While the quality of construction has been better than in many below-market projects, the monotonous and recognizable appearance has become an issue. As HPD's long-time director of planning for the Bronx puts it, "The two-tone brown-and-tan look, at the time, was unusual, actually a nice thing, good enough to be in Manhattan. [It] didn't look like affordable housing." But "now that so many of our projects have that look, not only in Melrose, it has come to designate just that."[83] To encourage variety HPD began encouraging developers to use more "twenty-first-century" materials, like glass.

Community amenities are now a priority for the neighborhood. According to Beatriz de la Torre, formerly at HPD, "Only this year has the Parks Department included capital funding to implement one of the three designated parks." At the same time, many of the heavily used and lovingly tended community parks that sprung up in the 1980s on abandoned infill sites are in danger of being developed for more housing. Another issue has been programmatic variety beyond maximizing unit counts. HPD does seem to be taking new risks, however. One of the last large parcels in northern Melrose Commons was awarded to Les Bluestone's Blue Sea, working with the Women's Housing and Economic Development Corporation (WHEDco) and Rogers Marvel Architects, for a Bronx Music Heritage Center, in part dedicated to live-work spaces for elder musicians and artists.

This new integrated approach to economics, design, and program in Melrose may have been inspired by HPD's sponsorship, together with the city's chapter of the American Institute of Architects, of a transparent, two-phase, architect-developer competition in 2005 for a site in the Bronxchester renewal area to create housing that is "affordable, sustainable, and replicable." The process prioritized design over economics, and perhaps more importantly, led to a subsequent review process that brought all relevant municipal agencies together in a weekly meeting to ensure that key goals were not watered down as the project was implemented.[84]

The result was Via Verde, "The Green Way," developed by the nonprofit Phipps Houses Group and the for-profit Jonathan Rose Companies, with a design by Dattner Architects of New York and Grimshaw Architects of London (fig. 6.37). Completed in early 2012, the exemplary quality of the design and program are obvious, beginning with the striking façade of prefabricated metal panels and sun-screening canopies. Its urban design is not formulaic, but makes the most of a long, narrow triangular site, combining a wide range of housing types into one large building that rises from low in the south to a twenty-story tower in the north, framing a shared courtyard. There are single-story apartments located above ground-floor townhouses accessed from exterior stairs; duplex apartments spanning one façade to the other, allowing for cross-ventilation (something made impossible by the double-loaded corridor model, which creates units facing one direction only) and reminiscent of Le Corbusier's Unité de Habitation; and tower living, where corridors and staircases are daylit. Socially, the building mixes lower-income households in rentals with middle-income families in for-sale co-op units.

6.37: Via Verde, 2014

Via Verde has achieved a status seldom attained by even market-rate multifamily housing in the United States: it has become a reference point for architects worldwide. But it has also provoked controversy. Built at a cost of $99 million, or $450,000 per unit—$100,000, or nearly 30 percent, more than most below-market housing organized by HPD, including at Melrose Commons—Via Verde has become a lightning rod for debate, bringing to the fore old disagreements about the role of design in below-market subsidized housing. On the one hand, much of the point of a constructive program (rather than one simply using vouchers) has always been architectural: to ensure not just lower costs but also better conditions. At the same time many housers have always felt uneasy about building below-market housing to high standards for fear that limited funds were being squandered on nonessential elements. Those who argue that Via Verde fails as a replicable model due to its cost, however, mistake the specific conditions of this building for the process that led to it. Indeed, the key strategy to be learned is the collaborative, open process that allowed for a project of such high quality. The long-term cost-benefit analysis of such projects, including on resident health, education, household income, and in terms of drawing further investment in the area, remains to be made.[85]

While the development of remaining city-owned parcels in Melrose Commons and Bronxchester is proceeding, Nos Quedamos has shifted its efforts away from construction. On the one hand this is due to the operational challenges of ownership, as it has outsourced the management of its buildings to specialists like Wavecrest and Grenadier Realty. On the other hand, the death of cofounder and long-time director Yolanda Garcia in 2005 reveals the instabilities of a type of organization that has no real political mandate (unlike that of a city community board), but depends on the charisma of its leaders to represent a neighborhood. The resulting difficulties are also emblematic of the inherent conflicts affecting an organization whose mission is fostering community in a nonprofit manner but is financially largely dependent on the fees generated through for-profit development.[86] Accordingly, the group has in recent years moved toward community building through human development by offering assistance in applying for social services, as well as classes on health, parenting, and environmental responsibility.

Histories of the South Bronx inevitably draw on and construct its mythology. Terms like "decline" and "fall" permeate discussions of the postwar era.[87] The more recent era of new construction and rehabilitation, meanwhile, is framed as a miracle: as "rebirth" or "resurrection."[88] But there is nothing miraculous about projects such as Melrose Commons and Via Verde. They are the product of diligent grassroots efforts by residents, local organizations, dedicated interest groups, and talented designers underwritten by political support and massive capital investment on the part of city, state, and federal governments. These programs, which have produced more than three thousand apartments at Melrose, are also the product of compromise, however. Although conceived as a corrective to the market—to provide what the market cannot—they are shaped by underlying assumptions that the market knows best what is needed and should ultimately benefit from the substantial public investment made. As with virtually all privately built below-market housing in New York City today, price restrictions are quickly fleeting. In the Nos Quedamos buildings developed with LIHTCs affordability restrictions end as early as 2018, and to extend them will require fresh subsidies.[89]
SUSANNE SCHINDLER

STOP

Conclusion: Challenges and Opportunities

New York City reformers pioneered the idea of below-market subsidized housing in the United States a century ago. Then, thanks to momentum generated during the New Deal, they built more of it than anywhere else. Between the 1930s and 1970s, in particular, the city found space and funds to create hundreds of thousands of below-market apartments of many shapes and sizes, and for many income levels. These places, some now nearly a century old, have long mattered to the city's well-being. At their best they provide secure places to grow old; spaces for cultural expression, leisure, and shopping; and safe, comfortable, and clean dwellings (fig. 7.1). Headlines have long told a mostly unhappy story of social dysfunction in affordable housing and, indeed, there have always been social and financial challenges. But as our contributors have shown, many below-market residents also live fulfilling, ordinary lives: rearing children, commuting to work, participating in community life. In many respects, and particularly in middle-income buildings, life is much like that in any city neighborhood.

But to maintain, let alone expand, the number of such homes for low- and middle-income families in a dense, expensive, big city like New York requires substantially more public subsidies than below-market housing enjoys today, locally or nationally. Since the crisis of the 1970s and the retrenchment of the welfare state, New York has lost ground, even with the addition of more than 120,000 Section 8 vouchers. The number of subsidized units has edged up, but has not kept pace with demand. Moreover, production has been characterized by shallower, shorter-term subsidies including private cross-subsidies; smaller-scale complexes; and programs prioritizing renovation, preservation of price and income restrictions, and sweat equity. In the meantime the economic inequality that produced alarming conditions a hundred

7.1: NYCHA maintenance workers, Polo Grounds Towers, Manhattan, 2014

years ago has returned. Simultaneously, other protections like rent controls have contracted. Without more robust efforts to preserve and construct new below-market housing, including deeply subsidized permanent housing like public housing, old scourges are resurfacing and the city will lose more of its middle and working classes to the suburbs and to other U.S. regions (fig. 7.2).

Below-market housing has always been, at heart, a liberal movement: those who support it believe deeply that working- and middle-class people have a right to quality accommodations, even in an expensive and dynamic city. The majority of New Yorkers still share this faith. They know how difficult it is for working people to find quality affordable apartments, and they have kept up pressure on politicians to deliver. The results include the 100,000 units preserved or constructed during Mayor Koch's Ten-year Housing Plan (1986–96) and the 105,000 units preserved and 55,000 constructed under Mayor Bloomberg's New Housing Marketplace Plan (2004–13). Even Republican Mayor Rudolph Giuliani (1993–2000), popularly associated with accelerating gentrification, built out Koch's plan.

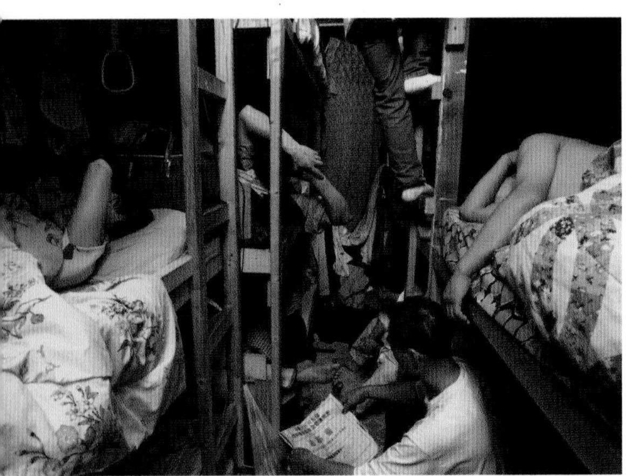

7.2: Chinese immigrants in tiny bunkrooms, Lower East Side, Manhattan, by Fred R. Conrad, 1996

These initiatives count many achievements. But they have not been especially effective in making New York City's housing market more affordable as a whole for the working or middle class; those lucky

7.3: Nine West African immigrants sharing an apartment, Flatbush, Brooklyn, by Ozier Muhammad, 1996

enough to get an apartment represent a fraction of those experiencing housing stress. Rent burdens, public housing waiting lists, and homelessness all rose in the last two decades of the twentieth century and first two decades of the twenty-first. Old troubles that recall the era of Jacob Riis—some potentially quite hazardous like overcrowding and the habitation of unauthorized basements and partitioned rooms—became serious problems again for the first time in decades. And not just in familiar locales like the Lower East Side, but also in new ones like the Bronx and Queens, where subdivision of apartments is endemic in many neighborhoods (fig. 7.3). Unfortunately, the deep subsidies that remedied these problems in the past and can remedy them again today have fallen out of favor in most of the country, even for public-private programs like Section 8 that once enjoyed support from many conservatives.

Challenges

A major area of concern today is the declining condition of low-income public housing. For the time being the NYCHA network remains functional. Some developments, such as those isolated in the Rockaways or East New York, suffer from high levels of social stress and disorder. Others, especially in Manhattan and middle-class sections of the boroughs, remain desirable. Systemwide the agency commands a waiting list of nearly 250,000 families (with another 100,000 on the waiting list, closed since 2007, for Section 8 vouchers, whose numbers have dwindled under President Obama). Yet the entire system is precarious and the question now on everyone's mind is whether New York will be able to avoid the fate of public housing in other American cities. For despite a remarkable record of success, the unfavorable national political climate has taken a major toll.

With 178,000 apartments and an official population of 403,000, NYCHA would be the twenty-seventh largest city in the United States as an independent entity. Many other big American cities, by contrast, have knocked down most of their public housing. Atlanta replaced all its low-income public housing except seniors-only units with a significantly smaller number of apartments in new mixed-income complexes and with Section 8 vouchers, scattering its most vulnerable populations to isolated sites. Often these are in far-flung aging suburbs with poor transit access and few social services. Chicago, too, has razed most of its high-rise projects, replacing the units with a mixture of low-rent low-rise complexes, mixed-income low-rise complexes, and vouchers.[1] So far, New Yorkers have resisted many calls, and great federal pressure, to do the same. NYCHA has replaced just two projects: four comparatively small towers at Prospect Plaza in Ocean Hill–Brownsville, originally built by a private developer in 1974 and now slowly undergoing redevelopment; and Edwin Markham Gardens (1943), a 360-unit, two-story garden apartment complex in Staten Island built as temporary housing for shipyard workers during World War II. Markham's wood-frame and stucco buildings, which were beyond repair, were replaced with 370 new low- and middle-income units between 2008 and 2012 (see fig. 0.33).[2]

New York has otherwise protected its public housing. In the 1970s and 1980s, when tenants and leaders in other cities were abandoning projects, ten thousand NYCHA staff held the line on disorder: porters and maintenance workers scrubbed graffiti, collected trash, and repaired elevators; housing police made daily vertical patrols; on site housing assistants collected late rents. Early federal modernization funds, boosted further when President Jimmy Carter allowed city- and state-financed developments to be absorbed into the federal program, financed successive waves of renovation including new windows, roofs, fixtures, apartment interiors, and playgrounds. Meanwhile, residents—while much maligned in the media for poor behavior—paid rents and helped keep their complexes and neighborhoods stable.

To aid in preservation, NYCHA continued its earlier practice of emphasizing tenant mixtures. Deconcentration of poverty, especially racialized ghetto poverty, became a major U.S. policy goal in housing in the 1980s and 1990s. But it had been a concern of New York housers as early as the 1920s. In the 1970s NYCHA administrators began giving preference to working families in certain developments to avoid concentration of tenants on public assistance. When the share of tenants on welfare climbed to 30 percent by the 1990s, the city began allotting half of all vacant apartments to households with at least one employed member. With the city's perennially tight housing market, and the perilous state of much private housing in many neighborhoods, working-class families lined up for NYCHA units. The dismantling of much of the New Deal system of public assistance under President Clinton with the Personal Responsibility and Work Opportunity Act of 1996—and Mayor Giuliani's aggressive efforts to reduce the share of the city on public assistance—further transformed NYCHA's tenancy. By 2013, 47 percent of apartments housed working families and only about 10 percent of families were on welfare. Approximately 88,000 NYCHA residents today have jobs in the formal sector, mostly the service industry. Many more are likely "NYCHApreneurs," who make money off the books by earning cash cutting hair, renting empty rooms, babysitting, housecleaning, and the like.

Despite these gains NYCHA remains heavily dependent on government aid, direct and indirect. The average family income of about $23,000 includes significant amounts of government payments: about 40 percent of households receive Social

Security, SSI, a pension, or veterans' benefits. New preferences for homeless families introduced in 2014 may push the system further in this direction.[3] With tenants paying an average of just $450 a month in rent, and a growing percentage of residents paying very little or nothing at all, federal support for annual operations must cover more than half the cost of maintaining the system. But appropriations fell sharply under presidents George W. Bush and Barack Obama, leading to staff cuts and operating deficits. Federal capital funding, essential for modernization of buildings, has also been slashed, leaving NYCHA administrators a deferred capital deficit in the billions of dollars. Deferred capital projects mean, on a day-to-day basis, that the millions of annual repairs by staff are frequently undone by systemic problems like crumbling brickwork and defunct plumbing. Despite approximately $7 billion of federal capital funds invested in NYCHA complexes since the 1990s a recent study found that in order to bring NYCHA to a high state of maintenance, an additional $17 billion are required.[4]

These many vulnerabilities were made all too clear when disaster struck New York in the fall of 2012. Hurricane Sandy flooded the ground level of developments housing approximately eighty thousand residents, causing hundreds of millions of dollars in damage to boilers and electrical systems. NYCHA administrators, the mayor, and regional federal officers raced to return displaced residents to their apartments by restoring basic power and heat, and did so within weeks. This engaged response contrasted sharply with that in New Orleans after Hurricane Katrina, in 2005, when local and federal officials used the damage to justify razing much of the city's public housing. A year after Sandy, however, twenty large developments in New York still depended entirely on temporary boiler systems. NYCHA's successful application for approximately three billion dollars in Federal Emergency Management Administration (FEMA) funds to renovate developments affected by the storm—for overhauling and weatherproofing major systems such as boilers, electrical systems, and building exteriors—has not settled questions about the long-term fate of developments in the flood zone.[5]

In spite of these challenges, there are some bright spots. Housing activists from such organizations as the Community Service Society, Community Voices Heard, the Teamsters Local 237 (representing NYCHA employees), and the Legal Aid Society, as well as tenants such as Ethel Velez at the Johnson Houses and Victor Gonzalez at Wise Towers have effectively pressured the city for better services and additional funds. In the first decade of the twenty-first century, NYCHA administrator David Burney took a big risk on the construction of community centers, like that at Van Dyke Houses by Olhausen DuBois Architects and Williamsburg Houses by Pasanella Klein Stoltzman & Berg Architects (fig. 7.4), to add color, light, and liveliness to otherwise dreary superblocks.[6] Many in the city's political class support renovation, in part because public housing can be found in every borough, and they have worked creatively to raise funds for capital improvements, most recently in the form of a city-sponsored bond for $700 million in 2013.

To survive in the era of federal retrenchment NYCHA has also begun to sell portions of its superblocks for new privately developed below-market housing. Reflecting design priorities of earlier eras, many NYCHA complexes occupy as little as 20 percent of their grounds, with the remainder given to lawns, playgrounds, and

7.4: Williamsburg Community Center, 2014

parking. At Forest Houses in the South Bronx, for example, this program allowed for the addition of 124 units in a new LEED Platinum-certified building with a roof-top greenhouse farm called Arbor House (2013), built by Les Bluestone's Blue Sea Development—while leaving the original project with acres of open space. Seeking to exploit this arrangement further, in 2013 NYCHA and Mayor Bloomberg (2002–13) announced a program to sell long-term ground leases at eight Manhattan sites. Lack of consultation with tenants, the fact that much of the housing was to be market-rate, and many other missteps provoked intense opposition. The reaction was so fierce that even the most generous offers to include more below-market units could not save it. The de Blasio administration and new NYCHA administrators, however, have reintroduced the possibility of building on certain NYCHA sites, both to bring aging designs in line with today's architectural fashions emphasizing the street grid, and to generate revenue. Indeed, one internal study determined that sale (rather than ground leasing) of just those eight pilot sites would have generated approximately $750 million dollars in revenue for the agency.[7] Mayor de Blasio is also experimenting with other types of privatization. In 2015 NYCHA finalized a plan to sell a 50 percent stake in six privately built section 8-based complexes that it manages to a group of private developers for $350 million. The new partners will invest an additional $100 million in renovations and have promised to protect current residents, with the understanding that they will be able to convert the complexes to market rents after thirty years with NYCHA's approval.[8]

The city's vast and unparalleled network of privately owned below-market subsidized housing also faces many serious challenges in the twenty-first century. City, state, and federal programs financed hundreds of thousands of apartments—in everything from garden apartments to massive high-rises—between the 1930s and mid-1970s. Since the 1980s hundreds of thousands more apartments have been produced by the decentralized housing network through renovation and new construction. Today, ambitious new projects like Hunter's Point South in Long Island City, Pacific Park (formerly Atlantic Yards) in Downtown Brooklyn, and Astoria Cove, which mayors Bloomberg and de Blasio played a large role in shaping, promise to add thousands more. As at NYCHA, attempts are also being to made rethink the superblock model; successful redevelopment of portions of private middle-income complexes like Park West Village on the Upper West Side, built as a Title I urban renewal project in the 1950s (fig. 7.5), indicate that additional retail, market, and below-market housing could be included on the grounds of many existing projects without unduly compromising quality of life.

7.5: Park West Village, 2014

But these efforts hardly address the depth of need among those earning even well above average incomes in New York City. As apartments have become eligible to exit rent-restricted systems many are leaving—including about half of all Mitchell-Lama rentals, along with many Mitchell-Lama co-ops, especially in Manhattan—and they are not being replaced quickly enough to reduce rising pressures on prices. Moreover, unlike Mitchell-Lama or even FHA's old limited-dividend and limited-equity program, LIHTCs (the most prolific program today) tend to require property owners to retain rent and income restrictions for only fifteen years. Even though many projects are developed using a range of other programs that extend those terms to thirty or forty years, it is only a matter of time before landlords leave the system as quickly as new stock is built.[9] As a result, advocates have found themselves running on a treadmill to preserve the housing they created just a few years before. Meanwhile, with its shallow subsidies, the decentralized system has difficulty producing units for low-income families, just as limited-dividend builders did in earlier eras.

Mayor de Blasio, like Mayor Bloomberg before him, has rightly focused on extending price restrictions in existing projects by offering new low-interest loans and tax abatements as a lure. And he is optimistic that his proposal, *Housing New York: A Five Borough, Ten-year Plan* (2014), can reinvigorate the city's commitment to below-market housing and generate the kind of dramatic results produced by programs of earlier eras. While more aggressive than Bloomberg's plan—it calls for over $41 billion in funds to be used for the construction of 80,000 apartments and extension of price restrictions at 120,000 more—its approach is still insufficient. It is incremental, despite calls to develop places like Sunnyside Yard, Queens, at a large scale reminiscent of projects like Stuyvesant Town (1949). It is also almost entirely dependent on a mixture of unstable federal grants, city debt, and old-fashioned "philanthropy-and-five-percent": private developers willing to accept limited profits for the greater good. Meanwhile, as under previous mayors, the city continues to grant enormous financial benefits to developers building mixed-income developments even when the number of moderate- and low-cost units is very small. What the city still lacks is a more robust and sustainable approach scaled to the unique needs, conditions, and capacities that distinguish New York from other U.S. cities.

Opportunities

The challenge of providing high-quality, below-market housing has evolved significantly in the past generation. Before the 1960s, substandard tenement housing, and the threats it once posed to health, and perhaps morals, defined housing debates and public policy. In the 1970s and 1980s it was urban crisis. Today New York has entered an exuberant new Gilded Age. The center of metropolitan gravity has shifted back to the city from suburbia, and following economist Saskia Sassen's "global cities" thesis, from other U.S. cities to New York.[10]

The city's sharp rise in income inequality, in particular, has complicated housing. Pay at the top in the United States has surged since the 1980s, but incomes for the working and middle classes have stagnated. In New York this means that co-op apartments on the Upper East Side that sold for double the price of a suburban house in Levittown in the late 1940s ($15,000, or $265,000 in 2013 dollars)—an era when the rich paid as much as 90 percent of their income in taxes—now sell for ten or twenty times as much. Although far less dramatic, prices relative to income have

risen in many more ordinary neighborhoods, too. This surge has been intensified by the gradual release of tens of thousands of privately built low- and middle-income units from price and income restrictions, as well as hundreds of thousands of units pricing out of rent control and rent stabilization. The problem is revealed most vividly, perhaps, in the fact that sixty thousand people now bed down in city shelters every night—roughly the same number who inhabit an entire city like Cheyenne, Wyoming. And this figure does not include the several thousand more on the streets, let alone the estimated hundreds of thousands of New Yorkers who live in cramped, dangerous dwellings (fig. 7.6).[11]

7.6: Improvised shelter, East New York, Brooklyn, 2014

To address these realities substantively will demand not just NYCHA land sales, ground leases, or public-private partnerships. Nor will Mitchell-Lama extensions, ten-year mayoral plans, philanthropy, and high-design examples like Via Verde (2012) or David Adjaye's Sugar Hill Housing (2014) suffice (fig. 7.7). What is needed are great infusions of capital for operating subsidies and new construction. The pioneers of below-market housing such as Clarence Stein never tired of pointing out that the problem of housing in cities like New York was not the result

7.7: Sugar Hill Housing, Manhattan, 2014

of short-term crises, or of greedy landlords and developers. The situation is fundamental to organizing a big city on a highly concentrated, centralized basis. Short of total decentralization—a goal that few housers today support given the challenges of service provision and transportation—there is only one true remedy for poor city housing conditions: a mixture of long-term, below-market-interest-rate loans, subsidized by the government; cash for operations and maintenance, especially for low-income housing; and low (abated) property taxes.

Housers and city leaders in the twenty-first century must think creatively about where to find and how to sustain such subsidies. Possibilities abound. The governor of New York State has at his disposal billions in surplus tax revenues and borrowing capacity—made possible in large part because of the global profits generated in New York City's financial sector. State housing programs such as Mitchell-Lama were once, and could be again, a massive help, not least since the high inflation that undermined the original program is no longer a problem. The city can levy new occupancy taxes on expensive pieds-a-terre, so many of which now seem to be owned by offshore investors who otherwise contribute little to the commonweal for the privilege of parking their money in New York City real estate. The mortgage-recording tax, which generates $1.5 billion for the city in good times and $500 million in bad, could be replaced by a transfer tax to capture benefit from the huge number of all-cash sales, including the 60 percent in Manhattan condominiums.[12] Organized labor can reconsider its resistance to nonunion labor in the below-market housing sector. The design professions and construction industries must continue to imagine how to make more housing with less money, without compromising quality of life, and to update old efficient formats like tower-in-the-park to suit new tastes. Indeed, it is hard to imagine large amounts of new housing in New York below-market or

7.8: HUD Secretary Shaun Donovan (center), Senator Charles Schumer (mid-right), Governor Andrew Cuomo (right), and Mayor Bill de Blasio (left) at Rebuild By Design event, Jacob Riis Houses, 2014

otherwise, without high-rises—if not on the order of Singapore, than at least on that of Starrett City.

Like a hundred years ago, however, perhaps the ultimate challenge for the city is to convince leaders at higher levels of government to support the cause (fig. 7.8). New York City has made good use of the subsidies it won from Washington and Albany over the past century and the city's decentralized network and NYCHA would do so again today. More crucially, the city cannot afford, and never really could, to pay for all the necessary below-market housing on its own.

New York City's leaders have been vocal critics of the federal retreat from funding of new below-market units and have lobbied hard to retain the subsidies that remain. But they have few allies. American skepticism toward government aid to the poor, particularly people of color, has undermined the notion of government housing as a positive force. In addition, the decentralized programs that replaced public housing have proven well-suited to much of the United States. In the absence of New York's multinational corporate headquarters, major financial exchanges, and global reputation as a secure place for off-shore real estate investment, housing in most places remains in line with local incomes. Periodic bubbles aside, cities like Denver and Phoenix do not face the affordability problem characteristic of global financial centers like New York. What gaps there are can be filled with voucher programs and shallow subsidies like LIHTCs. But these programs do not meet the needs or capacities of New York.

Beyond the broader conservative ascendency, the major roadblock to such a renewed effort is parochialism. Progressive California cities like Los Angeles and San Francisco aside, below-market housing is seen chiefly by Americans as a local, New York City problem. But leaders in Washington and Albany must be made to remember that however exceptional it may be, New York City is not an island unto itself. It is a bellwether of the nation. One in thirteen Americans still live in the New York metropolitan area, one in thirty-seven in the city, and 200,000 more arrive every year. The city needs a stable, healthy, and safe working and middle class to sustain its global competitiveness—not to mention that these citizens send far more tax revenue to Washington and Albany than they receive in expenditures. More so than ever New York is the nation's premier city, a key point of capital and cultural exchange and an important reflection of the American way. Its highs are the nation's, and so are its lows. Responsibility for alleviating its privations rests on the shoulders of us all.

Model Gallery III: Contemporary

Growing dissatisfaction with Modernist site planning and high-rise living among both tenants and leaders in the age of urban crisis provoked an exciting period of innovation in New York housing. Despite the great variety of approaches, one common theme was that architects and sponsors of nearly all the complexes shown here sought to return public spaces to tenants, either as access-controlled common areas or private yards and patios. Architects also experimented with new systems of circulation and massing in order to create more physical variety, while also cutting costs. Most of these changes coincided with the era's great shift in policy and financing for below-market subsidized housing. So while some experiments, like those of UDC, reflect the avant-garde priorities of architects, many others emphasize the more market-oriented desires of tenants, who helped to take charge of production, as suggested by the plain but prized row houses built by Nehemiah Houses and mid-rise apartment buildings developed at Melrose Commons. In reaction to the very ordinariness of this housing, designers have recently made efforts once again to assume a lead voice in below-market subsidized housing by staging competitions like that which produced Via Verde.

Riverbend

1968; 2BR = 930 square feet

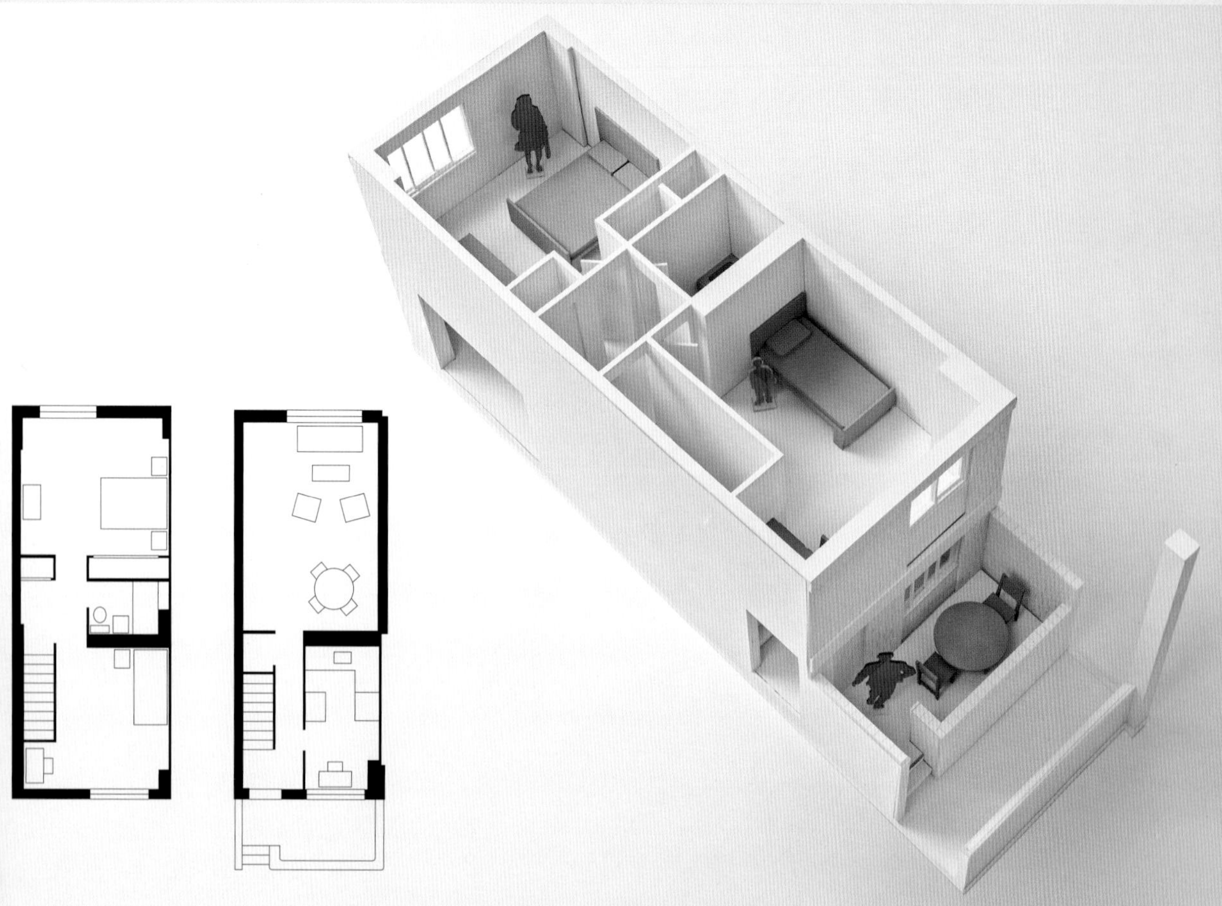

Riverbend, which reproduces the feel of row house living with economies possible only in high-rises, was designed as a vertically organized, high-rise set of two-story apartments. Units open to exterior corridors placed at every other floor and have private outdoor patios that lead to kitchens and serve as a transition zone between the shared walkway and the home. Units have cross-ventilation on the entry floor but a strong visual separation between living room and the kitchen and entry. Stairs to the second level, which contain the bedrooms, open from the foyer. Because of cost limits, apartments have relatively few windows. Although popular with their owners, the Riverbend solution was not widely replicated.

Eastwood

1976; 2BR = 900 square feet

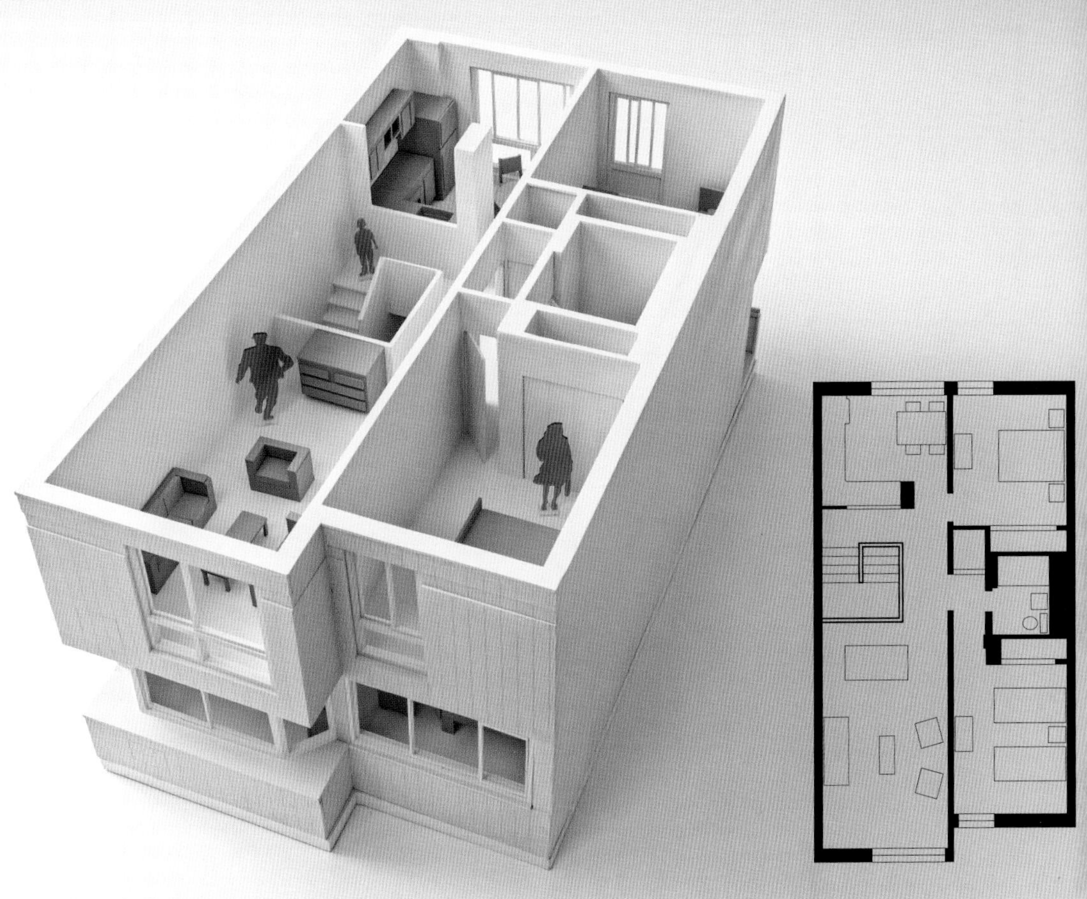

The designers of Eastwood attempted to engender feelings of community by arranging units along internal "streets in the sky." The spirit of innovation was just as pronounced within the units. From the "street," entrances led directly to private stairs going either up or down to the units, which sit above and below the public corridor. The stairways terminate in the center of each apartment in a foyer. From here, two parallel functional areas are accessed. One side leads to the kitchen, which reflecting the domestic informality of the 1970s is open to the stair and living room to promote visual connections, with large windows facing north and south. The other side leads to the bathroom and bedrooms. Despite the size of these units, the open plans, large windows, and unique locations appealed to many and have allowed the current landlord to command favorable market rents.

Nehemiah Houses

1982–; 2BR = 1,100 square feet

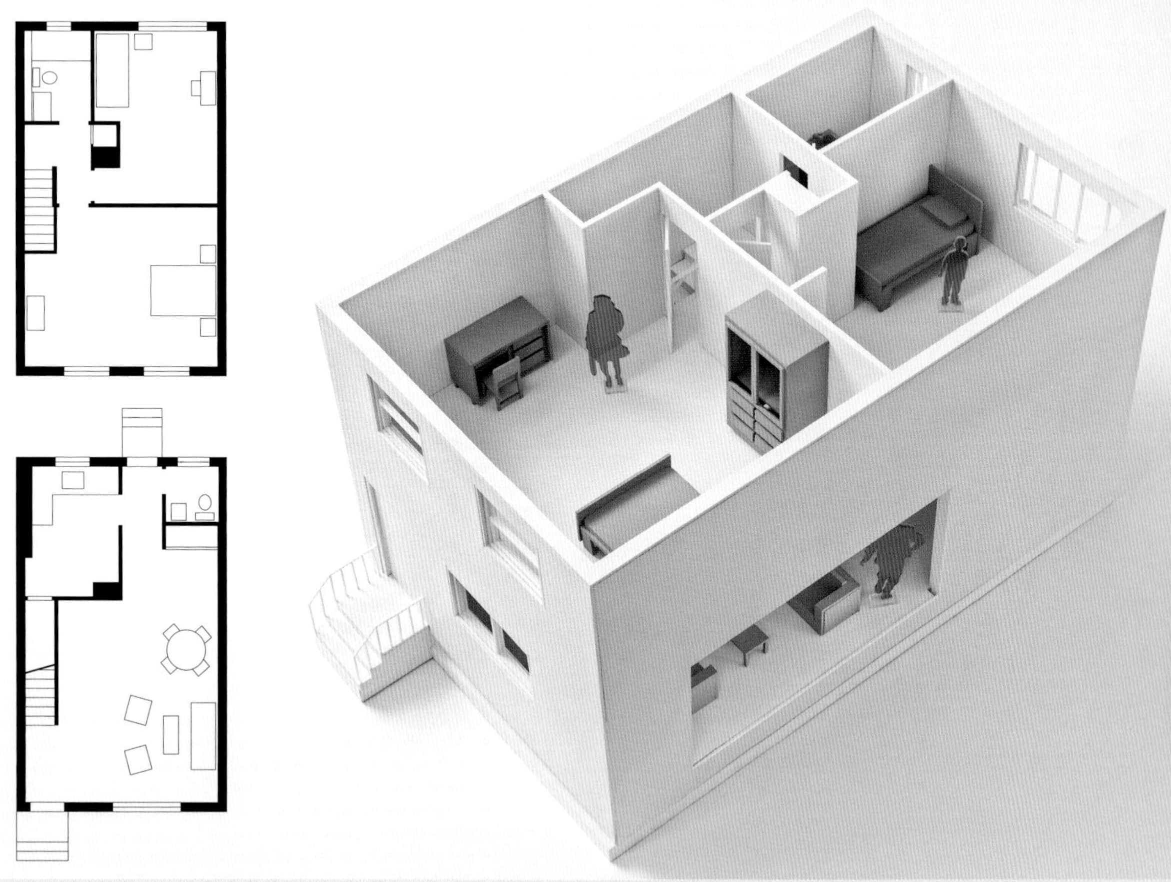

Responding to critiques of large-scale, high-rise development, Nehemiah sought to create units that maximized tenant control and pent-up demand for homeownership. No-frills row houses like these, with front and rear yards, gave residents more access to usable outdoor space than that enjoyed by many residents in older subsidized developments where securing public space against crime was a greater concern. Another advantage of these units is that they are highly flexible, with possibility for subdividing the upper level into anywhere from one to four bedrooms. Other than the stairs, kitchen, and bathrooms, the rest of the house is customizable.

Via Verde

2012; 2BR = 810 square feet

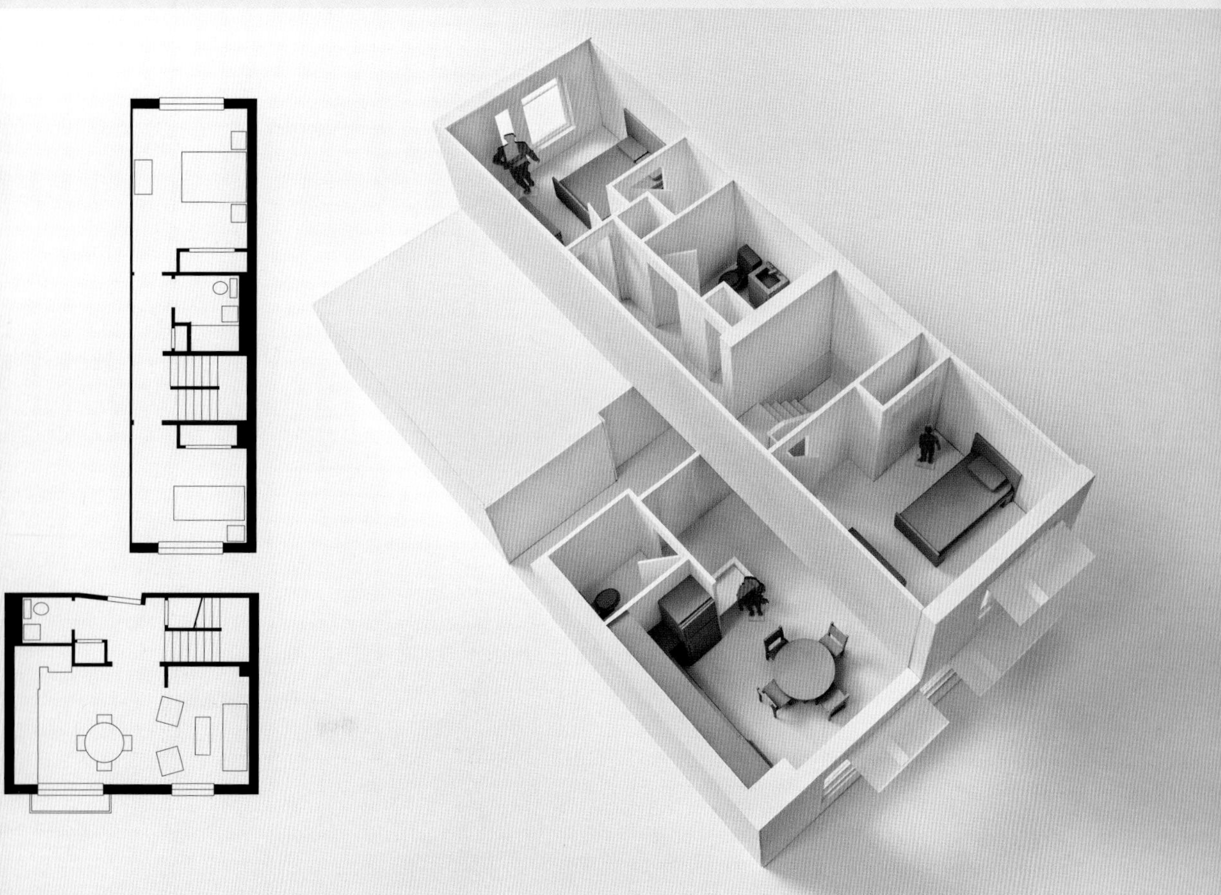

Via Verde, a showcase for cutting-edge architectural ideas about sustainability and community, rivals many market-rate units in size, unit cost, and amenities. In the main section of the building, which includes this two-bedroom unit, apartments are arranged in an interlocking duplex plan, accessed by double-loaded corridors. Units open to a kitchen and living-room area, with a balcony beyond. Upstairs are bedrooms, a second bathroom, and a second balcony off the larger bedroom. The open kitchen with no division to the living room creates an awkward lack of definition between these areas. Other features, however, like the built-in media center downstairs and the washing machine and dryer upstairs, rival those of new market-rate housing. MATTHIAS ALTWICKER, MATTHEW GORDON LASNER, NICHOLAS BLOOM

Notes

NYT = New York Times

Introduction

1. Lizette Alvarez, "Up and Out of New York's Projects," *NYT*, May 31, 2009: WE6.

2. On filtering see Richard Harris, "The Rise of Filtering Down: The American Housing Market Transformed, 1915–29," *Social Science History* 37, no. 4 (Winter 2013): 515–49.

3. On the origins of housing inequality in New York City see Elizabeth Blackmar, *Manhattan for Rent, 1785–1850* (Ithaca, N.Y.: Cornell University Press, 1989).

4. On the early tenants rights movement see, for example, Ronald Laswon, ed., *The Tenant Movement in New York City, 1904–1984* (New Brunswick, N.J.: Rutgers University Press, 1986).

5. Estimates based in part on Furman Center for Real Estate and Urban Policy, New York University and Institute for Affordable Housing Policy, *State of New York City's Subsidized Housing: 2011* (New York: Furman Center for Real Estate and Urban Policy, 2011). On FHA's postwar program data do not exist; for partial data see Ira S. Robbins and Marian Sameth, ed., *Directory of Large-scale Rental and Cooperative Housing with a Summary of Legislation Relating to Housing and Urban Renewal in New York City* (New York: Citizen's Housing and Planning Council of New York, 1957).

6. Lawrence J. Vale, *Purging the Poorest: Public Housing and the Design Politics of Twice-Cleared Communities* (Chicago: University of Chicago Press, 2013). On SROs generally in the United States see Paul Groth, *Living Downtown: The History of Residential Hotels in the United States* (Berkeley: University of California Press, 1994); Sam Davis, *Designing for the Homeless: Architecture That Works* (Berkeley: University of California Press, 2004).

7. On public housing outside New York, including narratives of failure and the transition away from it, see, for example, D. Bradford Hunt, *Blueprint for Disaster: The Unraveling of Chicago Public Housing* (Chicago: University of Chicago Press, 2009); Vale, *Purging the Poorest*; Joseph Heathcott, "The Strange Career of Public Housing: Policy, Planning, and the American Metropolis in the Twentieth Century," *Journal of the American Planning Association* 78, no. 4 (Autumn 2012): 360–75; Rhonda Y. Williams, *The Politics of Public Housing: Black Women's Struggles against Urban Inequality* (New York: Oxford University Press, 2004); Sudhir Alladi Venkatesh, *American Project: The Rise and Fall of a Modern Ghetto* (Cambridge, Mass.: Harvard University Press, 2000); Xavier de Souza Briggs, Susan J. Popkin, and

John Goering, *Moving to Opportunity: The Story of an American Experiment to Fight Ghetto Poverty* (New York: Oxford University Press, 2010); Katherine G. Bristol, "The Pruitt-Igoe Myth," *Journal of Architectural Education* 44, no. 3 (May 1991): 163–71; Alexander von Hoffman, "Calling Upon the Genius of Private Enterprise: The Housing and Urban Development Act of 1968 and the Liberal Turn to Public-Private Partnerships," *Studies in American Political Development* 27 (Oct. 2013): 165–94.

8. "Plan to Preserve Public Housing Survey Reveals Resident Concerns," *New York City Housing Authority Journal*, 43, no. 3 (Apr. 2011): 1.

9. On life in New York below-market housing see, for instance, Nicholas Dagen Bloom, *Public Housing That Worked: New York in the Twentieth Century* (Philadelphia: University of Pennsylvania Press, 2008); Matthew Gordon Lasner, *High Life: Condo Living in the Suburban Century* (New Haven, Conn.: Yale University Press, 2012), chapter 4; Samuel Zipp, *Manhattan Projects: The Rise and Fall of Urban Renewal in Cold War New York* (New York: Oxford University Press, 2010); Peter Eistenstadt, *Rochdale Village: Robert Moses, 6,000 Families, and New York City's Great Experiment in Integrated Housing* (Ithaca, N.Y.: Cornell University Press, 2010).

10. Ingrid Gould Ellen, "Spillovers and Subsidized Housing: The Impact of Subsidized Rental Housing on Neighborhoods," in *Revisiting Rental Housing: Policies, Programs, and Priorities*, ed. Nicolas P. Retsinas and Eric Belsky (Washington, D.C.: Brookings Institute, 2008).

11. For an overview of LIHTCs see David J. Erickson, *The Housing Policy Revolution: Networks and Neighborhoods* (Washington, D.C.: Urban Institute Press, 2009); Lawrence J. Vale and Yonah Freemark "From Public Housing to Public-Private Housing," *Journal of the American Planning Association* 78, no. 4 (Autumn 2012): 379–402; Edward L. Glaeser and Joseph Gyourko, *Rethinking Federal Housing Policy: How to Make Housing Plentiful and Affordable* (Washington, D.C.: AEI Press, 2008): 102–14; Katherine M. O'Regan and Karen M. Horn, "What Can We Learn about the Low-income Housing Tax Credit Program by Looking at the Tenants?," *Housing Policy Debate* 23, no. 3 (2013): 597–613.

12. Edward L. Glaeser and Bryce A. Ward, "The Causes and Consequences of Land Use Regulation: Evidence from Greater Boston," *Journal of Urban Economics* 65 (2009): 265–78.

13. Richard Plunz, *A History of Housing in New York City: Dwelling Type and Social Change in the American Metropolis* (New York: Columbia University Press, 1990).

14. See, for instance, Kenny Cupers, ed., *Use Matters: An Alternative History of Architecture* (Milton Park, U.K.: Routledge, 2013).

Chapter 1: Below-market Subsidized Housing Begins

1. Quotation from "Hem and Profit," *NYT*, November 29, 1896: 13. On low-cost housing generally in this period see Eugenie Ladner Birch and Deborah S. Gardner, "The Seven-percent Solution: A Review of Philanthropic Housing, 1870–1910," *Journal of Urban History* 7, no. 4 (Aug. 1981): 403–38; Jared N. Day, *Urban Castles: Tenement Housing and Landlord Activism in New York City, 1890–1943* (New York: Columbia University Press, 1999); Roy Lubove, *The Progressives and the Slums: Tenement House Reform in New York City, 1890–1917* (Pittsburgh: Pittsburgh University Press, 1962).

2. On the tenant movement see Robert Fogelson, *The Great Rent Wars: New York, 1917–1929* (New Haven, Conn.: Yale University Press, 2013); Joseph A. Spencer, "New York City Tenant Organizations and the Post–World War I Housing Crisis," in Lawson and Naison, eds., *The Tenants Movement in New York City, 1904–1984.* (New Brunswick, N.J.: Rutgers University Press, 1986).

3. Roy Lubove, *Community Planning in the 1920s: The Contribution of the Regional Planning Association of America* (Pittsburgh: University of Pittsburgh Press, 1963).

4. On Wood see Eugenie Ladner Birch, "Edith Elmer Wood and the Genesis of Liberal Housing Thought, 1910–1942," PhD diss., Columbia University, 1975.

5. Birch, "Edith Elmer Wood and the Genesis of Liberal Housing Thought, 1910–1942," 40–52.

6. On Stein see Lubove, *Community Planning in the 1920s*; Edward K. Spann, *Designing Modern America: The Regional Planning Association of America and Its Members* (Columbus: Ohio State University Press, 1996), chapter 4; Birch, "Edith Elmer Wood and the Genesis of Liberal Housing Thought, 1910–1942," 100 n. 8.

7. Quoted in Fogelson, *The Great Rent Wars*, 367.

8. Quoted in Lubove, *Community Planning in the 1920s*, 35.

9. On Governor Al Smith see political biographies such as Matthew Josephson, *Al Smith: Hero of the Cities: A Political Portrait: Drawing on the Papers of Frances Perkins* (Boston: Houghton Mifflin, 1969); Paula Eldot, *Governor Alfred E. Smith: The Politician as Reformer* (New York: Garland, 1983); Christopher Finan, *Alfred E. Smith: The Happy Warrior* (New York: Hill and Wang, 2002); and Robert Slayton, *Empire Statesman: The*

Rise and Redemption of Al Smith (New York: Free Press, 2001).

10. Quoted in "Model Homes Open," *NYT*, December 6, 1930: 17.

11. Quoted in "Gov. Smith Signs New Housing Bill," *NYT*, May 11, 1926: 1.

12. Louis Pink, *The New Day in Housing* (New York: John Day, 1928).

13. Matthew Gordon Lasner, *High Life: Condo Living in the Suburban Century* (New Haven, Conn.: Yale University Press, 2012), 97.

14. Lasner, *High Life*, 98–101, 143–46.

15. Laws of New York, Chapter 908 (1867); Chapter 85, Section 13 (1887).

16. For a history of the early apartment house see Elizabeth Collins Cromley, *Alone Together: A History of New York's Early Apartments* (Ithaca, N.Y.: Cornell University Press, 1990).

17. Among the basic general sources for tenement design and history are Lawrence Veiller, "Tenement House Reform in New York City, 1834–1900," in Robert W. DeForest and Lawrence Veiller, eds., *The Tenement House Problem*, vol. 1 (New York: Macmillan, 1903), 69–118; James Ford, *Slums and Housing* (Cambridge, Mass.: Harvard University Press, 1936); Anthony Jackson, *A Place Called Home: A History of Low-cost Housing in Manhattan* (Cambridge, Mass.: MIT Press, 1976); and Richard Plunz, *A History of Housing in New York City: Dwelling Type and Social Change in the American Metropolis* (New York: Columbia University Press, 1990). For the study of a specific tenement building, see Andrew S. Dolkart, *Biography of a Tenement House: An Architectural History of 97 Orchard Street*, 2d ed. (Chicago: Center for American Places, 2012).

18. Citizens' Association of New York, Council of Hygiene and Public Health, *Report of the Council of Hygiene and Public Health of the Citizens' Association of New York upon the Sanitary Conditions of the City* (New York: D. Appleton and Company, 1865), lxix.

19. "Prize Tenements," *NYT*, March 16, 1879: 6.

20. Charles Lockwood, "Quintessential Housing of the Past: Tenements," *NYT*, July 23, 1978: R1.

21. "Tenement House Show," *NYT*, February 10, 1900: 7.

22. For the Supreme Court case see Tenement House Department of City of New York v. Moeschen, 203 U.S. 93 (United States Supreme Court, November 12, 1906), and Judith A. Gilbert, "Tenements and Takings," *Fordham Urban Law Journal* 18, no. 3 (1990): 437–505.

23. For the 15,000 figure see City and Suburban Homes Company, *Twenty-third Annual Report* (1919), 4. Major sources for the history of the City and Suburban Homes Company are City and Suburban Homes Company, *Annual Reports*, 1896–1950; Lubove, *The Progressives and the Slums*; Andrew S. Dolkart and Sharon Z. Macosko, *A Dream Fulfilled: City and Suburban's York Avenue Estate* (New York: Coalition to Save City and Suburban Housing, Inc., 1988); Gail Harris, "City and Suburban Homes Company, Avenue A (York Avenue) Estate" and "City and Suburban Homes Company, First Avenue Estate" Designation Reports, New York City Landmarks Preservation Commission, 1990.

24. Ernest Flagg, "The New York Tenement-House Evil and Its Cure," *Scribner's Magazine* 16 (July 1894): 108–17.

25. "Care of Tenement House Properties," *NYT*, May 27, 1917: 33.

26. "Better Tenement Houses," *NYT*, November 22, 1896: 9.

27. *Model Homes* (New York: City and Suburban Homes Company, 1905), 14.

28. African Americans were listed as a separate nationality under the terminology "colored."

29. City and Suburban Homes Company, *Sixteenth Annual Report* (1912), 10–15.

30. "Methods Change in Management," *NYT*, May 14, 1939: RE6.

31. Allan Robinson, "Care of Tenement House Properties," *NYT*, May 27, 1917: 33.

32. "Flat $9.48 a Room," *NYT*, July 20, 1924: RE1.

33. Robinson, "Care of Tenement House Properties."

34. "New York's Famous Model Tenements Are Failures," *NYT*, October 27, 1912: SM1.

35. On Dunbar and Rockefeller generally see Lasner, *High Life*, 99–106, 108–9.

36. Kenneth W. Rose, "Partners in Housing Reform: The Apartment Developments of John D. Rockefeller, Jr., Charles O. Heydt, and Andrew J. Thomas," the Conference on New York State History, New York State Historical Association, Cooperstown, N.Y., June 8, 2007, 16.

37. Memorandum from Charles Abrams, consultant, and Wilfred S. Lewis, secretary, NYCHA to Members of the NYCHA, Subject: Acquisition of Dunbar Apartments, June 18, 1937, New York City Housing Authority Records, LaGuardia and Wagner Archive, LaGuardia Community College (hereafter NYCHAR).

38. "Dunbar Apts. Hit," *New York Amsterdam News*, October 10, 1936: 1; "Company Purchases Dunbar Apartments," *New York Amsterdam News*, November 6, 1937: 1; "Church's Part in Community Told at Meet," *New York Amsterdam News*, July 28, 1945: 6.

39. "Dunbar Housewives' League to Hold Exhibit," *New York Amsterdam News*, April 4, 1936: 6; "Tenants' League Fights Eviction of George W. Streator," *New York Amsterdam News*, May 13, 1939: 4; "Survey Shows Need for Better Housing,"

New York Amsterdam News, January 13, 1940: 4; Bill Chase, "All Ears," *New York Amsterdam News*, September 21, 1946: 8; "The Exotic Girls Score," *New York Amsterdam News*, April 3, 1948: 13.

40. Edward Wakin with photographs by Edward Letteau, *At the Edge of Harlem: Portrait of a Middle-class Negro Family* (New York: William Morrow, 1965), 15, 17.

41. Wakin and Lettau, *At the Edge of Harlem*, 11, 17, 25.

42. "Dunbar Apartments Sold," *New York Amsterdam News*, March 16, 1963: 1.

43. Dee Wedemeyer, "A Troubled Harlem Project," *NYT*, February 19, 1978: R1; Lee A. Daniels, "Harlem Co-op Conversion Plan Falters," *NYT*, December 2, 1983: B13; Selvin Michael, "Dunbar Apartments to Get a Facelift," *New York Amsterdam News*, September 1, 1984: 37; Jill Nelson-Ricks, "The Bank Knows Best for Harlem's Dunbar Houses," *City Limits* 9, no. 2 (February–March 1984): 8–11.

44. Alan S. Oser, "Switching to the Rental Track in Harlem," *NYT*, January 21, 1990: R7; J. Zamgba Browne, "Dunbar Apartments Get $7.5M for Renovations," *New York Amsterdam News*, December 21, 1996: 38; Heather Haddon, "Housing Wars," *The Independent* [New York] 87, May 21, 2006; Timothy Williams, "In Suit against Landlord, Tenants Make Unusual Accusation: Racketeering," *NYT*, July 12, 2007: B5; Eliot Brown, "Property: Pinnacle May Lose Harlem Site," *Wall Street Journal*, March 23, 2011: A20; Mireya Navarro, "Court Upholds a Settlement Affecting 20,000 City Renters," *NYT*, October 1, 2013: A21.

45. Personal interview with tenant Gina, April 19, 2013, conducted by Allison Blanchette and Marlon Willie.

46. Tanangachi Mfuni, "Dangers at Dunbar."

47. Personal interview with tenant Karen, May 12, 2013, conducted by Michael Fivis and Allison Blanchette.

48. Personal interview with tenant Ramona Ponce, May 8, 2013, conducted by Oksana Mironova; personal interview with tenant Gina.

49. Personal interview with tenant Barbara Nienaltowski, April 28, 2013, conducted by Oksana Mironova.

50. On Stein and his milieu generally, including efforts toward Sunnyside, see Kermit C. Parsons, "Collaborative Genius: The Regional Planning Association of America," *Journal of the American Planning Association* 60, no. 4 (Autumn 1994): 462–83; Clarence S. Stein, *The Writings of Clarence S. Stein: Architect of the Planned Community*, ed. Kermit Carlyle Parson (Baltimore: Johns Hopkins University Press, 1998), especially 97–98; Lubove, *Community Planning in the 1920s;* Carl Sussman, ed., *Planning the Fourth Migration: The Neglected Vision of the Regional Planning Association of America* (Cambridge, Mass.: MIT Press, 1976).

51. Lasner, *High Life*, 110–12.

52. Franklin Havelick, "Sunnyside Gardens: Whose Land Is It Anyway?" *New York Affairs* 7, no. 2 (1982): 70.

53. Havelick, *New York Affairs*, 73.

54. Marcus Brauchli, "If You're Thinking of Living in: Sunnyside," *NYT*, July 3, 1983: A7.

55. Constance Rosenblum, "Accessorized with Stroller and Rake," *NYT*, November 27, 2009: RE1.

56. Valerie Moylan quoted in Maggie Garb, "Suburbia Minutes from Midtown," *NYT*, June 26, 1994: G5.

57. Ellen Barry, "A Pocket of Queens Brimming with History, and Now Resentment," *NYT*, July 5, 2007: B3.

58. Lasner, *High Life*, 98–101. On the complex also see Elsie Danenberg, *Get Your Own Home the Co-operative Way* (New York: Greenberg, 1949): 62–70; Andrew S. Dolkart, "Homes for People; Non-profit Cooperatives in New York City 1916–1929," *SITES* 21–22 (1989): 30–42.

59. Abraham Kazan, "The Birth of the Amalgamated Housing Corporation," 1957, reprinted in "Reading #1," Co-op History/Discussion Club, July 12, 2009, www.columbia.edu/~hauben.

60. Pink, *The New Day in Housing*, 166.

61. Daniel Liebeskind in *At Home in Utopia*, dir. by Michal Goldman, Filmmakers Collaborative, 2008.

62. Harold Ickes, *Back to Work: The Story of PWA* (New York: Da Capo Press, 1973), 178–94.

63. "800% Land Value Rise Since '29," *New York Herald Tribune*, May 25, 1934.

64. Boulevard Gardens Buyers Committee, *Boulevard Gardens* (Woodside, Queens: 1991).

65. *The Boulevard Gardens Beacon*, no. 1, October 1935; Boulevard Gardens Buyers Committee, *Boulevard Gardens*.

66. "Prosperous Tenants to Lose Apartments," *NYT*, June 23, 1938: 23.

67. "Old PWA Loan Satisfied on Boulevard Gardens," *NYT*, January 1, 1941: 42.

68. Richard D Lyons, "Victory in Woodside; Status Quo," *NYT*, June 11, 1989: R1; see also "Now It's Time for Boulevard Gardens in Queens," *Daily News*, August 5, 1988: 16.

69. For the story of Mary Simkhovitch and NYCHA in more detail see Nicholas Dagen Bloom, *Public Housing That Worked: New York in the Twentieth Century* (Philadelphia: University of Pennsylvania Press, 2008), chapters 1–5; Mary Simkhovitch, "Standards and Tests of Efficiency in Settlement Work," *Proceedings of the National Conference of Charities*, June 1911, 1–3; "British Action in Slum Clearance," *New Republic*, reprinted in pamphlet by The National Public Housing Conference, September 26, 1934, 1–2.

70. Mary Simkhovitch, "The Story of Greenwich House," in National Federation of Settlements and Neighborhood Centers, *Settlement Goals for the Next Third of a Century: A Symposium* (Boston: 1926).

71. Ibid.

72. "Housing as a Permanent Municipal Service," Radio Address, WEAF, February 19, 1934, box 22, folder 92 (microfilm), Tamiment Collection (139), New York University.

73. Ibid.

74. See Joel Schwartz, "Tenant Unions in New York City's Low-Rent Housing, 1933–1949," *Journal of Urban History* 12, no. 4 (August 1986): 414–43, 420–21.

Chapter 2: Public Neighborhoods

1. For more details on NYCHA see Nicholas Dagen Bloom, *Public Housing That Worked: New York in the Twentieth Century* (Philadelphia: University of Pennsylvania Press, 2008); Joel Schwartz, *The New York Approach: Robert Moses, Urban Liberals, and Redevelopment of the Inner City* (Columbus: Ohio State University Press, 1993); Wendell E. Pritchett, *Brownsville, Brooklyn: Blacks, Jews, and the Changing Face of the Ghetto* (Chicago: University of Chicago Press, 2002); Gail Radford, *Modern Housing for America: Policy Struggles in the New Deal Era* (Chicago: University of Chicago Press, 1996).

2. "2,000,000 in Slums Face Housing Crisis," *NYT*, December 18, 1936: 21.

3. Edith Elmer Wood, *Housing Progress in Western Europe* (New York: E. P. Dutton, 1923); Louis Pink, *A New Day in Housing* (New York: John Day, 1928); Catherine Bauer, *Modern Housing* (New York: Houghton Mifflin, 1934); Herbert Undeen Nelson and Marion Lawrence Nelson, *New Homes for Old Countries* (Chicago: National Association of Real Estate Boards, 1937).

4. Quoted in Ira S. Robbins and Gus Tyler, *Reminiscences of a Housing Advocate* (New York: Citizens Housing and Planning Council of New York, 1983), 14.

5. Quoted in "10,000 Hear Mayor Say Unsafe Slums Will Be Wiped Out," *NYT*, April 9, 1934: 1.

6. "Open Drive to Build Low-Cost Homes," *NYT*, March 23, 1932: 15.

7. On these factions and debates see D. Bradford Hunt, "Was the 1937 U.S. Housing Act a Pyrrhic Victory?" *Journal of Planning History* 4, no. 3 (August 2005): 195–221; Alexander von Hoffman, "The End of the Dream: The Political Struggle of America's Public Housers," *Journal of Planning History* 4, no. 3 (August 2005): 222–53.

8. "City Housing Plans Urged to Add Jobs," *NYT*, March 28, 1930: 2; "Public Housing Asked by Workers," *NYT*, June 29, 1934: 19.

9. See Schwartz, *The New York Approach*, chapter 2.

10. "Public Housing Era Visioned by Mayor," *NYT*, July 9, 1936: 23; "LaGuardia to Seek Slum Clearance," *NYT*, November 26, 1933: 1.

11. Victor Bernstein, "City Seeking to Avert Shortage of Housing," *NYT*, January 3, 1937: E10.

12. "Drive Begins Jan. 1 to Abolish Slums," *NYT*, December 13, 1935: 8.

13. Alexander Garvin, *The American City: What Works, What Doesn't*, 3d ed. (New York: McGraw-Hill Education, 2014), 277–78.

14. "City-built Homes Will Open Dec. 3," *NYT*, November, 21, 1935: 3; Walter Gropius, "Minimum Dwellings and Tall Buildings," in *America Can't Have Housing* (New York: Museum of Modern Art, 1934).

15. "Housing Technique Is Rheinstein's Aim," *NYT*, January 21, 1938: 4; Alfred Rheinstein and Henry Pringle, "Why Slum Clearance May Fail," n.d., box 54A3, folder 8, New York City Housing Authority Records, LaGuardia and Wagner Archive, LaGuardia Community College (hereafter NYCHAR).

16. Editorial, "Government's Absurd Worship of a Low Density Fetish Defeats Public Housing," *News and Opinion*, February 6, 1939, box 54A3, folder 11, NYCHAR.

17. Robert Moses to Allan Harrison, July 12, 1940, NYC Parks, Robert Moses Papers, MN 22703, roll 3, City of New York Municipal Archives.

18. Clarence Stein, *Toward New Towns for America*, (Cambridge, Mass.: MIT Press, 1966): 204.

19. "City Builds Homes for 2943 Families," *NYT*, February 2, 1942: 17.

20. NYCHA, "Information on Kingsborough Houses," November 1941, LaGuardia Papers, roll 93, City of New York Municipal Archive. On other cities see, for example, D. Bradford Hunt, *Blueprint for Disaster: The Unraveling of Chicago Public Housing* (Chicago: University of Chicago Press, 2009); Alexander von Hoffman, "Why They Built Pruitt-Igoe," in *From Tenements to the Taylor Homes: In Search of an Urban Housing Policy in Twentieth-century America*, ed. John F. Bauman, Roger Biles, and Kristin M. Szylvian (University Park: Pennsylvania State University Press, 2000).

21. Joseph Heathcott, "'In the Nature of a Clinic': The Design of Early Public Housing in St. Louis," *Journal of the Society of Architectural Historians* 70, no. 1 (March 2011): 83–103, 83, 97; Hunt, "Was the 1937 U.S. Housing Act a Pyrrhic Victory?," 221–98; Lawrence J. Vale, *Purging the Poorest: Public Housing and the Design Politics of*

Twice-cleared Communities (Chicago: University of Chicago Press, 2013).

22. NYCHA, "Statistics on Tenants," October 7, 1935, box 53B3, folder 7, NYCHAR; Catherine Lansing, Daily Report, August 19, 1935, box 56E1, folder 4, NYCHAR.

23. For more details on the tenant selection controversies and community planning see Bloom, *Public Housing That Worked.*

24. Letter, Walter White (of the NAACP) to Nathan Straus, September 25, 1939, box 71B5, folder 3, NYCHAR.

25. Much of this article is based on primary documents housed in the Fiorello H. LaGuardia papers, LaGuardia and Wagner Archives, LaGuardia Community College. On LaGuardia and housing see also Bloom, *Public Housing That Worked*, 11–44; Robert Fogelson, *The Great Rent Wars: New York, 1917–1929* (New Haven, Conn.: Yale University Press, 2013), 140–73; Thomas Kessner, *Fiorello H. LaGuardia and the Making of Modern New York* (New York: Penguin, 1991), 292–341; Richard Plunz, *A History of Housing in New York City: Dwelling Type and Social Change in the American Metropolis* (New York: Columbia University Press, 1990), 207–46; Schwartz, *The New York Approach*, 25–60.

26. "10,000 Hear Mayor Say Unsafe Slums to Be Wiped Out," *NYT*, April 9, 1934: 1.

27. Martin Gottlieb, "New York Housing Agency Takes Bow at 50," *NYT*, June 25, 1984: A1.

28. "LaGuardia to Seek Slum Clearance," *NYT*, November 26, 1933: 1.

29. Kessner, *Fiorello H. LaGuardia and the Making of Modern New York*, 292.

30. On Abrams generally see A. Scott Henderson, *Housing and the Democratic Ideal: The Life and Thought of Charles Abrams* (New York: Columbia University Press, 2000); Murray Illson, "Charles Abrams, Worldwide Housing Expert, Dies," *NYT* February 23, 1970: 26.

31. Henderson, *Housing and the Democratic Ideal*, 58.

32. Bloom, *Public Housing that Worked*, 31.

33. Charles Abrams: Papers and Files, Department of Manuscripts and University Archives, Cornell University, 1975, 9–10.

34. Additional details on Harlem River Houses are available in Bloom, *Public Housing That Worked.*

35. NYCHA, Management Division, "Income Study of 4,832 Applications for Apartments," ca. 1936, box 78A7, folder 3, NYCHAR; "$4,219,000 Housing Goes to City Today," *NYT*, June 16, 1937: 25; "PWA Harlem Rent Set at $7 a Room," *NYT*, March 31, 1937: 24.

36. See, for instance, "11,500 Seek, 574 Get Model Apartments," *NYT*, August 19, 1937: 21; NYCHA, "Harlem River Houses Tenant Orientation Study," ca. 1937, NYCHAR; "Report of the Committee on the Selection of Tenants to the Harlem Housing Committee," November 20, 1935, box 55D5, folder 2, NYCHAR.

37. NYCHA, Management Department, Statistics Division, "Tenant Characteristics, 1968–1978," box 99A4, NYCHAR.

38. Quotation from Charlayne Hunter, "Tenants Praise Harlem Houses," *NYT*, September 29, 1975: 68. See also NYCHA, Research and Statistics Division, "Crime Index Complaints per 1000 Population," 1972–74, NYCHAR.

39. Site visits and personal interviews with NYCHA management, March 2013. Income levels and other statistics provided by Lisa Diaz, Federal Liaison and Senior Policy Advisor to the Chairman, NYCHA.

40. Some of this article is adapted from Sandy Zipp, "A Landmark Decision," *Metropolis Magazine* 23, no. 3 (November 2003): 34, 36. See also Bloom, *Public Housing That Worked*; Radford, *Modern Housing for America*; Plunz, *A History of Housing in New York City.*

41. Richard Pommer, "The Architecture of Urban Housing in the United States in the Early 1930s," *Journal of the Society of Architectural Historians* 37, no. 4 (December 1978): 249–56.

42. Bloom, *Public Housing That Worked*, 144–48; NYCHA, "Annual Report," 1938, 22, Annual Reports (1935–90), box 98D1, NYCHAR; NYCHA, "Project Statistics," 1947.

43. NYCHA, "Selection of Tenants for Housing Developments," February 23, 1939, box 70D6, folder 2, NYCHAR; "Housing Ceremony Set for Brooklyn," *NYT*, October 11, 1936: N8; "City Housing Aims Held Not Realized," *NYT*, June 6, 1938: 19.

44. NYCHA, "Number of Families at Federal Projects Shown by Racial Composition at Initial Occupancy and on June 30, 1954," box 63C7, folder 11, NYCHAR; NYCHA, Research and Statistics Division, "Special Tabulation of Tenant Characteristics," 1969–79, box 99A4, folders 1–11, NYCHAR.

45. NYCHA, Research and Statistics Division, "Crime Index Complaints per 1000 Population"; City of New York, Police Department, "Housing Bureau Crime Analysis," Compstat period ending May 11, 2014, www.nyc.gov.

46. Zipp, "A Landmark Decision."

47. NYCHA, "Development Data Book 2013," www.nyc.gov; NYCHA, "Project Statistics."

48. See, for instance, "City Housing Costs Cut by New Design," *NYT*, April 23, 1938: 17.

49. Frederick Lee Ackerman and William F. R. Ballard, "A Note on Site & Unit Planning," NYCHA, 1937; Karen A. Franck and Michael Mostoller, "From Courts to Open Space to Streets: Changes in the Site Design of U.S. Public Housing," *Journal of Architectural and Planning Research* 12, no. 23 (Autumn 1995): 186–220.

50. May Lumsden to Gerard Swope, December 9, 1940, box 54D2, folder 7, NYCHAR.

51. Bernard Brown, "The People Who Live There Want to Stay," *Long Island Star Journal*, March 4, 1940.

52. Quoted in Joseph Berger, "Her Film Project Happens to Be Her Project," *NYT*, December 14, 2005: B1.

53. "Housing Project on 1st Ave Started," *NYT*, March 3, 1940: 14.

54. Interview of Alfred Rheinstein, WNYC radio, August 11, 1939, box 54B4, folder 14, NYCHAR.

55. NYCHA, "Number of Families at Federal Projects Shown by Racial Composition at Initial Occupancy and on June 30, 1954"; NYCHA, "Tenant Characteristics, 1968–1978."

56. City of New York, Police Department, "Housing Bureau Crime Analysis," Compstat period ending May 11, 2014, www.nyc.gov.

57. Manuel Perez Rivaz, "Tenants Crusading for Decent Homes," *Newsday*, July 8, 1990; Samantha Henry, "A Good Rap," *Newsday*, August 5, 2001.

58. City Wide Tenants Council, press release, October 16, 1941, box 54D5, folder 2, NYCHAR; "Housing Authority Buys 2 Tenements," *NYT*, August 15, 1941: 31. See also news item released by City and Suburban Homes Company, August 14, 1941, and press release, October 6, 1940, box 54D5, folder 2, NYCHA; 1934 data quoted in NYCHA, "Statistics and General Information Amsterdam Houses," June 2, 1941, box 54D5, folder 2, NYCHAR; Marcy Sacks, *Before Harlem: The Black Experience in New York City before World War I* (Philadelphia: University of Pennsylvania Press, 2006).

59. "Oppose Extension of Housing Site," *NYT*, April 20, 1941: RE5; Allan Harrison to Gerald Swope, October 3, 1940, box 54C5, folder 18, NYCHAR; W. H. Tretter to Gerald Swope, June 20, 1941, box 54C5, folder 18, NYCHAR.

60. NYCHA, "Renting Progress Report," December 31, 1948, and January 7, 1949, box 67C1, folder 6, NYCHAR; Mr. Milton Saslow to P. Lapidus, August 6, 1948, box 67C1, folder 6, NYCHAR.

61. NYCHA, "Statistics and General Information Project: Amsterdam," June 2, 1941, box 54D5, folder 2, NYCHAR; "Housing Comes High," *The Sun*, April 15, 1941; personal interview with Henrietta Edwards, conducted by Fritz Umbach and Brittany McGee, October 6, 2006; Fritz Umbach, *The Last Neighborhood Cops: The Rise and Fall of Community Policing in New York Public Housing* (Newark, N.J.: Rutgers University Press, 2011): 171.

62. Thomas F. Farrel, "Object Lesson in Race Relations," *NYT*, February 12, 1950: SM16; personal interview with Hortense Vidal, conducted by author and Maria Figueroa, October 2006.

63. NYCHA, "Project Data Statistics," 1965–75, box 72A1, 72A2, NYCHAR.

64. On Lincoln Square see Samuel Zipp, *Manhattan Projects: The Rise and Fall of Urban Renewal in Cold War New York* (New York: Oxford University Press, 2010), chapters 4 and 5. On the changing socioeconomic geography of NYCHA see NYCHA, "Move-outs," March 1958, box 59D6, folder 5, NYCHAR; Neil Smith, *The New Urban Frontier: Gentrification and the Revanchist City* (New York: Routledge, 1996): 99–107; Pratt Institute, "Public Housing in New York City: Building Communities of Opportunity" (New York: Pratt Center for Community Development, 2009): 2, 11.

65. NORC data supplied by personal e-mail correspondence with NYCHA, October 2013.

Chapter 3: Public Housing Towers

1. For public housing nationally see works such as D. Bradford Hunt, *Blueprint for Disaster: The Unraveling of Chicago Public Housing* (Chicago: University of Chicago Press, 2009); William Moore, *The Vertical Ghetto: Everyday Life in an Urban Project* (New York: Random House, 1969); Rachel Bratt, "Public Housing: The Controversy and Contribution," in *Critical Perspectives on Housing*, ed. Rachel G. Bratt, Chester W. Hartman, and Ann Meyerson (Philadelphia: Temple University Press, 1986); John F. Bauman, *Public Housing, Race, and Renewal: Urban Planning in Philadelphia, 1920–1974* (Philadelphia: Temple University Press, 1987); John F. Bauman, Roger Biles, and Kristin M. Szylvian, eds., *From Tenements to the Taylor Homes: In Search of an Urban Housing Policy in Twentieth-century America* (University Park: Pennsylvania State University Press, 2000); Lawrence J. Vale, *From the Puritans to the Projects: Public Housing and Public Neighbors* (Cambridge, Mass.: Harvard University Press, 2000); Howard Husock, *America's Trillion Dollar Housing Mistake: The Failure of American Housing Policy* (Chicago: Ivan R. Dee, 2003); Edward G. Goetz, *New Deal Ruins: The Dismantling of Public Housing in the U.S.* (Ithaca, N.Y.: Cornell University Press, 2013); Donald Parson, *Making a Better World: Public Housing, the Red Scare, and the Direction of Modern Los Angeles* (Minneapolis: University of Minnesota Press, 2005); Sudhir Alladi Venkatesh, *American Project: The Rise and Fall of a Modern Ghetto* (Cambridge, Mass.: Harvard University Press, 2000).

2. Lee Cooper, "Postwar Plans Stress the Need to Rebuild Cities," *NYT*, July 25, 1943: RE1.

3. On postwar rent control see, for example, Joel Schwartz, "Tenant Power in the Liberal City,

1943–1971," in *The Tenant Movement in New York City, 1904–1984*, ed. Ronald Lawson (New Brunswick, N.J.: Rutgers University Press, 1986); and Roberta Gold, *When Tenants Claimed the City: The Struggle for Citizenship in New York City Housing* (Urbana: Illinois University Press, 2014).

4. Letter, Robert Moses to Arthur Hays Sulzberger, July 27, 1953, Box 91, Robert Moses Papers, New York Public Library.

5. On administrative and other changes in the Moses era see Nicholas Dagen Bloom, *Public Housing That Worked: New York in the Twentieth Century* (Philadelphia: University of Pennsylvania Press, 2008).

6. "City Lags in Help to Slum Tenants," *NYT*, April, 2 1954, 29; "20 Years of Public Housing," *NYT*, June 3, 1955: 22; "City Projects Add 40,000 Homes," *NYT*, November 25, 1955: 36; various letters, box 63D4, folders 10 and 11, New York City Housing Authority Records, LaGuardia and Wagner Archive, LaGuardia Community College (hereafter NYCHAR).

7. Letter, Robert Moses to Thomas Corcoran, June 20, 1946, Parks Commissioner Papers, MN107880, roll 35, City of New York, Municipal Archive; Letter, Robert Moses to Mayor William O'Dwyer, April 15, 1946, box 90, Robert Moses Papers, New York Public Library.

8. Letter, Robert Moses to Thomas Farrell, December 3, 1948, Parks Commissioner Papers, 107890, roll 52, City of New York, Municipal Archive.

9. NYCHA, "Report on the Program of NYCHA in Relation to Mayor Wagner's Platform Proposals," December 15, 1961, box 68B6, folder 6, NYCHAR.

10. On the U.S. tower-in-the-park see Eric Mumford, "The 'Tower in a Park' in America: Theory and Practice, 1920–1960," *Planning Perspectives* 10 (1995): 17–41; Matthew Gordon Lasner, *High Life: Condo Living in the Suburban Century* (New Haven, Conn.: Yale University Press, 2012), 74–76, 208.

11. See Richard Rosenthal, "The Challenge of Design," in *Fifty Years of Public Housing*, NYCHA (New York: NYCHA, 1985), box 74E5, folder 10, NYCHAR.

12. "Drive Opens Today to Better Harlem," *NYT*, May 24, 1942: 41.

13. A. H. Raskin, "Nonwhites Up 41% in City," *NYT*, November 19, 1957: 1.

14. On Chicago see Alex Kotlowitz, *There Are No Children Here: The Story of Two Boys Growing Up in the Other America* (New York: Doubleday, 1991); Arnold R. Hirsch, *Making the Second Ghetto: Race and Housing in Chicago, 1940–1960* (Chicago: University of Chicago Press, 1998); Thomas J. Sugrue, *The Origins of the Urban Crisis: Race and Inequality in Postwar Detroit* (Princeton, N.J.: Princeton University Press, 1996).

15. " 'Fact Sheets' List Housing Projects," *NYT*, February 7, 1965: R8.

16. "Project May Rise," *NYT*, October 4, 1954: 29.

17. John Sibley, "Village Housing a Complex Issue," *NYT*, March 23, 1961: 35.

18. Mumford quoted in Robert A. M. Stern, Thomas Mellins, and David Fishman, *New York 1960: Architecture and Urbanism between the Second World War and the Bicentennial* (New York: Monacelli, 1995), 72–74.

19. "More Slums, No Fewer," *NYT*, February 15, 1959: 51; Catherine Bauer, "The Dreary Deadlock of Public Housing," *Architectural Forum* 106 (May 1957): 140–42, 219, 221.

20. Letter, Robert Moses to Philip Cruise, August 17, 1951, box 68C2, folder 1, NYCHAR; letter, Philip Cruise to Robert Moses, August 23, 1951, box 68C2, folder 3, NYCHAR.

21. Charles Grutzner, "Shopping Scarce in City Projects," *NYT*, June 16, 1957: 74.

22. For the full standards see Bloom, *Public Housing That Worked*, 168–200; NYCHA, "Proposed Revision of Tenant Selection Policies and Procedures," December 14, 1961, box 65C8, folder 12, NYCHAR.

23. "Tenant Training Suggested Here," *NYT*, March 26, 1957: 28.

24. Robert F. Wagner, Jr., "Address to the National Conference on Social Welfare," May 27, 1962, box 68B6, folder 1, NYCHAR, 3.

25. See, for instance, NYCHA, "Annual Report," 1962, box 100A2, folder 12, NYCHAR.

26. To explore the argument that resident activism and policing played a crucial role in NYCHA success, see Fritz Umbach, *The Last Neighborhood Cops: The Rise and Fall of Community Policing in New York Public Housing* (New Brunswick, N.J.: Rutgers University Press, 2010).

27. See, for instance, Robert Tomasson, "Housing Projects Break Mold," *NYT*, December 9, 1973: 1; NYCHA, "Annual Report," 1968, box 60D8, folder 11m, NYCHAR; Harold Bell and Granville Sewell, "Turnkey in New York: Evaluation of an Experiment," Columbia University, Graduate School of Architecture, June 1969, Citizens Housing and Planning Council of New York archives; interview with John Simon, conducted by Marcia Robertson, July 24, 1990, NYCHA Oral History Project, NYCHAR, 12; Bloom, *Public Housing That Worked*, 152–67.

28. Alexander Burnham, "Mayor Cites Need of Housing Funds," *NYT*, May 1, 1963: 1.

29. Alexander Burnham, "Rockefeller Asks New Low-Rent Housing Policy," *NYT*, May 3, 1963: 16.

30. Robert F. Wagner, Jr., quotation from video recording, "Address at LaGuardia Community College, New York," November 30, 1987, NYCHAR.

31. Robert F. Wagner, Jr., "Text of Speech—Dedication of the First Rehabilitated Brownstone—West Side Urban Renewal Plan," October 9, 1962,

box 060006W, folder 25, Robert F. Wagner Documents Collection, Speeches Series, LaGuardia and Wagner Archives, LaGuardia Community College.

32. For criticism of the concentration of public housing by other officials see, for instance, "New York State Annual Report," 1951, box 61C6, folder 6, NYCHAR.

33. Bloom, *Public Housing That Worked*, 109–51; NYCHA, "Project Statistics," April 1950.

34. NYCHA, Research and Reports Division, "Number of Families at Federal Projects Shown by Racial Composition at Initial Occupancy and on June 30, 1954," box 63C7, folder 11, NYCHAR; NYCHA, Research and Statistics Division, "Special Tabulation of Tenant Characteristics," 1969–79, box 99A4, folders 1–11, NYCHAR.

35. NYCHA, "Crime Statistics for Jacob Riis," 1964, NYCHAR; NYCHA, Research and Statistics Division, "Crime Index Complaints per 1000 Population, 1971," 1972–74, NYCHAR.

36. Eric Pace, "Trend Seen in Robbery-Killings of Elderly on Lower East Side," *NYT*, September 11, 1971: 1; Joseph Fried, "Projects to Get More Protection," *NYT*, November 11, 1971: 53; Lesley Oelsner, "Rising Crime Stirs Fear on the Lower East Side," *NYT*, September, 22 1971: 51.

37. Ada Louise Huxtable, "Grass at Riis Giving Way to a Plaza," *NYT*, July, 14 1965: 39.

38. NYCHA, Management Department, Statistics Division, "Tenant Characteristics, 1968–1978," box 99A4, folders 1–11, NYCHAR.

39. Esther Fein, "For Families Struggling to Get By, City Projects Offer a Home for Hope," *NYT*, April 10, 1986: B1; Esther Fein, "At a City Project, Price of Survival Is Vigilance," *NYT*, July 10, 1986: B1; Ester Fein, "Managers Reviving a Project's Pride," *NYT*, April, 28 1986: B1.

40. "47 Tenants Settle in Two Projects," *NYT*, January 1, 1948: 29.

41. Site visits and personal interviews with NYCHA management, March 2013. Income levels and other statistics provided by Lisa Diaz, Federal Liaison and Senior Policy Advisor to the Chairman, NYCHA.

42. "City Aiding Tenants on New Housing Site," *NYT*, October 10, 1945: 31; "City Evictions Protested," *NYT*, October 16, 1945: 20.

43. NYCHA, "Project Statistics," April 1950.

44. NYCHA, "Number of Families at Federal Projects Shown by Racial Composition at Initial Occupancy and on June 30, 1954."

45. NYCHA, "Crime Statistics for Johnson Houses," 1964, NYCHAR; NYCHA "Crime Index Complaints per 1000 Population," 1–3.

46. Interview with Raymond Henson conducted by Marcia Robertson, August 6, 1990, box 1, NYCHA Oral History Project, NYCHAR, 14–15.

47. NYCHA, "Special Tabulation of Tenant Characteristics."

48. Personal interview with Ethel Velez, July 2013.

49. Site visits and personal interviews with NYCHA management, March 2013. Income levels and other statistics provided by Diaz, NYCHA.

50. City of New York, Police Department, "Housing Bureau Crime Analysis," Compstat period ending May 11, 2014, www.nyc.gov.

51. On the city-financed program see Bloom, *Public Housing That Worked*, chapters 2, 5, 6, and 7.

52. NYCHA, "Project Statistics," April 1952.

53. NYCHA, "Number of Families at Federal Projects Shown by Racial Composition at Initial Occupancy and on June 30, 1954"; NYCHA, "Crime Index Complaints per 1000 Population," 1–3; NYCHA, "Tenant Characteristics, 1968–1978."

54. Martin Gottlieb, "New York Housing Agency Takes a Bow at 50," *NYT*, June 25, 1984: A1; Curtis Taylor, "Home Work," *New York Newsday*, July 12, 1992.

55. Site visits and personal interviews with NYCHA management, March 2013. Income levels and other statistics provided by Diaz, NYCHA.

Chapter 4: Stabilizing the Middle

1. Elizabeth Collins Cromley, *Alone Together: A History of New York's Early Apartments* (Ithaca, N.Y.: Cornell University Press, 1990); A. K. Sandoval-Strausz, "Home for a World of Strangers: Hospitality and the Origins of Multiple Dwellings in Urban America," *Journal of Urban History* 33, no. 6 (September 2007): 933–64; Matthew Gordon Lasner, *High Life: Condo Living in the Suburban Century* (New Haven, Conn.: Yale University Press, 2012), chapters 1–3.

2. Gail Radford, *Modern Housing for America: Policy Struggles in the New Deal Era* (Chicago: University of Chicago Press, 1996); Catherine Bauer, *Modern Housing* (New York: Houghton Mifflin, 1934); D. Bradford Hunt, "Was the 1937 U.S. Housing Act a Pyrrhic Victory?," *Journal of Planning History* 4, no. 3 (August 2005): 195–221; Alexander von Hoffman, "The End of the Dream: The Political Struggle of America's Public Housers," *Journal of Planning History* 4, no. 3 (August 2005): 222–53.

3. Laura Bobeczko and Richard Longstreth, "Housing Reform Meets the Marketplace: Washington and the Federal Housing Administration's Contribution to Apartment Building Design, 1935–40," in *Housing Washington: Two Centuries of Residential Development and Planning in the National Capital Area*, ed. Richard Longstreth

(Chicago: The Center for American Places at Columbia College Chicago, 2010), 178.

4. Lasner, *High Life*, 134–37.

5. Data from Citizen's Housing and Planning Council of New York, *Directory of Large-scale Rental and Cooperative Housing: With a Summary of Legislation Relating to Housing and Urban Renewal in New York City* (New York: Citizen's Housing and Planning Council of New York, 1957).

6. Joel Schwartz, *The New York Approach: Robert Moses, Urban Liberals, and Redevelopment of the Inner City* (Columbus: Ohio State University Press, 1993), 120–21.

7. On the UHF see Lasner, *High Life*, 143.

8. Ira Henry Freeman, "City Plans Rise," *NYT*, September 29, 1969: 37.

9. "Text of Review by Mayor," *NYT*, September 22, 1957: 76; Warren Moscow, "Mitchell-Lama," Letter to the Editor, *NYT*, March 16, 1986: 12.

10. Thomas Ennis, "Aids to Housing," *NYT*, November 16, 1958: R1.

11. "Nonprofit Basis Urged for Co-ops," *NYT*, August 16, 1953: R6.

12. The federal programs were Sections 221(d)(3), 221(d)(4), and 236. Data from Furman Center for Real Estate and Urban Policy, New York University, "Subsidized Housing Information Project," database, datasearch.furmancenter.org.

13. Bobeczko and Longstreth, "Housing Reform Meets the Marketplace"; Lasner, *High Life*, 130–34, 137–43.

14. For a partial list of FHA complexes see Citizen's Housing and Planning Council of New York, *Directory of Large-scale Rental and Cooperative Housing*.

15. Lasner, *High Life*, 156.

16. David Andelman, "Co-op Conglomerates Advocated," *NYT*, September 27, 1970: R1.

17. "Abraham E. Kazan Dies at 82," *NYT*, December 22, 1971: 38.

18. Portions of this essay are adapted from Samuel Zipp, *Manhattan Projects: The Rise and Fall of Urban Renewal in Cold War New York* (New York: Oxford University Press, 2010). See also letter, Robert Moses to Thomas E. Dewey, March 22, 1943, roll 17, folder 010, Department of Parks, Robert Moses files, City of New York Municipal Archives.; Robert Fogelson, *Downtown: Its Rise and Fall, 1880–1920* (New Haven, Conn.: Yale University Press, 2001); Schwartz, *The New York Approach*, 70–72.

19. For a fuller account of this process see Zipp, *Manhattan Projects*, 77–83; Robert Moses, *Public Works: A Dangerous Trade* (New York: McGraw-Hill, 1970), 431; Arthur Simon, *Stuyvesant Town, USA: Pattern for Two Americas* (New York: New York University Press, 1970) 41, n. 5.

20. "Suggested Letter from Mr. Ecker to Assemblyman Mitchell"; letter, Moses to Jeremiah Evarts, March 2, 1943; letter, Moses to Ecker, March 5, 1943; letter, Moses to Dewey, March 22, 1943, roll 17, folder 010, Parks Department, Robert Moses Files, City of New York Municipal Archives.

21. See untitled agreement, February 1, 1943, and untitled Metropolitan Life press release, Stuyvesant Town, History and Plans, 1943–67, folder S14, Metropolitan Life archives, New York.

22. Edwin Burdell, "Rehousing Needs of the Families on the Stuyvesant Town Site," *Journal of the American Institute of Planners* (Autumn 1945): 17, 19; Rosamund G. Roberts, *3000 Families Move to Make Way for Stuyvesant Town : A Story of Tenant Relocation Bureau, Inc.* (New York: Felt, 1946): 9, 17, 6; Community Service Society, "The Rehousing Needs of the Families on the Stuyvesant Town Site," June 14, 1945.

23. "Stuyvesant Town," March 15, 1948, Stuyvesant Town-Statistics Folder, uncatalogued Stuyvesant Town materials, Metropolitan Life archives, New York; "Stuyvesant Town: Rebuilding a Blighted City Area," *Engineering News and Record*, February 5, 1948, 76. For Gas House District see letter, Stuyvesant Town Corporation to City Planning Commission, May 12, 1943, 4, roll 18, folder 14, 1943, Department of Parks, General files, City of New York Municipal Archives.

24. See Zipp, *Manhattan Projects*, 104–5.

25. See "Have You Studied the New Mass Homes?," *Home Furnishings Merchandising*, July 1947, 47–48; Zipp, *Manhattan Projects*, 134–35.

26. Zipp, *Manhattan Projects*, 83–113, 117–29, 145–54.

27. See, for instance, Linda Greenhouse, "Stuyvesant Town Aging with Grace," *NYT*, December 7, 1969: R1; Stephen Drucker, "The Oasis of Stuyvesant Town: Still Going Strong," *NYT*, September 6, 1984: C1.

28. For an account of controversies see Charles Bagli, *Other People's Money: Inside the Housing Crisis and the Demise of the Greatest Real Estate Deal Ever Made* (New York: Dutton, 2013).

29. Kirstin Aadahl quoted in Michael Powell, "A Former Bastion of Middle-class Housing Awaits Mayoral Help," *NYT*, June 10, 2014: A17.

30. Personal interview with tenants Perry and Brenda, April 27, 2013, conducted by Allison Blanchette and Michael Favis. On the suburban character see also Sylvie Murray, *The Progressive Housewife: Community Activism in Suburban Queens, 1945–1965* (Philadelphia: University of Pennsylvania Press, 2003), 30.

31. Personal interview with tenant Gloria Arra, April 27, 2013, conducted by Allison Blanchette and Michael Favis.

32. On "middle-income," FHA, and Bell Park Gardens generally see Lasner, *High Life*, 1–3, 119–22, 125–62. On Bell Park Gardens see

Andrea A. Krest, "The Postwar Garden Apartment: Housing for the Middle-Class in Bell Park Gardens, Queens," MS in Historic Preservation thesis, Columbia University, 1984.

33. Bell Park Gardens Community Council, *Bell Park Gardens Yearbook 1950–51*, 1951: 15.

34. Quoted in "Families Buying 'Garden' Suites," *NYT*, July 11, 1954: R1.

35. Krest, "The Postwar Garden Apartment," 69–70.

36. Barbara A. Smith, *Still Giving Kisses: A Guide to Helping and Enjoying the Alzheimer's Victim You Love* (Raleigh: Lulu, 2008), 39.

37. On going private, personal interview with tenant and board president Paul Stein, June 24, 2013, conducted by Oksana Mironova.

38. Personal interview with tenant Ellen, April 27, 2013, conducted by Allison Blanchette and Michael Favis.

39. Personal interview with tenant Gloria Arra.

40. On the term see display advertisement, Mitchell Gardens, *NYT*, February 18, 1951: R3; U.S., Congress, Senate, Committee on Banking and Currency, 83rd Congress, 2d Session, Housing Act of 1954: Hearings on S. 2889, S. 2938, and S. 2949 Part I, March 9–12, 15–19, 22–25, April 14, 1954 (Washington, D.C.: Government Printing Office, 1954), 979.

41. On Queensview and its designers generally see Matthew Gordon Lasner, "Architect as Developer and the Postwar U.S. Apartment, 1945–1960," *Buildings & Landscapes* 21, no. 1 (Spring 2014): 27–55, 39–40.

42. Schwartz, *The New York Approach*, 120–21, 126, 137–38; quotation 126.

43. Charles Abrams, *Forbidden Neighbors: A Study of Prejudice in Housing* (New York: Harper, 1955), 318.

44. Frederick Gutheim, "'Co-op' Owners' Improve Suites at Queensview," *New York Herald Tribune*, May 28, 1950: D5.

45. May Milstein, "Fifty Fleeting Years," and Israel Kugler, "Our Semi-Centennial," *Queensview News* 18, no. 1 (January 2000): 1; "Woman Brings Three Friends; 4 Buy Entire Floor of Co-op," *New York Herald Tribune*, March 20, 1949: D1; Richard Lincoln, "Middle Income Houses Said Gripped by Bias," *New York Amsterdam News*, March 22, 1952: 1; "Russian Visitors Decry TV Aerials," *NYT*, October 10, 1955: 29; William L. C. Wheaton, "Market Experience and Occupancy Patterns in Interracial Housing Developments: Case Studies of Privately Financed Projects in Philadelphia and New York City," report prepared for the Philadelphia Redevelopment Authority by the Institute for Urban Studies, University of Pennsylvania, July 1957; "Jews to Honor McKeldin in Brotherhood Ceremony," *New York Herald Tribune*, February 20, 1960: 12; Richard P. Hunt, "Atomic Question for the City," *NYT*, October 6, 1963: SM46, SM109.

46. Lasner, "Architect as Developer and the Postwar U.S. Apartment, 1945–1960," 40–43.

47. "Second Addition in Big Suites for Queensview," *New York Herald Tribune*, April 24, 1949: D1; Dorothy Barclay, "For Children: Parents Help at Cooperative Play School," *NYT*, July 26, 1951: 32.

48. George P. Crethan quoted in Nadine Brozan, "For Co-op Complexes, Complex Choices," *NYT*, February 3, 2002: J1. On the NORC see also Corey Kilgannon, "The Greatest Generation Learns about Great Safe Sex," *NYT*, February 14, 2007: B1; Ellen Hausknecht, "News from NORC," *Queensview News* 18, no. 3 (November 2000): 6; personal interview, manager Frank Marcovitz and Theresa Markevich, May 7, 2013, conducted by Oksana Mironova.

49. Kugler, "Our Semi-Centennial," 4.

50. Crethan quoted in Brozan, "For Co-op Complexes, Complex Choices." See also Alex Robbins, "Ten Years of Reconstruction," *Queensview News* 18, no. 3 (November 2000): 6; Michael Sullivan, "To Thine Own Self Be True," *Habitat* 181 (July/August 2002), 11–12; personal interview, Marcovitz and Markevich.

51. Personal interview, tenant Laura, April 25, 2013, conducted by Jennifer Yip and Gabriela Miller. See also personal interviews: tenant Diane, April 14, 2013, conducted by Sben Korsh and Ruth Lopez; tenants Joe and Migda Rivera, April 28, 2013, conducted by Gabriela Miller and Jennifer Yip; Marcovitz and Markevich.

52. Dan Shaw, "Habitats/Astoria, Queens: Handed Down from Grandmother to Grandson," *NYT*, March 2, 2008: RE4; Constance Rosenblum, "The Toys Are Gone, but It's Still Home," *NYT*, October 23, 2011: RE1; Alex Robbins, "Welcome, Neighbors," *Queensview News* 18, no. 1 (January 2000): 6.

53. On Kazan and housing generally see Abraham Kazan, *The Reminiscences of Abraham Kazan*, interview by Lloyd Kaplan, 1970, Oral History Research Office, Columbia University; Peter Eisenstadt, *Rochdale Village: Robert Moses, 6,000 Families, and New York City's Great Experiment in Integrated Housing* (Ithaca, N.Y.: Cornell University Press, 2010); Lasner, *High Life*.

54. Lasner, *High Life*, 98–101.

55. Abraham E. Kazan, "Cooperative Housing in the United States," *Annals of the American Academy of Political and Social Science* 191 (May 1937): 137, 138, 140.

56. Lasner, *High Life*, 118–19.

57. Quotation from editorial, "Community-minded Unionism," *NYT*, May 19, 1962: 26. On objections to redevelopment see also Paul Goldberger, "Raymond Hood and His Visions of

Skyscrapers," *NYT*, January 3, 1984: C11; Megan Costello, "Urban Legend: Jane Woods," *City Limits*, July 1, 2001. On Title I and Penn South generally see, for example, Kazan, *The Reminiscences of Abraham Kazan*, 404–15; Joshua B. Freeman, *Working-class New York: Life and Labor since World War II* (New York: New Press, 2000), 99–125; Hilary Ballon and Kenneth T. Jackson, eds., *Robert Moses and the Modern City: The Transformation of New York* (New York: W. W. Norton, 2007).

58. Joseph Malinconico, "Penn South Making 2 Decades of Success," *NYT*, June 5, 1983: R7.

59. Leonard Kriegel, "The Co-op: On Urban Planning and Socialist Dreams," *Dissent* 53, no. 2 (Spring 2006): 52–57, 53, 54.

60. Robert F. Wagner, Jr., "Text of Speech—Dedication of ILGWU Cooperative Houses," May 19, 1962, Robert F. Wagner Documents Collection, Speeches Series, box #06009W, folder 2, LaGuardia and Wagner Archives, LaGuardia Community College.

61. Quotation from Kriegel, "The Co-op," 54. See also Francis X. Clines, "Co-op Residents Prepay Taxes to Help the City," *NYT*, March 4, 1976: 22.

62. Personal interview, tenant William, April 28, 2013, conducted by Gabriela Miller and Jennifer Yip.

63. Tenant Florence quoted in "An Infinite Variety," in *Penn South Comes of Age: 21st Anniversary Journal*, ed. Arthur Vogel (New York: Penn South, 1983), 15, Tamiment Library and Robert F. Wagner Labor Archives, New York University. On moving to suburbs see Kriegel, "The Co-op," 55.

64. Tenant Sophie quoted in "An Infinite Variety."

65. Tenant Bella quoted in "An Infinite Variety." On politics see also Kriegel, "The Co-op."

66. Paula Brenner quoted in Clines, "Co-op Residents Prepay Taxes to Help the City." See also Glen Fowler, "$933,173 in Taxes to City Prepaid by Seven Co-ops," *NYT*, February 15, 1979: B3.

67. Quoted in Clines, "Co-op Residents Prepay Taxes to Help the City."

68. Quoted in Lisa W. Foderado, "Expiration of Tax Exemption Offers a Chance for Profits," *NYT*, October 19, 1986: R1. See also personal interview with Naomi Goldstein, Mario Mazzoni, and Walter Mankoff, June 7, 2013, conducted by Oksana Mironova; Malinconico, "Penn South Making 2 Decades of Success"; Nadine Brozan, "For Co-op Complexes, Complex Choices," *NYT*, February 3, 2002: J1.

69. On lotteries and the waiting list see personal interview with Naomi Goldstein, Mario Mazzoni, and Walter Mankoff.

70. Quotation from Foderado, "Expiration of Tax Exemption Offers a Chance for Profits." See also Walter Mankoff, oral history, ILGWU Heritage Project, ILGWU Collection, Kheel Center for Labor-Management Documentation and Archives, ILR School, Cornell University; Clines, "Co-op Residents Prepay Taxes to Help the City;" Edwin McDowell, "Big Chelsea Co-op to Vote on Staying a Nonprofit," *NYT*, March 30, 2001: B6.

71. Anita Altman, "The New York NORC-supportive Service Program" *Journal of Jewish Communal Service* 81, no. 3/4 (Spring/Summer 2006): 195–200; Andree Brooks, "Talking Aged Tenants: Some Need Help from Boards," *NYT*, March 1, 1987: R1; Co-op Learns to Age Gracefully," *NYT*, July 3, 1994: CV6; personal interview with Naomi Goldstein, Mario Mazzoni, and Walter Mankoff.

72. Tenant Georgio quoted in "An Infinite Variety." See also Tracey Schmitz, "An Urban Garden for Young and Old," *NYT*, April 21, 1988: C14.

73. Vivian S. Toy, "When Mom Is Just Floors Away," *NYT*, December 27, 2009: RE1; Vivan S. Toy, "Winning That One in a Million," *NYT*, March 2, 2008: RE1.

74. The only thorough history of Rochdale Village is Eisenstadt, *Rochdale Village*, which elaborates on all of the topics discussed in this essay. The book's major sources include Kazan, *The Reminiscences of Abraham Kazan*; the papers of Robert Moses in the New York Public Library; the UHF Collection in the Kheel Center for Labor-Management Documentation and Archives, ILR School, Cornell University; and approximately fifty original oral histories. See also Freeman, *Working Class New York*; Ballon and Jackson, *Robert Moses and the Modern City*; Lasner, *High Life*.

75. Eisenstadt, *Rochdale Village*, 17–19.

76. Display advertisement, *NYT*, January 8, 1961: RE5.

77. Harvey Swados, "When Black and White Live Together," *NYT*, November 13, 1966: SM47, SM102–20.

78. On the strike see Jerald Podair, *The Strike That Changed New York: Blacks, Whites, and the Ocean-Hill Crisis* (New Haven, Conn.: Yale University Press, 2002).

79. Nesbitt Benjamin, tenant since 1964, quoted in C. J. Hughes, "Living in Springfield Gardens, Queens," *NYT*, November 25, 2012: RE7.

80. Judith Perez, " 'Movin' On Up!': Pioneer African-American Families Living in an Integrated Neighborhood in the Bronx, New York," *Bronx County Historical Society Journal*, no. 43 (Fall 2006): 78.

81. Ian Frazier, "Utopia the Bronx: Co-op City and Its People," *New Yorker*, June 26, 2006: 54.

82. Steven V. Roberts, "Co-op City Blend of Races Sought," *NYT*, April 30, 1967: 31.

83. Roberts, "Co-op City Blend of Races Sought."

84. Memorandum, Ostroff to Riverbay Board, August 24, 1972, collection 6129, box 14, UHF Collection, Kheel Center for Labor-Management Documentation and Archives, ILR School, Cornell University.

85. Memorandum, Ostroff to Riverbay Board, 83–84.

86. Personal interview with Anne Sullivan, November 15, 2011.

87. "Co-op City Tenants to Withhold Rents," *NYT*, May 29, 1975: 39.

88. Steven V. Roberts, "Project for 6,000 Families Approved for Canarsie Site," *NYT*, June 28, 1967: 1.

89. Howard Husock, "Subsidizing Discrimination at Starrett City," *City Journal* 2, no. 1 (Winter 1992): 48–53; Harold M. Schultz, "Starrett City: Paradise Lost?," *The Urban Prospect* 13, no. 1 (2007): 2.

90. Personal interview with Bob Rosenberg, September 11, 2013.

91. Janny Scott, "A Sweeping Housing Plan Bedeviled by Racial Quotas," *NYT*, December 1, 2006: B6.

92. Howard Husock, "Occupancy Controls and Racial Integration at Starrett City (C)," Harvard University, Kennedy School of Government, Case Program, 964.0, 1990, www.case.hks.harvard.edu.

93. Personal interview with Bob Rosenberg.

94. Ibid.

95. Starrett City prospectus, New York Real Estate Brochure Collection, Avery Architectural and Fine Arts Library, Columbia University.

96. Personal interview with Bob Rosenberg.

97. Ibid.

98. Personal interview with Jean Lerman, September 24, 2013.

99. Jake Mooney, "On the Block, a Dream by the Sea," *NYT*, December 10, 2006: CY4.

100. Personal interview with Bob Rosenberg.

101. Spring Creek Towers, Office of Community Relations, "Spring Creek Towers Fact Sheet."

102. Personal interview with Jean Lerman.

103. Amanda Fung, "Affordable Housing Lives on at Starrett City," *Crain's New York Business*, July 29, 2009, www.crainsnewyork.com.

104. Personal interview with Jean Lerman.

Chapter 5: Housing Reimagined

1. Matthew Gordon Lasner, "Architect as Developer and the Postwar U.S. Apartment, 1945–1960," *Buildings & Landscapes* 21, no. 1 (Spring 2014): 27–55, 35–37. For critiques of public housing design see also Catherine Bauer, "The Dreary Deadlock of Public Housing," *Architectural Forum* 106 (May 1957): 140–42, 219, 221. NYCHA's Clason Point Gardens (1941) and many walk-up portions of larger developments citywide reflected a similar effort.

2. On Chicago see Jennifer S. Light, *The Nature of Cities: Ecological Visions and the American Urban Professions, 1920–1960* (Baltimore: Johns Hopkins University Press, 2009), chapters 4–5.

3. Jane Jacobs, *The Death and Life of Great American Cities* (New York: Random House, 1961), 150, 168. On Jacobs see also Suleiman Osman, *The Invention of Brownstone Brooklyn: Gentrification and the Search for Authenticity in Postwar New York* (Oxford: Oxford University Press, 2011), chapter 5; Max Page and Timothy Mennel, eds. *Reconsidering Jane Jacobs* (Chicago: American Planning Association, 2011); Samuel Zipp, *Manhattan Projects: The Rise and Fall of Urban Renewal in Cold War New York* (New York: Oxford University Press, 2010).

4. Charles Abrams, Henry Churchill, et al., "Book Reviews: Abattoir for Sacred Cows," *Progressive Architecture* 43, no. 4 (April 1962): 196, 200–210; 196.

5. Herbert Gans, "Urban Vitality and the Fallacy of Physical Determinism," in *People, Plans, and Policies: Essays on Poverty, Racism, and Other National Urban Problems* (New York: Columbia University Press; Russell Sage Foundation, 1993); Oscar Newman, *Defensible Space: Crime Prevention through Urban Design* (New York: Collier Books, 1973); Oscar Newman, *Housing Design and the Control of Behavior* (New York: Doubleday, 1980); Karen A. Franck and Michael Mostoller, "From Courts to Open Space to Streets: Changes in the Site Design of U.S. Public Housing," *Journal of Architectural and Planning Research* 12, no. 23 (Autumn 1995): 186–220.

6. Louis Winnick, "The Triumph of Housing Allowance Programs: How a Fundamental Policy Conflict Was Resolved," *Cityscape: A Journal of Policy Development and Research* 1, no. 3 (September 1995): 95–121; Joseph Heathcott, "The Strange Career of Public Housing," *Journal of the American Planning Association* 78, no. 4 (Autumn 2012): 360–75; David P. Varady and Carole C. Walker, "Vouchering Out Distressed Subsidized Developments: Does Moving Lead to Improvements in Housing and Neighborhood Conditions?," *Housing Policy Debate* 11, no. 1 (2000): 115–62.

7. Data from NYCHA, "About NYCHA Fact Sheet," www.nyc.gov.

8. Sydney Schanberg, "Gov. Offers a $6 Billion Plan to Rebuild Slums," *NYT*, February 28, 1968: 1.

9. Quoted in Martin Gottlieb, "From Public Housing to Private Incentive," *NYT*, January 27, 1985: E7.

10. "Urban Agreement Reached," *NYT*, May 22, 1969: 1.

11. Stephen Lefkowitz quoted in Joyce Pernick, "He Reshaped the Places We Live," *NYT*, April 24, 2000: B1.

12. On U.S. new communities see Nicholas Dagen Bloom, *Suburban Alchemy: 1960s New Towns and the Transformation of the American Dream* (Columbus: Ohio State University Press, 2001); Ann Forysth, *Reforming Suburbia: The Planned Communities of Irvine, Columbia, and the Woodlands* (Berkeley: University of California Press, 2005); Nicholas Dagen Bloom, "The Federal Icarus: The Public Rejection of 1970s National Suburban Planning," *Journal of Urban History* 28, no. 1 (November 2001), 55–71.

13. David Dunlap, "Edward Logue, Visionary City Planner, Is Remembered," *NYT*, April 23, 2000: 35.

14. Paul Goldberger, "New Urban Environment," *NYT*, May 18, 1976: 46; Yonah Freemark, "Roosevelt Island: Exception to a City in Crisis," *Journal of Urban History* 37, no. 3 (2011): 355–83.

15. Josh Barbanel, "The Low-rise Solution for the Poor," *NYT*, May 7, 1978: R1.

16. Martin Gottlieb, "UDC Chief Steering Agency into New Area," *NYT*, April 13, 1983: B1; Joyce Pernick, "He Reshaped the Places We Live," *NYT*, April 24, 2000: B1; Alan Oser, "How the UDC's Reach Came to Exceed Its Grasp," *NYT*, March 16, 1975: R1.

17. On WSURA generally see J. Clarence Davies III, *Neighborhood Groups and Urban Renewal* (New York: Columbia University Press, 1966); James Trager, *West of Fifth: The Rise and Fall of Manhattan's West Side* (New York: Scribner, 1987); Joseph Lyford, *The Airtight Cage* (New York: Harper & Row, 1966); Flavia Alaya, *Under the Rose: A Confession* (New York: Feminist Press at CUNY, 2001).

18. In 1972 SBNC estimated 1,649 low- and moderate-income units (NYCHA, NYCHA brownstones, Mitchell-Lama, Sections 221(d)(3) and 236) had been completed, with 997 in planning; in 1977 a neighborhood committee estimated 2,100 low-income units; and in 1982 it was reported there were 1,070 public housing units and approximately 1,000 below-market private units. See "1972 West Side Urban Renewal Area Site by Site Breakdown," folder: West Side Urban Renewal, Henry Joseph Browne Papers, Rare Book & Manuscript Library, Columbia University; City of New York, City Planning Commission, "Report of the City Planning Commission on the Fifth Amendment to the West Side Urban Renewal Plan," 1977, 32; Susan Baldwin, "West Side Urban Renewal Story," *City Limits* 12 (December 1982): 28.

19. "West Side Plan Opens New Vista," *NYT*, April 27, 1958: R1.

20. City of New York, City Planning Commission, "Urban Renewal," 1958.

21. On Father Browne's career, see "Crusader for Housing," *NYT*, May 25, 1965: 20; "Henry Browne, 61, Rutgers Professor," *NYT*, November 30, 1980: A44; and Alaya, *Under the Rose*, 168–86.

22. "Rabbi Wise Housing Dedicated; Mayor Backs Low-Income Units," *NYT*, December 15, 1964: 45; "West Siders Hail Housing Project," *NYT*, May 28, 1965: 20; "10-Year Renewal Stirs West Side," *NYT*, October 13, 1963: 1.

23. Clara Fox, *Vertical Neighborhood in an Urban Renewal Community* (New York: Goddard-Riverside Community Center, 1969), 12–15.

24. "Sponsors Named in Renewal Area," *NYT*, June 11, 1964: 37; "Commission Nathan Offers Program to Speed Up Construction in West Side Area," *Real Estate Builders Record and Guide* 98, no. 14 (October 1, 1966): 2.

25. On the movement see the documentary *Rompiendo Puertas (Break and Enter)*, dir. Newsreel, 1970.

26. Thomas Father Farrelly, "A Case of Urban Renewal," September 12, 1972, box 31, folder: West Side Urban Renewal, Henry Joseph Browne Papers, Rare Book & Manuscript Library, Columbia University; Tobias Armborst, Daniel D'Oca, and Georgeen Theodore, "NORCs in NYC," *Urban Omnibus*, March 17, 2010, www.urbanomnibus.net.

27. On Jacobs see Alice Sparberg Alexiou, *Jane Jacobs: Urban Visionary* (New Brunswick, N.J.: Rutgers University Press, 2006); Max Allen, ed., *Ideas That Matter: The Worlds of Jane Jacobs* (Owen Sound, Ontario: Ginger Press, 1997); Page and Mennel, *Reconsidering Jane Jacobs*; Timothy Mennel, Jo Stephens, and Christophe Klemek, eds., *Block by Block: Jane Jacobs and the Future of New York* (New York: Municipal Art Society and Princeton University Press, 2007); Anthony Flint, *Wrestling with Moses: How Jane Jacobs Took on New York's Master Planner and Transformed the American City* (New York: Random House, 2009).

28. Jane Jacobs, "The Missing Link in City Redevelopment," *Architectural Forum*, June 1956: 132–33; Jane Jacobs, "Downtown Is for People," *Fortune*, April 1958: 133–40, 236, 238, 240–42.

29. Jacobs, *The Death and Life of Great American Cities*, 1.

30. See Bauer, "The Dreary Deadlock of Public Housing"; Herbert Gans, "The Human Implications of Current Redevelopment and Relocation Planning," *Journal of the American Institute of*

Planners 25, no. 1 (1959): 15–26; Staughton Lynd, "Urban Renewal—For Whom?" *Commentary*, January 1961: 34–45.

31. Jacobs, *The Death and Life of Great American Cities*, 324.

32. Edith Elmer Wood, "A Century of the Housing Problem," *Law and Contemporary Problems* 137 (March 1934): 137–47.

33. Interview with Jane Jacobs, conducted by Leticia Kent, October 1997, Greenwich Village Preservation Archive and Oral History Project, Greenwich Village Society for Historic Preservation, www.gvshp.org.

34. Jacobs, *The Death and Life of Great American Cities*, 147.

35. Alexander Burnham, "Village Group Designs Housing to Preserve Character of Area," *NYT*, May 6, 1963: 1.

36. "West Village Group to Offer Housing Plan to City," *NYT*, February 2, 1969: 53.

37. Burnham, "Village Group Designs Housing to Preserve Character of Area"; Judith C. Lack, "Dispute Still Rages as West Village Houses Meets Its Sales Test," *NYT*, August 18, 1974: R1; Paul Goldberger, "Low-rise, Low-key Housing Concept Gives Banality a Test," *NYT*, September 28, 1974: 31.

38. Joseph P. Fried, "A 'Village' Housing Project Becomes Fiscal Nightmare," *NYT*, August 8, 1975: 58.

39. Albert Amateau, "Victory! West Village Houses to Become an Affordable Co-op," *Villager* 73, no. 4 (May 26–June 1, 2004); Julia Vitullo-Martin, "West Village Houses a Monument to a 1960s Development Battle," *New York Sun*, August 30, 2007.

40. Early on Lindsay commissioned reports on the city's housing quality and administration from Edward Logue and an appointed Commission on Urban Design. See City of New York, Office of the Mayor, Study Group on New York Housing and Neighborhood Improvement, "Let There Be Commitment: A Housing, Planning [and] Development Program for New York City," 1966; City of New York, Mayor's Commission on Urban Design, "The Threatened City: A Report on the Design of the City of New York," 1967.

41. Lawrence Halprin and Associates, *New York, New York: A Study of the Quality, Character, and Meaning of Open Space in Urban Design* (San Francisco: Chapman Press, 1968).

42. City of New York, Housing and Development Administration, "Record of Submissions and Awards Competition for Middle-income Housing at Brighton Beach, Brooklyn," 1968; Denise Scott Brown and Robert Venturi, "Co-Op City: Learning to Like It," *Progressive Architecture*, February 1970: 64–73.

43. Herbert Muschamp, "Samuel M. Brody, 65, Architect of Housing Complexes, Is Dead," *NYT*, July 30, 1992: D25; "Town Houses in Sky Planned for Harlem," *NYT*, May 30, 1965: R1; "Board Approves 200 Houses in the Sky," *New York Amsterdam News*, July 31, 1965: 51.

44. Personal telephone interview and e-mail correspondence with architect Kimbro Frutiger of Davis Brody, October 2013; personal telephone interview with Richard Ravitch, October 28, 2013.

45. Peter Blake, "Riverbend Houses: The Impossible Project," *Architectural Forum* 131, no. 1 (July/August 1969): 46–55; contemporary assessment gathered at Riverbend community meeting, October 2013.

46. Alexander may have been instrumental in getting Riverbend started. See "Riverbend Houses Start Upward Monday," *New York Amsterdam News*, June 4, 1966: 43; "Townhouse in Sky? That's Riverbend," *New York Amsterdam News*, April 8, 1967: 43. Davis quoted in "The Evolving Urban Architecture of Davis, Brody & Associates," *Architectural Record* 152 (August 1972): 97–106. On design and marketing see display advertisement, *New York Amsterdam News*, September 25, 1965: 51; Poppy Cannon White, "Moving Back to Harlem," *New York Amsterdam News*, June 18, 1966: 17; Lou LuTour and Jose Ananias, "Global Portraits," *Philadelphia Tribune*, August 9, 1966: 13.

47. See Alison Smithson and Peter Smithson, "An Urban Project," *Architects' Year Book* 5 (1953) 48–55.

48. Alison and Peter Smithson, *Without Rhetoric: An Architectural Aesthetic, 1955–1972* (Cambridge, Mass.: MIT Press, 1973). See also Reyner Banham, *The New Brutalism: Ethic or Aesthetic* (New York: Reinhold, 1966).

49. Blake, "Riverbend Houses"; "The Evolving Urban Architecture of Davis, Brody & Associates," *Architectural Record*.

50. John Morris Dixon, "41-year Watch," *Oculus* 70, no. 1 (Spring 2008): 47; Kimbro Fruitiger, "No More Paradigms: The Challenge of Riverbend Houses," *DOCOMOMO US New York Tri-state Newsletter*, (Summer 2009) 1, 6.

51. Juan Forero, "Worlds of Difference in Facing Strike Threat; Harlem Tenants Are Used to Pulling Together," *NYT*, April 18, 2000: B1.

52. The key source on Northside Center and the role of Kenneth and Mamie Clark in the development of Schomburg Plaza is Gerald Markowitz and David Rosner, *Children, Race, and Power: Kenneth and Mamie Clark's Northside Center* (Charlottesville: University Press of Virginia, 1996).

53. On the transformation of East Harlem see Samuel Zipp, *Manhattan Projects. The Rise and Fall of Urban Renewal in Cold War New York* (New York: Oxford University Press, 2010), part IV;

Christopher Bell, *East Harlem Remembered: Oral Histories of Community and Diversity* (Jefferson, NC: McFarland, 2012), 117–18. Projects in Central Harlem include: Johnson Houses (1948), Forest Houses (today: Rev. Dr. Martin Luther King, Jr., Towers; 1954), Jefferson Houses (1959), and Taft Houses (1962). In East Harlem: Clinton Houses (1956), Carver Houses (1958), and Lehman Houses (1963).

54. Quoted in Markowitz and Rosner, *Children, Race, and Power*, 218.

55. Ibid.

56. A rendering of Edgar Tafel's proposal is published in Markowitz and Rosner, *Children, Race, and Power*, n.p.

57. Eric Pace, "New Name Given to the 110th St. Area," *NYT*, September 7, 1965: 41.

58. City of New York, City Planning Commission, "Milbank Frawley Circle Area—1966 Urban Renewal Program," brochure, 1966; Markowitz and Rosner, *Children, Race, and Power*, 220; "Mayor Pinpoints 3 Renewal Areas," *NYT*, September 20, 1966: 1; Charles G. Bennett, "2 Renewal Areas Chosen under New Policy," *NYT*, November 3, 1966: 28.

59. Steven V. Roberts, "Negro-Latin Feud Hurting Harlem," *NYT*, February 25, 1968: 45; Markowitz and Rosner, *Children, Race, and Power*, 221; "190-acre Renewal in Lower Harlem Gets U.S. Approval," *NYT*, June 3, 1967: 37.

60. John Sibley, "Rockefeller Plans for Slums Voted," *NYT*, April 10, 1968: 1; Markowitz and Rosner, *Children, Race, and Power*, 223.

61. Markowitz and Rosner, *Children, Race, and Power*, 223–24.

62. Steven V. Roberts, "Negro-Latin Feud Hurting Harlem," *NYT*, February 25, 1968: 45; Markowitz and Rosner, *Children, Race, and Power*, 226–28.

63. On the rift between Puerto Ricans and African Americans in this area see Arlene Davila, *Barrio Dreams: Puerto Ricans, Latinos, and the Neoliberal City* (Berkeley: University of California Press, 2004).

64. The City Planning Commission approved the plan in April 1970: Maurice Carroll, "'Harlem Gateway' Plan Passed by Commission," *NYT*, April 30, 1970: 37; Markowitz and Rosner, *Children, Race, and Power*, 229–30. On the legal battle to stop the evictions on the future site of Schomburg Plaza see Alfonso A. Narvaez, "A Housing Group Fights Evictions," *NYT*, April 9, 1971: 35; Prudencio T. Feliciano et al., Plaintiffs, v. George Romney, Secretary of the Department of Housing and Urban Development, et al., Defendants, United States District Court, S. D., New York, July 19, 1973, www.leagle.com.

65. Markowitz and Rosner, *Children, Race, and Power*, 231–32.

66. On the cornerstone ceremony see "Schomburg Plaza Dedication Is Set for Thursday, May 17," *New York Amsterdam News*, May 12, 1973, B13; on the opening ceremony see Charlayne Hunter, "Housing Is Dedicated at Schomburg Plaza," *NYT*, December 18, 1974: 47.

67. Mamie Clark's plan to reserve one-third of the apartments for whites was also opposed by community members who wanted all the affordable units reserved for nonwhites. On the occupancy plans, Markowitz and Rosner, *Children, Race, and Power*, 233–34; Charlayne Hunter, "Hopes and Fears on Rise with New Harlem Skyline," *NYT*, November 20, 1974: 41.

68. Schomburg Plaza received several awards in recognition of its design excellence: Honor Award Excellence in Design, Municipal Arts Society, 1973; Design Award, New York State Chapter of the American Institute of Architects, 1973; and the Albert S. Bard Award, City Club of New York, 1975. In 1968 NYCHA engaged Gruzen & Partners to oversee and upgrade the architectural designs for fifty-four Model Cities Program sites. Gruzen was also responsible for several UDC projects, including five for which it alone has design credit: 106th Street and Fifth Avenue (1969) in Manhattan; Rainbow Center (1969) in Niagara Falls; Southeast Loop (1969) in Rochester; Ten Eyck (1970) in Albany; and Seven Pines (1972) in Yonkers. Gruzen & Partners teamed with Castro-Blanco, Piscioneri & Feder on the Lindsay Bushwick Houses, Brooklyn (1971), another UDC project, and Castro-Blanco on its own designed the UDC-sponsored Williamsburg Houses (1970).

69. I am grateful to Jordan L. Gruzen for sharing both his recollections of the project (interview in August 2013) and the few surviving project files of Gruzen & Partners. For a published recollection of Jorden Gruzen about the use of twin towers, see David Dunlap, "Even Now, a Skyline of Twins," *NYT*, November 2, 2001: E35.

70. Sam Howe Verhovek, "3 Jump to Death and 4 Others Die in Apartment Blaze," *NYT*, March 23, 1987: 1; Eileen Markey, "Foreclosure Threat Looms over Thousands of City Apartments," *Gotham Gazette*, June 22, 2009.

71. This essay is drawn from the forthcoming book Lizabeth Cohen, *Saving America's Cities: Ed Logue and the Struggle to Renew Urban America in the Suburban Age* (New York: Farrar, Straus, & Giroux). Logue's papers are housed at Edward Joseph Logue papers, Manuscripts and Archives, Yale University (hereafter "Logue Papers").

72. On New Haven see Douglas Rae, *City: Urbanism and Its End* (New Haven, Conn.: Yale University Press, 2003); Robert A. Dahl, *Who Governs? Democracy and Power in an American City* (New Haven, Conn.: Yale University Press, 1961); and Allan R. Talbot, *The Mayor's Game: Richard*

Lee and the Politics of Change (New York: Harper & Row Publishers, 1967); Jeanne R. Lowe, *Cities in a Race with Time: Progress and Poverty in America's Renewing Cities* (New York: Random House, 1967), 405–551.

73. On Boston, see Thomas H. O'Connor, *Building a New Boston: Politics and Urban Renewal 1950–1970* (Boston: Northeastern University Press, 1993); Lawrence W. Kennedy, *Planning the City upon a Hill: Boston since 1630* (Amherst: University of Massachusetts Press, 1992); Boston Redevelopment Authority, "Seven Years of Progress: A Final Report by Edward J. Logue, Development Administrator, Boston Redevelopment Authority," August 1967; Langley Carleton Keyes, *The Rehabilitation Planning Game: A Study in the Diversity of Neighborhood* (Cambridge, Mass.: MIT Press, 1969).

74. City of New York, "Let There Be Commitment."

75. Eleanor L. Brilliant, *The Urban Development Corporation: Private Interests and Public Authority* (Lexington, Mass.: D.C. Heath, 1975); Louis K. Loewenstein, "The New York State Development Corporation: A Forgotten Failure or a Precursor of the Future?," *Journal of the American Institute of Planners*, 44 (July 1978): 261–73; New York State Urban Development Corporation Symposium & Exhibition Committee, "Policy and Design for Housing: Lessons of the Urban Development Corporation 1968–1975," www.udchousing.org.

76. New York State Moreland Act Commission on the Urban Development Corporation and Other State Financing Agencies, "Restoring Credit and Confidence: A Reform Program for New York State and Its Public Authorities," March 31, 1976.

77. Quotation in letter from Edward J. Logue to John Goldman, May 27, 1982, box 107, folder "Manufactured Housing Correspondence," 1985 Addition, Logue Papers. For Charlotte Gardens, see Alexander Hoffman, *House by House, Block by Block: The Rebirth of America's Urban Neighborhoods* (New York: Oxford University Press, 2003), 18–39; Jill Jonnes, *South Bronx Rising: The Rise, Fall, and Resurrection of an American City* (New York: Fordham University Press, 2002).

78. Linda Corman, "Former BRA Head Takes Another Look at the City He Helped Plan," *Banker & Tradesman*, October 21, 1987: 6.

79. David W. Dunlap, "Edward Logue, Visionary City Planner, Is Remembered," *NYT*, April 23, 2000: 35.

80. Myles Weintraub and Marco Zicarelli, "The Tale of Twin Parks," *Architectural Forum* 138 (June 1973): 52–55; Clayton Knowles, "Lindsay Will Face Crisis on Budget," *NYT*, November 11, 1965: 49; Charles Morris, *The Cost of Good Intentions: New York City and the Liberal Experiment, 1960–1975* (New York: McGraw-Hill, 1980): 18, 119.

81. Vincent Scully, "Preface," in *Pasanella and Klein: Public and Private Interventions in the Residential Field*, ed. Alessandra Latour (Rome: Kappa, 1987).

82. City of New York, Housing and Development Administration, "Twin Parks: Vest Pocket Housing," December 7, 1967. See also memorandum, Marion Scott to Edward Logue, May 16, 1972; letter, Ronald Clare to Rev. Paul Matson, April 24, 1973; memorandum, Ronald Clare to file, June 20, 1973, box 291, folder: Twin Parks 1972, Logue Papers.

83. Clayton Knowles, "Governor Speaks on Bronx Housing," *NYT*, October 1, 1970: 35.

84. Paul Goldberger, "Twin Parks, an Effort to Alter the Pattern of Public Housing," *NYT*, December 27, 1973: 39.

85. Although UDC continued to have an active role through the leasing period, it became, in effect, insolvent by 1975. See Yonah Freemark, "The Entrepreneurial State: New York's Urban Development Corporation, an Experiment to Take Charge of Affordable Housing Production, 1968–1975," Master's in Urban Planning thesis, Massachusetts Institute of Technology, 2013.

86. "7 Housing Units and State Agree on Arrears Plan," *NYT*, March 12, 1982: B3.

87. Data from Furman Center for Real Estate and Urban Policy, New York University, "Subsidized Housing Information Project," database, datasearch.furmancenter.org; Daniel Beekman, "Ex-Met Vaughn Hits It Out of Park with Deal to Fix Up Two Bronx Apartment Buildings," *New York Daily News*, December 17, 2010; Omni New York, "Twin Parks," www.onyllc.com/property/twin-parks.

88. On original design intent and current conditions see Susanne Schindler and Juliette Spertus, "The Landscape of Housing: Twin Parks Northwest 40 Years On," *Urban Omnibus*, November 6, 2013.

89. Portions of this essay first appeared as Karen Kubey, "Low-rise, High-density Housing: A Contemporary View of Marcus Garvey Park Village," *Urban Omnibus*, July 18, 2012, and in the exhibition "Low Rise High Density," Center for Architecture, New York, April 25–June 29, 2013.

90. Edward Ranzal, "Ground Is Broken in Brownsville on U.S.-aided Housing Project," *NYT*, November 22, 1972: 39.

91. Museum of Modern Art, *Another Chance for Housing: Low-rise Alternatives; Brownsville, Brooklyn, Fox Hills, Staten Island* (New York: Museum of Modern Art, 1973): 38.

92. Kenneth Frampton, *Reminiscences of Kenneth Frampton*, interview by Karen Kubey,

2008, Oral History Research Office, Columbia University.

93. Suzanne Stephens, "Compromised Ideal: Marcus Garvey Park Village Housing, Brooklyn, N.Y., 1973–76," *Progressive Architecture* 60 (October 1979): 50–53; Kenneth Frampton, "U.D.C. Low Rise High Density Housing Prototype," *Architecture D'aujourd'hui* 186 (1976): 15–21.

94. Susan Saegert and Gabrielle Bendiner-Viani, "Making Housing Home: Marcus Garvey Village, Brownsville, Brooklyn and Urban Horizons, The Bronx," *Places* 19 (2007): 72–79; Anna Fogel, "Marcus Garvey Village: Towards a New Housing Prototype," BA thesis, Harvard University, 2007.

95. New York State Urban Development Corporation, "General Development Plan: Schedule 2," 1969, Roosevelt Island Operating Corporation archive (hereafter RIOCA). On Roosevelt Island generally see also, for example, Freemark, "Roosevelt Island."

96. Robert Campbell, "Interview with Sert" [1980], in *Josep Lluís Sert: The Architect of Urban Design 1953–1969*, ed. Eric Mumford (New Haven, Conn.: Yale University Press, 2008); Joe Moran, "Imagining the Street in Post-war Britain," *Urban History* 39, no. 1 (February 2012): 1966–86.

97. Memorandum, Paul Byard to Edward Logue, "Welfare Island Programming," July 1, 1970, Roosevelt Island Historical Society (hereafter RIHS); New York State Urban Development Corporation Symposium and Exhibition Committee, symposium transcript, "Policy and Design of Housing: Lessons of the Urban Development Corporation 1968–1975," April 18, 2005, www.udchousing.org; Linda Greenhouse, "After 5 Months, the Crisis Mood at U.D.C. Gives Way to a Steady Salvage Operation," *NYT*, July 24, 1975: 26; Eastwood prospectus, 1976, RIHS; memorandum, Tino Calabria, City of New York Human Resources Administration, "Next Taskforce Meeting," December 27, 1973, RIHS.

98. Display advertisement, *NYT*, January 28, 1975: 2; Anthony Bailey, "Manhattan's Other Island: Roosevelt Island," *NYT*, April 24, 1974: SM32; Joseph Fried, "Roosevelt I. Real Estate Agent Replaced," *NYT*, February 7, 1976: 34.

99. Roosevelt Island Operating Corporation, "A Rather Brief Briefing on Roosevelt Island," October 1995, RIOCA; personal interview with Judith Berdy, Roosevelt Island Historical Society, October 8, 2013.

100. Quoted in New York State Urban Development Corporation Symposium & Exhibition Committee, symposium transcript, "Policy and Design for Housing: Lessons of the Urban Development Corporation 1968–1975, Operations, How the UDC Program Worked," panel 1, June 11, 2005, 13–14.

101. Mendes Hershman, "Is There a Future for State Involvement?," *Urban Land*, April 1977; Judith Cummings, "Two Blazes on Roosevelt Island Being Investigated as Suspicious," *NYT*, July 9, 1977: 11; Robin Hermann, "Roosevelt Island Is a Paradise to Some, a Prison to Others," *NYT*, January 25 1979: B1; George Goodman, "Bungled Housing to Be Repaired," *NYT*, January 25, 1982: 39.

102. Roosevelt Island Operating Corporation, "A Rather Brief Briefing on Roosevelt Island"; "Backing Eastwood's Public Safety Issue in Rent Hike," *Main Street WIRE*, February 10, 2001: 1, 6.

103. New York State Urban Development Corporation, "Policy and Design of Housing."

104. City of New York, "Mayor Announces Agreement between Owners and Tenants," press release #123-04, May 20, 2004, www.nyc.gov; "Eastwood Residents OK Owner Privatization Plan," *Main Street WIRE*, August 24, 2005: 1, 8.

105. "Eastwood Tenants Reorganize; Building Has a Modernization Plan," *Main Street WIRE*, November 11, 2006: 10; Joseph Chiara, "Housing Trends on the Island," *Main Street WIRE*, October 16, 2004; Urban Homesteading Assistance Board, "Tracking the Sales of Five Former Mitchell-Lamas," 2007, www.uhab.org/newsroom; C. J. Hughes, "Roosevelt Island: An Island Joins the Mainstream," *NYT*, September 2, 2007: RE7.

106. New York State Public Service Commission, case 08-E-0838, "Order Reinstating Submetering Approval at Northtown Roosevelt with Conditions," October 28, 2011, www.dps.ny.gov; Robert Laux-Bachand, "Westview Residents Turn Out to Be Heard at DHCR Rent Hearing," *Main Street WIRE*, February 10, 2001: 1, 7; Dick Lutz and Larry Harris, "Inertia and Disincentives May Be Keeping Heating Costs High Here," *Main Street WIRE*, January 28, 2012: 1, 12; Dick Lutz and Larry Harris, "Sample Bills for Submetered Electricity Are Alarming Many Living at 510–580," *Main Street WIRE*, October 16, 2004: 1, 8.

107. This article draws on Lilian M. Knorr, "Youth and Cities: Planning with Low-income Youth and Urban Youth Cultures in New York City and Paris," PhD diss., Massachusetts Institute of Technology, 2014. On the topic generally also see Nelson George, *Buppies, B-Boys and Bohos: Notes on Post-Soul Black Culture* (New York: Da Capo Press, 2001); Tricia Rose, *The Hip Hop Wars: What We Talk about When We Talk about Hip Hop—And Why It Matters* (New York: Basic Books, 2008).

108. Jeff Chang, *Can't Stop Won't Stop: A History of the Hip Hop Generation* (New York: St. Martin's Press, 2005); Ivor L. Miller and Robert Farris Thompson, *Aerosol Kingdom: Subway Painters of New York City* (Jackson: University Press of Mississippi, 2002).

109. Personal interview with Grandmaster Caz, March 21, 2013.

110. Personal interview with Maria Fernandez, March 20, 2013.

111. Lisa T. Alexander, "Hip-Hop and Housing: Revisiting Culture, Urban Space, Power, and Law," *Hastings Law Journal* 63 (2012): 803–66.

112. Jay-Z, *Decoded* (New York: Spiegel & Grau, 2010): 7.

113. Personal interview with Orlando Torres, April 3, 2013.

114. Personal interview with Bonz Malone, March 24, 2013.

115. Ibid.

116. Brendan Frederick, "Mobb Deep's Queensbridge Classics," *XXL Magazine*, April 2006.

117. Jay-Z, *Decoded*, 155.

Chapter 6: The Decentralized Network

1. David J. Erickson, *The Housing Policy Revolution: Networks and Neighborhoods* (Washington, D.C.: Urban Institute Press, 2009), 35.

2. Jack Rosenthal, "Suburbs Abandoning Dependence on City," *NYT*, August 16, 1971: 1.

3. Martin Gottlieb, "A Decade after the Cutbacks," *NYT*, June 30, 1985: 1.

4. Robert McFadden, "Abraham Beame Is Dead at 94," *NYT*, February 11, 2001: 1.

5. "Why the South Bronx Is Burning," *NYT*, June 20, 1975: 34.

6. Michael Sterne, "In Last Decade, Leaders Say, Harlem's Dreams Have Died," *NYT*, March 1, 1978: B15.

7. Citizens Housing and Planning Council of New York, "The Future of Real Estate Tax Exemptions for Affordable Housing in New York City," December 2011, chpcny.org/.

8. "City's Housing Problem: To Bulldoze or Rehabilitate?," *NYT*, Feb 18, 1968: R1.

9. Suleiman Osman, *The Invention of Brownstone Brooklyn: Gentrification and the Search for Authenticity in Postwar New York* (Oxford: Oxford University Press, 2011); Sharon Zukin, *Loft Living: Culture and Capital in Urban Change,* paperback ed. (New Brunswick, N.J.: Rutgers University Press, 1989); Matthew Gordon Lasner, *High Life: Condo Living in the Suburban Century* (New Haven, Conn.: Yale University Press, 2012), 265–66; William C. Apgar and Mark Duda, "The Twenty-fifth Anniversary of the Community Reinvestment Act: Past Accomplishments and Future Regulatory Challenges," *Federal Reserve Board of New York Economic Policy Review*, June 2003: 169–91; Sarah Kass, "Demand for Affordable Housing Helps Slow Redlining," *NYT*, November 13, 1988: A18.

10. Alexander Garvin, *The American City: What Works, What Doesn't*, 3d ed. (New York: McGraw-Hill Education, 2014), 279; "Self-help Housing: The Story of the Urban Homesteading Assistance Board," *Urban Omnibus*, December 19, 2012; Fergus Bordewich, *NYT*, February 10, 1980: R1; John Krinsky and Sarah Hovde, *Balancing Acts: The Experience of Mutual Housing Associations and Community Land Trusts in Urban Neighborhoods* (New York: Community Service Society of New York, 1996), 152–56.

11. On Los Desperados see Kathleen Teltsch, "Once Desperate, a Bronx Housing Group Earns Praise," *NYT*, October 30, 1987: B1.

12. On the system nationally see Erickson, *The Housing Policy Revolution*; Alexander von Hoffman, "Calling upon the Genius of Private Enterprise: The Housing and Urban Development Act of 1968 and the Liberal Turn to Public-Private Partnership," *Studies in American Political Development* 27 (October 2013): 165–94.

13. Alan Oser, "Phasing Out Centralized Management," *NYT*, February 2, 1992: LIR5.

14. Alan Finder, "Nonprofit Community Groups," *NYT*, March 11, 1990: 33.

15. Alan Finder, "Renovation Program Is Running Out of Abandoned Housing," *NYT*, April 16, 1990: B5.

16. Alan Finder, "Nonprofit Community Groups," *NYT*, March 11, 1990: 33.

17. On LIHTCs generally see, for example, Jean L. Cummings and Denise DiPasqual, "The Low-income Housing Tax Credit: An Analysis of the First Ten Years," *Housing Policy Debate* 10, no. 2 (1999): 251–307.

18. Lydia Chavez, "Out of the Ashes," *NYT*, June 14, 1987: 1; Garvin, *The American City*, 342–45; Alan S. Oser, "New York Slashing an Array of Programs," *NYT*, April 5, 1992: R5; Michael Lappin, "Affordable Housing," letter to the editor, *NYT*, March 22, 2012.

19. Philip Shenon, "Taste of Suburbia Arrives in the South Bronx," *NYT*, March 19, 1983: 1; Alan S. Oser, "Lessons from One-family Housing in the South Bronx," *NYT*, April 21, 1985: A18; Teltsch, "Once Desperate, a Bronx Housing Group Earns Praise."

20. Robert Esnard quoted in Anthony de Palma, "The Nehemiah Plan: A Success, but . . . ," *NYT*, September 27, 1987: R1.

21. Quoted in Lynette Holloway, "At Melrose Court, Progress in Shades of Teal," *NYT*, May 8, 1994: CY9.

22. Michelle Murphy, "A Developer Goes Home to Tackle a New Project," *NYT*, December 7, 2003, 4; Sam Davis, *Designing for the Homeless: Architecture That Works* (Berkeley: University of California Press, 2004), chapter 1.

23. See Edward G. Goetz, *New Deal Ruins: The Dismantling of Public Housing in the U.S.* (Ithaca, N.Y.: Cornell University Press, 2013); Lawrence J. Vale, *Purging the Poorest: Public Housing and the Design Politics of Twice-Cleared Communities* (Chicago: University of Chicago Press, 2013).

24. Lee Dembart, "Carter Takes 'Sobering' Trip to South Bronx," *NYT*, October 6, 1977: 1; Michael Sterne, "A Loan and Some 'Sweat Equity' Create an Oasis amid Desolation," *NYT*, October 7, 1977: 6.

25. See Robert Kolodny (assisted by Marjorie Gellerman), *Self Help in the Inner City: A Study of Lower Income Cooperative Housing Conversion in New York* (New York: United Neighborhood Houses of New York, 1973).

26. Michael Garrison, "Peoples Development Corporation," *City Limits*, June–July 1976, 3.

27. Quotation from Interfaith Adopt-a-Building newsletter (1973), box 15, folder: Adopt a Building 4, Ronald Lawson Tenant Movement in New York City files, Tamiment Library and Robert F. Wagner Labor Archives, New York University. See also, for example, Robert Schur and Virginia Sherry, *The Neighborhood Housing Movement: A Survey of the Activities and Services Provided by Non-profit Community-based Organizations to Residents of Low- and Moderate-income Communities in New York City* (New York: Association of Neighborhood Housing Developers, 1977).

28. Osman, *The Invention of Brownstone Brooklyn*, 230–31; City of New York, Mayor's Policy Committee, "Housing Development and Rehabilitation in New York City," November 1974, 1; Michael Goodwin, "City-owned Houses Come Complete with Pandora's Box," *NYT*, January 7, 1979: E6.

29. Task Force on City Owned Property, "The Report on the Task Force on City Owned Property," March 29, 1978, Urban Homesteading Assistance Board.

30. Quotations from Alexandra Christy, *Self Help, in Our Own Words: Our First Fifteen Years, 1974–1988* (New York: Urban Homesteading Assistance Board, 1989), 10.

31. Ibid., 7.

32. On Starr's life see, for example, Jack Rosenthal, "The Contrarian," *NYT*, December 30, 2001: SM49; Bruce Lambert, "Roger Starr, New York Planning Official, Author and Editorial Writer, Is Dead at 83," *NYT*, September 11, 2001: C17.

33. Roger Starr, "Our First Housing Project," *NYT*, December 3, 1960: 22.

34. "City Hall Critic Gets State Post," *NYT*, November 11, 1971: 29.

35. Joseph P. Fried, "City's Housing Administrator Proposes 'Planned Shrinkage of Some Slums,'" *NYT*, February 3, 1976: 35; "Minority Caucus Bids Starr Quit," *NYT*, March 5, 1976: 13. For Starr's most extended discussion of planned shrinkage, see Starr, "Making New York Smaller," *NYT*, November 14, 1976: SM32.

36. Most of this essay is based on original fieldwork. For more on Nehemiah and Brownsville see Samuel Freedman, *Upon This Rock: The Miracles of a Black Church* (New York: Harper Collins, 1993); Wendell E. Pritchett, *Brownsville, Brooklyn: Blacks, Jews, and the Changing Face of the Ghetto* (Chicago: Chicago University Press, 2002).

37. Personal interview with Sarah Plowden, July 9, 2013.

38. Jill Shook, *Making Housing Happen: Faith-Based Affordable Housing Models* (St. Louis: Chalice Press, 2006), 196.

39. Anthony DePalma, "The Nehemiah Plan," *NYT*, September 27, 1987: R1.

40. DePalma, "The Nehemiah Plan"; John M. Doyle, "Grass-roots 'Nehemiah Plan' Builds Working-class Homes in Urban Wasteland," Associated Press News Archive, September 28, 1985, www.apnewsarchive.com/1985; personal interview with Carmelia Goffe, June 11, 2013.

41. Personal interview with Pat Worthy, June 26, 2013.

42. Archinet, "Alexander Gorlin Architect, Project Portfolio, Nehemiah Spring Creek Housing," www.archinect.com.

43. Personal interview with Linda Boyce, July 11, 2013.

44. "Block 2007," ca. 1988–89, box 42, folder 41, R61, series XII, subseries C, Abyssinian Baptist Church Records, Abyssinian Baptist Church, New York (hereafter ABC); "Adam Clayton Powell Jr. Bould.," map, ca. 1988–89, box 42, folder 41, ABC; Sheila Rule, "Crossroads for Harlem," *NYT*, November 21, 1980: B3.

45. Frank White III, "The Yuppies Are Coming," *Ebony*, April 1985: 155; Simon Anekwe, "Harlem Church to Build $5M Housing for Seniors," *New York Amsterdam News*, October 18, 1986: 18; Rev. Robert A. Clemetson and Roger Coates, eds., *Restoring Broken Places and Rebuilding Communities: A Casebook on African-American Church Involvement in Community Economic Development* (Washington, D.C.: National Congress for Community Economic Development, 1993), 32–34.

46. On CDCs, see, for example, Neil R. Peirce and Carol F. Steinbach, *Corrective Capitalism: The Rise of America's Community Development Corporations* (New York: Ford Foundation, 1987); Alexander Von Hoffman, *House by House, Block by Block: The Rebirth of America's Urban Neighborhoods* (New York: Oxford University Press, 2003); Michael Leo Owens, "Doing Something in Jesus' Name: Black Churches and Community Development Corporations," in *New Day Begun: African American Churches and Civic Culture in Post-Civil Rights America*, ed. R. Drew Smith (Durham, NC: Duke University Press, 2003), 215–47; Preston Washington, *God's Transforming Spirit:*

Black Church Renewal (Valley Forge, PA: Hudson Press, 1988), 99–108.

47. For a contemporaneous account of gentrification in Harlem in this era, see Richard Schaffer and Neil Smith, "The Gentrification of Harlem?," *Annals of the Association of American Geographers* 76, no. 3 (September 1986): 347–65; "Abyssinian Studio," ca. late 1987, box 42, folder 43, ABC.

48. See William Julius Wilson, *The Truly Disadvantaged: The Inner City, the Underclass, and Public Policy* (Chicago: University of Chicago Press, 1987).

49. Through the 1990s, Abyssinian received about a third of its support from banks and intermediaries, 10 percent from corporations and foundations, and the remainder from public sources. See Owens, "Doing Something in Jesus' Name," 233.

50. "Become a Harlem Homeowner at West One Three One Plaza," ca. 1993, box 42, folder 30, ABC; "West One Three One Plaza: Condominiums in the Heart of Harlem," ca. 1993, box 42, folder 30, ABC; "Stop Paying Rent!" ca. 1993, box 42, folder 30, ABC; Shankar Vedantam, "Dream Homes in Harlem," *New York Newsday*, n.d., box 211, folder: Grants Files 1994 Abyssinian Development Corporation, Vincent Astor Foundation Records, Manuscripts and Archives Division, New York Public Library.

51. Sam Roberts, "Poor Gain, Rich Gain a Lot," *NYT*, March 20, 1994: CY6.

52. Craig Horowitz, "The Anti-Sharpton," *New York*, January 26, 1998, 28–31, 90–91; Peter Noel, "The Sins of Reverend Calvin Butts," *Village Voice*, October 27, 1998; Timothy Williams, "God and Neighborhood: Powerful Harlem Church Is Also a Powerful Harlem Developer," *NYT*, August 18, 2008: B1; Alan Feuer, "Stress of Harlem's Rebirth Shows in School's Move to a New Building," *NYT*, February 2, 2004: B1; Graham Rayman, "The (Very) Earthly Pursuits of Rev. Calvin O. Butts III," *Village Voice*, April 17, 2013.

53. This essay is adapted from portions of Jonathan Soffer, *Ed Koch and the Rebuilding of New York* (New York: Columbia University Press, 2010). On the plan see also Susan D. Wagner to Robert Esnard, "Status of the Recommendations in the Report by the Mayor's Panel on Affordable Housing and the Blue Ribbon Panel Report," January 12, 1987, 21-52-14, Koch Papers, LaGuardia and Wagner Archives (hereafter "Koch papers"); City of New York, Department of Housing Preservation and Development, "The Ten Year Housing Plan: Fiscal Years 1989–1998," n.d. (1989?), City of New York, Municipal Library.

54. Yvette Shiffman and Nancy Foxworthy, "Producing Low-income Housing in New York City," typescript, Community Service Society of New York, January 1985, Bobst Library, New York University, 2–3; Felice Michetti, "The New York City Capital Program for Affordable Housing," in *Housing America: Mobilizing Bankers, Builders and Communities to Solve the Nation's Affordable Housing Crisis*, ed. Jess Lederman (Chicago: Probus, 1993), 199–213, 201–3; Abraham Biderman, *Reminiscences of Abraham Biderman*, interview by John Metzger, 1992, Oral History Research Office, Columbia University, 42, 45.

55. Paul A. Crotty, *Reminiscences of Paul A. Crotty*, interview by John Metzger, 1992, Oral History Research Office, Columbia University, 60–61, 180–81; Robert Esnard to Edward I. Koch, April 4, 1985, 21-52-6, Koch papers; Biderman, *Reminiscences of Abraham Biderman*, 43; "Cuomo Signs Bill to Build New Housing Using Excess Funds from 2 Authorities," *Bond Buyer*, April 11, 1986; David L. A. Gordon, *Battery Park City: Politics and Planning on the New York Waterfront* (Amsterdam: Gordon and Breech, 1997), 91–93; Louis Uchitelle, "New York Is Seen Nearing Its Debt Limits," *NYT*, October 9, 1988: 42.

56. Wagner to Esnard, "Status of the Recommendations"; Herbert Sturz to Edward I. Koch, February 20, 1985, 21-52-4, Koch papers; Edward I. Koch to Robert Esnard, February 25, 1985, 21-52-4, Koch papers; Charles J. Orlebeke, *New Life at Ground Zero: New York, Home Ownership, and the Future of American Cities* (Albany: Rockefeller Institute Press, 1997), 125; Crotty, *Reminiscences of Paul A. Crotty*, 71–72.

57. Wagner to Esnard, "Status of the Recommendations"; Orlebeke, *New Life at Ground Zero*, 124–27; Michael deCourcy Hinds, "Affordability, How's New York Doin'?," *NYT*, November 15, 1987: R1; Michael H. Schill, Ingrid Gould Ellen, and Ioan Voicu, "Revitalizing Inner-City Neighborhoods: New York City's Ten Year Plan," *Housing Policy Debate* 13, no. 3 (2002): 529–66, 536; personal interview, Abraham Biderman, June 10, 2009.

58. Personal interview, Abraham Biderman.

59. Clarence Norman to James Harding, May 19, 1987; Paul Crotty to James Harding, July 16, 1987, 23-57-1, Koch papers.

60. Michetti, "The New York City Capital Program for Affordable Housing," 203, 11; on the SRO controversy see Soffer, *Ed Koch and the Rebuilding of New York*, 278–80.

61. On AAFE's history, see Asian Americans for Equality, "Our History," www.aafe.org; Peter Gee, Douglas Nam Le, Richard Lee, Jo-Ann Yoo, and Christopher Kui, "The Struggle for Quality Affordable Housing in New York City," *Asian American Policy Review* 21 (2010–11): 9–17; "Chinatown Journey: From Protesters to Developers, *NYT*, January 12, 2003: RE1; Eva Neubauer Alligood, Alisa R. Drayton, and Ashrufa Faruqee, "Asian Americans for Equality," *Shelterforce* 85 (January–February 1996), www.nhi.org.

62. "Asians Picket Building Site, Charging Bias," *NYT*, June 1, 1974: 33.

63. Les Shaver, "Koo's Community-oriented Vision Shapes Enterprise," *Multifamily Executive*, February 2009.

64. Personal interview with Thomas Yu, Managing Director of Real Estate & Development, DMCDC, June 23, 2014.

65. "Christopher Kui, Executive Director, Asian Americans for Equality," *Philanthropy News Digest*, August 13, 2002.

66. "What a Difference Two Decades Makes," *NYT*, January 12, 1997: CY4.

67. Suffolk Homes is discussed at length in David Listokin and Barbara Listokin, "Asian Americans for Equality: A Case Study of Strategies for Expanding Immigrant Homeownership," *Housing Policy Debate* 12, no. 1 (2001): 47–75.

68. On efforts to persuade the city to add an accessory dwelling unit category and inducement to landlords to legalize basement apartments and maintain affordable rents see Rachana Sheth and Robert Neuwirth, *New York's Housing Underground: A Refuge and Resource* (New York: Pratt Center for Community Development and Chhaya Community Development Corporation, 2008).

69. Listokin and Listokin, "Asian Americans for Equality," especially 52–57.

70. On AAFE's Rebuilding Chinatown Initiative, see Robert Weber, "Building Trust," *Shelterforce*, 146 (Summer 2006), www.nhi.org; on the gentrification of Chinatown, see Bethany Y. Li, Andrew Leong, Domenic Vitiello, and Arthur Acoca, *Chinatown Then and Now: Gentrification in Boston, New York, and Philadelphia* (New York: Asian American Legal Defense and Education Fund, 2013).

71. Richard Lee and Christopher Kui, *Demolition through Intentional Neglect: A Tactic of Predatory Landlords to Demolish Rent-regulated Housing* (New York: Asian Americans for Equality, 2011).

72. A comprehensive history of supportive housing is provided by the Supportive Housing Network of New York, "History of Supportive Housing," www.shnny.org.

73. Urban Pathways, "What Is Supportive Housing," www.urbanpathways.org; "Locked In: The Costly Criminalization of the Mentally Ill," *Economist*, August 3, 2013.

74. Personal interview with Fred Shack, September 23, 2013. Information on residents and practices at Hughes provided by Urban Pathways.

75. City of New York, Department of Housing Preservation and Development, "HPD Design Guidelines for Supportive Housing," February 2012, www.nyc.gov.

76. Graham Shane, "Restoring the Urban Dream," *Bauwelt* October 2012: 18–21; "Susanne Schindler & Affordable Housing in New York," Bauwelt Movie No. 11, produced in cooperation with Deutsche Welle, dir. Werner Herzog, 2012, www.bauwelt.de/themen/videos.

77. City of New York, Department of Housing Preservation and Development, and Supportive Housing Network of New York, "A Survey of Common Spaces in Supportive Housing Projects," typescript, August 2011, www.shny.org.

78. On the Bronx see Evelyn Gonzalez, *The Bronx: A History* (New York: Columbia University Press, 2004); Marshall Berman, *All That Is Solid Melts into Air: The Experience of Modernity* (New York: Simon and Schuster, 1982); Richard Plunz, *A History of Housing in New York City: Dwelling Type and Social Change in the American Metropolis* (New York: Columbia University Press, 1990), epilogue; Jim Rooney, *Organizing the South Bronx* (Albany: State University of New York Press, 1995).

79. Tom Angotti, *New York for Sale: Community Planning Confronts Global Real Estate* (Cambridge, Mass.: MIT Press, 2008); von Hoffman, *House by House, Block by Block*, 20–76; Jerilyn Perine and Michael H. Schill, "Reflecting on New York City's Housing Policy: 1987 to 2004," in *Neighborhood Renewal & Housing Markets: Community Engagement in the US & UK*, ed. Harris Beider (Oxford: Blackwell, 2007), 91–114; Jill Jonnes, *South Bronx Rising: The Rise, Fall, and Resurrection of an American City*, 2d ed. (New York: Fordham University Press, 2002).

80. City of New York, Department of Housing Preservation and Development, "Bronxchester Request for Proposals," 2012, www.nyc.gov.

81. Magnus Magnusson quoted in "Social Housing beyond NYCHA," panel discussion organized by the Forum + Institute for Urban Design, New York, June 26, 2014.

82. Personal interview with Magnus Magnusson, February 2012.

83. Personal interview with Ted Weinstein, June 2014.

84. Mark Ginsberg, Lance Jay Brown, and Tara Siegel, *The Legacy Project: New Housing New York. Best Practices in Affordable, Sustainable, Replicable Housing Design* (Shenzhen: Oscar Riera Ojeda, 2013).

85. Quantitative and qualitative analysis of buildings by HPD, including Via Verde, is being funded by the MacArthur Foundation: MacArthur Foundation, "Why Housing Matters," www.macfound.org.

86. Personal interview with Anthony Winn, COO of Nos Quedamos, June 2014; Winnie Hu, "Ex-director of Charity Is Charged in Theft," *NYT*, October 9, 2013: A26; Reginald Mack, "Melrose Reviving: The Exploration of a Grassroots and Transformative Urban Renewal Process in

Melrose Commons," Master's thesis, Pratt Institute, 2010; James DeFilippis and Susan Saegert, eds., *The Community Development Reader* (New York: Routledge, 2012); Rob Rosenthal and Maria Foscarinis, "Community Development Corporations: Challenges in Supporting a Right to Housing," in *A Right to Housing: Foundation for a New Social Agenda*, ed. Rachel G. Bratt, Michael E. Stone, and Chester Hartman (Philadelphia: Temple University Press, 2006); Justin Steil and James Connolly, "Can the Just City Be Built from Below?: Brownfields, Planning, and Power in the South Bronx," in *Searching for the Just City: Debates in Urban Theory and Practice*, ed. Peter Marcuse et al. (New York: Routledge, 2009), 172–93.

87. Jonnes, *South Bronx Rising*; Gonzalez, *The Bronx*.

88. von Hoffman, *House by House, Block by Block*; Jonnes, *South Bronx Rising*.

89. Personal interview with Anthony Winn.

Conclusion: Challenges and Opportunities

1. See, for example, Lawrence J. Vale, *Purging the Poorest: Public Housing and the Design Politics of Twice-cleared Communities* (Chicago: University of Chicago Press, 2013).

2. Eileen Elliott, "Welcome Back: Markham Gardens Residents Prepare to Move Back Home," *NYCHA News*, www.nyc.gov.

3. HR&A Advisors for NYCHA, "Economic Impact of the New York City Housing Authority in New York City and State," September 12, 2013, www.nyc.gov.

4. HR&A Advisors for NYCHA, "Cost of Rehabilitation versus the Cost of Replacement across NYCHA's Portfolio," August 16, 2013, www.nyc.gov.

5. Greg B. Smith, "17 Months after Hurricane Sandy, NYCHA Residents Are Still Waiting for Repairs," *New York Daily News*, March 11, 2014; Cara Buckley and Michael Wilson, "In New York's Public Housing, Fear Creeps in with the Dark," *NYT*, November 2, 2012: A1.

6. Jayne Merkel, "Fine Tuning: How the New York City Housing Authority Makes Housing Work," in *Architectural Design Home Front: New Developments in Housing*, ed. Lucy Bullivant (London: Wiley, 2003), 70–81; David Dunlap, "Community Centers Open Up, with Glass and Air," *NYT*, November 14, 2002: B3; James S. Russell, "Red Hook Center for the Arts, Brooklyn," *Architectural Record* 189 (March 2001), 136; Richard Plunz, "Endgame: in the Bubble," *Lotus International 47* (2011), 90–103.

7. This report was not released to the public. A former top-ranking NYCHA official provided details of the report to Nicholas Bloom, summer 2014. On critique see, for example, Tom Angotti and Sylvia Morse, "Keeping the Public in Public Housing," Hunter College Center for Community Planning and Development, January 2014, www.hunter.cuny.edu.

8. Laura Kusisto, "New York City to Sell Public-housing Stake," *Wall Street Journal*, December 7, 2014; Chris Pomorski, "Public Private Partnership Aims to Save Section 8 Units from 'Demolition by Neglect,'" *New York Observer*, February 10, 2015.

9. Of the 31,224 units using LIHTCs put into service fifteen or more years ago (in 1998 or earlier) in New York City, 26,229, more than 84 percent, remained below-market in late 2014: Furman Center for Real Estate and Urban Policy, New York University, "Subsidized Housing Information Project," database, datasearch.furmancenter.org.

10. Saskia Sasen, *The Global City: New York, London, Tokyo* (Princeton, N.J.: Princeton University Press, 1991).

11. On current challenges see, for example, Mireya Navarro, "As New York Landlords Push Buyouts, Renters Resist," *NYT*, July 10, 2014: A1; Constance Rosenblum, "Middle-class Lament: Rent," *NYT*, June 1, 2014: RE1; Sean Capperis et al., "State of New York City's Housing and Neighborhoods in 2013," Furman Center, New York University, furmancenter.org; City of New York, Department of Homeless Services, "Daily DHS Shelter Census," www.nyc.gov.

12. City of New York, Office of Management and Budget, "Tax Revenue Forecasting Documentation: Financial Plan Fiscal Years 2012–2016," by Joshua Goldstein and Rodney Chun, April 22, 2013, www.nyc.gov/omb, 93; City of New York, Office of Management and Budget, "February 2015 Financial Plan, Fiscal Years 2015–2019," www.nyc.gov/omb, 18, 22, 50; Jonathan Miller, "Manhattan Home Sales Are NOT 80% All-cash (They Are 45%), *Matrix Blog*, Miller Samuel, May 17, 2014, www.millersamuel.com.

Contributors

Matthias Altwicker LEED AP AIA is chair of architecture and associate professor at the New York Institute of Technology School of Architecture and Design. He is principal and founder of Matthias Altwicker Architect in New York City; the work of the firm has won numerous awards and has been published and exhibited internationally.

Hilary Ballon is university professor, deputy vice chancellor, and NYU Abu Dhabi professor of urban studies and architecture at New York University. Her books include *The Paris of Henri IV: Architecture and Urbanism* (Architectural History Foundation/MIT Press, 1991); *Louis Le Vau: Mazarin's College, Colbert's Revenge* (Princeton University Press, 1999); *New York's Pennsylvania Stations* (Norton, 2002); *Robert Moses and the Modern City: The Transformation of New York*, ed. with Kenneth T. Jackson (Norton, 2007); and *The Greatest Grid: The Master Plan of Manhattan, 1811–2011*, ed. (Museum of the City of New York/Columbia University Press, 2012).

Nicholas Bloom is associate professor of social science, chair of interdisciplinary studies, and director of the urban administration program at the New York Institute of Technology. His books include *Suburban Alchemy: 1960s New Towns and the Transformation of the American Dream* (Ohio State University Press, 2001); *Merchant of Illusion: James Rouse, America's Salesman of the Businessman's Utopia* (Ohio State University Press, 2004); *Public Housing That Worked: New York in the Twentieth Century* (University of Pennsylvania Press, 2008); and *Metropolitan Airport: JFK International and Modern New York* (University of Pennsylvania Press, 2015). He is co-editor of *Public Housing Myths: Perception, Reality, and Social Policy* (Cornell University Press, 2015).

Lizabeth Cohen is Howard Mumford Jones professor of American studies and dean of the Radcliffe Institute for Advanced Study at Harvard University. Her books include *Making a New Deal: Industrial Workers in Chicago, 1919–1939* (Cambridge University Press, 1990) and *A Consumers' Republic: The Politics of Mass Consumption in Postwar America* (Knopf, 2003).

Andrew S. Dolkart is director of the Historic Preservation Program and the James Marston Fitch associate professor of historic preservation in the Columbia University Graduate School of Architecture, Planning, and Preservation. His books include *Morningside Heights: A History of Its Architecture and Development* (Columbia University Press, 1998); *Biography of a Tenement House in New York City: An Architectural History of 97 Orchard Street* (Center for American Places, 2006); and *The Row House Reborn: Architecture and Neighborhoods in New York City, 1908–1929* (Johns Hopkins University Press, 2009).

Peter Eisenstadt is an independent historian. His books include *Rochdale Village: Robert Moses, 6,000 Families, and New York City's Great Experiment in Integrated Housing* (Cornell University Press, 2010). He served as editor-in-chief of *The Encyclopedia of New York State* (Syracuse University Press, 2005) and is co-author of *Visions of a Better World: Howard Thurman's Pilgrimage to India and the Origins of African American Nonviolence* (Beacon Press, 2011).

Yonah Freemark is project manager at the Metropolitan Council in Chicago. His writing has appeared in the *Journal of the American Planning Association* and the *Journal of Urban History*.

Brian Goldstein is assistant professor of architecture at the University of New Mexico. His writing has appeared in the *Journal of Urban History* and in *Summer in the City: John Lindsay, New York, and the American Dream* (Johns Hopkins University Press, 2014).

Richard Greenwald is dean of arts and sciences at Brooklyn College. His books include *The Triangle Fire, the Protocols of Peace, and Industrial Democracy in Progressive Era New York* (Temple University Press, 2005). He is co-editor of *Labor Rising: The Past and Future of Working People in America*, ed. with Daniel Katz (New Press, 2012), and *Sweatshop USA: The American Sweatshop in Historical and Global Perspective* (Routledge, 2003).

Jennifer Hock is an instructor at the Maryland Institute College of Art. Her writing has appeared in the *Journal of Urban History*, the *Journal of the Society of Architectural Historian, Places,* and *Atomic Dwelling: Anxiety, Domesticity, and Postwar Architecture* (Routledge, 2012).

Benjamin Holtzman is a historian who writes about social and political life, capitalism, cities, movements, and race in the twentieth-century United States. His work has appeared in *Space and Culture, New Politics, Radical Society, Business History Review,* and several edited collections.

Christopher Klemek is associate professor of history at the Columbian College of Arts and Sciences at George Washington University. His books include *The Transatlantic Collapse of Urban Renewal: Postwar Urbanism from New York to Berlin* (University of Chicago Press, 2011). He is co-editor of *Block by Block: Jane Jacobs and the Future of New York* (Municipal Art Society, 2007).

Lilian Knorr is a postdoctoral research associate at the Woodrow Wilson School for Public and International Affairs at Princeton University. She is an urban policy and planning scholar who writes about the relationship between youth, the state, and the built environment.

Jeffrey Kroessler is associate professor at the Lloyd Sealy Library, John Jay College. His books include *New York Year by Year: A Chronology of the Great Metropolis* (New York University Press, 2002) and *The Greater New York Sports Chronology* (Columbia University Press, 2010).

Nancy H. Kwak is associate professor of history at the University of California–San Diego. Her writing has appeared in the *Journal of the American Planning Association*; *Flammable Cities: Urban Conflagration and the Making of the Modern World* (University of Wisconsin Press, 2011); and the forthcoming *Public Housing Myths: Perception, Reality, and Social Policy* (Cornell University Press, 2015).

Karen Kubey is an architect and former executive director of the Institute for Public Architecture in New York. She is co-founder of the New York City chapter of Architecture for Humanity and New Housing New York, a design competition. Her writing has appeared in *Urban Omnibus*.

Matthew Gordon Lasner is associate professor of urban studies at Hunter College. He is author of *High Life: Condo Living in the Suburban Century* (Yale University Press, 2012). His writing has also appeared in the *Journal of the Society of Architectural Historians*, *Buildings & Landscapes*, *Places Journal*, the *Journal of Urban History*, the *Journal of American History*, *Planning Perspectives*, the *New York Times*, *Robert Moses and the Modern City: The Transformation of New York* (Norton, 2007), and *Making Suburbia: New Histories of Everyday America* (University of Minnesota Press, 2015).

Steven A. Levine was coordinator for educational programs at the LaGuardia and Wagner Archives.

Nadia Mian is an instructor in the Department of Technology, Culture, and Society, New York University Polytechnic School of Engineering. She is co-editor of *Ecologies of Faith in New York City: The Evolution of Religious Institutions* (Indiana University Press, 2013).

Karina Milchman is a housing planner at the Metropolitan Area Planning Council in Massachusetts.

Mariana Mogilevich is an independent scholar. Her publications include writing on architecture and the built environment in the John Lindsay era in *The City Lost and Found: Capturing New York, Chicago, and Los Angeles 1960–1980* (Princeton University Art Museum; Yale University Press, 2014); *Summer in the City: John Lindsay, New York, and the American Dream* (Johns Hopkins, 2014); *Use Matters: An Alternative History of Architecture* (Routledge, 2013); *Future Anterior*; and *Candide: Journal of Architectural Knowledge.*

Stephen Petrus is an Andrew W. Mellon research fellow at the New-York Historical Society and co-author, with Ronald D. Cohen, of *Folk City: New York and the American Folk Music Revival* (Oxford University Press, 2015). Petrus is a twentieth-century urban historian and is currently writing a political and cultural history of Greenwich Village in the 1950s and 1960s.

Annemarie Sammartino is associate professor of history at Oberlin College. Her books include *German Studies in North America*, ed. with Keith Alexander (German Historical Institute, 2004), and *The Impossible Border: Germany and the East, 1914–1922* (Cornell University Press, 2010).

David Schalliol is a photographer and assistant professor of sociology at St. Olaf's College. He is author of *Isolated Building Studies* (Utakatado [Japan], 2014). His photographs have appeared in *The Poorhouse* (Southern Illinois University Press, 2012); the National Film Board of Canada (NFB)'s *Highrise: Out My Window* (2010); the NFB/*New York Times* coproduction, *A Short History of the Highrise* (2013); *Places Journal*; *Dwell*; and *American Sociologist.*

Susanne Schindler is an architect, writer, and editor. She is author of *Inszenierte Moderne: Zur Architektur von Fritz Bornemann*, with Nikolaus Bernau (Jovis, 2003), and co-author of *Growing Urban Habitats: Seeking a New Housing Development Model* (William Stout, 2009).

David Smiley teaches in the Columbia Graduate School of Architecture, Planning, and Preservation. His books include *Sprawl and Public Space: Redressing the Mall*, editor (National Endowment for the Arts/Princeton Architectural Press, 2002) and *Pedestrian Modern: Shopping and American Architecture, 1925–1956* (University of Minnesota Press, 2013).

Jonathan Soffer is professor of history in the Department of Technology, Culture, and Society, New York University Polytechnic School of Engineering. His books include *General Matthew B. Ridgway: From Progressivism to Reaganism, 1895–1993* (Praeger, 1998) and *Ed Koch and the Rebuilding of New York City* (Columbia University Press, 2010).

Fritz Umbach is associate professor in the Department of History at John Jay College of Criminal Justice. His books include *The Last Neighborhood Cops: The Rise and Fall of Community Policing in New York Public Housing* (Rutgers University Press, 2011).

Nader Vossoughian is associate professor at the New York Institute of Technology School of Architecture. His books include *Otto Neurath: The Language of the Global Polis* (Nai [Rotterdam], 2008).

Samuel Zipp is associate professor in American studies and urban studies at Brown University. He is the author of *Manhattan Projects: The Rise and Fall of Urban Renewal in Cold War New York* (Oxford University Press, 2010). He has written articles and reviews for a number of publications, including the *New York Times, Washington Post, Nation, Reviews in American History, Baffler, Metropolis, American Quarterly, American Literary History, Journal of Urban History, Cabinet,* and *In These Times.*

Index

Note: Page numbers in italic type indicate illustrations.

Illustration Credits

We thank the following libraries and individuals for permission to reprint the illustrations in this volume. Numbers refer to figures, unless otherwise indicated.

Matthias Altwicker and Christopher Alvarez, model galleries I, II, III (plans)
Matthias Altwicker and Alexander MacVicar with Christopher Alvarez and Kevin Kawiecki (models), Eduard Hueber/archphoto (photographs), model galleries I, II, III
Avery Architectural and Fine Arts Library, Columbia University, 5.3, 5.11; The New York Real Estate Brochure Collection, 1.19, 4.1, 4.5, 4.8, 4.9, 4.17, 4.38, 5.18
Lo-Yi Chan, 5.1, 5.25
Citizens Housing & Planning Council of New York Archives and Library, 5.10
Cornell University Library, 2.16; Hip Hop Collection, 5.34, 5.35, 5.36; Kheel Center, 4.26
William Fellows, 5.23
Harvard Art Museums/Fogg Museum, Transfer from the Carpenter Center for the Visual Arts, Social Museum Collection, 1.10, 1.12
Harvard University, Frances Loeb Design Library, 4.6
Craig Hodgetts, 5.28
Nancy Kaye, 6.20
LaGuardia and Wagner Archives, LaGuardia Community College, CUNY, 2.8, 2.14, 2.23, 2.25, 3.4, 4.28; the New York City Housing Authority Photograph Collection, 0.1, 0.3, 1.6, 1.27, 2.3, 2.6, 2.12, 2.13, 2.15, 2.17, 2.19, 2.20, 2.21, 2.22, 2.26, 2.27, 2.28, 3.1, 3.3, 3.5, 3.8, 3.9, 3.13, 3.14, 3.15, 3.17, 3.18, 3.21, 4.3, 4.4, 4.29, 5.4, 5.12, 5.17, 6.18
Joe Lapal/Top of the Court, 4.16, 4.18
Matthew Gordon Lasner, 1.5, 4.19, 5.30,
Library of Congress, Prints & Photographs Division: HABS, 1.14, 1.15; New York World-Telegram and the Sun Newspaper Photograph Collection, 5.13; WPA Posters, 2.4, 2.5
LIFE Picture Collection/Getty Images, 6.5
Margaret Logue, 5.7, 5.8, 5.22
Grace Madden, 6.8
Norman McGrath, 5.19, 5.20
Nadia Mian, 6.23
Marc Miller, 4.25, 4.33
Michael Moran, 6.13
Museum of the City of New York, 1.1, 1.3, 1.4, 1.7, 1.8, 1.9, 1.11, 1.22, 1.24, 2.2, 4.12
Steven Nessen, 2.24
The New York City Housing Authority, 0.7, 2.7, 3.7, 3.12, 3.19, 3.22, 7.8
The New York Public Library, Astor, Lenox and Tilden Foundations: General Research Division, 2.9, 2.10, 2.11, 3.6, 3.10, 3.11, 4.2, 4.7; Science, Industry & Business Library, 1.25
The New York Times/Redux: 0.2, 0.9, 4.14, 4.32, 5.5, 5.9, 5.14, 5.15, 5.16, 6.1, 6.3, 6.4, 6.6, 6.9, 6.12, 6.14, 6.16, 6.21, 6.22, 6.29, 6.30, 6.34, 6.35, 7.2, 7.3

Minna Ninova, 0.4
Anthony Pangaro, 5.26
Penn South, 4.28
Queensview, 4.21, 4.23
Rockefeller Archive Center, 1.13
Roosevelt Island Historical Society, 5.31
Mel Rosenthal/The Image Works, 6.2
David Schalliol, 0.5, 0.6, 0.8, 0.10, 0.11, 0.12, 0.13, 0.14, 0.15, 0.16, 0.17, 0.18, 0.19, 0.20, 0.21, 0.22, 0.23, 0.24, 0.25, 0.26, 0.27, 0.28, 0.29, 0.30, 0.31, 0.32, 0.33, 0.34, 0.35, 0.36, 1.18, 1.20, 1.21, 1.23, 1.26, 2.18, 3.16, 3.20, 4.10, 4.11, 4.13, 4.15, 4.22, 4.24, 4.27, 4.30, 4.31, 4.35, 4.36, 4.37, 5.21, 5.24, 5.29, 5.32, 5.33, 6.7, 6.11, 6.17, 6.19, 6.24, 6.25, 6.26, 6.27, 6.28, 6.31, 6.32, 6.33, 6.36, 6.37, 7.1, 7.4, 7.5, 7.6, 7.7
Nancy Siesel, 6.10
U-HAB, 6.15
United States, Federal Emergency Administration of Public Works, 2.1
United States, National Archives, 3.2, 5.6
University of California, Environmental Design Archive, Berkeley, Vernon DeMars Collection, 5.2
Alan Zale, 4.34